Piano Roles

Three Hundred Years of Life with the Piano

James Parakilas

with

E. Douglas Bomberger

Martha Dennis Burns

Michael Chanan

Charlotte N. Eyerman

Edwin M. Good

Atsuko Hirai

Cynthia Adams Hoover

Richard Leppert

Ivan Raykoff

Judith Tick

Marina Tsvetaeva

Mark Tucker

Gretchen A. Wheelock

Stephen Zank

Foreword by

Noah Adams

Yale
University
Press
New Haven
and London

Piano *Roles*

Parts of Chapter 4 are adapted from Mark Tucker, *Ellington: The Early Years* (Urbana and Chicago, 1991), including all citations from primary sources, printed by permission of University of Illinois Press; and Judith Tick, *Ruth Crawford Seeger: A Composer's Search for American Music* (Oxford, 1997), including all citations from primary sources, printed by permission of Oxford University Press.

"Piano after War" by Gwendolyn Brooks (p. 329), copyright 1945 by the author. Reprinted by her permission.

Designed by Nancy Ovedovitz and set in Bodoni Book type by B. Williams & Associates, Durham, North Carolina. Printed in the United States of America by R.R. Donnelley & Sons Company, Willard, Ohio.

Library of Congress Cataloging-in-Publication Data
Parakilas, James.
Piano roles : three hundred years of life with the piano / James Parakilas . . . [et al.]
   p.   cm.
Includes bibliographical references and index.
ISBN 0-300-08055-7 (cloth : alk. paper)
1. Piano—History.   2. Music and society.   I. Title.
ML650.P37   2000
786.2'09—dc21   99-29430

A catalogue record for this book is available from the British Library.

The paper in this book meets the guidelines for permanence and durability of the Committee on Production Guidelines for Book Longevity of the Council on Library Resources.

10 9 8 7 6 5 4 3 2 1

In tribute to the teachers who gave us our first piano lessons:

Rita Bunn (Ivan Raykoff)
Linnie Chronister (Edwin Good)
Helen Dickson (Gretchen Wheelock)
Mary Cecilia Robinson Eyerman (Charlotte Eyerman)
Judith Hancock (Mark Tucker)
Kitarō Hirai (Atsuko Hirai)
Carolyn B. Jackson (James Parakilas)
Sr. Mary Lawrence (Richard Leppert)
Mildred Lyon (Stephen Zank)
Mr. Meyers (Martha Dennis Burns)
Edna Peterson (Julie Carlson)
Athea Roberts (Cynthia Adams Hoover)
Mary Rouse (Douglas Bomberger)
Nancy Russell (Jane Costlow)
Helen Tulin (Judith Tick)
Mrs. Weiss (Michael Chanan)

Contents

When I was fifty-one I took the deepest breath of my life and bought a piano. I would set out to learn to play, and keep a journal. My Steinway upright arrived in January. When Christmas Eve came, I put on a tuxedo and lit a candle and surprised my wife by playing "Träumerei"—I'd been secretly practicing.

That moment stays luminous in memory: Schumann's transcendent melody, the trembling of my fingers as I searched for the chords, the snow falling outside the window, the wet release of our tears, and the piano's gleam in the candlelight.

As the year had progressed, I'd worried that I was more attracted to the piano itself than to the music. My trusty Steinway Model 1098 was fine, but should I have bought that six-foot-ten-inch grand that whispered in my ear when I touched a few keys? And how is it that I can visit a friend's house and become captivated by the sweet sound of an old oak upright saved from the junkyard?

But when Vladimir Horowitz made his homecoming trip to the Soviet Union in 1986 his piano—having been hoisted out the window of his New York apartment—traveled with him on the plane to Moscow. Glenn Gould constantly searched for a piano that would match his memory of the Chickering in his parents' lakeshore cottage. The singer-songwriter Julie Gold wrote her hit "From a Distance" on the morning after she was reunited with her childhood piano—a Knight upright. And in the movie theater, we suffer with Ada in *The Piano* when she and her daughter travel from Scotland to New Zealand for an arranged marriage. When she arrives, her piano is left abandoned on the beach. After it's retrieved, a blind tuner comes. He sniffs the air near the keys. "Scent? And salt, of course." Ada's obsession with the instrument is the soul of the film. Jerry Lee Lewis—famous for "Whole Lotta Shakin' Going On"—sometimes used lighter fluid to torch the piano after his shows, but that's a different sort of obsession, and perhaps it could be seen as a tribute to the frenetic showmanship of Franz Liszt, about whom Moritz Gottlieb Saphir wrote: "Daunted pianos lie around him; torn strings wave like flags of truce."

The notes that I kept during my first months of learning became a book. It was a story mostly of misadventure, of mistakes and false starts and lapses of logic, but by year's end I was playing, and playing an instrument that I'd come to love.

And now I'm blessed—almost every day—by letters from readers. They write with their piano stories. They tell me about the music they've challenged themselves to learn. And they tell me about the instruments they've known:

- A red wooden toy piano about fourteen inches long that my parents bought me for my sixth birthday
- A six-foot restored Knabe grand

- A used Baldwin Acrosonic spinet
- A new Yamaha vertical in cherry with lovely Queen Anne legs
- A handy little upright Winter
- A sun-faded, tone-deaf Wurlitzer
- An old Gulbranson with its beautifully elaborate woodwork
- A Katholnig, several Streichers, a Graf, a few Pleyels, an Erard, a Clementi, even a Blüthner
- A glorious new Steinway B (We could've bought a new airplane!)
- A 1906 Krannich and Bach, green in color, but a jewel on the inside

The fondest memories seem to be of the $125 pianos, or the ones painted pink, or white with seashell decals, and it does seem to be true that if you have three friends and can borrow a pickup truck, you can be a piano player. And then you can be a better one. "Action begins with fantasy," a reader told me. Another wrote to invite me to a recital. "The hall seats three hundred. Maybe only my family will show up. Who cares? For $175 I have the hall for the entire day. I could very easily lock the doors and play that nine-foot Steinway all by myself."

The piano is an instrument of dreams made from wood and ivory and brass and iron and copper and steel and felt. It is a gift to us from craftsmen and artists of many generations, many countries. The story is told in the pages that follow. Read on—and play!

Piano Roles

*T*n Irving Berlin's *Stop! Look! Listen!*—which opened on Broadway on Christmas Day, 1915—the song "I Love a Piano" was staged as a lavish production number: the singer Harry Fox and the chorus girls, accompanied by six pianists on six pianos, strutted in front of a giant keyboard that reached across the stage. Like Leporello in Mozart's Catalog Aria, who declares Don Giovanni's love for women "of every form, rank, and age," the soloist here offers his own musical catalog of pianos and reasons why he adores them so:

> I love to stop right
> beside an Upright,
> Or a high toned Baby Grand.

"I love to run my fingers o'er the keys," he sings, but he loves listening to the piano as much as playing it—

> I love to hear somebody play
> upon a piano,
> A grand piano,
> It simply carries me away.

He loves the great solo performance—

> When Paderewski comes this way,
> I'm so delighted,
> If I'm invited
> To hear that long-haired genius play—

but he is no less fond of the pianist who takes on humbler roles:

> At her best I detest the soprano,
> But I run to the one at the piano,
> I always love the accompaniment.

And though the piano music he mentions is all as "high-toned" as a Baby Grand —or as Don Giovanni's countesses and baronesses—his taste evidently runs just

Introduction

James Parakilas

Still photograph from the movie *King of Jazz*, directed by John Murray Anderson, 1930. Magnifying the keyboard and multiplying the players made the power of music visible in the staging of Irving Berlin's "I Love a Piano" on Broadway in 1915. A decade and a half later, Hollywood adopted the device to the same effect in *King of Jazz*, an early Technicolor extravaganza, when the Paul Whiteman orchestra sat atop the giant piano, joined by five pianists (but not enough keys), to play *Rhapsody in Blue*.

as much to Upright music (as Don Giovanni's did just as much to chambermaids) because the song that he is singing and those six pianists are playing is itself in a lowbrow, though then phenomenally popular, style: the jaunty march style that Berlin had blithely mislabeled "ragtime" in his big hit of four years earlier, "Alexander's Ragtime Band."

The singer of "I Love a Piano" lets us know that he didn't always love the piano. "As a child," he tells us right at the beginning, he "went wild when a band played," preferring especially the clarinet and the trombone. Only when he reached sexual maturity, in other words, did he begin his love affair with the piano. But D. H. Lawrence, in the poem "Piano" that he wrote only a few years before Berlin's song, describes a love of the piano that was formed in childhood and that remains strong precisely through its power to reawaken these youthful memories:

> Softly, in the dusk, a woman is singing to me;
> Taking me back down the vista of years, till I see
> A child sitting under the piano, in the boom of the tingling strings
> And pressing the small, poised feet of a mother who smiles as she sings.

The speaker of Lawrence's nostalgic poem (which he wrote just after his own mother's death) is less exclusively a piano man than the singer of Berlin's song is; far from "detesting the soprano," he treats the piano as hardly more than an adjunct to the sound of her voice in his memory. On the other hand, he is choosier in his devotion to the piano than is Berlin's singer. Or rather, his emotional attachment to the piano rests on his ability to keep one set of piano experiences isolated in his memory from any others, including others that might be musically more splendid:

> In spite of myself, the insidious mastery of song
> Betrays me back, till the heart of me weeps to belong
> To the old Sunday evenings at home, with winter outside
> And hymns in the cozy parlour, the tinkling piano our guide.

> So now it is vain for the singer to burst into clamour
> With the great black piano appassionato. The glamour
> Of childish days is upon me.

But even as Lawrence chooses to honor, to glamorize, the "tinkling" parlor piano over the "great black piano appassionato" of the public stage, he can demonstrate his choosiness only by admitting the public piano onto the stage of his

First page of the sheet music of Irving Berlin's "I Love a Piano" from *Stop! Look! Listen!* New York, 1915

I LOVE A PIANO

by IRVING BERLIN

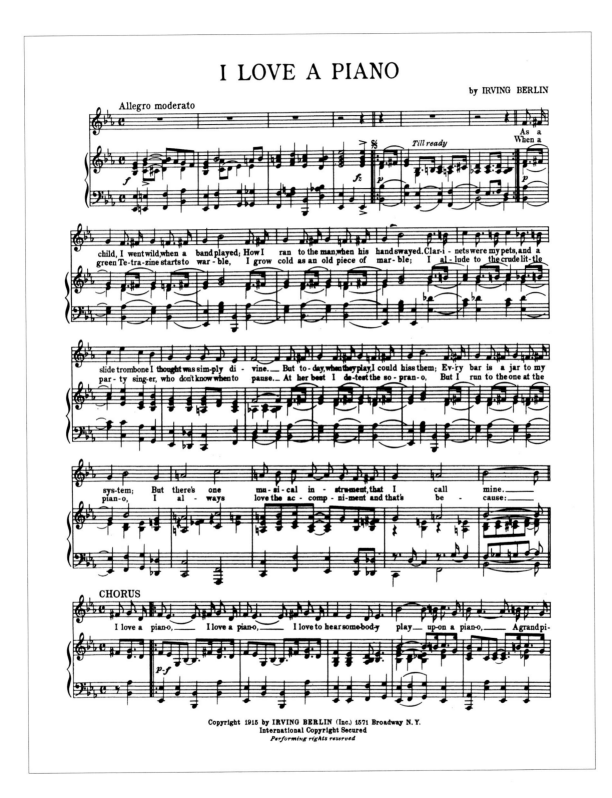

poem for contrast. However selective an attachment to the piano he may be describing, he defines that attachment by reminding his readers of the same larger culture of the piano that Berlin embraces so indiscriminately: the piano that belongs in different ways to public and private life, to highbrow and lowbrow music making, to soloists and accompanists, amateurs and professionals, schooled and unschooled, to women and men, adults and children, to rich and poor, to players and listeners of every race: the piano that is found on both sides of all the social boundaries that it has itself helped to define.

The theme of this cultural history of the piano is that the piano has always exhibited a unique power to act as a cultural go-between, as a medium through which social spheres that stood in opposition to each other could nonetheless nourish each other. It is not just that the piano has somehow proven an adaptable enough instrument to serve for both parlor hymn singing and the Paderewski concert; it is that through the piano, each of those social activities makes the other possible. The workaday functions of the piano—the theatrical tryouts, the weekly choir rehearsal, the daily practicing, along with the Sunday evening hymn singing—have always been sustained by the foretaste, aftertaste, or imaginary taste that they give people of grander or more public or more glamorous musical worlds. And conversely, the life of public music—theater, church, and concert music—in the industrial world has always been sustained by the pianos of the workaday world, the pianos on which those public performances were prepared as well as the ones on which paying audience members developed their musical interests and drummed into their ears and hearts whatever public music was destined to last. Long after the giant keyboard in *Stop! Look! Listen!* was taken down from its Broadway stage, the sheet music of "I Love a Piano" was being played on parlor uprights across America and around the world.

The piano has served as a cultural go-between because musically it is a particularly adaptable instrument. It is more of a machine than most musical instruments are, and as a machine it lacks much personality. Furthermore, for the latter half of its history it has been a mass-produced machine, so that any piano, even the most expensive, is apt to be less individual in sound than a hand-made mbira from Zimbabwe or violin from Cremona. But personality and individuality aren't the piano's game; its gift is for impersonating other musical natures. Although its sound comes from the decaying notes of hammered strings, it impersonates the sustained singing of the human voice. With a single set of strings, it evokes the harmony of a choir, the textural richness of an orchestra, and the rhythmic impe-

4

tus of a dance band—a range of impressions that a pipe organ can hardly match with a roomful of pipes. Like a movie projector, the piano envelops an audience in its illusion. Played by itself, it puts whole worlds of musical sound at the fingertips of one player. Joining other instruments or voices, it supplies whatever they need to make their illusion complete.

But the adaptability of the piano to a host of social spheres and roles is not simply the result of ingenious mechanical design. It is equally the result of ingenious commercial exploitation. The piano is the instrument, the product, around which the modern entertainment industry was created. All the mutually reinforcing, social-boundary-crossing systems by which giant media corporations today market their products grew out of marketing systems created a century or two ago around the piano. Piano builders invented the virtuoso concert tour, along with the publicity blitz that promoted it. Publishers of piano music created the musical

Gustave Caillebotte, *Jeune homme jouant du piano* (Young man playing the piano), 1876, depicts the private side of piano playing. A conservatory student, the artist's brother, is shown practicing at home.

press, and they learned to dictate not only what music pianists performed, but sometimes even what works opera houses staged. And the man who at his death was called "The Father of the Pianoforte" was not the one who invented the instrument, Bartolomeo Cristofori (1655–1732), but the one who, a century later, figured out how to link instrument sales, printed music, journal subscriptions, concert tickets, piano lessons, musical keepsakes—and dreams—so that they all promoted one another: Muzio Clementi (1752–1832).

In a sense, what Clementi and other founders of the entertainment industry discovered was that if the piano was promoted as a symbol of social behavior and social distinction, it could be made an obligatory part of social life. No social distinction was more crucial to this process than that between women and men. Women like Lydia Beardsall Lawrence—the mother "who smiles as she sings" in D. H. Lawrence's poem—did not, as girls, choose between learning the piano and learning the clarinet or the trombone, even if they "went wild when a band played." They learned the piano because doing so was central to the education of girls in their social world. And when Lydia grew into a would-be schoolteacher and then a mother who ran a small shop out of her home, piano playing was a skill that fit into her whole life, as it did not into that of her coal-miner husband. This isn't to say that the piano was exclusively a female instrument. In fact, for the entertainment industry to work—for the domestic and public realms of the piano to maintain their symbiotic existence—young Lydia Beardsall in Kent and young Ignacy Paderewski in Podolia, and for that matter young Scott Joplin in Texas, all had to be practicing their pianos at the same time.[1]

This book describes the roles that the piano has played in the life of its culture, because telling the story of those roles is a way to discover what the piano has meant in that culture. The story begins with Cristofori's act of invention three centuries ago, with the questions of what the piano was invented to do and how its original purpose and design match the uses to which it was eventually put. It ends with an investigation of the changing social meanings of the piano today, when even as the electronic media have extended the cultural reach of the piano worldwide, those same media as well as electric and electronic instruments have usurped many roles that the piano once played.

This is a far larger and less personal story than those that Berlin or Lawrence tell about loving the piano. It is the story of the social, ideological, and imperial systems, as well as the industrial, commercial, and communications systems, that have conditioned the musical experience of millions of people. At the same time, it is the story of how the personal experience of sitting at a piano has shaped the world we live in. The authors of this book hope that all readers who "love a piano" will be able to locate their own experiences within this larger story.

Most sections of chapters in this book are titled, and their author is identified under the title. The untitled introductory sections in each chapter (except chapters 2 and 8) are by James Parakilas.

In 1700, the year by which the first piano had been built, European musical life was full of stringed keyboard instruments—spinets, virginals, clavichords, and harpsichords, among others—some providing quiet pleasure in private chambers, others holding their own in crowded opera pits, church choirs, and court orchestras.[1] Why, then, was a new kind of stringed keyboard instrument needed? And once it was built, how did it come to displace its predecessors? Did the piano improve on what they did, or fulfill a different need?

The violin likewise was born into a world full of other bowed instruments. But because the violin was not invented at a single time and place, we cannot interpret that instrument as a particular person's response to a particular need. With the piano, though, we have not only an inventor to point to, but even an indirect report of his thoughts about his invention. That inventor was Bartolomeo Cristofori, who served as instrument maker to the crown prince Ferdinando Maria de' Medici of the grand duchy of Tuscany and who produced in Florence by 1700 a piano, or "Arpicembalo . . . di nuova inventione, che fa' il piano, e il forte" (a harpsichord, of new invention, that plays soft and loud), according to a court inventory of that date. In some respects Cristofori's piano (it was to take more than a century for the name to be reduced to that form) was no more of a "new invention" than the violin had once been; it embodied no greater innovation or sophistication in acoustical design, for instance, than the violin. Why, then, was the phrase "di nuova inventione" applied, in a document as humble as an inventory, to the piano, as it is not likely ever to have been to the violin?

The difference is that in the time between the creation of the two instruments, a change of consciousness had occurred that historian of technology John Rae has called the "invention of invention."[2] Cristofori himself embodied this new consciousness: he had a hand in publicizing the piano as his invention, and as a result of this publicity—not just of the design itself—the world accepts him today as the inventor.[3] In accepting that claim, the world has also embraced the underlying, modern premise that allows the piano to be considered an invention at all: that the design of a musical instrument can be considered intellectual property.

Although it was a modern move for an instrument maker to put himself forward as an inventor, Cristofori did it in what seems like a bizarrely unmodern way. A modern inventor, after all, would take out a patent on his creation. Cristofori could have done that; in fact, Florence was the city where the first known patent in Western history had been granted, almost three centuries earlier. But a Florentine patent would have given his invention no protection outside Tuscany; inter-

Piano by Bartolomeo Cristofori, Florence, 1722 (Museo degli Strumenti Musicali, Rome)

9

national patent agreements lay far in the future. From our modern perspective, though, it is still surprising to find Cristofori allowing a prominent man of letters to print an article in a Venetian cultural journal announcing the invention of the piano, describing its musical virtues, and detailing its construction in word and drawing. Why would an inventor give his secrets to the world in this way, without taking any steps to profit from them?

One part of the answer is that Cristofori's capacity to profit from his innovation was, from a modern perspective, severely limited by the means of production and marketing available to him. Cristofori's piano is one of the most impressive examples of machine design and construction from its age, but it was a machine built largely of wood and leather parts that needed to be cut and shaped and joined with hand tools by a skilled artisan. Further, it was a luxury furnishing enclosed in a case that was decorated by other expert hands. A piano of this kind is not an object that lends itself to mass production even today, and in 1700 neither the concept nor the tools of mass production had been devised. Like other complex machines of its day, the piano was a product that could be manufactured only in small workshops, where a single craftsman and a few assistants produced on a tiny scale.

Because Cristofori was fortunate enough to be in the service of a rich and music-loving prince, he had the luxury of building one piano after another over the course of several decades, adapting and developing his original design as he proceeded. He was able to train assistants, some of whom would in time carry on his project in their own workshops. Connected as he was to a prominent royal patron, he was even able to sell a few of his pianos to a monarch some distance away: the king of Portugal. But even if Cristofori had had the capacity to turn out pianos at a great rate, there was no commercial mechanism by which he could have marketed them on a wide scale. He may have lived at the beginning of the age in which a musical instrument could be thought of as an invention, but it was still a time when expensive musical instruments were produced on commission from individual patrons. It was to be more than another century before, in the words of Arthur Loesser—whose ageless book *Men, Women, and Pianos: A Social History* will be cited here many times—"mankind speculated in the crazy custom of first making things on a vaguely huge scale and then trying to induce people to buy them."[4]

In terms of production and marketing, then, Cristofori lived in a not so modern world. But in terms of communication on a "vaguely huge scale," his world was rapidly assuming a modern form: the piano appeared just when Europe was beginning to conduct a good part of its intellectual life in the pages of periodicals. If Cristofori had no means of making and selling his pianos on a large scale, he seems to have discerned, or been persuaded, that through the medium of the press he could at least achieve glory across Europe for his invention. And in what Stewart Pollens has described as the "earliest known interview of a musical instrument maker," he made his bid for that glory by the means his age made available to him: he released such a detailed description of the construction of his invention that instrument makers far and wide could duplicate his work and discover for themselves what a remarkable achievement it was.[5]

Cristofori entrusted this information to a writer whom the historian Eric Cochrane has called the "noisiest gadfly of the Italian Republic of Letters," Scipione Maffei, who gave Cristofori all the publicity he could have dreamed of.[6] Maffei published his article on the Cristofori piano in 1711, not in his own journal, but in the most fashionable new intellectual journal on the Italian peninsula, the *Giornale de' letterati d'Italia* of Venice, and then reprinted his article eight years later in a collection of his own poetry and prose, also published in Venice. In 1725, appearing in German translation in Johann Mattheson's *Critica musica*, the article may have helped stimulate the making of pianos in the German lands.

Today this article is a godsend not just to scholars and builders of historic instruments, for whom it provides an invaluable complement to the evidence of the three surviving Cristofori pianos (which have suffered varying amounts of well-intended reconstruction over the centuries), but also to anyone trying to understand the need that this instrument had been built to fulfill. Given that Maffei was a visitor from northern Italy who had probably never heard the instrument or much about it until he walked into the Medici palace, it seems reasonable to assume that he was agreeing to serve as Cristofori's mouthpiece. In that role he explained and defended Cristofori's work, not just to those everywhere who had not yet heard of the instrument, but also to those who evidently had heard it and had pronounced themselves unimpressed.

Maffei's strategy is to compare the new instrument favorably to the traditional harpsichord, not on its own terms but on new ones: it succeeds in doing something that the harpsichord was never designed to do. He begins by reminding readers that one of the sources of singular delight that music lovers feel at hearing "grand concertos in Rome" is the effect of "the soft and the loud" that expert musicians make in performing those works, "either in the propositions and responses, or when the level of sound is allowed to drop little by little, through artful diminution, and then suddenly returns at full blast." But, he writes, whereas bowed in-

The pictures on these two pages show stringed keyboard instruments put to different musical uses in different settings around 1700.

Emanuel de Witte's *Interior with a Woman, Playing the Clavecin* (seventeenth century) captures the atmosphere in which a player in a quiet domestic space could commune with herself musically on a spinet, a small instrument with a harpsichord action. (Museum Boijmans van Beuningen, Rotterdam)

The role of the full-scale harpsichord in the spectacle of court opera is illustrated in Pietro Domenico Olivero's *Opera Performance in Turin* of 1740 (detail), showing two harpsichords contributing to the basso continuo part and providing musical direction to the whole production. (Museo Civico, Turin)

Between the extremes of quiet domestic playing and full-blown operatic spectacle is the music making depicted in one of several paintings called *A Musical Conversation* by Marcellus Laroon the Younger, ca. 1760, showing a harpsichord being played in a small group of instruments and voices, for a small company. (Yale Center for British Art)

The newest member of the keyboard family, the piano, in a splendidly decorated and splendid-sounding example built by Manuel Antunes of Lisbon in 1767 (America's Shrine to Music Museum, University of South Dakota). Where would this newcomer fit into the musical scene?

struments like the violin are excellent at creating "this differentiation and alteration of sound," the harpsichord is entirely incapable of such subtleties. It is just this want that Cristofori has supplied "perfectly" with his new instrument: by applying different kinds and degrees of force to its keys, the player can control "not only the volume, but also the diminution and variety of the sound, as if on a cello."[7]

In these few sentences Maffei describes the need for a keyboard instrument that can take full part in the great stylistic revolution of music in his day. The effects that he mentions define the musical style that we now call Baroque—above all, the musical language of opera, which had swept all Italy and much of Europe off its feet in the century since its birth, and of other fashionable genres of the era, including the "grand concertos" of Arcangelo Corelli and others that at the time of Maffei's writing had distinguished the musical scene in Rome for several decades.

The first of the effects that Maffei describes is a Baroque rhetoric of musical phrases: a rhetoric of phrases that build on each other and engage each other like the sentences of an oration or the arguments of two speakers in a dramatic dialogue. These are the possibilities that Maffei (a dramatist himself) suggests in his phrase "propositions and responses." The harpsichord, with its plucking mechanism that attacked every string with a distinct ping and with unvarying force, was superb at creating a clear imitation of that complex overlapping and interweaving of functionally equal, sometimes melodically identical phrases characteristic of sacred vocal music as well as of madrigals and other secular music of the sixteenth century and earlier. But in attempting to contrast one phrase against the next in the "proposition and response" style, the harpsichord was at a disadvantage. By coupling and uncoupling the instrument's different sets of strings or by other mechanical devices, a harpsichordist could change the volume of sound between one phrase and another, but those were cumbersome devices appropriate only for special effects. The piano was much better suited for the pervasive changes in volume from phrase to phrase that the new Baroque style demanded.

The second effect Maffei mentions has to do with contrast within

Opposite: Anonymous portrait of Bartolomeo Cristofori, 1726, formerly in the Staatliches Institut für Musikforschung, Berlin. The portrait is reproduced from a photograph made before World War II, when the painting was destroyed. It was the only known portrait of Cristofori and probably the earliest representation of a piano.

Drawing of the hammer mechanism of a Cristofori piano from Scipione Maffei's article "Nuova invenzione d'un gravecembalo col piano e forte," as it appeared in *Giornale de' letterati d'Italia*, 1711

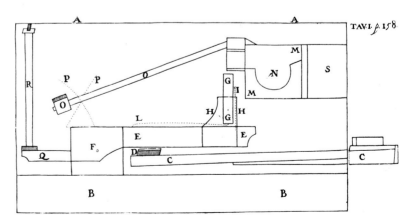

phrases as well as between them: gradual as well as sudden changes in the volume of sound. The particular effect he describes—letting the sound diminish gradually and then coming back abruptly to full volume—could be achieved by violins, or by singers, either on a single note or chord or in a succession of notes or chords. With both the harpsichord and the piano, there is no way to manipulate the volume of a single note or chord once it has been played. The difference between the two comes when a change of volume is wanted in the course of successive notes or chords. Here, the harpsichord is helpless because its quills pluck a string with fixed force, no matter how hard the key is struck. The piano, on the other hand, has hammers that can strike its strings as forcefully or gently as the player strikes the keys, so that each note or chord can be a little or a lot softer or louder than the one before.

Though Maffei describes here a particular and sensational effect, his description of it can be understood as raising the larger issue of how a keyboard instrument can "shape" a melodic phrase. The solution depends utterly on the style of melody under consideration. If it is a question of reproducing plainchant on a keyboard instrument, for instance, the organ is better suited than any stringed keyboard, because its constancy of air supply suits a melodic style that demands comparatively little differentiation in volume or other sound qualities either during a note or from one to the next. But the style that Maffei is referring to depends on extreme differentiation, and of many kinds, between one note of a melody and another. Any single "proposition" or "response" in an opera or concerto of his day may use a variety of contrasts—of long and short notes, sustained and gasping breath, dissonant and consonant harmonization, bright and dark color, as well as loud and soft volume—to create suspense and resolution, to provide emphasis at a certain point, and to give the whole phrase a distinctive stamp.

When it came to reproducing melodies of this sort at the keyboard, harpsichordists were not lacking in resources. Even though the notes at their disposal all sounded with equal force, they could emphasize one over another with ornaments. Even though those notes all died away very quickly from the instant they were plucked, the player could sustain a single note, in effect, by trilling on it. And speeding up a scale could create the illusion of a crescendo, just as accompanying a single note of a melody with a thick chord could make it seem louder than the others in the same phrase.

But the piano offered more resources for this purpose. Being able to play one note louder than the next gave the player the means not just to emphasize one note over another, but also to make it audible longer than another. In fact, for the purpose of sustaining a note, the piano had an advantage over the harpsichord quite distinct from its control over volume: whereas the harpsichord string, plucked by a quill, pings sharply and then decays abruptly, the piano string, glanced against by a rounded and relatively soft-surfaced hammer (covered with leather on the earliest pianos, later with felt), has both less ping on the attack and a slower decay thereafter, so that a single held note can give an impression of being "sung." This difference, perhaps subtle in Cristofori's and other very early pianos, became considerable as the instrument developed. In fact, the responsiveness of the hammers to the keys allowed players on the piano, by varying their "touch"—the character and not just the force of their stroke—to produce a tremendous range of characters and colors as well as volumes of sound on a single note—as if on a cello, as Maffei suggests.

Besides these advantages in shaping a contrast-laden melody, the piano gave its player the means to highlight a melody over its accompaniment. A harpsichordist playing a two-manual instrument can highlight the melody by playing it on one manual and the accompaniment on the other, but this is a mechanical effect that leaves no room for subtlety. On the piano, the distinction can be made by touch, flexibly and sensitively. The touch is instilled, not instinctive—all those who have ever had piano lessons can no doubt still hear their teachers calling to them, "Bring out the melody!" This practice, now deeply entrenched in the art of piano playing, belonged to the instrument from the start. Once Cristofori had invented a mechanism that allowed notes on a keyboard to be played more or less loudly, notes struck simultaneously could of course be differentiated in volume just as easily as notes struck successively. But beyond that, it can be seen in Maffei's language that the need to highlight a single melody within a complex texture played by one player at a keyboard was intrinsic, not incidental, to Cristofori's project: the musical style that he invented his piano to perform was a style in which a single melody needed to stand out, so that the music as a whole could suggest a single voice issuing a "proposition" or a "response."

All in all, Cristofori's invention, as represented in Maffei's report, seems so perfectly suited to the music of its day that it comes as a surprise to learn that it had detractors. "Some professionals," as Maffei tells us next, "have not given this invention all the applause that it merits." First, they don't appreciate what it took to create this marvel, and second, they find its sound "too soft, and dull" (literally, "obtuse"). Further on, Maffei explains that the instrument has been found "not to have a big sound, and not to have as much strength as other harpsichords." It is instructive for us that Maffei rehearses these objections and responds to them: his doing so reminds us that the piano he is talking about—quieter than a harpsichord—is a very different thing from any modern piano. Moreover, these objections make him turn from the musical style that necessitated the piano to the performing situations in which it was needed.

Maffei responds to the criticism by conceding that the piano is quieter than a harpsichord, without acknowledging that that is a defect. When you first put your hands to the piano, he says, it may indeed sound soft and dull to you, but in the long run it produces a less tiresome sound. Turning from the player's experience to a listener's, he adds that it turns out to be "even more exquisite to hear the instrument at a distance." If this seems an odd thing to write immediately after conceding how quiet the instrument is, perhaps Maffei is implicitly comparing the piano not to the harpsichord but to the clavichord, an instrument at which keyboard players had long been able to play one note louder than another. The trouble with the clavichord was that it was not at all "exquisite at a distance": it was inaudible. Maffei may be announcing that this is not just another clavichord.

But still, he has conceded that it is quiet on the whole, and so it is "properly a chamber instrument, and not adaptable for use in church music, or in a large orchestra. . . . It certainly succeeds perfectly at accompanying a singer, and at supporting another instrument, and even in a modest ensemble, although that isn't the principal use for which it is intended, which is rather to be played solo, like the lute, the harp, the six-stringed viols, and other instruments of the greatest delicacy."[8] This must be the most telling statement any eighteenth-century source makes to us about the piano. Not only does it oblige us, against our habit, to think of the piano as an instrument for more intimate music making than the harpsichord; it also gives us the means to relate musical style to musical use when we consider the need the piano was invented to fulfill.

After all, the piano was capable, according to Maffei, of emulating the "grand concertos" played in Rome, often in churches—but those were exactly the sort of ensemble and hall for which the piano was "not adaptable." Those concertos called for a keyboard instrument in the orchestra's continuo group, to provide bass and harmony for the other instruments, and the keyboard part was normally played on harpsichord. The harpsichord may have lacked the rhetorical and dramatic expressiveness of the violin-family instruments that made up most of the ensemble, but it could leave that expressiveness to them. It had a different function to perform: providing rhythmic leadership and a harmonic framework for the rest of the ensemble. In fact, the harpsichord was there for the other musicians more than for the audience, and its pinging notes were ideal for catching the ears of the other musicians spread out in the choir of a church, or in the pit and on the stage of an opera house, cutting through the rest of the music as well as the noise of the audience. It is hardly surprising that the harpsichord retained its place in the orchestra for nearly the duration of the eighteenth century, even as it lost out to the increasingly powerful-sounding piano in other settings. As late as 1791, for instance, when Haydn presented his latest symphonies in London, he himself presided over the performances from the harpsichord. (That was pretty much the end of the line for the harpsichord, however: the next year, in the same orchestral series, Haydn switched to the piano.)[9]

Still, when Maffei describes the relationship of the piano to an orchestra, he is not describing the piano taking a role within an orchestra. Because the piano had the expressive powers that the harpsichord lacked, it could imitate the effects of the orchestra as a whole—largely the effects of massed string instruments—just as it could imitate the effects of the singers in an opera or a choir. But it would imitate them on its own terms, on its own intimate scale, in its own proper space. It would transport the rhetoric and drama of music making in the opera house or church into the private chamber. By Maffei's account, this power to transport a musical effect into a new setting was the main selling point of the new instrument. In fact, it has remained a main selling point of the piano. The sheer volume of sound that allows a modern concert grand to stand up to an orchestra in the piano concertos of Brahms and Tchaikovsky is hardly anticipated in Cristofori's pianos. But the power of a piano to imitate orchestral fury in a sonata of Beethoven, to mimic the intricacies of vocal ornamentation in a Chopin nocturne, to stand in for the orchestra in a vocal or choral or instrumental rehearsal, to reproduce the styles of many different musical repertories in a music theory or music apprecia- tion classroom—that power, Maffei would have us believe, was present from the very beginning in Cristofori's idea of the piano and his initial realization of it.

Courtly Cultivation

The year of Cristofori's death, 1732, marks the end of a third of a century in which the piano was developed and promoted, mostly by Cristofori himself. It is also the year that the first music was published for the piano, marking the beginning of a second third-century during which instrument makers and musicians explored the potential of the new instrument within the courtly setting for which it had been conceived. That is, although the piano was transported to several different countries during the first two-thirds of the eighteenth century, in all those coun- tries it stayed within a tiny circle of royal and aristocratic patrons and the key- board builders, players, singers, and composers connected to their courts. There it continued to serve as a solo instrument or as accompaniment to individual singers or instrumentalists, in performances given in the intimate setting of courtly chambers.

Among the first courts to which the piano traveled was the royal court in Lisbon. The Portuguese king and queen, João V and Maria Anna, were unstinting patrons of Italian music who brought to their court many Italian opera singers and orchestral musicians, the composer and harpsichordist Domenico Scarlatti, and some of Cristofori's pianos. The king's younger brother, Dom António de Bragança, who had spent time in Italy and had studied harpsichord there with Scarlatti, now became the dedicatee of the first music published for the piano, twelve solo sonatas composed by Lodovico Giustini, an organist in the Tuscan city of Pistoia, and printed in Florence in 1732. Another music lover of high rank completes the courtly circle in which these pieces were created: Dom João de Seixas da Fonseca, a cleric from Brazil who enjoyed favor with popes and royalty and was living in Florence at the time, signs the dedication to Dom António as the publication's patron.

It is important to bear this charmed circle in mind when thinking about what the publication of Giustini's sonatas represents. For example, it can in no sense be considered a commercial publication. Otherwise the title page would hardly describe these works as "Sonatas for soft-loud harpsichord, commonly called the one with little hammers."[10] Even at the very end of the eighteenth century, when the piano was clearly driving the harpsichord into oblivion, title pages of keyboard music quite regularly claimed that the works being offered for sale were suitable for either piano or harpsichord. What publisher, after all, would want to turn away even a small part of the potential market for a publication? But when the Giustini sonatas were published, the market for piano music consisted of literally a handful of piano owners. Why, then, would the publisher of these sonatas describe them as suitable for only that instrument? Perhaps we should begin by asking why they were published at all. The best answer seems to be that publication in this case represents a gesture of magnificent presentation to a royal musician, rather than an act of commercial promotion.

Likewise, when we examine Giustini's music, it is helpful to bear in mind that the composer was not creating piano music for sale to the general musical public but participating in an experiment in musical expression on an instrument that was the plaything of the Tuscan and now the Portuguese court. To ask, as many writers have, whether Giustini succeeded in creating an idiomatic piano style in these pieces is to disregard this situation. His sonatas are better understood as

Lodovico Giustini, *Sonate da cimbalo di piano, e forte* (Florence, 1732): the first page of the Dolce from Sonata 6 and the second page of the Corrente from Sonata 7. In the Dolce, the composer uses indications of "soft" *(piano* or *pia.)* and "loud" *(for.)* to distinguish one phrase from another, "proposition" from "response." In the first line of the Corrente, he directs the player to decrease the volume gradually (*pia.* for "soft," followed by *più pia.* for "softer"), even as the chords get thicker; on the harpsichord, the thickening of chords would necessarily have the opposite effect, increasing the volume.

demonstrations, for those in the know, of what Cristofori's soft-loud harpsichord could do that no ordinary harpsichord could. And it was by taking the piano through a tour of every possible style of harpsichord music, not by creating any new style, that Giustini thought to test the new instrument and put the old one to shame. Accordingly, successive movements in these sonatas turn from the learned contrapuntal style to long-established dance styles and then to the fleet up-to-date manner that we associate with the keyboard music of Domenico Scarlatti. There is even considerable imitation of fashionable styles of violin figuration: wouldn't Cristofori and Maffei have been pleased![11]

For the demonstration to be effective, the performer needed to try the contrasts of soft and loud notes that the piano was built to provide. The composer indicated those contrasts by marking *piano* and *forte* liberally throughout the twelve sonatas. (In any movement *piano* appears first, but never right at the beginning, so that we have to assume that *forte* indicates the default volume and *piano* is the special effect.) In many places, answering phrases—Maffei's "propositions and responses"—are distinguished from each other by the markings *piano* and *forte;* in others, gradual or sudden changes are marked within phrases—here following Maffei's description of a level of sound that is allowed to drop little by little, through artful diminution, then suddenly returns at full blast. (The terms *crescendo* and *diminuendo* not being standard in scores at the time, Giustini uses graded terms—"soft" followed by "softer"—apparently to suggest a gradual change of volume.) All through these sonatas, it is striking how systematically Giustini places his *piano* and *forte* indications against the musical grain: where a thickening of the chords would produce an increase in volume on a harpsichord, he writes *piano;* where a move from a lower register to a higher one would produce a decrease in volume on a harpsichord, he writes *forte.* In other words, he is not just showing what the piano and only the piano can do; he is flaunting it.

For thirty or so years after this publication, there was apparently no other music published explicitly for the piano. That is no sign that the piano was falling into disfavor; it simply indicates that the instrument and its musical repertory continued to develop almost entirely in courtly circles, a market too small to support musical publication, except in special circumstances. What the courtly quarters of the piano did fortuitously provide was attention from a couple of the greatest keyboard composers of the era. One of these was Domenico Scarlatti, who may have used the pianos of the Portuguese royal family when he was in their service in Lisbon and certainly had use of some in Spain, where he lived the last three decades of his life (after his student, the Portuguese princess Maria Bárbara, married into the Spanish royal family). But there is little direct evidence of what Scarlatti thought of the piano in general or as a medium for his hundreds of keyboard sonatas. He published just one collection of those sonatas, in 1738, with the indication that they were for harpsichord (*gravicembalo*), but that simply reminds us that the buying public for keyboard sonatas then included almost no piano owners.

Johann Sebastian Bach had a briefer, though serious, acquaintance with the piano. The Saxon keyboard builder Gottfried Silbermann, who built pianos on the model of Cristofori's in the 1730s, showed one to Bach, who suggested improvements that Silbermann seems to have achieved by 1747, when Bach visited the Prussian court in Potsdam and played before Frederick the Great on the king's Silbermann pianos. In fact, it was on a Silbermann piano that Bach apparently improvised the fugue that he later wrote down as the three-part Ricercar in the *Musical Offering*—though when he published that work, there was no more of a piano-owning public to pitch it to than there had been for Scarlatti, and consequently there was no reason to advertise any part of it as suitable for the piano. His receptivity to the new instrument is strikingly expressed, however, by the fact that two years later, already in his mid-sixties, he acted as a sales agent for Silbermann's pianos. Equally striking is that his son Carl Philipp Emanuel, with whom he was visiting in Potsdam, presided over the royal collection of Silbermann pianos as Frederick the Great's keyboard master, yet continued to prefer the intimate expressivity of the clavichord long after his father showed favor to the piano.

Aside from its brush with these great composers, the piano in its courtly phase kept company with great singers. Two castrati, Carl'Antonio Zanardi and Francesco de Castris, were the first owners of Cristofori pianos outside the Florentine ruling family, and one of the greatest eighteenth-century singers, the castrato Farinelli, owned a piano built by a pupil of Cristofori that he told Charles Burney was his favorite keyboard instrument to play and compose for in his retirement.[12] It seems appropriate that opera singers would have been among the first musicians to appreciate the dramatic and lyrical capacities of the piano.

Going Public

The fortunes of the piano changed dramatically in the final third of the eighteenth century. Suddenly, during the 1760s, pianos began to be heard in public concerts, and keyboard publications began to specify the piano, usually as an alternative to the harpsichord. There are notices of public performances on the piano in Vienna from 1763, in London from 1766, and in Paris from 1768.[13] Further, the piano is named as a suitable medium—along with the harpsichord—on the title page or in the preface of collections of solo sonatas published by Johann Gottfried Eckard in Paris and by Johann Christian Bach and John Burton in London between 1763 and 1766.[14] Why did the piano suddenly burst onto the scene in so many places and ways at once?

One reason the piano began to appear in public concerts is that it had finally made its way to cities where such concerts occurred. Concert series like the Bach-Abel concerts in London or the Concert Spirituel in Paris, where the piano was heard in the 1760s, had no equivalent in Florence, Rome, Lisbon, Madrid, and Potsdam, where the piano had been found until then. But public performance on the instrument cannot be fully understood in isolation from other developments. Not only did the publication of piano music begin in Paris and London at the same time, but piano manufacturing arrived in those cities then as well. And in London especially, pianos were not being built primarily for use in a royal court, as had been the pianos of Cristofori, Silbermann, and other builders in Florence, Portugal, and Spain. The London piano industry was started in this period by German immigrant builders like Johannes Zumpe who had developed square pianos—smaller instruments with simpler mechanisms than the "grand" pianos of Cristofori, Silbermann, and the other earliest builders. Whereas a piano of the Cristofori type was a great luxury, the German builders in London were producing a cheaper version that you didn't have to be a king to afford.

But making a cheaper product for a bigger market required more public means of promotion. And what better way to promote the piano in London, where subscription concerts were a principal recreation of the upper classes, than to present the well-known keyboard players of the day performing on it? Correspondingly, from the perspective of concert organizers, what better way to attract new subscribers than to give them the opportunity to hear a new instrument that they might then go out and buy? It is in keeping with the whole subsequent history of the instrument that at this moment, when the piano first appeared in public, the public piano and the domestic piano were already being used to promote each other.

The promotion of the piano, as an instrument both to buy and to hear, was in turn supported by the sale of music designated as suitable for the piano. If that music had been labeled simply "for the piano," it would presumably have appealed only to buyers who already owned pianos. But to label it "for the harpsichord or piano," as a great deal of the keyboard music published in the last third of the eighteenth century was labeled, was to invite harpsichord owners to buy the music, take it home, play it on their harpsichord, and find themselves wishing they had a piano. The frequent markings of *piano* and *forte*, often in passages where a contrast in volume would obviously be effective, was a continual reminder to harpsichordists of what they were missing, just as the regular showing of the NBC peacock, spreading what was obviously meant to be seen as a rainbow of feathers, was to owners of black-and-white televisions in the early days of color broadcasting. But this music provided subtler incentives to wish for a piano as well.

"Pianism," as Katalin Komlós writes, "is not merely a matter of dynamic signs," and in her survey of the "harpsichord or piano" music of this period, she shows brilliantly how such early works as sonatas by Eckard and Johann Christian Bach whetted the appetites of consumers for pianos. The individual lines of the music often need articulation and shading of a vocal nature that only the piano can provide; similarly, accompaniments that would be overbearing or wearing

Johann Christian Bach, *Six Sonatas for the Piano Forte or Harpsichord,* Op. 5 (London, 1766): first page of Sonata 2. Harpsichord owners who bought these sonatas would have found, at least in the first four of them, reason to think the music better suited to the piano than to the harpsichord. On this page, they would have wanted to know how the piano, with its capacity for loud and soft playing, would realize the symphonic effect of the opening lines, which alternate between blasting, "whole-orchestra" chords and lyrical, soloistic phrases.

on the harpsichord can be kept in balance on the piano. In fact, when harpsichordists bought themselves a piano, they needed to be taught the new art of "bringing out the melody." Komlós quotes Charles Burney issuing precisely that instruction to performers in the preface to a set of piano (or harpsichord) duets that he published in 1777: "Each Performer should try to discover when he has the *Principal Melody* given to him, or when he is only to *accompany* that Melody; in order, either to make it more conspicuous, or merely to enrich its harmony."[15] Paying attention to such instructions would be one way for new piano owners to learn to get the most out of the instrument, as well as the music, that they had purchased, but going to concerts and hearing what the professionals could do with the same instrument, and even the same music, was no less important. In that way sales of music, as of instruments, promoted ticket sales.

The square pianos that Zumpe and other London builders were making created the distinction between a domestic and a concert piano—a theoretical distinction anyway, although it was not until 1771 that Americus Backers advertised the first English grand piano, and scholars have consequently speculated that some at least of the earliest concert performances in London may have been given on square pianos.[16] Music for the piano likewise came in domestic and concert varieties, or amateur and professional varieties—not necessarily the same distinction. But the boundaries existed to be crossed. Amateur players filled the concert halls to hear the professional players, and although in one sense the amateurs might have needed a distinct repertory of music to play, suited to their own level of competence, in another sense they might have wanted to play—or at least try to play—the music that they had heard performed in concerts. As a result, although one can speak of amateur and professional genres of piano music, nothing illuminates the culture of the piano in this period more than to see where these generic boundaries break down.

The accompanied sonata, for instance (or piano sonata with an added part for a violin or some other instrument), has been tactfully described by Simon McVeigh as "essentially an amateur domestic medium, designed for lady pianists of moderate skill and gentlemen string-players of yet more slender accomplishment." McVeigh also describes, however, an exceptional case of an accompanied sonata performed in public by two virtuosos.[17]

Piano duets were another essentially amateur genre, an eminently sociable medium of domestic music making that also allowed the piano to show off its capacity for imitating the complexity and power of orchestral music. What, then, are we to make of the publication in 1793 of the *Grand Overture for Two Performers on*

One Piano Forte by Jan Ladislav Dussek, the great Bohemian virtuoso then resident in London, "As Performed at Mr. Salomon's and other Concerts by the Author and Madam Dussek"? Publications in this period and long thereafter often carried "as-performed-by" phrases on their title pages, as if to assure amateur customers that what they were buying and taking home to play was exactly what they had heard the composer perform in concert, not some watered-down version designed for amateurs like . . . themselves. This particular duet might be considered a public work in a domestic genre, transportable "back" into the domestic realm through the medium of publication. Or perhaps, because the Dusseks were a married couple, besides being two formidable pianists, their performance of a duet "at Mr. Salomon's and other Concerts" could be considered a public staging of their domestic relationship.

Title-page engraving by Johann August Rosmaesler for Franz Seydelmann, *Six Sonatas for Two Persons at One Clavier* (Leipzig, 1781), showing a duet being played on a square piano in a domestic setting

The piano concerto, at the other end of the spectrum, was among the most public of genres, except that concertos were published for amateur consumption in solo, and perhaps simplified, versions: the more musically ambitious of Jane Austen's characters play "concertos" when they are called on to grace a dinner party with a piano solo. The solo sonata crossed the border between public and private performance from the other side. Both in England and on the Continent, it was often called a "lesson," which suggests not just that its function was domestic, but also that it served as a private exercise in self-improvement. Nevertheless, solo sonatas figured on concert programs. Perhaps the musicians who gave public performances of their own sonatas—some of which could have counted as amateur music if considered simply in terms of their difficulty—did so partly to promote sales of the music to their audiences.

Amateurs might buy the most difficult music for themselves, just as virtuosos might appear in public playing music that they had composed for amateurs. Muzio Clementi, who began appearing in London concerts in the 1770s, taught himself tricks at the keyboard that no other player of the time could duplicate, in particular dazzling passages of octaves and thirds. The three solo sonatas that he published in his Op. 2 collection in 1779 display these tricks with a vengeance; the first of them, in fact, became known as his "celebrated octave lesson." Why, then, did he publish these three virtuosic sonatas in a collection that alternated them with three amateur-style sonatas for keyboard, accompanied by flute or violin? A cynical explanation would be that he was hoping to sell the same work to both professional and amateur buyers, knowing that each type of player would have no use for part of what was in the collection.

But a more sympathetic explanation can be constructed with a little attention to the psychology of ownership. Musical amateurs don't buy only what they can easily play. For musicians who were comfortable playing the three accompanied sonatas in Clementi's Op. 2, it might have been an occasional temptation and challenge to have a go at the three virtuosic solo sonatas—at least when no one else was listening; the "octave lesson," after all, may have been "celebrated" not just as a feat performed by Clementi himself, but also as a test of other players' more modest accomplishments. Or it may have been a desirable item for musical amateurs to buy and display on their music stands, as a sign of their musical culture, just as people buy best-sellers to put on their coffee tables or leather-bound classics to put on their shelves, whether or not they ever expect to read them.

That Clementi in a sonata publication of 1779 should have been able to play the idea of the amateur pianist off against the idea of the professional—and the idea of domestic piano music off against the idea of public piano music—is in itself a sign of how rapidly the piano had established the characteristic web of functions that would become its hallmark. A quarter-century earlier it had been an experimental instrument known in just a few courtly musical establishments, unheard and almost unheard-of in the great capitals of Paris, London, and Vienna. Now it was driving keyboard makers in those cities to experiment with devices that would make the harpsichord more like a piano; indeed, by the end of the century, production of harpsichords was to stop altogether. Ironically, it was the culture of the harpsichord that had made the rapid progress of the piano possible. It was much easier to switch from playing harpsichord to playing piano, after all, than to learn the piano from scratch. In fact, the harpsichord seems to have been the instrument on which Clementi conceived the virtuosic sonatas of his Op. 2 and on which he gave the first public performances of them, yet as those sonatas became famous—and as the harpsichord dropped from the scene—they were soon being remembered as the first truly pianistic music.[18]

The piano was creating such a versatile role for itself that the older stringed keyboard instruments, including the harpsichord, were coming to seem overly specialized. As a result, the piano seemed indispensable even before it became very widely distributed. In 1779 it was still very much an instrument of the elite and of professional musicians who performed for this highbrow audience; all across Western Europe there were still more harpsichords than pianos. But the piano had a tremendous momentum in the musical marketplace because of what Maffei had identified seventy years earlier as its salient feature: its unsurpassed capacity to transfer expressive effects from one musical medium, one place, one kind of performance, to another.

Charles Hess.

PATENTED
JUL 17.1866

Convertible bed room piano.

CLASSIFICATION
56.413
DIVISION.

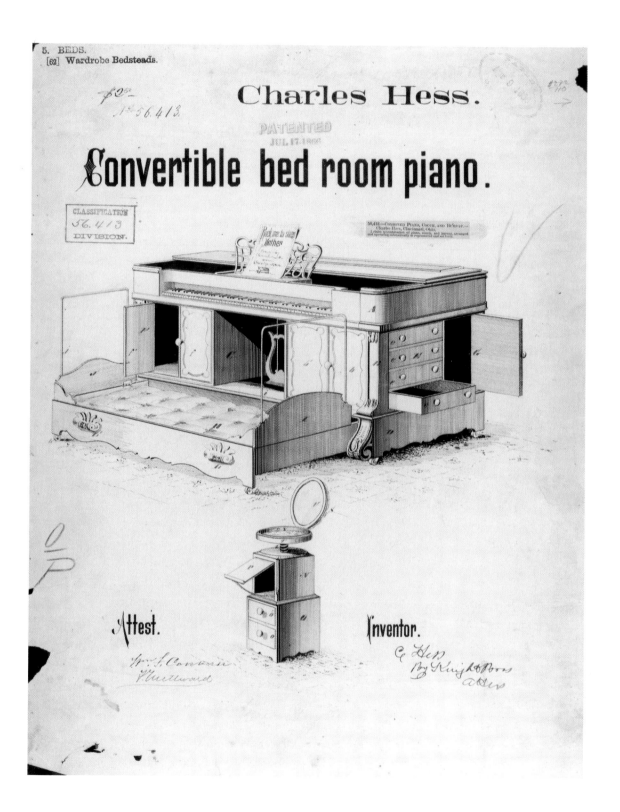

Attest.

Inventor.

*T*n the beginning, the clientele was wealthy and noble, the workshops small. From the start, it was important for piano makers to have influential clients, links with leading performers (who were often also composers), an understanding of technologies applicable to instrument building, and a savvy sense of both production techniques and marketing opportunities. In all the major developments in piano making to be considered here—starting with the invention—this same configuration of factors came into play.

Who, then, drove the invention of the piano at the beginning of the eighteenth century? Was it the wealthy patron? The enterprising instrument maker? A clue is found in Scipione Maffei's still extant notes from his 1709 interview with Cristofori for his article on the invention of the piano. The notes begin with a sentence that raises the question of what role Cristofori's chief client—Prince Ferdinando de' Medici—played in the creation of the piano:

> Bortolo Cristofali [*sic*] of Padua, employed by the Lord Prince, invented the harpsichord with soft and loud without incentive from anything else (ha inventato senza motivo avuto da altra cosa il cimbalo col piano e forte).[1]

This language could mean that Cristofori claimed to have invented the piano without copying anyone else's design—a claim for himself as inventor that fits with the language he put on the nameboards of all three of his surviving pianos: "Bartholomeus de' Christophoris patavinus inventor faciebat Florentia."[2] It could equally mean that this invention was not undertaken at the behest of his royal employer. Maffei did not quote the remark in his article, and we may guess from that that he, unlike Cristofori himself, did not wish to emphasize the independence of the grand prince's harpsichord maker.

In a certain sense, Cristofori's dependence on his employer was undeniable. Prince Ferdinando paid his salary, which allowed him the luxury of developing his idea for the piano; in the end, producing one model after another, he worked on the project for more than three decades. Cristofori's connection to the Medici court also provided him with other important customers for his pianos, from Cardinal Ottoboni in Rome to King João V of Portugal, and directly or indirectly with the opportunity to have his pianos played and admired by renowned musicians like Scarlatti and Farinelli. And, in the beginning at least, Cristofori's employment at the Medici court provided him with a place to work. In Maffei's notes we read that Cristofori began his career in Florence in 1688 working in a large, noisy room (most likely the Uffizi's Galleria dei Lavori) with more than a hundred other

Two **Designing, Making, and Selling Pianos**

Edwin M. Good and Cynthia Adams Hoover

Charles Hess, drawing of a convertible bedroom piano for a U.S. Patent Office application, April 9, 1866. No indication has been found that this invention was ever manufactured. (Smithsonian Institution)

artisans. He found that wearying and complained to the prince; by 1690 he seems to have worked at home, calling on cabinet makers, assistants, and apprentices from time to time for help in completing his instruments.[3]

Whatever Cristofori thought up, then, he had to be able to build himself in his home workshop, with occasional help from a few others, using the materials and tools available to an artisan of that day. And if his claim to credit as the inventor of this new instrument was to be credible, he had to design it so that he and other builders could reproduce the plan and had to construct it so that far-flung owners could keep their pianos in working order without his help. We cannot appreciate the inventiveness of his concept without considering the conditions of production and use under which he worked.

And what was the nature of that concept? Cristofori gave the musical world a keyboard instrument with a hammer action that varied the volume of sound—and that worked consistently. The weight of the player's finger on the piano key sent the hammer flying free to strike the string with corresponding speed. The free flight and gravity made the hammer bounce away from the string after striking it, as it needed to do to allow the string to keep vibrating (if the leather facing of the hammer had simply pushed against the string, it would have produced only a thud). With relatively little weight on the key, the hammer flew relatively slowly and the resulting sound was soft (piano); with a harder push, the hammer flew

Front of a piano built by Bartolomeo Cristofori in 1722, showing the maker's nameboard over the keyboard. The inscription reads, "Bartolomeo Cristofori, Paduan, inventor, made [it], Florence, 1722." (Museo degli Strumenti Musicali, Rome)

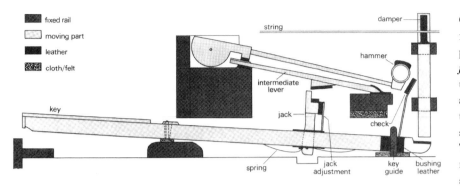

fixed rail
moving part
leather
cloth/felt

string
damper
hammer
intermediate
lever
key
jack
check
spring
jack
adjustment
key
guide
bushing
leather

Cristofori action from the 1726 piano in Leipzig. Depressing the *key* raises the *jack* to push up the lip under the *intermediate lever*, the left end of which touches the hammer shank, pivoted at the left. The lever pushes the hammer shank hard enough to send the *hammer* flying to the *string*. As the key rises, the *spring* on the jack (under the key) and the key's motion combine to move the jack sideways so that it misses ("escapes") the lip's return to rest. When the key is released, the spring returns the jack to its position under the lip. The *check* catches the hammer as it falls back from the string, releasing it when the key is released. The right end of the key as it rises pushes up the *damper* from the string.

faster and the sound was loud (forte). With practice and sensitivity, a performer could make subtle gradations in volume, much as a singer or violinist could.

The harpsichord, as we learned in Chapter 1, is not equipped for such nuances in volume. A plectrum plucks the string, and the loudness of a note is determined by the mass of the plectrum. The performer can affect the loudness of the instrument only by coupling sets of strings together so that one key causes two or three strings to be plucked at once, or by playing thicker chords. The clavichord, on the other hand, is sensitive to touch. Pressing a key brings a brass strip (a tangent), set in the end of the key, up against the strings, which makes them vibrate. The speed of the contact allows gradations of loudness—or perhaps we should say, of softness. The clavichord's whispered elegance, in fact, was suited almost exclusively to solo playing, or perhaps to accompanying the softest singing. Cristofori's piano, too, suffered from softness, or so it was charged by the detractors cited by Maffei in his article. But Maffei defended the instrument's sound in the right setting; with a small group of instruments, a single instrument, or a voice, he wrote, or best of all by itself, "it succeeds perfectly."

To reach this level of perfection, Cristofori had to overcome a series of design problems posed by his unique hammer action. The first, mentioned above, was the problem of escapement: how could the hammer be sent flying freely so that it did not stay up against the string even if the player's finger kept holding the key down? Cristofori's solution is shown here in an illustration. It is a complex machine, but it works cheerfully in repeating the movements consistently many times a minute.

The free-flying hammer caused a second problem: it applied more energy to the string than did a harpsichord plectrum. In order for the string to resist being knocked out of tune, or even broken, it needed to be under greater tension.[4] Cristofori employed the same lengths of strings that he used in harpsichords, but

33

thicker strings to withstand the greater tension. Heavier strings under higher tension added stress on the instrument's framing and bracing. Cristofori side-stepped this difficulty in two ingenious ways that, because they were concealed, came to light only a few years ago. First, he strengthened the case, the box in which the instrument rested, by adding a heavy inner lining and by attaching a rail that held the outer ends of the strings firmly to that strengthened case. With the assistance of a stout block in front that held the tuning pins, the case became a formidable resister of string tension.

The working of the soundboard was also threatened by the increased tension of the strings. To make the instrument audible, the strings' vibrations were transmitted through a hardwood bridge glued to the soundboard, which spread the vibrations across its expanse and reproduced them. So much vibrating surface disturbed the air enough that the sound could be heard even at a distance. But if the soundboard were to take up any of the string tension, it could be distorted and its function disturbed. So Cristofori did something that no other piano maker has done, as far as we know: he mounted the soundboard on an inner wall, separated from the case wall by a spacer. In that way, the soundboard's vibrations were not hindered.[5]

The Shapes of Pianos to Come
Edwin M. Good

Cristofori's pianos were the size and shape of a harpsichord, though their mechanism was radically different. In the decades after Cristofori's death in 1732, other instrument builders made pianos, or piano-like instruments, in radically different sizes and shapes, as well as with mechanisms unlike Cristofori's. Some were vertical instruments reaching nearly nine feet from the floor. Others, called "square" pianos but really rectangular, were the size and shape of clavichords, with the strings strung diagonally in the case rather than perpendicular to the keyboard. This proliferation of designs represented the adaptation of several traditional keyboard designs—designs for instruments that were vastly different from each other in complexity, price, the musical functions for which they were suitable, and the kinds of people who bought and played them. In other words, although the workshops of piano makers remained small, their clientele soon diversified.

We might look back on these various early pianos and think we see the shape of grands and uprights to come. The variety of shapes that early pianos took can certainly remind us that in three centuries, the piano has never found a single ideal or all-purpose shape, like that of the violin or the sitar. Being less movable than most instruments, having to fit a variety of locations, and being called on to play a variety of roles, the piano has always needed to come in a variety of shapes.

Upright piano by
Domenico del Mela, 1739
(Luigi Cherubini Conser-
vatory, Florence)

The earliest upright piano we know was made in 1739 in the village of Gagliano, near Florence, by Domenico del Mela, a priest who was perhaps a friend of
Cristofori's.[6] The piano has a somewhat odd-looking case slightly over six and a
half feet tall and sits on a stand that lifts it another two and a quarter feet. The
strings are hung slightly diagonally, with the longest along the left side of the
case. The instrument is about the size of a Cristofori piano, but its mechanism is
not at all the same. It looks as if the flat surfaces of the hammers never had leather
covering, and that would suggest that it made quite a jangling sound. Instruments
like these were also made in Germany in the mid–eighteenth century; Christian
Ernst Friederici of Gera claimed to have built the earliest German uprights,
which he called "pyramid pianos" because of their symmetrical shape. But little
is known of the musical purposes for which they were designed or to which they
were put.

A more popular piano-like instrument in the German-speaking lands—and
one that came in both vertical and clavichord shapes—was the pantalon. The
pantalon took its name from an enormous zither played with hand-held mallets by
Pantaleon Hebenstreit, a successful virtuoso in the early 1700s. The mid-century
pantalon was a smaller instrument with a keyboard; it had small wooden hammers
with no covering and no dampers, although some makers devised ways to damp
the strings. The instrument was able to play all gradations of loudness, but it had
little expressive subtlety; nonetheless, many listeners found its undamped wash
of sound bewitching. One legacy of the pantalon to the piano was the use of tone-
changing stops, such as mutes that softened and "harp" stops that hardened the
sound.

The pantalon and the clavichord, both popular in Germany, influenced the
invention of the square piano. In fact, a recent study by Michael Cole argues persuasively that what have been taken to be the earliest square pianos are misiden-
tified pantalons.[7] If Cole is correct, the square piano was invented by Johannes
Zumpe, a German builder from Fürth, near Nuremberg, who came to London in
the 1750s. He worked for the harpsichord maker Burkat Shudi until 1761, when he
established his own shop in Princes Street, Hanover Square, "at the sign of the
Golden Guittar." There he first made guitars and other plucked-string instruments that were small, affordable, and favored by young ladies. By 1766 he was
making pianofortes that were also small, affordable, and appealing to upper-class
women.

Zumpe's square pianos are so much like clavichords in layout, size, and
shape that we most naturally suppose that he founded the design on the earlier

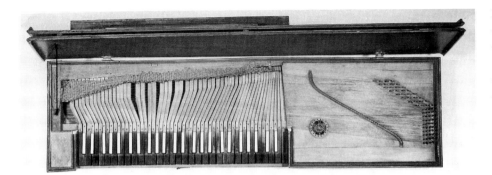

Plan views of an eighteenth-century clavichord by an unknown German builder and *(below)* a square piano by Johannes Zumpe, London, 1770 (Smithsonian Institution)

instrument. But his pianos used a sturdier case and considerably heavier strings than those in clavichords, and a much thicker bridge, necessary for the heavier strings. His action, having no intermediate lever, may have been derived not from Cristofori's piano action, but from the very simple action of a pantalon. The leather-covered hammers were hinged with leather on a rail. Zumpe used hand stops to raise the dampers, and in about 1770 introduced a harp or buff stop. Some other makers in England borrowed more stops from the pantalon to alter the tone.

If a square piano seems small and simple compared with a Cristofori or an early-eighteenth-century upright, its clientele, initially, was most exalted. The arrival of the young, musical Princess Charlotte in September 1761 from the small north German court of Mecklenburg-Strelitz to become queen to George III has been called "the catalyst that accelerated the pianoforte revolution in Britain."[8] Among the German musicians who migrated to London in her wake was Johann Christian Bach, who came in May 1762 to compose opera, to establish concert series, and soon to become the queen's music master. From Mecklenburg-Strelitz itself came

Pianos for Sale
Cynthia Adams Hoover

37

instrument maker Gabriel Buntebart, who joined in partnership with Zumpe by 1768. Zumpe designed the pianos; he and Buntebart made them; Bach composed for them, played them (in one of the earliest recorded London public solo piano performances on June 2, 1768), and sold them.

The nature of the revolution was that the piano became, for the first time, a popular instrument rather than a courtly curiosity. Both Queen Charlotte and her brother had Zumpes (mostly likely acquired through J. C. Bach and Buntebart). But it was not enough for Zumpe to have the patronage of the queen and her brother; he used it to promote sales of his instruments. He did not often advertise, except by listing his address on the front board over the keyboard of his instruments. Like piano makers through the whole history of the instrument, he instead relied heavily on the endorsement of players: J. C. Bach and Charles Burney played that role for him. In 1770 in Paris Burney found that Bach had provided a Zumpe for Madame Brillon, the talented Parisian who was a friend of Boccherini and Benjamin Franklin. Burney and "John" Bach also helped Diderot acquire a Zumpe (at eighteen guineas) for his daughter in the early 1770s.[9]

When Zumpe changed the location of his shop, however, he did resort to advertising, inserting the following notice in the *General Advertiser* (February 1, 1780):

> Mr. Zumpe, the inventor of the Small Piano-Forte and Maker to her Majesty and the Royal Family . . . begs leave to acquaint the Nobility & Gentry, that he has just compleated a New Improvement with different Pedals, that makes the Piano-forte perfect in every degree, which hitherto it never was; and also prevents that instrument from going out of order, which was always the case before.[10]

Note that second only to Zumpe's claim to have invented the small piano comes his claim to be the maker of choice for the royal family. Also, note the clientele that he addresses: "the Nobility & Gentry." Even at sixteen to eighteen guineas, about one-third the cost of a good harpsichord, a square piano was a luxury item.[11] But no matter how luxurious the item, Zumpe had created a new relationship between maker and buyer when he started producing pianos in quantity (no matter how small the quantity) and offering them on the open market (no matter how elite the market). This is made clear by the last line of Zumpe's advertisement, in which he claims to have discovered how to make pianos so that they do not go out of order. Evidently the crucial factor that made Zumpe's piano marketable was not its low price, but the reliability of operation derived from its simplicity of design.

English nobles and gentlemen might be richer than Medici princes, but they still had no Cristoforis on staff to repair and regulate their pianos.

Zumpe clearly had a fashionable hit on his hands. As Charles Burney wrote:

> There was scarcely a house in the kingdom where a keyed instrument had ever had admission, but was supplied with one of Zumpe's piano-fortes for which there was nearly as much call in France as in England. In short he could not make them fast enough to gratify the craving of the public. Pohlmann, whose instruments were very inferior in tone, fabricated an almost infinite number for such as Zumpe was unable to supply.

Yet the scale of production with which Zumpe caused this sensation was not great; according to Michael Cole, it was just over fifty pianos a year. As Burney observes, when Zumpe could not keep up with the demand, other makers offered their wares, apparently with Zumpe's blessing.[12]

In the 1770s other craftsmen, many of them German immigrants, set up shop in London in response to the growing demand for pianos. In 1775 another maker of

Johan Zoffany, *George, 3rd Earl Cowper, with His Wife and the Family of Charles Gore*, 1775. The social prestige of the Zumpe square piano is demonstrated by the place of the instrument in this painting commemorating a marriage uniting two upper-class English families. (Yale Center for British Art)

German origin, John Behrent, placed an advertisement in the Philadelphia papers that is probably the earliest known announcement of a piano made in America.

> JOHN BEHRENT, Joiner and Instrument Maker, living in Third-street continued, in Campington, directly opposite Coates' Burying-ground, Has just finished for sale, an extraordinary fine instrument, by the name of Piano Forte, of Mahogany, in the manner of an harpsichord, with hammers, and several changes: He intends to dispose of it on very reasonable terms; and being a master in such sort of work, and a new beginner in this country, he requests all lovers of music to favour him with their custom, and they shall not only be honestly served, but their favours gratefully acknowledged, by their humble servant, John Behrent.[13]

In Paris, Sébastien Erard, a builder who later contributed much to the development of the piano, began building square pianos sometime around 1777. Johann Andreas Stein, an organ builder in Augsburg, experimented with a new action on grand pianos, winning Mozart's praise when he visited in 1777.[14]

Back in London, the harpsichord maker John Broadwood sold his first square piano in 1780, his first grands in 1785.[15] By the end of the eighteenth century, as its piano clientele expanded, the Broadwood firm was dividing its account books into two categories: (1) the regular customers (no doubt the "Nobility and Gentry") to whom the firm regularly sold instruments and for whom it regularly tuned (tuning provided a steady income for many makers when sales were slow); and (2) the Chance Trade—people who walked into the showroom on Great Pulteney Street.[16] The Chance Trade probably included daughters and their newly middle-class parents eager to emulate a more refined style of life.

Well into the nineteenth century, as pianos became affordable by members of the middle class, they remained out of reach for most members of the working class—including many of the workers who produced them. In England the price of a fine grand in the early 1800s was as much as £84 (or four-fifths of a skilled workman's annual salary of £100), that of a square about 18 guineas to as much as £30. In New York in 1854, a Steinway square sold for $550, when the annual wage of a skilled worker ranged from $625 to $1,000, and the yearly expenses for a workingman's family of four were $600.[17]

Often a music teacher would recommend a purchase (for 10 to 15 percent commission), a practice that Philadelphia piano maker and importer Charles Taws denounced in newspapers in the 1790s as bribery.[18] In spite of Taws's protests, the practice of commissions and discounts (up to 50 percent to a system of hand-picked agents in various cities and towns) continued in the trade, even until present times. Builders sought to improve their reputations and increase their sales through gifts or loans of pianos for famous players to use in concerts. Thomas Broadwood (one of John's sons and successors) presented a grand to Beethoven in 1817. Some players remained loyal to one maker, like Chopin to Pleyel pianos; others changed allegiances or, like Liszt, seemed to enjoy playing on many makes of pianos. As the demand for pianos increased, makers worked hard to keep up with orders. As James Shudi Broadwood (another son of John) wrote in 1798 to a wholesaler wanting his order filled, "Would to God we could make them like muffins!"[19]

As piano makers did indeed begin to "make them like muffins," continuity of production became as important as scale and speed. Cristofori's piano production had died with him. Zumpe, after an amicable dissolution of his partnership with Buntebart, arranged for two journeymen cabinetmakers from his home town, Frederick and Christian Schoene, to join his shop in the late 1770s, and in 1782 he turned his business over to them and retired a wealthy man, listing himself as "Gentleman." But continuity was perhaps best assured by marrying well, if not the former master's widow or daughter, at least someone with a modest dowry and good health to provide many children for carrying on the business. Perhaps the best example of marrying well is John Broadwood, who with his marriage in 1769 to Barbara Shudi (the daughter of his employer, harpsichord maker Burkat Shudi), gained a wife, a business partnership, and the beginning of a piano dynasty that flourished through the nineteenth century. Johann Andreas Stein is remembered not only for his finely crafted pianos, but also for the continuation and development of his tradition through pianos built in Vienna by his son Mattheus Andreas and by his daughter Nannette Streicher, her husband Andreas, and their progeny. The importance of family is also evident in the history of later piano firms like Chickering & Sons and Steinway & Sons in the United States and Bechstein in Germany. This family tradition was noted, though in terms that ignored the crucial part played by daughters, in a comment made by one member of the piano trade in 1921: "Absence of male issue has brought down many a fine business."[20]

The Workshop
Cynthia Adams Hoover

What kind of workshops and showrooms did builders like Zumpe and Broadwood and Stein have? Many of the shops were small. Not unlike modern-day makers of harpsichords and fortepianos, the master craftsman usually used the same location for workshop, living quarters (not only for his family but also often for his assistants), and showroom (which in England was often in the dining room).[21] Some shared quarters with other craftsmen, including cabinetmakers; the 1774 New York advertisement of John Sheybli, listed and shown as an organ builder in the rare illustration seen here of a shop interior, also claimed that he made "fortepianoes" and had "one hammer spinnet" for sale.[22] Some makers established smaller showrooms visible through display windows from the street or placed their instruments with music dealers who sold a variety of goods. Others, like the Broadwoods, expanded to nearby houses and to property in adjoining mews and alleys. This crazy-quilt pattern of shops was true even in New York for the Steinways before they built their first factory (in 1860).[23]

At first, the typical shop included the master craftsman, one or more journeymen, and apprentices. Records of early piano workshops are sketchy, but inventories of modest piano makers show that shops had from two to at least six workbenches.[24] The traditional seven-year apprenticeship (wherein the master entered into a legal agreement to provide food, clothing, lodging, some schooling, but no pay) was often shortened to fewer years if observed at all, especially in America.[25] The goal of the apprentice was to work long enough to earn the title and independence of the journeyman. The journeyman aspired to become a partner with his master or to establish his own shop. Many masters sought to prosper enough to live away from the shop (even in a country estate), to invest in other enterprises like real estate, and to acquire wealth and position so that they and their sons could become "gentlemen" and highly respected members of their community.

In the period of preindustrial craft, the weekly or annual production depended as much on the number of workers as it did on shop routine. In 1784 John Broadwood sold thirty-eight harpsichords and 133 square pianos; by 1794 the firm made five hundred grand pianos and more than

Advertisement of John Sheybli, organ builder in New York who shared the workshop of Mr. Samuel Prince, cabinetmaker. From *New-York Gazette and Weekly Mercury*, October 10, 1774. This rare view of the interior of a shop shows on the left a worker at his bench with his tools arranged on the wall. (Smithsonian Institution)

JOHN SHEYBLI, ORGAN-BUILDER, At Mr. Samuel Prince's, cabinet-maker, in Horfe and Cart-ftreet, New-York;

MAKES, repairs and tunes all forts of organs, harpfichords, fpinnets and Fortepianoes, on the moft reafonable terms.

N. B. He has now ready for fale, one neat chamber organ, one hammer fpinnet, one common fpinnet.

a thousand squares. (The last harpsichord was made in 1793). John Geib, a London organ and piano maker who moved to New York in 1797, advertised in 1800 that in London his company had made eight to ten pianos a week (about five hundred a year) and, in addition to church and chamber organs, had already made 4,910 pianos (grand and small) and about four hundred "organized pianos" (a combination of a square piano and a small pipe organ). During the partnership of Jonas Chickering and James Stewart in Boston between 1823 and 1826, their production expanded from fifteen to thirty pianos a year. The Steinways claimed that in Germany they had made about ten pianos a year before the family came to America in 1850.[26]

When shops were small, nearly everyone working in them eventually learned the entire "art, Trade & Mystery" of making pianos. The master or the senior journeyman oversaw the more crucial tasks like gluing and installing the soundboard or regulating the instrument.[27] As the shop grew, some journeymen began to spe-

Piano wareroom of Loud & Brothers in Philadelphia, ca. 1825 (Library Company of Philadelphia)

Keith's Music & Umbrella Store in Boston, 1845, from the back cover of *Ole Bull Violin Instruction Book: A Complete School for the Violin* (Boston, 1845)

Nameboards from two late-eighteenth-century square pianos built in New York, one by John Geib & Son, the other by Whaites & Charters. The similarity of design suggests that the two makers worked with the same nameboard painter. (Smithsonian Institution)

cialize in making cases or doing other piece work. They often signed the piece they completed as a matter of pride and evidence of completion. Sometimes, too, the shop books reveal who worked on what part; the early Steinway factory books, for instance, listed William Steinway as the bellyman (soundboard installer), Henry Jr. as the finisher, and Charles as the regulator. Sometimes part of the work was completed outside the shop. Certainly brass work was purchased elsewhere, and possibly some of the decorations on nameboards were completed by specialists who made similar designs for several makers. By 1852 Chickering was obtaining his keyboards, wire, and iron frames from others.[28]

Each experienced worker had his own workbench and set of tools. Although the shop owner often provided the bench, each worker was required to provide his own tools, which he may have mounted over his bench (see the Sheybli workshop illustration) or stored and transported in a special chest designed with compartments and drawers. At a time when a foreman's annual earnings in England were about one hundred pounds, the tools of a senior workman might be worth seventy pounds. Without tools, a journeyman had no work or trade; they defined his livelihood and status as a craftsman. In the event that journeymen lost their tools in a shop or factory fire, entire communities, including artisans from competing shops, rallied to help the workers replace them.[29] The journeymen developed such precision using their tools that they could produce nearly uniform parts. And because their skills were transferable, the journeymen were free to move from shop to shop, although some worked for the same employer for decades. Others, however, sometimes found themselves out of work because of financial depressions, the seasonal nature of the piano trade (busiest in late fall before Christmas), and the influx of immigrant workers and unskilled novices willing to take lower pay.[30]

In New York during the 1830s, several trades formed unions in an attempt to force employers to pay a standard price for similar work. The Journeymen Piano-Forte Makers formed a society that published in 1835 the *New-York Book of Prices for Manufacturing Piano-Fortes* for "better regulating and equalizing their prices . . . to the mutual advantage of both the Employer and the Employed." In about 110 pages, the journeymen described and priced almost every step in making four kinds of pianos: two types of squares (plain and German) and two upright or cabinet pianos. No grand pianos are priced, which might suggest that few were being made. All men were required to work by the piece, except those with functions

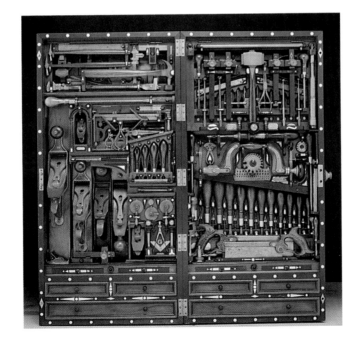

Piano maker's tool chest and tools, 1890–1920. The chest, made of materials used in piano construction (ivory, ebony, mahogany, mother-of-pearl), may have been constructed by the piano maker who owned it, H. O. Studley of Quincy, Massachusetts. (Robert Gilson)

like "Fly-Finishing," on which workers were not to work more than ten hours a day. The journeymen were to furnish their own candlelight. No prices are given for tuning and regulating; according to statistical wage data from 1863 to 1880 about the Steinway workers, tuning and regulating were higher paid than the other functions listed in the *Book of Prices*. The highest Steinway pay went to foremen, clerks, and salesmen.[31]

As production increased, workers specialized further. Contemporaries of Conrad Graf in Vienna reported that in the 1830s Graf's factory had organized the work into eight divisions. The Broadwood factory, with three hundred to four hundred or more workers making twenty-five hundred to three thousand instruments a year in the 1830s and 1840s, was reported to have divided the manufacture of the piano into forty-two separate steps in 1851, expanding to fifty-eight departments by 1867. A visitor to the Chickering factory in Boston reported in 1852 that the hundred workmen in the finishing department divided the work into twenty different departments, each man always doing the same task. "For example, the man who makes *hammers* never does anything else," for as many as thirty years. But even the hammers were divided into four tasks: woodwork, hinges and joints, leathers, and fitting the hammers in place. "This minute subdivision of labor secures, of course, the greatest possible uniformity and perfection."[32]

Grand and Would-Be Grand Pianos
Edwin M. Good

Cristofori called his invention neither "piano" nor "grand" but "harpsichord (*cimbalo*) . . . with soft and loud." The term "grand piano" was introduced in 1777 in Robert Stodart's application for an English patent for a combination piano-harpsichord.[33] To call this instrument "grand" was simply to distinguish it as "large" from Zumpe's type of little square. But Stodart did not invent what we may call the grand piano. That had been done earlier in the 1770s in both Germany and London.

The process began as early as 1725, with the German translation of Maffei's article about Cristofori. Gottfried Silbermann in Dresden read the article and proceeded to copy the instrument described in it. He finally succeeded to the point that, in 1747 or so, King Frederick the Great of Prussia bought a number of his instruments, and Johann Sebastian Bach not only played one at the Potsdam court but also signed his name as agent on the sale of a Silbermann piano to Count Branitzky of Białystok.[34] Silbermann's instruments were just like Cristofori's, and shared their quiet sound and other limitations. As the piano became more popular, makers both in England and on the Continent began to make adjustments to the harpsichord-shaped piano to make it more adequate to new needs. The "grand" piano developed into an instrument that answered the acoustical demands of concert settings, the musical needs of professional musicians and serious amateurs, and the social needs of the rich and powerful. By the early nineteenth century the grand gave the word *piano* its ideal (if not its ordinary) meaning. Smaller types of instruments, especially squares, continued to account for a much greater share of production and sales, but more and more they were designed to emulate the touch and sound of grands.

Professional performance on the piano differed between London and Germany, public concerts counting for more in London and courtly gatherings for more in Germany and Austria. Accordingly, the design of grand pianos took different directions in the two areas, the English makers pursuing above all greater power of sound and the Germans greater fleetness and subtlety in the response of the instrument to the player's touch. The crucial demarcation in grand piano design during the late eighteenth century, then, was the difference between the English and German actions, although there were also important differences in the design of the case, the stops, and other features.

The English designers gave their action a direct-blow design instead of Cristofori's intermediate lever. The action used in the 1772 Americus Backers grand in the Russell Collection at Edinburgh University—the earliest surviving English grand—was modified somewhat in Robert Stodart's patent of 1777. That design, adopted by John Broadwood when he began to make grands in 1785, be-

English grand action from a Broadwood piano, 1799. As the *key* rises, the *hopper* is pushed against a notch in the hammer shank, propelling the *hammer* to the *string*. As the hopper rises, its projection slides along the *set-off*, which forces the hopper to pivot to the right, and its top moves to the right of the notch when the hammer falls back to the *check*. The right end of the key pushes the *damper* off the string. When the key is released, the *spring* brings the hopper back to its original position.

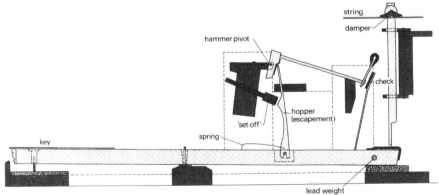

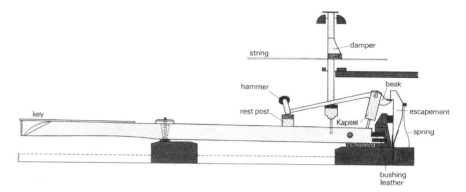

"Viennese" grand action, by Johann Andreas Stein, ca. 1785. The *hammer* with its shank is pivoted in the fork-shaped *Kapsel*. The *beak* is positioned under the projection on the *escapement*. As the *key* rises, the beak's position forces the hammer to pivot up to the *string*, and as it drops back, the beak catches on the front surface of the escapement. When the key is released, the *spring* on the escapement allows the beak to return to its original position in the notch. The damper lifter, mounted on the key, pushes the *damper* off the string as the key rises. Later designs added a check to catch the hammer.

came the standard in English and some French pianos for about one hundred years.

The English grands typically had two stops: a damper lifter and a keyboard shift or una corda, worked by pedals attached to the front legs of the instruments, the damper pedal on the right and the una corda on the left. The damper stop had been introduced to the piano by Gottfried Silbermann. It was taken up also by the pantalon makers, who, like Silbermann, used hand stops for the dampers. In both, the stop raised all the dampers at once, so that the player could obtain more resonance than was available by holding down individual keys. The una corda stop had been introduced by Cristofori. His pianos had a knob on the cheek of the keyboard by which the entire keyboard could be moved sideways so that the hammers would strike only one of the two strings for each note. This is sometimes thought of as a "soft" stop, but sounding one rather than both of the strings for a given note produces more difference in timbre than in volume. In the 1772 Backers piano and some Broadwoods, the two pedals give a distinctly pigeon-toed look. Later the pedals were attached to a frame under the middle of the keyboard, which in the nineteenth century often took the symbolic shape and name of a lyre. Today pedals remain the conventional method of activating stops.

What became the Viennese rival to English grand piano design emerged about the same time—the 1770s—but probably in Augsburg, not Vienna, in the workshop of Johann Andreas Stein. The case of a Stein piano is not so deep as an English one and makes the instrument look more fragile, although it is not. The reason is simple: Stein's A-frame brace, combined with cross braces, kept his grands from warping on their right cheek as English pianos were prone to do. For stops, Stein and other German and Viennese makers preferred knee levers, tucked inconspicuously under the front of the case below the keyboard, to the English pedals. After 1800, they switched to pedals, and the stops on their pianos proliferated wildly. On some pianos, uprights as well as grands, we find up to seven pedals, including a buzzing "bassoon" stop, a muting "moderator," and a thumping and jingling military stop ("Janissary"), along with the less ephemeral damper lifter and una corda stop.[35]

More important, however, was the introduction of the Stein action, which has

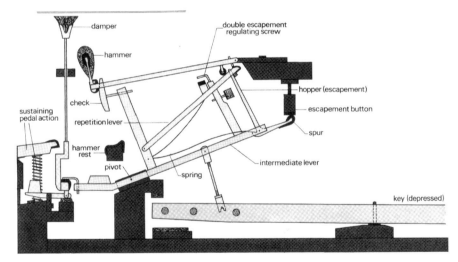

Erard "double escapement" (or "repetition") action, 1822. The diagram shows the *key* depressed, after the *hammer* has struck the *string* and been caught by the *check*. The wippen, which joins the key and the *intermediate lever*, pushes the lever up as the key rises. That raises the *hopper (escapement)* against the round projection under the hammer shank, called the "knuckle," propelling the hammer to the string. As the hopper pushes the knuckle, the *spur* is stopped against the *escapement button*, forcing the hopper to pivot to its right, and the knuckle settles back on the *repetition lever*, pushing it down slightly. As the key is released, the hopper moves left, and the *spring* makes the repetition lever push the knuckle up so that the end of the hopper returns under it and the stroke can be repeated before the key is completely released—hence the name "repetition action." The key's rising makes the left end of the intermediate lever push down against the damper assembly, which pulls the damper down from the string.

come to be known as the Viennese grand action (see illustration). This action was lighter, more responsive to the touch, and therefore conducive to more subtlety of expression than the English action. Later, however, it was made heavier, as pianos increased in size and strings in girth.

In the long run (that is, by the beginning of the twentieth century), piano manufacturers came to a fairly universal agreement that favored the English tradition over the Viennese in action design as well as choice of stops. But in the meantime, the Viennese tradition of design produced the pianos for which the classic repertory of piano music was composed: Haydn, Mozart, Beethoven, Schubert, and Schumann were all most familiar with the light, responsive action of German and Austrian pianos. One of the great challenges in studying the history of the piano, then, is to understand how the piano itself evolved away from the instrument of the Viennese and German masters at the very time that their music was becoming established as the most prestigious body of piano music.

Both English and German grand pianos grew in range and size even during the 1790s, when Broadwood, reportedly at the urging of Jan Ladislav Dussek, the darling of the London concert stage, began to construct grands with a range of five octaves and a fifth. A few makers in Vienna, Anton Walter among them, increased the range one step beyond five octaves, to the G two octaves and a fifth above middle C. In that same decade Broadwood even made a six-octave grand on special order, but only around 1810 were many grands given that six-octave, C to C, range. In Austria and Germany, the move to six octaves tended to be from the F two octaves and a fifth below middle C. Such a range was used by Beethoven in his later works and often by Schubert.

The leading French maker, Sébastien Erard, made an experimental seven-octave grand in the 1820s, which became the standard range until about the 1880s. But Erard's greatest importance for the grand stemmed from his design of a replacement for the English action. Pianists had complained that the English action was stiff and could not give rapid repetition. Erard patented in 1821 what he called a "repetition" or "double escapement" action (see illustration). With Erard's design, a virtuoso no longer needed to choose between the power of the English action and the speed of the Viennese. And virtuosos, impressing ever larger audiences with the wonders they could perform on Erard pianos, were the ones who sealed the reputation of that action. It was a long time, however, before Erard's action—somewhat improved by pianist and piano manufacturer Henri Herz in about 1840—overcame resistance in every piano-manufacturing country to become the standard grand piano action.

In the meantime, upright and square pianos were busy catching up with the grands. One way to catch up was to make an upright piano as big as a grand, capturing the advantages of its large soundboard, long strings, and resulting full tone, but taking up much less floor space in a home than a grand. An example was the "upright grand Piano-forte in the form of a bookcase" patented by William Stodart (Robert's son) in 1795. Stodart's rectangular case (and those of similar pianos by other English makers) had space above the shorter treble strings for shelves to hold music, busts of Roman heroes, or other knick-knacks (see the photograph of the Broadwood upright grand piano in Chapter 3). The German and Austrian counterpart was the "giraffe," so called for its external resemblance to that marvelously unwieldy beast. Unlike the English upright grands, these pianos had cases extending down to the floor, making for more stability with no loss of instrumental quality.

Turning a grand piano upright was not, however, going to put the piano within the reach of people who could not afford a grand. The enormous expansion of the piano market in the nineteenth century depended on the creation of smaller pianos, and in 1800 two experiments in small vertical pianos were made in Germany and America. The Ditanaklassis, a bit more than five feet high, was designed by Matthias Müller, using an action modeled on Stein's. Müller also had the bright idea, seen in some earlier Viennese grands, of combining two instruments in one case, with the keyboards facing each other, and the hammers striking strings on either side of a single soundboard. In the same year, John Isaac Hawkins, an English engineer in Philadelphia, patented a "Portable Grand Piano," which was vertical and only fifty-four inches tall. Its unique action used a counterweight to encourage the hammer to fall away from the string. Hawkins also introduced metal bars as bracing behind the soundboard, an innovation that had no immediate successors but that preceded by some years the successful introduction of iron. Hawkins puffed his piano a bit by calling it both "portable" and "grand." Portable it is, with handles on the sides of an elegant case; grand (even in the sense of "big") it is not.

In the second decade of the nineteenth century, the era of the smaller upright began in earnest, with the "cottage piano" by Robert Wornum of London heralding a recognition that the middle class could now emulate the wealthy in the arts and own very good pianos that would fit their more modest homes and budgets. Wornum's improved upright "tape-check" action in 1826 has continued in modified form right to the present. But it did not solve problems of responsiveness and touch, and until recently the upright action has never been very satisfactory.

"Portable Grand Piano"
by John Isaac Hawkins,
Philadelphia, 1801
(Smithsonian Institution)

Wornum's early cottage pianos were only forty-one inches high, shorter than most modern uprights. To fit strings of a length that would give a tone approaching the decent, he hung them diagonally in his very short case.

Henri Pape of Paris attained even more miniaturization than Wornum. His "piano consoles" were only about thirty-six inches high, so they took up little floor space and hardly any room against a wall. To achieve a tone that would be acceptable in the age of the grand piano, Pape devised a scheme of "cross-stringing" in the late 1820s. Here the longest bass strings ran diagonally from lower left to upper right, while the shorter treble strings ran in the opposite direction, and the longer ones crossed above the others. By this scheme Pape not only squeezed longer strings into his tiny piano than he could have otherwise, but he also arranged that the bridge for the lower strings could be located where they would resonate more richly. The irony of Pape's innovation is that while he devised it to enable a small piano to sound more like a big one, it was eventually adopted in grand piano design as well, to make grand pianos sound even grander.

Meanwhile, the square piano continued its career. In 1786 John Geib, then still working in London, patented an action for the square piano that contained the intermediate lever that made the actions of Silbermann pianos so responsive; at last there was an escapement for square pianos. To keep up with grands, squares also grew bigger and bigger, with wider keyboard ranges, heavier hammers, thicker strings, and louder tone. These changes created problems in the square that were solved only with the introduction of iron. But before examining that development, let us return to the subject of how pianos were produced.

The Industrial Revolution was defined by new exploitations of energy sources (especially steam power), raw materials, and machinery to produce goods; new organization of work through the division of labor and specialization of jobs; improved transportation and communication; and a general application of science to industry. Wealth and power were redistributed; class and labor were redefined. A worker changed from a "handicraft worker with tools" to "a machine operator subjected to factory discipline." At times, in order to deal with the new patterns of authority, the working class joined together in unions for bargaining strength.[36]

Because the Broadwood company led the world in numbers of pianos produced in the mid–nineteenth century and had its factory in England (sometimes dubbed "the workshop of the world"), one might expect it to have led in adopting new industrial methods. But the company was slow to do so. In 1842 George Dodd published an account of a visit to the Broadwood factory at Horseferry Road, Westminster, which the company had leased in 1823. He described how the buildings and rooms were arranged in a way that reflected a logical system for production. The crucial lumber piles were carefully aged and dried in one area. In other portions of the factory, an impressive number of workrooms carefully divided by piano styles and functions resembled cabinetmakers' shops with stoves and fireplaces for warming glue. The keyboards were cut with a framed saw, the fretwork by a fret saw, and the planks with pit saws. All were hand operated.[37]

Dodd summed up his visit with the observation that "the piano-forte manufacture is one in which nothing but highly skilled manual dexterity can make and adjust the numerous pieces of mechanism involved in it; and those workmen who possess this skill are not likely to be supplanted by any automatic machinery." When the Broadwood factory burned down in 1856 (the tools lost were valued between three thousand and four thousand pounds), a new factory of the same design was built in the same leased location. No modern machinery for woodworking was added. With the abundance of skilled labor, the Broadwood family thought that their traditional (and conservative) craft-based method would continue to serve them well in their production of about twenty-five hundred pianos each year. But as one economic historian pointed out, "even Broadwood's elaborate division of labour achieved an annual productivity of only seven pianos per man, no higher than that of small firms." Not until 1902, when Broadwood built a

The Factory

Cynthia Adams Hoover

53

Illustrations of a key-cutter and a fret-cutter at work in the Broadwood & Sons piano factory, London, from George Dodd, *Days at the Factories* (London, 1843)

new factory in the East End, did it use machinery and adopt a production-line system.[38]

In contrast, some American firms eagerly adopted many of the principles of the Industrial Revolution. Jonas Chickering, a Boston manufacturer who had begun as a humble apprentice in 1818, built a piano factory in Boston in 1838 with financial backing from John Mackay, a wealthy shipping merchant. By the early 1850s, Chickering had expanded to three other locations: two in nearby Lawrence, where one made keyboards and the other—its machinery powered by the Merrimac River—was devoted to seasoning, sawing, and planing lumber; the third was a veneering factory in Boston. The main factory burned on December 1, 1852, four years before the Broadwood fire.[39]

When he rebuilt, Chickering, unlike Broadwood, chose to celebrate the industrial changes. Visitors to the new factory were led first to the shining new steam engine, "a marvel of graceful motion" that provided power for the machines and heat for the entire building. Instead of cutting the rough lumber with pit saws, the workmen used large new sawing and planing machines. They also used a steam-powered jigsaw for cutting fretwork for music desks. A steam-powered elevator (described by one writer as large enough to hold a "comfortable-sized dinner party" with ease) carried from floor to floor men, lumber, and work in progress.[40] Other American piano manufacturers, even smaller companies like Boardman & Gray in Albany, New York, built factories using steam power and machines.[41] Steinway & Sons, Chickering's rival at the top of the piano-making line, built a steam-powered factory in 1860 (at what is now Park Avenue between 52nd

Above: Scenes from the new Chickering Pianoforte Manufactory in Boston, from *Frank Leslie's Illustrated Newspaper,* April 16, 1859. Note that here the fret cutting is done with a power-driven saw. Note also the use of child labor in the action room.

View of the Engine Room at the Chickering factory, Boston, from *Scientific American,* October 26, 1878

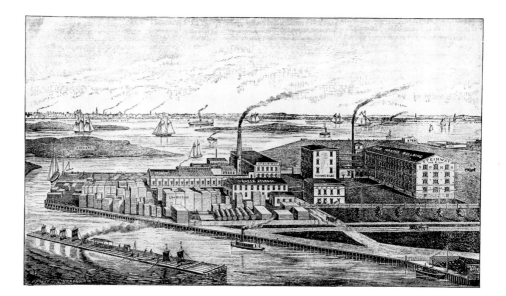

Steinway & Sons factory in Astoria, Long Island, New York, from an 1888 Steinway catalog

and 53rd in New York City), expanding in the 1870s to Astoria, New York, with a factory and company town and in 1880 to a factory in Hamburg, Germany. Eventually what became known as the American System of manufacture was adopted by piano companies around the world.

Did the new machinery and steam power obviate the need for skilled workers? Not at all. The piano industry retained through the years many jobs that required skilled human dexterity and judgment. One writer observed as late as 1981 that "the most complicated machine in the Steinway factory is the finished grand piano." Yet in the same publication, another writer described the Yamaha factory in Hamamatsu, Japan, where robots carried pianos along an assembly line to speed the production of several hundred thousand pianos each year.[42]

The Iron Frame
Edwin M. Good

It did not take a factory system of manufacture to bring iron into piano frames. We have already seen that Hawkins tried iron braces in the frames of his tiny uprights in 1800. The demand for ever-louder sound in pianos of all sorts led to ever-increasing tension on strings. Coupled with the inconvenience caused by the ease with which pianos of the day went out of tune, this made evident the need for stronger framing. Sooner or later, someone would think of making metal frames. The power of the Industrial Revolution was that it shaped the attitudes of those who decided whether or not to accept this innovation. To build pianos with steam-powered tools was one thing; to put a cast-iron frame at the center of the instru-

Piano construction today is a blend of hand and automated workmanship. These two photographs from the Yamaha piano factory in Hamamatsu, Japan, show a worker adjusting the filler block by hand during inner rim construction, and a computer-controlled robotic key-level sensing device.

ment, making the product itself a modern if miniature factory of sound, rather than a fully hand-crafted artwork in wood, was quite another. The debate over whether to accept the change was lengthy and vigorous.

Pianos of different shapes showed the strain of increased string tension in different places. Squares tended to respond to the diagonal arrangement of the strings by warping upward at the right front and left back corners, even with thicker boards on the bottom and a stout oaken spine.[43] Grands tended to take on an alarming warp at the right cheek, where the case curves inward. English and French grands tended to warp more than German and Viennese ones, which were mostly kept in good shape by their sturdy A-frame bracing.

Soon after Hawkins's experiment with iron braces, other builders, in England especially, tried other ways to provide efficient iron braces for the grand. In 1808, Broadwood attempted to run iron tension bars from the pin block in front to the string plate, at the other end of the strings, but he was unable to attach them securely.[44] In 1820, James Thom and William Allen, employees of William Stodart in London, took out a patent for a metal compensation frame. It was a system of nine metal tubes bolted into the pin block and the string plate, and its avowed function was to compensate for strings' tendency to go out of tune because of changes in the atmosphere. The tubes were made of the same material as the strings below them, iron in the top and brass in the lower bass, so that they would contract and expand with temperature changes at the same rate as the strings. The only problem with this strategy was that pianos go out of tune not because of temperature changes but because of changes in humidity. The Thom-Allen frame in fact functioned as a compression frame, resisting the string tension. Throughout this period of experimentation, many felt certain that iron in the piano would ruin the tone.

Alpheus Babcock patented the one-piece metal frame in 1825. Babcock, a very talented Boston craftsman—less talented in business, unfortunately—received his patent on December 17, 1825, to manufacture "the frame, to which the strings of the piano forte are attached, of cast iron, wrought-iron, brass composition metal, or some other metal, or compound of metals, suitable to this purpose."[45] The piano for which Babcock designed this frame was a square, which was in fact the only kind of piano he ever made, although the patent text claims that the patent applies to any piano "now in use, or which has been, or can be invented." It is hardly surprising that an American inventor would have carried out the idea in a square piano, because that was the type that dominated the American market at the time. But Babcock, after engaging in battles with other manufacturers over the ownership of the idea in the early 1830s, went to work for Jonas Chickering from 1837 until his death in 1842. Chickering, who had the business savvy that Babcock lacked and who built pianos of every type, took up the iron frame and made a commercial success of it, first in square pianos and then in grands, which he became the first to build with iron frames in 1840.[46]

The iron frame meant that string tension could be increased with relative impunity: heavier strings, longer strings, strings of stronger material—steel was still too expensive for piano strings until Henry Bessemer invented his process in 1856. But it was some time before everyone came to use full iron frames. Technological history has many examples of the lapse of time between innovation and success. An invention that seems by hindsight to be inevitable and natural may take decades or even centuries of debate or suppression before it comes to general adoption. Cristofori's piano is one case in point. The iron frame is another. Henry Fowler Broadwood took the advice of his scientist friend Dr. William Pole, who warned Broadwood to steer clear of the iron frame lest he harm the tone and add to the weight and cost of his pianos. Albert-Louis Blondel, who had directed the Erard company since 1873, said as late as 1927 that the opinion against one-piece iron frames, long held by Erard, was founded on perceptions of tone quality.[47] By the time it became the norm, the nature of the grand piano had been altered by still other innovations.

The patent for the first cross-strung grand piano was given to Henry Steinway, Jr., in 1859. The idea of cross-stringing was developed, as we have seen, by Henri Pape in the 1820s as a device to allow small uprights to emulate the rich sound of the grands of the period. To introduce the idea into grand pianos was not to emulate any other kind of piano, but to push the concert sound of the piano into new territory. The Steinway sound that was going to set the industry standard was to be louder, richer, and more blended (less differentiated in timbre across its range)

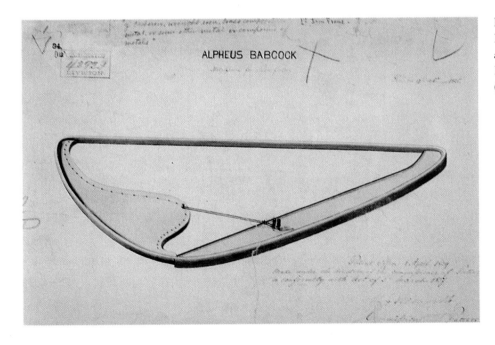

Patent drawing of a Babcock square piano with a one-piece metal frame, December 17, 1825 (Smithsonian Institution)

than previous piano sounds. But that innovation in sound was not achieved by cross-stringing alone. It was achieved when Steinway brought cross-stringing together with a number of earlier changes in piano design (see illustration, p. 62), all of them invented by other builders and several of them pioneered on squares or uprights rather than grands: Babcock's one-piece iron frame, already patented by Chickering for straight-stringing on grands; the split bridge, invented by Broadwood about 1790; felt-covered hammers, pioneered by Henri Pape around 1830; the agraffe, a method of securing strings at the tuning-pin end used by Erard in 1808; and the full present-day range of seven octaves and a third, AAA-c⁵, already known in many pianos for some time.

This was a cluster of innovations that supported one another, not a set of unrelated devices that served disparate purposes. Together they produced a grand-piano sound that filled larger concert halls than ever before and by the end of the nineteenth century was inspiring new kinds of musical expression from composers and performers. It also became the sound that the manufacturers of smaller pianos needed to emulate. By the 1860s, most European makers had discontinued making squares, and American makers finally followed their lead by the end of the century. Makers of uprights have persisted. In fact, although the grand defined the ideal sound for all pianos, the upright has continued to dominate the market.

Promoting the Piano
Cynthia Adams Hoover

In the nineteenth century, there were those who felt that they could produce pianos more quickly and more cheaply than the established suppliers. In 1860 Joseph Hale, a shrewd Yankee and energetic manufacturer who had worked as a carpenter and run a successful pottery business in Worcester, Massachusetts, came to New York to enter the piano trade strictly out of commercial interest. In his forthright manner, he accused the established makers of charging an extravagant price for a piano with a fashionable name, and claimed that he wanted to offer "to the middle and industrial classes a good instrument at a cheap rate," causing a democratic revolution that would "make a piano as easily procured as a cooking-stove or a sewing machine."[48]

Hale bought piano cases, keys, actions, and other parts from specialists at low prices for cash and had pianos assembled in his large New York factory. He was willing to put any name on the nameboard, including names like "Stanley & Sons" that resembled those of leading makers. Needless to say, the established piano oligarchy opposed his approach, charging Hale with cheap workmanship and with turning out instruments "like so much sausage-meat." Hale ignored his competitors' charges and, with attention to "business, strict economy, and cash purchases," produced in 1879 about seventy-two hundred pianos, which he sold for about one-third the price of the established pianos. Further, he rejected the agency system with its exclusive dealerships and sought markets in the expanding American West, where dealers could have his instruments with their names stenciled on them.[49]

Leading manufacturers like Steinway & Sons, who relied on family name and prestige, elitist advertising, and the sponsoring of famous performers on tour and in their own concert halls, were threatened by Hale's challenge. Even within the Steinway family, the outspoken and inventive eldest brother, Theodore, thought that his brother William was charging too much. In a letter to William, he wrote that in Germany a Bechstein piano cost 350 marks retail, a Steinway 700 marks wholesale. He insisted that they stop underwriting artists, use Steinway Hall for a wareroom, and reduce dealer markup: "My boy, a piano is a piano, a little better or not does not make a difference with people." But, as one recent Steinway historian has written, William chose class, not mass; he gambled instead on Americans' "nagging sense of cultural inadequacy."[50]

Dun financial reports throughout the years rated Hale as a safe and flourishing businessman, who at his death in 1883 left an estate of nearly $2 million. Alfred Dolge, historian of the American piano trade and quite possibly a supplier of piano hammers and soundboards to Hale, wrote in 1911 that Hale had forever changed the piano industry in America, opening up the market with commercial manufacturing and marketing techniques, or as another writer put it, fighting in "a philosophical war of high quality and refined art, or pretensions to it, against volume production and popular taste." As Dolge wrote, "the tremendous increase of output, from 25,000 pianos in 1869 to 350,000 in 1910, was only made possible through the educational, artistic and advertising propaganda by makers of high-grade pianos on the one hand, and the aggressive selling methods of the makers of commercial pianos on the other."[51]

W. W. Kimball of Chicago, one of Hale's biggest clients, was a master at developing aggressive marketing methods and selling pianos in the West. A native of Maine, Kimball first tried his hand at real estate and insurance in Decorah, Iowa, where daily he saw scores of covered wagons passing through, filled with families eager to settle the land. When he moved to Chicago in 1857, he began what became a very profitable piano business by trading some Iowa land for four square pianos. Like Hale, Kimball anticipated the needs of the pioneers, many of them European immigrants with a long tradition of music making. Like Hale, Kimball wanted to sell instruments (as an 1880s Kimball sales promotion stated)

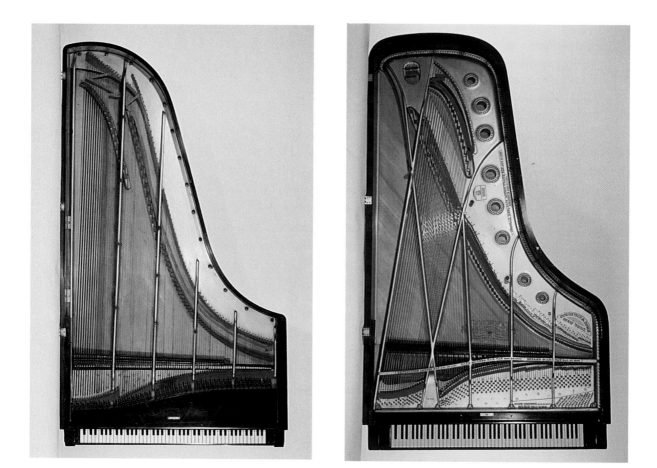

Plan views of a straight-strung 1857 Steinway grand (*left*) and a cross-strung 1892 Steinway grand (Smithsonian Institution)

Opposite: Cartoon of Joseph Hale, from *Music Trade Review*, New York, November 18, 1876

that were "within the reach of the farmer on his prairie, the miner in his cabin, the fisherman in his hut, the cultivated mechanic in his neat cottage in the thriving town." Both the piano and its country cousin the reed organ were to provide the Kimball customer "an influence which refines his home, educates his children, and gladdens his daily life like a constant ray of sunshine on his hearth."[52]

Kimball offered his instruments through installment buying, as did D. H. Baldwin, a Cincinnati dealer who also built a profitable and lasting piano firm. Baldwin, taking his cue from the Singer Sewing Machine Company, hired sewing machine salesmen in 1872 to carry out the installment plan with pianos. Salesmen were paid on commission, not salary. Buyers signed a contract with a salesman and paid a small down payment with terms for regular payments until the bill was paid in full (usually one to three years). The title to the instrument remained with the manufacturer until full payment. For some hard-nosed dealers, a late payment

MUSIC TRADE REVIEW.

Vol. III.—No. 2. NEW YORK, NOVEMBER 18, 1876. Whole No. 26.

"Hail to the Chief!"

could mean the purchaser's loss of the instrument and all that had been invested in it. But more generous dealers considered this practice unscrupulous. As one New York dealer wrote in 1882, "a colored man is telling me of his experience, where he has paid $50 each on three separate organs, only to have them taken away from him and his money forfeited because the payments were a few days in default. In five years' experience we have not a single transaction of that kind, and we have many times refunded money paid in excess of a low rental, taking back the instrument, but always with the cheerful consent of the customer." In the 1920s, the Baldwin Company urged dealers through its house magazine to follow the collection system of automobile companies by requiring large down payments and large monthly installments so that the customer had a real equity in the purchase. Even the best of credit risks suffered the "humiliation of repossession" when they failed to keep up payments during the Depression in the 1930s.[53]

The more aggressive dealers in the West were both jobbers (wholesalers) and retailers. Some Kimball wholesalers would go on the road with a full line, set up a sale in a promising town, and "after closing out a number of instruments at good prices go around to some druggist or furniture dealers" and persuade them to take the remaining stock on consignment. The head of the Kimball wholesale department, E. S. Conway from Wisconsin, set up a system of traveling salesmen who, according to some in the trade, sometimes coerced good agents into mortgaging themselves to the "Kimball System." As an editorial in an 1886 New York publication charged, "The W. W. Kimball system is to the music trade what the Standard Oil is to the oil trade," an accusation that might have seemed even more true once Kimball began manufacturing its own pianos in 1888. But W. W. Kimball and others in the trade saw Conway as a natural-born salesman, "fresh from the farm himself, with manure still on his heels," more like the successful salesman "who was willing to load a piano or organ on a wagon, drive into the country, unload his piano or organ at some farm house, and play and demonstrate it in hope of making a sale."[54]

Mail-order firms also supplied modest homes with pianos. Some, like Sears, Roebuck and Montgomery Ward, offered pianos and reed organs along with bicycles, buggies, furniture, clothing, sewing machines, and many other goods. Although the 1896 Sears catalog listed four upright piano styles ranging in price from $125 to $179 (reed organs sold at $38.95 to $51, a "Stradivarius" violin at $5.95, bicycles as high as $78.95, a three-piece Bedroom "Suit" at $13.95), the 1902 edition listed only one, the "New American Home" at $98.50, or about one-fifth of the annual earnings of a non-farm worker in 1900. Guaranteed for twenty-five years, the 1902 pianos were made "by the largest and most reputable makers of high grade instruments in the country" of carefully selected hard rock maple, finished (not veneered) in mahogany or fancy burl walnut "so cleverly made that it is with difficulty that you can tell them from the natural wood." The tone was "full, round and powerful, at the same time sweet and melodious." Railroad freight costs for the 800-pound piano from Chicago to Butte, Montana, were $3.10 per 100 pounds; to Allentown, Pennsylvania, $0.73 per 100 pounds. The 1926 Montgomery Ward catalog offered "Windsor" pianos with player action ($398 or $485) or without the player action ($284). Terms were $10 to $25 down with $10 to $15 a month, no interest.[55]

Other mail-order firms stressed the savings gained by eliminating the retail dealer. Williams Organ & Piano Company of Chicago offered the "Epworth Piano" to a select group, especially preachers, 150 of whom are listed on the inside cover of their 1902 catalog. The preachers were listed because they were widely known and "as a class are educated, cultured and critical people, and of limited means." The four upright styles shown are made from complete scales and patterns purchased in 1893 "from a certain well-known German piano manufacturer." The "Improved Practice Pedal" allowed the learner "to practice the usual exercises, scales, arpeggios, and other finger gymnastics to develop technical skills, without wearing the hammers or annoying the family." The "List Prices" ranged from $470 to $600; the "Net Factory Price" (which was lower) would be sent in a personal letter, so "no one, excepting those directly involved, need know the price you pay."[56]

All these firms were caught up in building the consumer culture, in which people sought fulfillment through buying. As citizens grew more prosperous, they added to their purchases not only pianos but also the emerging competition for their time and money: the bicycle, phonograph, automobile, radio, and movies. Piano manufacturers and dealers scrambled to respond and to stay afloat. For the household without musical talent, the player piano offered musical enjoyment without practice. "Easy to Play" read the Gulbransen advertisement with the Gulbransen Baby pressing on the pedals, a trademark as famous as Nipper, the Victor dog. One writer suggests that in America, where the piano had been a pastime primarily for females and foreigners, the player appealed directly to American-born men. Total production of all types of pianos in America hit its peak in 1909 with nearly 365,000 (player pianos made up about one-eighth of this total). By 1923, the balance had shifted: of the 347,414 pianos produced, nearly three-fifths (205,556) were players.[57]

Throughout this tremendous expansion of the market, the high-grade piano manufacturers continued to produce and sell quality instruments and to enhance their reputations through "educational, artistic, and advertising propaganda," as Dolge wrote.[58] Some companies, like Chickering & Sons and Knabe, managed to survive the financial crises of the 1890s by joining in 1908 the newly formed American Piano Company, a corporation that marketed all kinds of pianos, from concert instruments to mass-produced commercial ones. The Baldwin Piano Company began to produce high-grade pianos that won prizes and found their place in wealthy homes. In England, Broadwood built its first factory with a production-line system in 1902 but never regained its world prominence. On the continent, Bechstein in Germany and Bösendorfer in Austria produced some of the most prestigious pianos made. Yamaha in Japan produced its first upright in 1900, its first grand in 1950.

Steinway & Sons grew during the 1920s, even though pianos were being "literally pushed from the parlor to the spare bedroom, the basement or the garage." Through a sustained campaign begun in the nineteenth century, the company claimed association with important people of wealth and nobility. Their instruments continued to be preferred by leading performers. They were made by "artisans," not assembly line workers. Steinway, along with its high-end piano manufacturing colleagues, sought to convince the public that in the fast-changing twentieth century, pianos provided a way to rear children in the cultivated tradition. The company needed to be persuaded that tasteful advertising in popular magazines like the *Saturday Evening Post* would convey this message without putting them in a class with patent medicines.[59]

The Atwood Piano Loader, patented in 1917 and manufactured in Cedar Rapids, Iowa. Its publicity claimed that "one Atwood Loader, one Ford car, and one man will sell more pianos than any six of the best Piano salesmen that ever walked in shoe leather." (Smithsonian Institution)

Toward this end, by 1900 the directors of Steinway & Sons hired the respected Philadelphia advertising firm of N. W. Ayer & Son to help them launch a national advertising campaign. The copy of these ads always linked the name of Steinway with quality, creating "the patina and panache of excellence and luxury." The Ayer firm sought a change from the earlier piano advertisements showing prosperous factories and portraits of bearded proprietors (as Loesser wrote, the piano industry's own version of the "Smith Brothers" of cough drop fame), or "lovely ladies sitting at pianos in lovely drawing rooms." The new image would be the great pianists and composers who had played Steinway pianos through the years. "The Instrument of the Immortals," young copywriter Raymond Rubicam called them in one of advertising's most inspired phrases, which he linked with portraits of great celebrities, in a national series of four-color advertisements. For decades this tasteful, elevated campaign sealed the association of Steinway with the revered themes of family, art, music, and excellence. One satisfied customer writing to the Steinways in 1936 confirmed the success of the campaign. In telling of her joy in playing her piano, she wrote, "God speaks through every Steinway."[60]

Easy to play—easy to sell— easy to keep in good order.

Nationally priced—nationally advertised—nationally esteemed.

GULBRANSEN
Player-Piano
GULBRANSEN-DICKINSON CO., 3242 W. Chicago Avenue, CHICAGO

One of the successful advertisements for the Gulbransen Player-Piano, with the Gulbransen Baby showing how "easy to play" the instrument is

In the face of rapid changes in culture and products, the Steinway company chose to appeal to the nostalgia of a seemingly immutable good: the Steinway grand that virtuosos had trusted for years. Much like the Broadwood company's earlier reluctance to adopt the one-piece iron frame, this choice represented a conscious and class-based marketing decision. Other manufacturers, however, have embraced newer technologies. Although the workings of the conventional—or as some call it, acoustic—piano have for the most part remained unchanged in the twentieth century, its outward appearance has been reconceived at times to make the most of new materials. High-impact plastics, for instance, useful for car bodies and space travel, have allowed designers to imagine new piano looks and shapes. The Schimmel see-through piano is one example: in this design, the transparent plastic case allows a clear view of all the innards, including the bobbing hammers and dampers. The instrument was made to be set in a bar on the ocean liner *Queen Elizabeth II,* and perhaps bar patrons, well along in the evening, would find the motion fascinating. A more interesting shape is represented by another Schimmel

New Bottles for Old Wine
Edwin M. Good

67

PADEREWSKI PLAYING THE MINUET

STEINWAY
THE INSTRUMENT OF THE IMMORTALS

"THE perfection of the modern Steinway is the triumph of love of profession, and to it, I pay my tribute of admiration and esteem" . . . These are the words of Ignace Paderewski, beloved poet of the piano, who comes today to Steinway Hall, just as he came years ago, echoing the choice of Wagner, Liszt, Rubinstein and other masters who preceded him, for the Steinway, "the instrument of the immortals," the piano without a peer.

Naturally, we are proud of the fact that great artists of the pianoforte, visiting Washington in concert, look to this establishment—exclusive local distributors of the Steinway for 64 years—for the instrument that reflects their own matchless genius. The Steinway heads our quality line of products, which includes the superbly beautiful Brambach and Vose grands. Victrolas, Victor records, music and musical instruments of every type.

STEINWAYS PRICED FROM $875 UP
BRAMBACH GRANDS FROM $635 UP
TERMS MAY BE ARRANGED WITH US

E. F. DROOP & SONS CO., 1300 G St.

Advertisement by N. W. Ayer & Son for "Steinway —The Instrument of the Immortals" (Smithsonian Institution)

design, the "Pegasus" grand. Imitating the weightlessness of flight, it stands partly on a clear plastic support located under the soundboard. The lid, with its "hood ornament" depicting Pegasus, is raised not on a stick but by an electrically controlled lift, which can be set at any angle. The "Pegasus" was sold by mail order for $150,000.

While experiments in exterior design have been lavished on the grand, innovation in mechanical design, such as there has been, has focused on the upright. David Klavins of Bonn, Germany, designed an upright more than twelve feet tall,

Schimmel "Pegasus" grand piano, pictured on the cover of a mail-order catalog

Below: Part of the Fandrich upright action, showing the repetition spring and individually adjustable hammer return spring that help simulate the performance characteristics of a grand piano

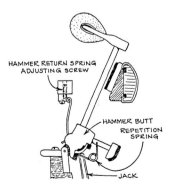

accommodating strings long enough to give extremely fine tone without cross-stringing, as well as a soundboard large enough to create a rich sound. It is therefore an experiment in sonority, at the expense of the usual concessions to practicalities of space. A different experiment, by Darrell Fandrich of Seattle, Washington, addresses a persistent problem in the design of upright pianos: the standard upright action, based on Robert Wornum's 1826 "tape-check" action, is always harder for the pianist to control than the action of a grand. Fandrich's design is intended to make an ordinary-sized upright feel like a grand piano instead of a toy. The very fact that resourceful inventors continue to attack old and unsolved problems in piano design gives reason to believe that the piano is still playing a dynamic role in its culture.

Other manufacturers in the twentieth century have turned technology to the creation of radically new capabilities, such as sound storage and reproduction. The first of these inventions to come into its own was the player piano (see inset following this chapter). In the later twentieth century, sound storage and reproduction were brought to the piano by new means: computer-driven player mechanisms and the application of digital analysis to the sound of electronic keyboards.[61]

The Digital Revolution
Edwin M. Good

An early digital player was the "Piano-corder," which recorded digitally to a tape what the player played and could be played back immediately. The digital signal was converted to an analog signal sent to solenoids, which operated levers that worked the piano's action. It was possible to play prerecorded tapes on this machine. The onset of the compact disc has revolutionized this technique; now several brands of players can record directly from the pianist's performance to a CD. Yamaha was early off the mark with its Disklavier, and the American companies PianoDisc and QRS/Pianomation have developed slightly less complete systems. In all three of these, the signals from the CD (or floppy disk) trigger solenoid switches that move the keys. Only the Yamaha has means to operate all three pedals of a grand; the other two operate the damper pedal only. A different mode of player is the Gulbransen KS20 MIDI Keyboard Controller, which uses optical sensors instead of switches to record the key position and the velocity of the stroke. It is said that this provides better control and reproduction, especially of volume. All these systems contain MIDI features, which provide a software interface with a computer for recording and editing. (MIDI, or "Musical Instrument Digital Interface," is an industry-wide standard for software and hardware that connects instruments to such digital implements as computers.) In all four types, the owner is also given the option of playing prerecorded CDs, floppy disks, or computer-stored performances.[62]

The electronic keyboard resembles a piano, but it is not a piano. Nevertheless, recent incarnations of the instrument start from an actual piano in order to synthesize piano sound. Although in the 1970s and 1980s engineers and others engaged in synthesizing instrumental sounds were successful at capturing the sound of some instruments, synthesis of the piano sound proved elusive. Consequently, some of the earliest electronic keyboards had a barely recognizable piano sound. Other versions sidestepped the issue completely. Yamaha, for example, had an electronic grand, the CP-80, which was an acoustic piano complete with repetition action, strings, and dampers, but no soundboard. Its extremely short strings ran across piezoelectric pickups, which converted the vibrations into electronic signals to an amplifier. But an inferior piano with inferior tone, even helped by the best amplifier, gives an inferior piano sound.

The CP-80 gave way in time to Yamaha's Clavinova, which, like most other keyboards, uses "sampled" sound. Basically, sampling requires recording the sound of some notes of a fine piano—ordinarily a grand—converting the signals to digital form, and editing them in two ways: first, to produce all the pitches of an eighty-eight-key piano (for some keyboards, fewer than eighty-eight); and second, to simplify within an acceptable range the complexities of the vibration patterns by "sampling" those patterns on a computer at certain extremely small time intervals.[63] The resulting tone is hardly distinguishable from that of a normal piano, even to a well-trained ear. The sampled tones are encoded to a processor chip, and the software inside the instrument produces the right sound for each note. The instruments usually are programmed with a sustaining pedal.

Despite some characteristic faults of touch, tonal decay, and volume control, these electronic keyboards can make quite a satisfactory substitution for a piano in a variety of music, including classical. Nevertheless, the point of discussing them here is not that they produce piano sound; it is that they store piano sound. Someone must strike a key on a piano to allow the sampling process to begin.

It is worth noticing, too, that electronic keyboards retain the traditional pattern of black and white keys. Their keyboards are indistinguishable in appearance from those used since the eighteenth century in pianos and before that in harpsichords, clavichords, and organs. That symbolic connection to the tradition is important. However different from a piano the inside of a keyboard might look, the outside is familiar to anyone who has ever sidled up to a piano, except that you have to plug it in, turn it on, and select the right voice, volume level, and other tonal parameters. The persistence of keyboard design represents savvy marketing on the part of the makers. But then, the piano has been crossing musical boundaries like this throughout its history.

The Player Piano

Michael Chanan

*Instrument makers are people with a special facility of imagination that is little
recognized. Perhaps because they are technologists freed from the usual function-
alism of technology, they are adept at imagining crossovers, at combining features
from different families of instruments to come up with something new—like the
saxophone, the invention of the Belgian instrument maker Adolphe Sax in the
1840s, a hybrid that combines the body of a brass instrument with a clarinet
mouthpiece to create a unique new sonority of its own. A similar process produced
the player piano, although here the aim was not a new sonority but something
altogether different, mechanical reproduction, in which the principle of pneumatic
action is used for activating the keys by means of air admitted through perfora-
tions in a roll of paper, thus dispensing with the pianist. The original player piano
betrayed the simplicity, to the technologist, of the basic idea: a contrivance called
a "piano player" was wheeled into position in front of an ordinary piano so that a
row of wooden "fingers" projected over the keyboard. Inside this surreal device, a
punched paper roll operated by a handle activated the release of air that set in
motion the wooden fingers that struck the notes on the keyboard. Small mechanical instruments of this type were on sale in New York by the end of the 1870s.*

*This is not the first time that someone has thought of using a punched paper
roll to drive a musical—or other—mechanism. Neither the aim nor the means were
entirely new, and the prehistory of what would later be called the pianola is a
revealing one because it exemplifies a trait that is little appreciated in orthodox
musical histories: the fact that the engineering of musical instruments is highly
integrated with the broader history of technology. The eighteenth-century craze
for automata elicited water organs—Mozart and Haydn both composed pieces for
them—in which a pattern of holes in a sheet of paper was used to set the pegs on a
rotating cylinder that operated valves that released the air that sounded the pipes.
This principle, derived from the medieval Mechelen carillon, was used by the son
of an organ builder, Basile Bouchon, in an attempt to solve the problems of productivity in the silk industry in Lyons by means of automation by applying the
idea to the silk loom. When the technique was improved by Jacques de Vaucanson,
the master maker of automata, the silk weavers responded to the threat of automation with riots, and Vaucanson's mechanism was abandoned; until in 1800 a silk
weaver called Joseph Marie Jacquard put it together again with minor improvements, which included replacing paper with punched cards. Again the workers*

threatened by automation rioted, and like the English Luddites smashed the new machines. In America, within years of its application to the player piano, Herman Hollerith took the idea of punched cards and added electrical sensors in order to tabulate the results of the American census. This, in the twentieth century, became the favored method for the insertion of data in mechanical calculators and early electronic computers, which in subsequent decades would have, in turn, a major impact on the piano.

The pianola evolved from the Jacquard loom by stages. In due course a Frenchman named Peytre came up with a perforated paper music roll for barrel organs, while in London, around 1825, Clementi made a "self-acting pianoforte" using a barrel-organ mechanism activated by a powerful spring. The Paris piano maker Henri Pape experimented with the idea in the middle of the century; in 1863, a French patent was granted to J. B. Napoléon Fourneaux for a pneumatic piano called the Pianista—almost a good name, Arthur Loesser remarks, but too human-sounding for a machine that was crank-operated;[1] a more effective model was produced by the German company Welte in 1887, and ten years later, an American engineer named Edwin Scott Votey patented a version called the Pi-anola, which became the generic term for the instrument. The instrument took off, encouraging conventional piano makers, big and small, to produce player pianos of their own, which superseded Votey's still fairly cumbersome mechanism. (Captain Scott took a London-made Broadwood model to the Antarctic in 1910 and played it on the ice at his first base camp.) By now the mechanism was built into the body of the piano, levers and pedals were added to control the tempo and loudness, and a foot treadle was appended to drive the pneumatic system. By careful use of the treadle and levers for tempo control, it was possible to produce quite satisfactory "performances." Further improvements modified even this elementary dose of musicianship by incorporating devices that could approximate the performing nuances of an artist, like tempo changes, crescendos, diminuendos, and other dynamics. In time, the whole thing came to be powered by electricity, and coin-operated pianolas were placed in amusement centers and dance halls.

These instruments could reproduce a recorded performance with a fair amount of accuracy, enough to be endorsed by leading pianists. Piano rolls were made by figures as varied as Alfred Cortot, Claude Debussy, Sergei Rachmaninoff, Artur Rubinstein, and, among popular artists, George Gershwin (many can now be heard on CD), and either sold or rented, anticipating the methods of the market for videos many decades later. In short, what started as little more than a souped-up music box had been transformed into a real adjunct of musical culture. In 1891 a Texas newspaper described a new player piano as a novelty that "enables the cook to furnish music for her mistress's guests using the same technique employed for grinding coffee."[2] On the eve of World War I, a spokesman for the Perforated Music Company claimed that "A man buys a player, and the first month he plays ragtime. Then he goes rapidly through the comic opera, till he reaches Chaminade and MacDowell. Often he gets no further than that, but an increasing percentage go on to the classics."[3] Two years after the war, as distinguished a figure as the doyen of English music critics, Ernest Newman, would write a little book in praise of it.[4] The truth is that the pianola served genuine musical desires: it not only brought music to people and places without it, it also disseminated music that was too difficult for the amateur and seldom heard in the concert hall. It even attracted composers to experiment in music that transcended the limitations of the human hand, including Stravinsky's Etude for Pianola (1917) and Paul Hindemith's Toccata for Mechanical Piano (1926).

The vogue for the pianola declined with the growth of radio, the introduction of electrical recording, and the coming of the talkies. By 1932 it was no longer being made, but a special niche in twentieth-century music is occupied by the figure of Conlon Nancarrow, who was to devote himself almost entirely to elaborate works for player pianos that are among the most teasing and delightful creations of mid-century experimentalism. While the pianola may have encouraged musical appreciation, it did not turn people into pianists, or so one might suppose. Gershwin, however, owed the pianola a particular debt. He was six years old—the

Aeolian Pianola piano player (New York, ca. 1900), showing the mechanical fingers that would play the keys of a piano (Smithsonian Institution)

year is 1904—when he stood on Harlem's 125th Street "outside a penny arcade listening to an automatic piano leaping through Rubinstein's Melody in F. The peculiar jumps in the music held me rooted."[5] Six years later, when their parents bought a piano, his brother Ira discovered that his younger sibling could already play it: George had found a player piano "at the home of a friend on Seventh Street" and used it to teach himself. Another half-dozen years, and he supplemented his income as the youngest of piano pounders for Tin Pan Alley by making piano rolls himself; he later made one of Rhapsody in Blue—*which can now be heard on CD married to a modern recording of the orchestral accompaniment. "I remember being particularly impressed by his left hand," writes Ira, hinting that his brother's unusual way of learning to play the piano may have had something to do with his distinctive touch at the keyboard.*[6]

uzio Clementi did it all. By the age of fourteen, in 1766, he had been appointed to a position as a church organist in Rome, his native city, and was composing both keyboard and sacred vocal music. At that point he was scooped up by a rich Englishman, Peter Beckford, who paid Clementi's father to let him bring the boy to his estate in Dorset, where in addition to providing musical entertainment, Clementi spent long hours, for seven years, turning himself into a keyboard virtuoso with unprecedented skills. Thereupon he set out for London, where he made a name and fortune for himself as a performer and composer of keyboard music. He performed to sensational effect in other European capitals as well, taught some of the greatest pianists of the next generation, and created pedagogical works of lasting value for piano students, from beginners to the most advanced. Investing his earnings in a piano-manufacturing and music-publishing firm, he became a leader in building a piano-centered musical culture, in England and across Europe, around a combination of English pianos and the music of his Viennese contemporaries, Haydn, Mozart, and Beethoven. Four years older than Mozart, he was still active in business, if no longer in performing or composing, after the deaths of both Beethoven and Schubert.

Clementi's musical life will be used here as a frame for telling the story of the piano in what is now routinely called the Classical period. The point of choosing this frame, however, is not simply that Clementi's career touched all facets of piano life. It is more apt to claim that in this period he was more thoroughly and deeply involved than any other single person in revolutionizing the musical culture of Europe around the piano. He played all of his roles on one side of that process, as a producer and marketer of music, performances, instruments, instruction, and opinion. On the other side stood the public, which played a complementary role in this cultural revolution by adapting itself to new practices. The public's side of the story will be told in a later part of this chapter, using as a focal point the work of Jane Austen, a writer who represented musical life in Clementi's time and country from the perspective of the consumer. But the story is all one story: Clementi, who desperately wanted to be as great a performer as Mozart, as great a composer as Beethoven, discovered his real genius in providing a whole social class with the means of recreating public musical experiences for itself at home; and Austen tells us what it meant, what it felt like, when members of that class put those means to use.

Take the case of Clementi's virtuosity. He was a child prodigy in Rome, but prodigious in his general musicianship and compositional talent more than in his

James Parakilas and Gretchen A. Wheelock

John Smart, *The Misses Binney*, 1806, a portrait of two sisters, one of them at an English grand piano, playing from the *Ranelagh Treasury* (evidently a collection, designed for domestic performance, of music popularized in the great rotunda of Ranelagh Garden in London—see Chapter 6) (Victoria and Albert Museum Picture Library, London)

D. Orme sculpsit

Engraving of Muzio Clementi by D. Orme (Yale University Music Library)

keyboard playing. By the time he had spent his seven years practicing the harpsichord in the isolation of Dorset and was making his name as a keyboard player in
London, starting in 1775, he was in his twenties, no longer a child. But during this
period, keyboard and other instrumental virtuosos in London, as in other European capitals, were largely children, women, foreigners, and the blind—in other

Faustine Parmantié, etching of Maria Theresia Paradis, 1784

Below: Michel-Barthélémy Ollivier, *Thé à l'anglaise* (Afternoon tea in the Salon of the Four Mirrors at the Temple, with the whole court of the Prince of Conti listening to the young Mozart), 1766. The painter exaggerates the impression of musical freakishness by making the ten-year-old Mozart look even younger than he was. (Musée du Louvre, Paris)

AT the Great Room in Spring-Garden, near St James's Park, Tuesday, June 5, at Twelve o'Clock, will be performed a grand Concert of

Vocal and Inftrumental MUSIC.

For the Benefit of Mifs MOZART of Eleven, and Mafter MOZART of Seven Years of Age, Prodigies of Nature. This Method is therefore taken to fhew to the Public the greateft Prodigy that Europe or that even Human Nature has to boaft of. Every Body will be ftruck with Admiration to hear them, and particularly to hear a young Boy of feven Years of Age play on the Harpfichord with fuch Dexterity and Perfection. It furprifes all Underftanding or all Imagination; and it is hard to fay whether his Execution upon the Harpfichord, and his playing at Sight, or his own Compofitions, are moft aftonifhing. His Father brought him to England, not doubting but that he muft meet with Succefs in a Kingdom, where his Countryman Handel received during his Life-time fuch particular Protection.
† Tickets, at Half a Guinea each, to be had of Mr Mozart, at Mr. Couzin's, Hair-Cutter, in Cecil-Court, St. Martin's Lane.

words, musicians whose gifts could be touted as miraculous. The Mozart children had been presented in this light when they visited Paris and London in the mid-1760s: they were made to perform musical tricks for the public, and they were subjected to tests of their musical abilities by local authorities, who pronounced them freakish. Likewise, the keyboard player Maria Theresia Paradis, though as the daughter of the Hapsburg court secretary she came from privileged circumstances, was presented as a freak—a performer who was young, female, foreign, and blind—in her tours to Paris and London. The public that paid to hear and gawk at these performers connected their prodigious musical abilities to something "alien" about them—their nationality or youth or handicap—and thus enjoyed their playing without wondering why they themselves, with a little more practice, couldn't produce the same results.

Clementi's virtuosity was of a different sort. He lacked freakish characteristics (even his foreignness must have lost something after those seven years in Dorset), and the only miracle he offered the public was his miraculous industry. His specialty was to play passages in thirds, sixths, and octaves faster and more accurately than anyone else could, and he had acquired that specialty by dint of practicing eight hours a day for years, as he let everyone know. Even Mozart's dismissive assessment of Clementi backhandedly concedes the effects of Clementi's assiduous practicing. In Vienna in 1781, after competing as the local keyboard champion against the visiting celebrity Clementi before Emperor Joseph II, Mozart reported: "His forte is passages in thirds. Other than that, he doesn't have a kreutzer's worth of feeling or taste—in a word, a mere machine."[1] But Clementi was able to exploit his brand of virtuosity precisely because it showed what an ordinary mortal could achieve by hard work. Unlike Mozart, who usually published the keyboard works he composed for amateurs and left unpublished the virtuosic works he composed for himself, Clementi published the works with which he himself created the greatest sensations, such as his "octave lesson" and other solo sonatas in Op. 2, in effect challenging the general run of keyboard players to practice until they could play them. The result was that more than fifty years later he could claim, in an article supplied anonymously by his publicity operation to the English music journal *The Harmonicon,* that his Op. 2—

> though it is now, from the immense progress which manual dexterity has made in the last sixty years, within the powers of even second-rate performers—was, at the period of its production, the despair of such pianists as J. C. Bach and Schroeter, who were content to admire it, but declined the attempt to play what the latter professor declared could only be executed by its own composer, or by that great performer of all wonders, and conqueror of all difficulties, the Devil.[2]

Clementi's virtuosity, in other words, had two faces: that displayed to the public in his own concert performances, and that marketed to amateurs playing at home. And if Mozart had no use for this double-faced virtuosity, Beethoven among others did: an admirer of Clementi, Beethoven followed his lead in publishing virtuosic piano sonatas for the mass market.

Even though Clementi was no child prodigy, he took his virtuosity on tour. In 1781, on his first tour away from England, Clementi had the English keyboard builder John Broadwood ship him a harpsichord and a piano to perform on in Paris.[3] This apparently innocent act marks a noteworthy change in the marketing of virtuosity, as well as of pianos. Earlier in the eighteenth century, keyboard builders like Cristofori occasionally sent instruments to a foreign country, to fill orders from royal patrons like the king of Portugal. Royal patrons may have ordered instruments for the musicians in their employ to play, but it was the patron, not the builder or performer, who controlled the transaction. In the case of Clementi in Paris, though, the performer and the builder appear to have engaged in a collaborative form of speculation. Clementi evidently wanted to present his playing on the instruments that he knew and liked best. Broadwood must have seen Clementi's tour as an opportunity to open a market for his instruments in Paris, which lagged behind London in the manufacture of pianos. This collaboration, forged in the late eighteenth century, marked a permanent change in the landscape for both manufacturers and performers. Ever since this shipment of instruments across the Channel, piano makers and pianists have never stopped promoting each other.

Within ten years of shipping instruments to Clementi, Broadwood's firm was producing on the order of five hundred pianos a year, ten times the number produced by any other piano builder either in London or elsewhere. If the firm was manufacturing pianos on an unprecedented scale, the owners needed to think in unprecedented ways about how to expand the market for pianos. The Broadwoods' thoughts carried them, it seems, into strategies not only for making upper-class English families all believe that they needed a piano, but also for creating an international market for the company's products. In 1817, for instance, the Broadwood company sent a grand piano as a gift to Beethoven in Vienna. Scholars have long wondered how Beethoven's writing for piano changed as a result of his composing for this latest in English pianos rather than for the Viennese pianos to which he was accustomed. But it is also worth asking what the Broadwood company was up to when it donated the instrument. Viennese piano builders were then Broadwood's chief rivals in the international market, and planting this English piano in the home of the most prestigious living Viennese composer was in effect pushing Broadwood's product right into the heart of its competitors' market.

Meanwhile Clementi himself had become engaged in the building of pianos. In 1798 he invested enough of his earnings from performing on the piano, composing for the piano, and teaching the piano to become a partner with John Longman in a company that made pianos and published music, largely for the piano. He was said to have helped design the pianos that bore his name. Starting in 1802, he traveled to the Continent no longer as a virtuoso performer but as a sales agent for his own pianos and a scout for music that his company might publish. Even before then, Clementi pianos were being promoted in Hamburg by another virtuoso, Jan Ladislav Dussek, who moved there from England in 1800, had a Clementi piano sent to him, and performed on it. Dussek was so impressive on this instrument that he soon found himself asking the company to send a couple of pianos for him to sell to some "Amateurs" who, having heard him, were "very anxious of possessing a Like instrument."[4] However tiny the scale of promotion was in this case, the story reveals the nature of the virtuoso's power as a promoter. When Dussek sold Clementi pianos to amateurs, just as when Clementi published his own piano sonatas, he was playing to the desire of those amateurs to emulate the public performance of the virtuoso in the privacy of their own homes.

It was unusual for one businessman both to build pianos and to publish music, as Clementi did. Other music publishers, for instance, also published maps or art engravings or wallpaper; their products were united by a common means of production. Piano building and music publishing were two very different modes of production, but each of the products could promote sales of the other. Clementi and his partners were thinking not in terms of producing products for an existing

Vertical grand piano, John Broadwood & Sons, London, ca. 1815. Grand pianos, like squares, were built and sold largely for placement in homes, though they could be carried into public performance spaces as needed. Building a grand vertically, as was often done in the early nineteenth century, only enforced the domestic nature of the instrument. This was a piece of furniture that needed to stand against a wall of a room, and the vacant space within its elegantly squared-off cabinet had shelves for the family's music library. (Smithsonian Institution)

market, but about expanding the market in domestic music making by providing a set of products that demanded each other. Clementi himself not only had a hand in the design of his company's pianos and the choice of music it published, but he also ensured that the two lines of products together would promote the piano as a fixture of musical life. Almost his first act on behalf of the company, for instance, was to create the introductory piano tutor, or method book, that it published in 1801: *Clementi's Introduction to the Art of Playing on the Piano Forte.* Here he was, the most famous virtuoso in England, later to compose the monumental *Gradus ad Parnassum* for aspiring virtuosos, and he entered the piano pedagogical market with a work for beginners. Evidently he was thinking that a musical culture—and market—built around the piano could grow only as the number of piano players multiplied.

Increasing the number of piano players meant teaching adults as well as children, introducing to the instrument those who had never learned to play any keyboard as well as converting those who had grown up playing the harpsichord. Clementi was far from alone in this field. The preface to one of the many keyboard methods published in London at this time shows how an enterprising author played on the desire of adults to keep up with the times, in this case by offering them a shortcut:

> This Book owes its Publication to an Accident. A Gentleman, having a Music-Master to teach his Niece, had an Inclination (though at an advanced Age) to acquire a few easy Tunes for his Amusement; he learned the Gamut, and attempted the First Lessons; but found that neither his Sight, nor Recognition of the Notes, would permit him to proceed. Unwilling to give up the Attempt, he got the Song of the Dead of the Night, and transposed the Notes into capital Letters, by which he acquired that Tune, and three others in one Month, God save the King, Logan O'Bucan, and Yeo, yeo, yeo! not perfectly, nor sufficiently well to play in Company, but with sufficient Melody to please himself; and from the First of the Attempt, instead of attending to Sounds without Words or Meaning, he played by the Words and Notes til he brought them to speak the Sense and Melody of the Tune, and that with Pleasure to himself, from the very First of the Attempt. This induced him to consider whether the Public might not be benefited by this Accident.[5]

Clementi's *Introduction,* far more ambitious than this, addressed to young and old alike, furnishing no shortcuts, nevertheless offers the same ideology of self-improvement. In fact, would-be buyers of the *Introduction* learn from the title

Page of lessons from Muzio Clementi's *Introduction to the Art of Playing on the Piano Forte* (London, 1801), showing a mix of original and transcribed music by composers "ancient" (J. S. Bach—in the unlabeled line at the top of the page—and Corelli) and modern (Clementi himself—in the Prelude in C-sharp Minor—and Haydn)

page that they will be cultivating the highest musical taste as they develop their skills at the piano; instead of acquiring "a few easy Tunes for [their] Amusement," they are to be taken through "Fifty fingered Lessons . . . by Composers of the first rank, Ancient and Modern." That doesn't actually exclude "easy tunes" for "amusement": the lessons include arrangements of popular theater songs of the day, like "Fal, lal, la" from Stephen Storace's *The Cherokee,* and an unpretentious waltz by an aspiring young Viennese composer of the day named Beethoven. But it also includes arrangements of movements from the chamber music of Corelli and oratorios of Handel, along with keyboard pieces by Scarlatti, both J. S. and C. P. E. Bach, and Mozart. The *Introduction,* in other words, shows piano students the full range of musical experiences that the piano can open up to them, from the classic to the popular and from orchestral and vocal transcriptions to the natively pianistic. Contrast this idea of what it is to learn the piano with the approach that harpsichord teachers had long taken, an approach exemplified by François Couperin in his *Art de toucher le clavecin,* published in 1716: all the examples are his own, and he promises to teach students "to succeed in executing my pieces well."

Couperin's harpsichord method also provides a useful reference point for considering how the concept of marketing in music publishing had grown in less than a century. Couperin, as organist and harpsichord teacher to the French court, held as prestigious a position as any European keyboard composer could have wanted in 1716, yet his method was available to the public only from his home in Paris and the shop of the music dealer Henry Foucault, likewise in Paris; furthermore, it went through only two editions, in 1716 and 1717. Clementi's company, by contrast, put his *Introduction* through a dozen printings and editions in England in the remaining three decades of the author's career; and during the eight years immediately following the initial English publication, he himself traveled around Europe—barely avoiding the worst fighting of the Napoleonic Wars—and made arrangements with publishers in several countries, with results that included the first of dozens of foreign editions of the *Introduction.*[6]

Couperin's harpsichord method, published only in Paris, became known to only a few experts outside France in the decades after its publication; Clementi's piano method, largely because of his marketing endeavors, was bought and used by many students and teachers across Europe and the United States. Nor was it the only work of its period circulated on such a scale. Louis Adam's *Méthode de piano du Conservatoire* of 1804, similar in concept to Clementi's *Introduction,* had a comparably wide distribution. Whereas the Clementi benefited internationally from its author's prestige as a performer and a marketing campaign that promoted piano learning alongside piano buying, international sales of the Adam were enhanced by the prestige of the newly founded Paris Conservatory where Adam taught—the first national institution anywhere devoted to the production of pianists.

In publishing his own music, too, Clementi thought internationally. Copyright laws in England had protected music since the early eighteenth century, but not until the Berne Convention of 1886 was there to be any international copyright agreement protecting a composer's rights outside the country of copyright. After the conclusion of the Napoleonic Wars in 1815, therefore, Clementi became one of the first composers to secure copyright in several of the biggest music-buying markets by arranging for virtually simultaneous publication of his piano works by his own company in London and by other publishers in Paris and Leipzig.[7] Chopin, among other composers, later followed exactly the same practice.

Simply publishing one's music, however, was no guarantee that it would sell. The next step was to get it publicized. For this purpose, fortunately, there was just beginning to be a musical press—a number of journals devoted specifically to the promotion of musical culture and musical products (see the section on the musical press, p. 93). The most important journal of this kind at the very beginning of the nineteenth century was the *Allgemeine musikalische Zeitung*, founded in 1798 by Gottfried Christoph Härtel, the owner of the Leipzig music publishing house of Breitkopf & Härtel. It will hardly surprise anyone to learn that Clementi's music generally earned rave reviews in the house journal of the publisher who issued the German editions of that music. It can be disconcerting, however, to learn that after the journal printed a review praising a performance of a Clementi symphony, Breitkopf & Härtel sent Clementi & Company a note thanking it for providing the "review . . . for insertion into the musical journal we publish."[8] Even the crudest distinction between a press release and a review—between publicity and disinterested evaluation—was not observed. We find here the beginnings of the ethical problem caused when the producers of cultural products own the media entrusted to comment on them. The problem, as we know, has persisted and grown. The most powerful and long-lived music journals have continued to be those owned by music publishers, presumably because music publishers had a unique incentive to keep the public interested in their wares.

Given his commercially enterprising spirit, it may seem strange that Clementi never founded his own music journal. But he might well have felt that he didn't need one. By the 1820s several music journals were being published in England, such as the *Quarterly Musical Magazine and Review* and the *Harmoni-*

con, and their pages were filled with mostly positive reviews of Clementi company publications. A number of forces undoubtedly kept these journals in Clementi's "camp"—his status as the leading national figure in music, his various collaborations with the editors of these journals in the tightly knit London musical world, and the sheer quantity of material his firm provided as grist for their reviewing mill. These forces determined what was written in those journals about him, his own compositions, and the publications of his firm just as surely as if he had owned the journals himself, though perhaps in a more subtle way. His influence over the press—the power that suppliers of cultural products exert over the opinion expressed in cultural journals—constitutes still another ethical problem bequeathed to society by the commercial arrangements of Clementi's musical world.

The publication of reviews in journals should not be taken to mean that customers were necessarily buying piano music in an open market, any more than they always do so today. It is true that during the eighteenth century, consumers in the larger European cities could increasingly visit music shops to examine music publications. The shops, however, and even the music lending libraries that served as an alternative, were generally storefronts of the publishers themselves, and although they might carry some publications by other publishers, perhaps especially foreign ones, the customer in those shops and lending libraries may have had an experience more like shopping in a neighborhood bakery than in a supermarket.

Furthermore, although music consumers might be guided by reviews when they bought music from a shop or ordered it from a publisher's catalog, in many cases they bought music about which they could know nothing. They subscribed to publication projects that were announced in the press—an experience of paying for a product not only before the reviews were in, but even before it existed. And like members of mail-order book and record clubs in the twentieth century, they subscribed to periodicals that consisted entirely of music to be performed at home. It would be hard to convey how important periodical publications were to musical life and commerce—and no doubt especially to consumers like Jane Austen who lived in places where there were no music shops—at the end of the eighteenth century and well into the nineteenth. Subscribers to a periodical received, once a month or at some regular interval, a piece or collection of music chosen for them by the editors of the periodical. The contents of these periodicals give a remarkable picture of the printed music that great numbers of music lovers owned and performed in their homes.[9]

Although there were periodicals of music for guitar or flute or harp, the music

THE MUSICAL LOUNGE,

AND

APOLLO CIRCULATING LIBRARIES,

AT

D. CORRI's,

MUSIC SELLER TO THE ROYAL FAMILY,

No. 28, HAY MARKET,

AND AT

T. JONES's, No. 23, *Bishopsgate Street*,

Where every SUBSCRIBER will be GRATUITOUSLY entitled to the full Amount of their Sub-
scriptions in Printed Music, either at the Time of subscribing, or at any Period within the
Term subscribed for, at the Option of the Subscriber, from the Catalogue published by
CORRI or JONES.
And also be accommodated, at either of the above Houses, with Apartments, and Instruments
of every Description, for the Purpose of trying Music.
In Addition to which, every Annual Subscriber will have free Admission to CORRI's Quarterly
PRIVATE CONCERTS, at his Great Room, Hay-Market.

THE above Libraries will contain several Numbers of the most celebrated and extensive Selections of Ancient and Modern
Works, both Vocal and Instrumental, in Print and Manuscript, which will be continually increasing, by the Addition of the
most esteemed Compositions that may hereafter be published in every Part of Europe, on the following Terms, viz.

	£.	s.	d.		£.	s.	d.
For a Year	2	2	0	A Quarter	1	1	0
Half a Year	1	11	6	Single Book, per Day	0	0	6

To be paid at the Time of subscribing at either of the above Libraries.

(SEE REGULATIONS THE OTHER SIDE.)

A Musical Journal will be published every MONDAY for the Voice, Piano Forte, Harp, Flute, Violin, and Tambourine,
constructed on a Plan entirely new, by D. CORRI, (Price 1s. 6d.)

N.B. The Musical Academies for Voice, Piano Forte, &c. will be continued as usual, by Mr. and Mrs. CORRI, at the above Places.

Frettell & Postle, Printers, 54, Great Windmill-Street, Hay-Market.

Advertisement from a London music lending library, ca. 1800. In the details of this sheet it can be seen how the Corri family, like Clementi, conducted several musical enterprises that promoted one another. Subscribers to the lending library were entitled to Corri musical publications (which they could try out on instruments provided for the purpose) and admission to the Corri concert series. They were also encouraged to purchase even more music by subscribing to the Corri music periodical. (British Museum, London)

The climactic pages from *The Battle of Prague* by Francis Kotzwara (František Koczwara), as it appeared in James Harrison's *Piano-Forte Magazine* (London) in 1798. This was neither the first nor the most elegant publication of the work, but it was an important one in making it one of the best-selling pieces of the era,

especially in the English-speaking world. It may seem odd to find "God Save the King" at the moment of victory in a work commemorating a battle between Austria and Prussia, but Kotzwara, born in Prague and living in the British Isles when he wrote the work, evidently knew his market.

appearing in periodicals was largely for the piano: songs with piano accompaniment, opera selections with piano accompaniment, orchestral music arranged for piano, solo piano music, and piano music with accompaniments for other instruments. The Viennese periodical *Pot Pourri für das Forte-Piano,* published by Thaddäus Weigl from 1804 to 1813, for example, was filled with Viennese ballet music (some of it by Weigl himself), transcribed for piano; here is a musical product that we hardly associate with Beethoven's Vienna. One of the periodicals, the *Piano-Forte Magazine* of London, which was published from 1797 to 1802, even came with vouchers, a complete set of which was meant to be cashed in for a piano.

Music shops and lending libraries, music journals, and music periodicals allowed owners of pianos to keep up with everything that was new and fashionable in their musical world from their own parlors. Musical publications also taught these same piano owners to steep themselves in the music of the past and present that was bound to endure through the ages. Here again Clementi was in the forefront, marketing the idea of musical classics at the piano. His *Introduction* embodies the idea, revolutionary at the time, that music students should form their technique from the very beginning on the music of "Composers of the first rank, Ancient and Modern." He relentlessly pursued Beethoven in Vienna for works to publish, hoping for a share in the honor and profit of promoting him to the stature of a modern master. And in 1830, at age seventy-eight, he found a new way of marketing the immortality of masters living and dead when he brought out the first of a series of "keepsake" albums called *Apollo's Gift.* The album contains, amid a varied collection of printed music, a group of facsimiles of the musical handwriting of the greatest musical masters of the day—Haydn, Mozart, Beethoven, Weber, and Clementi himself. These were short examples of their compositions in their own hand, rather clumsily traced onto lithographic plates. At a time when reverence for the musical handwriting of the masters was a relatively new form of composer worship, Clementi was already engaged in mass producing the necessary relics.

Turning the works of Haydn, Mozart, and Beethoven into a permanent canon—into "classical music"—while they were still alive or barely dead was an act of marketing, and Clementi played a leading role in it. From a commercial point of view, it was a brilliant idea, allowing publishers—along with performers, teachers, and others—to profit by the same works year after year and decade after decade, instead of constantly needing to find and risk their resources on new material. According to D. W. Krummel, in fact, "the concept of the musical monument, of permanent value to several generations of purchasers, allowed for long-term investment, and probably lengthened the life of publishing firms."[10] Clementi's contribution to the idea, characteristically, was to help bring it into the home—into piano instruction, onto the family piano music stand, and into the collection of cultural relics that a respectable family could take pride in owning.

Clementi lived through the French Revolution and its international aftermath, through the Industrial Revolution and its reordering of economic and social life. His own career symbolizes, better than that of any other musician of the period, a comparable revolution in musical culture. It was like the French Revolution in that it involved a transfer of cultural power from the old ruling class that had previously owned the opera houses, the orchestras, and even such experimental keyboard instruments as the piano, to a widening, if still small, circle of the population thinking of itself as "the people." It was comparable to the Industrial Revolution in that it involved new means of producing and distributing cultural goods—pianos, printed music, journals, systems of education and opinion—on a mass and international scale. In this cultural revolution Clementi showed a particular genius for understanding how apparently different systems of production and marketing could be coordinated so that each promoted and expanded the others: concert life and domestic music making; piano manufacture and piano instruction; music publishing, musical journalism, and the musical canon. Instead of being called the Father of the Pianoforte, as he was during his lifetime, he should perhaps be known as the Father of the Entertainment Industry, because the principle of tie-ins, of interrelated promotions on which today's entertainment industry depends, is fully realized in his enterprises. The difference is that in his enterprises, during his lifetime, the whole musical entertainment industry revolved around the piano.

To understand the role that music journals have played in cultural life, you need to imagine a world in which no radio or recordings exist to spread the sounds of new and unfamiliar music to a wide audience, public concerts of any sort are confined for the most part to major cities, hardly any schools or universities offer courses in music appreciation, and books on the history and criticism of music are few. Into this world the Leipzig music publishing house of Breitkopf & Härtel introduced its *Allgemeine musikalische Zeitung* (Universal music newspaper) in 1798. The remarkable range of its coverage betrayed an ambitious program to educate the musical public. In its weekly issues, subscribers could read serialized treatises on questions of music theory and practice, serialized biographies

Interlude: The Piano and the Musical Press
James Parakilas

93

of great musicians, reports on musical life in various European cities and countries, reviews of operatic premieres and concert performances, reviews of music published by Breitkopf & Härtel or by other publishers but available through them, and reports on new musical instruments or developments in the design of familiar ones. For readers whose musical horizons were dominated by local performers and who had been accustomed to a haphazard acquaintance at best with whatever was new in music outside their own locality, their subscriptions to *AMZ* must have provided an astonishing sense of being plugged in to an international musical life pulsing with new ideas, new personalities, new experiences. Once this journal had proved its worth with readers of German, it was not long before comparable music newspapers were started in English, French, and other European languages.

To realize how thoroughly the rise of the music journal depended on the conquest of the parlor by the piano, it is necessary simply to browse through a few issues of such nineteenth-century music journals as *AMZ, Harmonicon,* or *Revue et gazette musicale de Paris.* This survey would reveal that the greatest space in these journals was taken up by reviews and listings of, and advertisements for, music publications, the overwhelming majority of them requiring a piano to perform. Even the reviews of operatic or choral or orchestral performances are followed by announcements and reviews of piano arrangements of those works. And all these journals included with every year's subscription a number of musical supplements—a few pages of printed music, almost always requiring a piano to perform, often illustrating a subject discussed in the pages of the journal, yet suitable to grace the music stand of the subscriber's piano long after they had completed their service in illustrating the article.

The pages printed here from the *Allgemeine musikalische Zeitung,* for instance, include the editor's foreword to an article from 1800 on Hungarian folk dance. The article itself describes the typical Hungarian dance band as consisting of violins, string bass, and cimbalom; the supplement then gives several examples of the music played by those bands, in an arrangement for the piano. In this case, the piano is expected to represent the sounds of a whole ensemble, one distinguished by the timbre of the cimbalom, an instrument that the subscriber may never have heard. It was all in a day's work for the piano.

A century later, editors of music journals still presumed that their readers could take music examples to a piano and play them. Evidence for this can be found in a series of articles by Arthur Farwell, "Keeping in Touch with World's Musical Growth through the Piano," that appeared in *Musical America* beginning

94

ALLGEMEINE

MUSIKALISCHE ZEITUNG.

Den 28ten May   No. 35.   1800.

ABHANDLUNG.

Ueber die Nationaltänze der Ungarn.

Tanz und Musik sind wahrscheinlich die ältesten Künste; Nationaltänze und Volkslieder (lange in der Anwendung verbunden) wahrscheinlich die ältesten Ueberbleibsel derselben — und zwar nicht nur nach der zählenden Chronologie der Weltgeschichte, sondern auch nach der schätzenden Chronologie der Kultur-Geschichte der Nationen. Nationaltänze und deren Musik, Nationallieder und deren Melodien kennen zu lernen, muß nicht nur dem Musiker und Kunstliebhaber, sondern auch dem Gelehrten, z. B. dem Antiquar, Geschichtforscher, Geschichtschreiber — ja auch überhaupt dem gebildeten Menschen nicht gleichgültig seyn. Nicht nur der erste kann aus den Eigenheiten, die alle Nationaltänze, Volkslieder und deren Musik haben — aus dem immer so ganz Ausgezeichneten der Melodie, des Rhythmus, der Einschnitte, der Schlußfälle u. s. f. seine Ideen bereichern, seinem Genius neue Schwingen ansetzen, um sich, wo es so gut gethan ist, über die oft nur gar zu willkührlich unter uns gesezten, und nicht selten mit Ketzereifer der infalliblen Kirche vertheidigten Schranken zu erheben; sondern auch der zweyte und dritte können aus der Kenntniß derselben neue interessante Betrachtungen über den Geist und die Eigenheiten der Nationen überhaupt, und über die unvertilgbaren, nur immer in andern Farben hervorspielenden Grundzüge der Charaktere der Völker anstellen. Gewiß, jede Nation schildert sich selbst, unwillkührlich, aber darum nur desto treffender, in ihren Tänzen, mit deren Musik, und ihren Volksliedern: aber viel-

leicht in den ersten am allerzuverlässigsten. Man denke, um Etwas davon gleich vor Augen zu haben, nur etwa an die mit Galanterie entgegenkommende, aber mit Ehrerbietung doch nur ferner sich annähernde Menuett der Franzosen; an die gemäßigte Fröhlichkeit, geistreiche Abwechselung, und Dauer *in* Abwechselung der Anglaise; an das wilde Stürmen und die dürftige Einförmigkeit der schottischen Tänze; an das Gravitätische und dann in Gluth übergehende der spanischen Fandango's und Bolero's; an das Grimassierende, Verzerrte, und ganz Geschmacklose der Reste jüdischen Tanzes bey Festen dieser Nation in manchen Ländern; an das Lautfröhliche, kräftig und gleichmäßig Aushaltende, aber dabey allerdings Einförmige des deutschen Tanzes, und *an die Musik* aller dieser verschiednen Arten — freylich alle, wie sie unter dem Volke selbst sind, und nicht, wie unsre feine Welt diese und jene heut'ges Tages in Musik sezt und tanzt! Und will man noch einen Schritt weiter gehen, so beobachte man, wie z. B. der Deutsche die Menuett oder Anglaise in Musik und Tanz abändert und vorträgt; wie der Franzos mit der Anglaise verfährt und den deutschen Ländler, wo er nur kann, verschmähet — kurz, wie eine Nation von der andern wohl das und jenes annimmt, aber überall ihr Eigenes damit amalgamiert, und nun gerade dadurch (wie es beym eigentlichen Amalgamieren geschiehet) ihr Eigenes desto sicherer zu Tage legt.

Diese und noch manche ähnliche Gedanken, zu deren Verfolgung sich ja wohl einmal weitere Gelegenheit in diesen Blättern finden wird, veranlaßten mich, die Redaktion zu vermögen, verschiedene, durch Wissenschaften und für Musik gebildete Männer auswärtiger Nationen um Nach-

2. Jahrg.

No. IV.

Beylage zur allgemeinen Musikalischen Zeitung.

IX

Ungarische Nationaltänze.

Two pages from *Allgemeine musikalische Zeitung*, May 28, 1800

in 1910. The first of these, from November 5, carried the subtitle "How Students May Know What the Leaders of the Great National Schools of Composition Are Doing—The Difference between 'Learning How to Play' and Really Understanding the Best in Music," followed by an editor's note explaining that the series would show "how one may become acquainted with the new music of the various national schools through the piano." The article began:

> One's piano is a kind of magic mirror which is capable of reflecting to one the whole musical world from classic times to the present, and throughout all lands. It requires only that one put the music on his piano-rack and play it, or, at least, play at it. The tone of the orchestral instruments may not be there; vocal tone may not be there, or the sound of the chorus; but there is the melody, there is the harmony, and there is the rhythm—the three tangible factors that make up music. The soul is there, too, if we can get it out. Through our piano we can get into touch, more or less intimate, with everything from a Greek scale, or a two-step, to Beethoven's Ninth Symphony, or a tone poem of Strauss. In short, we can take the whole world of music into our lives through our piano.

Austen and the Domestic Life of the Piano
James Parakilas

In the eighth chapter of *Pride and Prejudice*, Charles Bingley, having marveled at how "very accomplished" all the young ladies of his day are, is challenged by Mr. Darcy to define a higher standard of "accomplished" by which to take a woman's measure. He responds:

> A woman must have a thorough knowledge of music, singing, drawing, dancing, and the modern languages, to deserve the word; and besides all this, she must possess a certain something in her air and manner of walking, the tone of her voice, her address and expressions, or the word will be but half deserved.

In a discussion being carried on largely by two men speaking in the presence of women, it is striking how Bingley defines female accomplishments as a set of attributes for men to admire. Music is the first of these attributes, a position it earns elsewhere in this and other Austen novels, where young women are frequently called on to demonstrate their accomplishment at the piano, either by playing solos or by accompanying themselves as they sing. Their playing always "places" them—defines their upbringing and their character—in the eyes of men as well as of other women, and even in their own eyes.

The piano rose to prominence in late-eighteenth-century musical life because playing it became a necessary accomplishment for a growing class of women. As Arthur Loesser writes, "the history of the pianoforte and the history of the social status of women can be interpreted in terms of one another."[11] England led in the creation of the new piano culture. It was the country where the largest number of pianos was built and where the commerce in piano music was strongest—even if the best composers for the piano were centered in Vienna—because it had the most highly developed economy in the Western world and therefore the economy

Johan Zoffany, *Colonel Blair with His Family and an Ayah*, 1786(?). Almost as soon as English families began buying pianos, they began taking them around the world with them, whatever the trouble of transporting them and maintaining them in unaccustomed climates. Zoffany was one of several English society painters who spent years in India, recording how the leaders of the English commercial and military forces there replicated the essential features of their domestic life; one of those features was that their daughters learned to play the piano for them.

with the largest number of families able and willing to furnish their daughters with piano lessons. Although upper-class families from Paris to St. Petersburg and from Boston to Buenos Aires were also furnishing their daughters with piano lessons, in those places there were proportionally fewer such families.

The daughters of the most prosperous classes, as Bingley's sentences imply, were educated under quite a different system from the sons, or from daughters of the less prosperous classes, and piano lessons formed just one element of that system. Bingley makes female education seem like something of a lark, but in fact what he describes is a remarkably demanding and expensive course of studies to be lavished on a class of people who were expected to make no direct contribution through their own labor to the income of their families. What's more, when Bingley is finished with his account, Mr. Darcy ups the ante by asserting that "to all this she must yet add something more substantial, in the improvement of her mind by extensive reading." In a world where literacy at any level was considered not a universal birthright but a skill to be acquired as needed for position, profession, or religious practice, it marks a cultural revolution that an English gentleman of 1797 (the year *Pride and Prejudice* was completed) could expect any lady of his acquaintance not just to be literate, but to be a serious reader.[12] Piano playing should be considered alongside this "extensive reading" and what Bingley calls the "thorough knowledge . . . of modern languages" as part of the remarkable program of literacy—broadly construed—that formed the foundation of upper-class female education.

Of course, real-life piano players like Austen herself may have played the piano by ear sometimes; some of them may never have learned to read notes very successfully, despite years of lessons, just as some never got very adept at reading in French or spelling in English. But the system by which they were taught music—singing as well as playing the keyboard—was very much a literacy of notes, a system of learning to read notes and translate them into sounds. It was a literacy far more complex and difficult to master than that of letters. It required years of lessons from a music master who taught from method books and other printed or handwritten scores (Austen herself copied out a great deal of borrowed music for her own use). Some music masters visited their students' homes to give the lessons; others taught in boarding schools. Austen, the daughter of a clergyman, received instruction from within the clerical world, which had been the source of most literate education since the Middle Ages: the assistant organist at Winchester Cathedral came to her home, the rectory in nearby Steventon, to teach her the piano. He was doing so when she was twenty and at work on *Pride and*

Prejudice.[13] It is hard to imagine, furthermore, that the opportunity of learning to play the piano was given in this period of history to many people who were not highly literate in every sense. In chapter 31 of the novel, when Lady Catherine De Bourgh invites Mrs. Collins to come to her house every day and practice on the piano in her maid's room, Austen is letting us know how rich and pretentious Lady Catherine is, to have such a well-educated, such a literate, maid.

An upper-class woman didn't play the piano for money; in fact, having so great a gift for music that it was marketable could be just as much a problem for her as having none at all. The accomplishments of upper-class women were designed to demonstrate to the world that the men of their families didn't need them to be gainfully employed. After marrying and childbearing, according to Richard Leppert, "the greatest challenge faced by females of the leisured classes was how to be leisured." It was a challenge, he says, that gave men and women different

Christopher Villem Eckersberg, *The M. L. Nathanson Family,* 1818. Among countless family portraits that wealthy people in this period had painted of themselves, this offers a particularly clear representation of a family life familiar to us from Austen's novels: a society of siblings, presided over by their mother, in which one elder sister at the piano provides endless entertainment for all the others; the father seems little more than a visitor to this society. (Statens Museum for Kunst, Copenhagen)

Diana Sperling, *Newport Pagnell. Mrs. Hurst Dancing*, watercolor from an album, September 17, 1816. Drawing and watercoloring were accomplishments of upper-class women, just as were singing, dancing, and playing the piano. Here one accomplishment is used to record the enjoyment of others. (Estate of Neville Ollerenshaw)

experiences of time: "Time for the male was a developmental parameter lived socially. For women, time was non-developmental and lived familially."[14] A young woman might care about "development" as she practiced the piano, and her teacher surely would, but her family might care only that she kept at it.

In a sense the most helpful thing Austen's novels tell us about the relationship between women and the piano comes in a passage of *Pride and Prejudice* that is not about music at all. It comes in chapter 37, when Lady Catherine says to Mrs. Collins: "I cannot bear the idea of two young women travelling post by themselves. It is highly improper. You must contrive to send somebody. I have the greatest dislike in the world to that sort of thing.—Young women should always be properly guarded and attended, according to their situation in life." Being "properly guarded and attended" meant that women, especially young women, stayed home a great deal. In fact, throughout Austen's novels we see women mostly in the safety of a home, visiting one another, sometimes attended by the men of their families; we see the men only when the women see them, which is to say that we hardly ever catch a glimpse of them producing the wealth on which this family life depends. The family piano was a piece of furniture—and in the course of the com-

ing century it became an increasingly heavy and immobile piece of furniture—at the center of a domestic realm to which women were bound.

In England especially, the primary home of an upper-class family was apt to be a country seat. During the proper season, the family migrated to London or to Bath, where some or all could hear concerts and operas. In London the women might visit Clementi's music store or Corri's Musical Lounge and Apollo Circulating Libraries—along with Broadwood's or Clementi's piano showroom—and acquire arrangements for piano of the hit numbers from those concerts and operas. The piano served as a means for women to keep their families abreast of the latest in their musical culture, as well as to remind them of old favorites. But it may have played a particularly important role when the family had returned to its country house. From there women could make frequent trips to the post office, where the latest issue of a music periodical or music journal might await them.[15] In the long evenings at home, the piano was a means by which one woman could provide songs and piano pieces for everyone else in the house to enjoy, there being no concerts or operas to hear, or provide music for a single couple or a whole party to dance to, there being no balls to attend. Playing the piano was an activity,

Thomas Rowlandson (1756–1827), *Reflections, or the Music Lesson*. For the age-old theme of young couples carrying on their flirtations under the nose of a parent or guardian or elderly husband, the piano provided simply a new stage; even the role of the music master was an ancient one for the brazen lover. Rowlandson drew several versions of this scene, although he did not provide the mirror for the incriminating "reflections" in all of them. For a treatment of the theme by Daumier, see Chapter 5. (Yale Center for British Art)

Cassandra Austen, portrait of Jane Austen, ca. 1810 (National Portrait Gallery, London)

a form of work, that a young woman performed for her family's recreation; it was not just a way to fill her own time.

Austen's novels are full of women performing for their families, but the overriding activity in her fictional world is courtship. The female accomplishment of playing the piano, as Bingley's account makes clear, was understood by everyone as one way that a young woman could catch the fancy of the right man. In this sense, Austen's fiction mirrors the real world of the era, and it is especially valuable for reconstructing so vividly that most vulnerable stage in a young upper-class woman's life when she was poised between the control of her parents and that of the husband she was trying to win. During this period, the young woman was simultaneously and continuously under the scrutiny of both suitor and parents. The domestic piano, although it was one of her means of seduction, was firmly planted in the center of her parents' house or some other home where members of the older generation could supervise her seducing. In chapter 31 of *Pride and Prejudice*, the piano at Lady Catherine's house allows Elizabeth Bennett, as she plays, to enter into conversation with Mr. Darcy, whom we have been prepared to believe she is destined to marry. They become so engaged in sparring with each other that she neglects to keep playing, with the result that they are "interrupted by Lady Catherine, who called out to know what they were talking of. Elizabeth immediately began playing again."

For some young women, the role of the piano in courtship wholly determined their relationship to the instrument. Elizabeth Bennett's sister Mary, for one, practiced without cease to compensate for being less than beautiful. But others could put the piano to more private purposes as well. In fact, privacy was itself an especially female domain, though not always an easy domain for women to secure to themselves. For Elizabeth (again in chapter 37) "not a day went by without a solitary walk, in which she might indulge in all the delight of unpleasant recollections," but elsewhere in the story those solitary walks bring censure on her. Playing the piano was a safer and more acceptable form of solitude, no doubt because it was less removed from supervision—a form of privacy without actual solitude.

In chapter 6 of *Persuasion*, for instance, we learn that Anne Elliott, the heroine of the novel,

> knew that when she played she was giving pleasure only to herself; but this was no new sensation: excepting one short period of her life, she had never, since the age of fourteen, never since the loss of her dear mother, known the happiness of being listened to, or encouraged by any just appreciation or real taste. In music she had been always used to feel alone in the world.

In this Anne resembles her creator. Jane Austen's own life at the piano was described in a memoir by her niece, Caroline Austen:

> Aunt Jane began her day with music—for which I conclude she had a natural taste; as she thus kept it up—tho' she had no one to teach; was never induced (as I have heard) to play in company; and none of her family cared much for it. I suppose, that she might not trouble them, she chose her practising time before breakfast—when she could have the room to herself—She practised regularly every morning—She played very pretty tunes, *I* thought—and I liked to stand by and listen to them.[16]

Because Austen's fiction concentrates so exclusively on the piano playing of women at the marriageable age, it is particularly precious to have this testimony about the author herself at an age when marriage had passed her by and to learn that the end of the courtship period didn't need to mean the end of a woman's piano playing.

The extremely narrow social focus of Jane Austen's fiction allows her, paradoxically, to reveal everything about the social life of the piano at precisely the moment and in precisely the social world where that life began. And because she was there and told it all, her fiction provides a perfect standpoint from which to measure, in subsequent fiction, changes and continuities in the representation of the piano in people's lives.[17]

Precisely a century after *Pride and Prejudice*, for instance, Anton Chekhov, in the short story "Ionych" (1898), described that same moment when a young woman's piano playing attracted a young man's notice. As in Austen's novels, the setting is both domestic and rural, and the parents of the young woman, Yekaterina, are both encouraging and policing. One difference is that in the century since Austen wrote, pianos have become sturdier, the music for them has become

A Literary Excursus: Fictional Pianos

James Parakilas

103

more strenuous, and young ladies have been allowed to expend more physical energy in playing, so that the young doctor from the neighboring village who is first encountering her in this scene can be seduced, as no Austen hero could be, by the sight of her working up a sweat at the piano:

"And now, Kitty, you play something," said Mr. Turkin to his daughter.

The lid of the grand piano was raised, the music books lying there in readiness were opened, and Yekaterina sat down and struck the keys with both hands; then she struck them again with all her might, and again and again; her shoulders and bosom shuddered, she went on striking the keys in the same place, and one could not help feeling that she would go on hitting the keys till she had driven them into the piano. The drawing-room filled with thunder; everything thundered—the floor, the ceiling, the furniture. Yekaterina was playing a difficult passage, interesting just because it was difficult, long and monotonous. Listening to it, Startsev imagined rocks falling from the top of a high mountain, falling and falling, and he wished they would stop falling quickly, while he found Yekaterina, rosy with the exertion, strong and energetic, a lock of hair falling over her forehead, very attractive indeed. After a winter spent in Dyalizh among peasants and patients, to be sitting in a drawing-room looking at this young, exquisite, and probably pure creature and listening to these noisy, tiresome, but none the less cultivated sounds, was as pleasant as it was novel.

"Well, Kitty, you played as never before tonight," said Mr. Turkin with tears in his eyes after his daughter had finished, and he quoted the words addressed to the Russian eighteenth-century playwright Denis Fonvisin: "You can die now, Denis, you'll never write anything better!"

They all surrounded her, congratulated her, expressed their admiration, assured her that they had not heard such music for a long time, while she listened in silence, a faint smile playing on her lips, and her whole figure expressed triumph.

"Wonderful! Excellent!"

"Excellent!" Startsev said too, giving in to the general enthusiasm. "Where did you study music?" he asked Yekaterina. "At the conservatoire?"

"No, I'm only just now trying to get into the conservatoire. For the time being I'm taking lessons from Mrs. Zavlovsky."

"Were you at the secondary school here?"

"Oh, no," Mrs. Turkin replied for her, "we had tutors for her at home. At a secondary school or at a boarding school there might be bad influences. While a girl is growing, she must be under the influence of her mother alone."

"I'll go to the conservatoire all the same," said Yekaterina.[18]

The opportunity available to Yekaterina for going to the conservatory and making a career of her piano playing is another difference between Chekhov's world and Austen's. The piano promises to liberate her professionally—as playing it liberates her physically—from traditional notions of the feminine. But as the story unfolds, the increased range of opportunities open to young women in Chekhov's day simply creates new opportunities for heartbreak on every side: Yekaterina rejects Startsev's hand to go to conservatory, but then comes home to live out a dreary spinsterhood as he, not far away, lives out a dreary bachelorhood. Still another century later, in Elfriede Jelinek's *The Piano Teacher* (1983), the piano serves its traditional role as the instrument of seduction for a woman who teaches piano at the Vienna Conservatory, but at the same time becomes, in the hands of her mother—an appalling descendent of those policing parents we find in Austen and Chekhov—the means of imposing a life of cloistered professionalism on the daughter; in turn the daughter can express her frustration only through sexual acts destructive to her lover, her mother, and herself.

In James Weldon Johnson's novel *The Autobiography of an Ex-Colored Man* (1912), the theme of the piano as an instrument of courtship is given two twists: the piano-playing protagonist, the light-skinned child of a black mother and a white father, uses the piano as a means of "passing" as well as of seducing, and this protagonist is male. Here the mother doesn't live long enough to supervise her son when he reaches the age of courtship; instead she plays a role that we don't find in Austen or Chekhov or Jelinek, but that many women took on when their own days of playing to be noticed were over and they settled into motherhood: she drew her child into a love of music through her own playing. Johnson's account of this process shows the mother connected to both sides of a racially divided musical culture—a position she passes on to her son. At the same time the narration, by the son, has the same sentimentality as D. H. Lawrence's narration of *his* mother's playing in the poem "Piano." Johnson writes:

> Always on Sunday evenings she opened the little square piano and picked out hymns. I can recall now that whenever she played hymns from the book her *tempo* was always decidedly *largo*. Sometimes on other evenings, when she was not sewing, she would play simple accompaniments to some old Southern songs which she sang. In these songs she was freer, because she played them

by ear. Those evenings on which she opened the little piano were the happiest hours of my childhood. Whenever she started toward the instrument, I used to follow her with all the interest and irrepressible joy that a pampered pet dog shows when a package is opened in which he knows there is a sweet bit for him. I used to stand by her side and often interrupt and annoy her by chiming in with strange harmonies which I found on either the high keys of the treble or the low keys of the bass.

Later in life the protagonist becomes a famous ragtime player in New York. But when he meets and falls in love with a woman who is "as white as a lily," he—passing as white—serenades her with Chopin. Then when he reveals his racial identity to her along with his love for her, she takes fright and leaves him. But after a separation they meet by chance, and it is over Chopin that they reunite:

Later in the evening she went to the piano and began to play very softly, as if to herself, the opening bars of the Thirteenth Nocturne. I felt that the psychic moment of my life had come, a moment which, if lost, could never be called back; and, in as careless a manner as I could assume, I sauntered over to the piano and stood almost bending over her. She continued playing, but, in a voice that was almost a whisper, she called me by my Christian name and said: "I love you, I love you, I love you." I took her place at the piano and played the Nocturne in a manner that silenced the chatter of the company both in and out of the room, involuntarily closing it with the major triad.[19]

He takes over the female role of pianist-seducer—quite literally here by supplanting the woman he loves on the bench—only to turn it into a role of male assertiveness ("silencing the chatter of the company")—and here Johnson is playing on the turn from "feminine" to "masculine" character in the course of that Thirteenth Nocturne, the C Minor Nocturne of Op. 48. At the same time, he gives himself

William Holman Hunt, *The Awakening Conscience*, 1853. Hunt's painting tells its story of would-be seduction at the piano with greater narrative detail than a Rowlandson drawing or any of the nineteenth-century French images discussed in Chapter 5; nevertheless, ever since the painting was first exhibited, there have been disputes about just what story it tells. Like the fictions of Flaubert, Tolstoy, and Johnson, it violates artistic conventions about love scenes at the piano: it is the man who is seated at the piano, and he is seated so as to suggest that he barely meant to play at all; the woman, whose "conscience" is "awakening," moves to break free of the piano—that symbol of domestic propriety—in order to restore propriety. In the words of Richard Leppert (*The Sight of Sound*, p. 194), "this unsettling picture is the dark reverse image of the cult of domesticity." (Tate Gallery, London)

over to white music—the Chopin nocturne—at the very moment that he triumphantly sees his blackness accepted by the white woman he loves.

Two nineteenth-century stories break out of Austen's fixation on the moment of courtship to explore the piano as a symbol of sexuality in the lives of married women: Gustave Flaubert's novel *Madame Bovary* (1857) and Leo Tolstoy's novella *The Kreutzer Sonata* (1889).[20] In both works the husband, at the time of marriage, assumes the parental role of supervising his wife's virtue, and the piano becomes a weapon by which she might assert her independence from that supervision. For Emma Bovary the piano belongs, along with novels, to the dream realm of romance to which she longs to escape from her boring, provincial marriage. But when she persuades her husband to pay for her to take weekly piano lessons in the city, the piano is a ruse: instead of meeting her piano teacher there, she meets her lover. The pretense only sets off suspicions and therefore more supervision, more deceits, debts, and in the end her suicide.

In *The Kreutzer Sonata* too the wife dies violently, but at the hands of her jealous husband. This is another case of an unhappily married woman who finds relief from her unhappiness in playing the piano, but here the suspicious husband has arranged for her to play duets with a violinist whom he has met and about whom he later reports, "I disliked him from the first glance. But curiously enough a strange and fatal force led me not to repulse him, not to keep him away, but on the contrary to invite him to the house." The wife's music making, in other words, is in this case the husband's insane device for leading his wife into a musical relationship that he can then imagine as an affair, thereby driving himself into such a jealous rage that he kills her. Along the way he attributes to the music that she and the violinist play together a terrible power to awaken and unleash sexual feelings: "Take that Kreutzer Sonata for instance, how can that first presto be played in a drawing-room among ladies in low-necked dresses?"[21] It is in effect the same seductive power that the parents in Austen's novels thought they could cultivate in their daughters through piano lessons, without letting it get out of control; here, though, the husband believes that music is so irresistibly seductive that to his mind the mere idea of its seductiveness—without any proof of a seduction—justifies an uncontrolled and fatal jealousy.[22]

In all this fiction the piano itself is an ordinary instrument, a mere pawn in the play of human identities and relationships. In August Wilson's play *The Piano Lesson* (first performed in 1987), by contrast, the piano itself is a remarkable creation, carved with a family's history, full of spirits from the family's past, controlling the family's destiny. But this remarkably imagined idea of a piano nevertheless connects to the rest of this tradition of fictional pianos in that it, too, puts the piano at the center of family tensions. Carved by a slave with his family's history, but at his owner's order, the piano becomes not just a possession but also a symbol of the family's need for self-possession after emancipation, when the former slave owners continue to own the piano: "Boy Charles . . . be talking about taking it out of Sutter's house. Say it was the story of our whole family and as long as Sutter had it . . . he had us. Say we was still in slavery."[23] The struggle over ownership of the piano costs one family member his life and leaves the surviving members at odds over what to do with it: one plays it for a living and then leaves it, another wants to sell it and buy land with the money, and Berniece, who has possession of it, wants to keep it but not play it, until the moment comes when she needs to exorcise the ghost of past struggles over the piano by playing it. In the end, this story is more remarkable for its musical family than for its magical piano: every member of this family is in one way or another a player of the piano, and the family piano is in one way or another an obstacle to every member's liberation. *The Piano Lesson* creates its family dynamic without resort to the usual fictional structure in which *not* playing the piano—owning it and listening to others play—marks some family members' power over those who do play.

The Classical Repertory Revisited: Instruments, Players, and Styles
Gretchen A. Wheelock

Surveys of piano literature from 1770–1820 typically, and understandably, focus on core repertories of the solo sonata and the concerto by the Viennese masters—Mozart, Haydn, and Beethoven. Rarely, however, do they address these works in terms of the instruments that inspired them or the venues in which they were played and heard. Here I take a closer look at these long-familiar works from a more broadly historical and contextual perspective, giving due attention to the diversity of instruments, venues, and players for which they were written and their influence on style and genre in this period.

During the last three decades of the eighteenth century, when the piano underwent its most rapid development in technology and production, a commensurate growth in the quantity and diversity of published music for the instrument took place, as did a gradual specialization of keyboard genres and styles for an expanding market of consumers, both amateur and professional. Publishers eager to accommodate the broadest possible spectrum of keyboard players most often advertised their offerings as suitable "for the Harpsichord or Piano Forte," even for works that were undeniably written to exploit the idiomatic possibilities of the newer instrument. Although composers were themselves often complicit in this marketing strategy, they also increasingly favored the piano for its unique range of expressive and dynamic effects. Moreover, distinctive styles of playing and writing for the piano emerged in response to marked differences in the mechanism and sound of Viennese and German instruments versus English ones. And in Vienna itself, the distinctive qualities of one builder's instruments in comparison with another's were appreciated as suitable for particular kinds of players and styles.

Perhaps the most significant development in composition for the piano, however, had to do with an increasing divergence of music written for a predominantly female market of amateur players in domestic settings from that meant for performance by professionals and virtuosos in public and semi-private concerts. Just as in the gradual and often blurred distinction between music written for harpsichord and that for piano, one cannot draw clear lines separating these broad categories, as there is an overlapping of style and technical demands within genres of each. But the piano concerto's identification with virtuosity and public performance eventually assured its status as a vehicle for the male professional—most often the composer himself. The piano sonata, on the other hand, had a more varied and changing profile: while associations of the solo and accompanied keyboard sonata with domestic music making of female amateurs persisted throughout the period, the works of Beethoven, Clementi, Dussek, and others around the turn of the century promoted new directions and expectations for performers within these genres as well.

"For the Harpsichord or Piano-forte"

Judging from the large outpouring of easy pieces and tutors published for the beginning keyboard student, the question of whether one sat at the harpsichord or the fortepiano seems hardly relevant. In England and on the Continent, a flood of pastiche sonatas and simple sonatinas, variation sets, and simplified arrangements of works originally intended for other media offered a growing market of consumers the means to refine their earliest efforts on whatever keyboard instrument was at hand. Instruction books, largely occupied with the development of technical facility—hand position, fingering, and the like—do not begin to address aspects of expression specific to the piano until a decade after the turn of the century.[24] By this time, as we shall see, the idiomatic capabilities of the "new" instrument had been variously exploited by Haydn, Mozart, Beethoven, and others, who captured its expressive potential in increasingly precise notation. In the course of that development, emerging genres and styles of piano music were increasingly bound up with the particular instruments and players they served.

Although Mozart used the term *fortepiano* only once in a score (for the D Major "Coronation" Concerto, K. 537, of 1788), preferring instead the generic *cembalo*, he seems to have written the vast majority of his keyboard works with the piano in mind. Whereas one may encounter in his autographs entire movements without any dynamic markings, it was Mozart's habit to add these, along with many more expressive details of articulation, in preparing his works for publication. Music intended for public consumption needed to be more "instructive" than that used for one's own students or performances. Thus we find as well more richly composed-out embellishments in places where the improvising composer-performer would need to provide models for the anonymous consumer: varied returns of themes, spontaneous-sounding lead-ins at anticipatory fermatas, embellished repeats, and the like. Whereas the piano idiom is apparent rather later in Haydn's keyboard writing, we also find this increasingly specific notation in his works, especially those published after 1780.

Mozart's sensitivity to the fortepiano's responsiveness in clean damping, dynamic shading, singing line, and subtle articulations is already evident in his earliest set of sonatas, composed in Munich in 1774. (See, for example, the Andante of the C Major Sonata, K. 279, mm. 11–22; the Adagio of the F Major, K. 280, mm. 1–8; and, especially, the Andante amoroso of the B-flat Major, K. 281, mm. 1–8, shown here.) The opening movement of the A Minor Sonata, K. 310, composed in Paris in 1778, provides the only instance of *pp* and *ff* indications in his keyboard sonatas (mm. 58–69), but Mozart's notation of both intimate and symphonic uses of the piano extends far beyond dynamic indications to embrace countless details of subtle nuances in articulation and scoring.

Wolfgang Amadeus Mozart, Sonata, K. 281. Andante amoroso, mm. 1–8

Evidence of a shift from a harpsichord or clavichord idiom to one that favors the piano is less decisive in Haydn's keyboard output, but in his sonatas of the 1780s and 1790s I will describe changes in style that reflect his acquaintance with both Viennese and English pianos. As for Beethoven, there can be no question of the intended instrument for one whose response to a broad spectrum of Viennese and English pianos stretched their mechanical and expressive capabilities to the limit. Even so, publishers of the first editions of his sonatas continued to offer harpsichord as an option up to and including the C Minor Sonata, Op. 13 ("Pathétique"), and even for later works. Apart from the earlier Op. 49 "Sonates faciles," considered by Czerny as "useful for less accomplished players," Beethoven's keyboard works signal a decided break from both harpsichord and music for dilettantes.

Even if the amateur at home may have ignored the idiomatic potential of distinctive keyboard styles, the choice was not simply a matter of harpsichord versus piano. Quite apart from the differences between "squares" and "grands," the particular qualities of pianos made by individual builders called forth distinctive styles of writing and playing suited to the particular strengths of each. The visitor Johann Schönfeld, for example, whose impressions of Vienna's musicians were published in 1796, compared the pianos of four different builders in that city alone: "The sound of Schanz's pianos is not as strong as Walter's instruments, but it is just as clear and for the most part, more pleasing. They also have a lighter action owing to their shallower key dip, and the keys are not so wide . . . they are almost copies of the Fortepiano made by the Augsburg artist, Stein."[25] Production of the pianos by Johann Andreas Stein that Mozart came to know in Augsburg continued in Vienna at the firm of Stein's daughter, Nannette Streicher, whose instruments are also mentioned by our reporter: "They do not have the strength of Walter's, but in evenness of sound, clarity, and a gentle sweetness that seems to float, they are matchless. The sounds blend together; the action needs a light touch, resilient fingers, and a sensitive heart." Of particular interest in this same commentary are the writer's remarks about pianos in relation to players of the day:

> We seem to have two types of great pianists. One of these loves to treat the ears to a powerful clamor. So they play with a full sound and extraordinary speed; they practice the fastest scales and octaves. All of this demands strength and composure . . . [and] a fortepiano that will not snap. For this kind of virtuoso, we recommend the Walter fortepiano. The other type of great pianist seeks nourishment for the soul and loves not only clear but also soft, sweet playing. These pianists can choose no better instrument than a Streicher, or the so-called Stein variety.

To find such a wealth of different instruments of distinctive characters in a single city is as remote from the experience of today's players as the "Stein variety" is from the Steinway.

Accustomed as we are to public concerts devoted entirely to piano sonatas, perhaps even those of a single composer, the notion of the piano sonata as composed largely for pedagogical use and for private, domestic music making—frequently with ad libitum accompaniments and often played on the harpsichord—is as foreign to us as our performance practices would be to the eighteenth-century listener. The distinctively pianistic solo sonatas heard in recital today emerged gradually in a variety of performance contexts, many of which might not be considered "performances" in any modern sense. Haydn's output of keyboard sonatas over some forty years allows us to trace that development across a range of instruments—clavichord, harpsichord, and fortepianos of both Viennese and English makers. Because publishers were eager to sell Haydn's music to the broadest possible market, they often advertised his keyboard works—even his latest compositions—as suitable for either harpsichord or fortepiano. Although the players of Haydn's day were apparently content to put his music on the rack of whichever of these was at hand, modern scholars and performers have been attentive to the relationship of notation to idiom in trying to sort out which instrument may be best suited to the demands of a given piece. But how might consumers and venues of performance be reflected in the styles of Haydn's keyboard compositions?

Haydn spent his early years as a student and freelance composer in the imperial city of Vienna before taking up his position with the Esterházy family in 1761. His earliest sonatas, most often called "divertimenti" or "partitas," all include a minuet as one of two, three, or four short movements that are simple in texture and design, and full of the triplet and trill figures and Alberti bass patterns typical of Viennese keyboard style in the 1750s and early 1760s. László Somfai has characterized such sonatas as "Liebhaber" sonatas, that is, graceful and easy pieces meant for the fingers of students and music lovers of modest accomplishment.[26]

Haydn's sonatas of the late 1760s and early 1770s are more individual in expression, explore a greater range of keys, and exploit more fully the keyboard idiom. The famous C Minor Sonata, Hob. xvi:20, dates from this period, a time in which Haydn was experimenting with more serious and dramatic elements of the so-called *Sturm und Drang* style in his quartets and symphonies as well. In the more intimate domain of keyboard genres, we might speak instead of the *empfindsamer Styl*—the sensitive style—associated with C. P. E. Bach, whose works Haydn knew and admired. His dynamic indications imply that Haydn intended the C Minor Sonata for a touch-sensitive instrument, perhaps the clavichord, as A. Peter Brown and Somfai suggest. The amazing breadth and intensity of expression in the outer movements of this work may make it seem to us an unlikely candidate for this softest and most intimate of keyboard instruments, but the clavichord was highly regarded for its unique expressive capabilities. And, as Brown reminds us, C. P. E. Bach used pianissimo and fortissimo indications in his most famous and idiomatic piece for the clavichord, the "Abschied vom Silbermannischen Clavier." In any case, it seems clear that the C Minor Sonata represents a departure from harpsichord writing. When he came to publish the work in 1780, nearly ten years after its composition, Haydn no doubt considered it suitable for the fortepiano, for by this time the newer instrument was well known in Vienna. Even so, it's worth noting that before 1780 only two works published in Vienna offered fortepiano on the title page as an alternative to the harpsichord, and both listed it as the second choice.[27]

Apart from this anomalous C Minor Sonata, few of Haydn's keyboard works before 1780 have any dynamic markings, and there is little reason to suppose that they were written with the fortepiano in mind.[28] It is in the "Auenbrugger" sonatas (Hob. xvi:35–39), published in 1780 with the addendum of the much earlier Hob. xvi:20 discussed above, that we find more signs of a piano idiom. Putting aside this earlier sonata, which Haydn himself noted was "the longest and most difficult" of the group, some scholars have regarded these sonatas as aimed at pleasing a wider public. Our own judgment of the set may be colored somewhat by the familiarity of both its opening work, the C Major Sonata, Hob. xvi:35, and the D Major, Hob. xvi:37. There is certainly an exuberance and directness of rhythmic energy in many of the opening and closing movements of this set, but the sonatas in C-sharp Minor, Hob. xvi:36, and E-flat Major, Hob. xvi:38, demonstrate what Elaine Sisman has called "the peculiar digressive style that gives to so much of Haydn's piano music the quality of informal speech."[29]

Franz Joseph Haydn, Sonata, Hob. xvi:36. Moderato, mm. 21–26

Haydn, Sonata, Hob.
XVI:35. Allegro con brio,
mm. 132–36

The opening of Hob. XVI:36 confirms this experience of Haydn's music as a spontaneous living in the moment, of feeling free to take the roundabout way, to linger when it strikes one's fancy, and to return to an earlier spot, now seen in a different light. Spontaneity of gesture is a hallmark of Haydn's style, and the fact of solo performance underscores the freedoms of whimsy and the fantastic, even seeming forgetfulness. The range and rapid changes of dynamic effects in this first movement, as well as in that of Hob. XVI:35, contribute to such an impression, and point as well to the touch-sensitive capability of the fortepiano. (Shown here, for example, are the opening movements of Hob. XVI:36, mm. 21–26, and Hob. XVI:35, mm. 132–36.) In this respect, Haydn may well have sought to address not simply a wider public but also a growing preference for music that suited the new instrument.

With the sonatas of the mid-1780s and 1790s, we can speak of a fully realized fortepiano style. These are also the years of the incredible series of Haydn's mature "accompanied Sonatas," or piano trios, as we call them. Unlike the solo sonatas, which Haydn composed throughout his life, the trios divide rather remarkably into an early group of twelve from the 1760s, and a late group of twenty-eight, written from 1784 on. The term "accompanied Sonatas" is a fitting description of these works in Haydn's oeuvre, because the piano dominates as the leading and often self-sufficient voice—the genre itself arose from the practice of adding accompanying violin or flute and cello parts ad libitum. Indeed some of the Haydn sonatas we know as solo works were published in their day with accompaniments added by others—the Haydn enthusiast Charles Burney, for one. This practice reminds us of the social nature of informal music making in the eighteenth century, in which friends and family could become listeners and players in turn, depending on the instruments and players at hand.

Haydn's accomplishments in this genre seem even more remarkable when measured against J. P. Milchmeyer's comments on the dubious virtues of accompanied sonatas in those days: "As for sonatas with an accompanying part, they have the advantage that now and then, after the solos, one can relax; also, since the attention of the listener is divided between two persons, a slight mistake is not as noticeable as it is in pieces without accompaniment."[30] Few of Haydn's trios allow moments of relaxation for the pianist. The late works especially are brilliantly virtuosic, exploiting the full idiomatic range of the instrument. They are also among the most harmonically adventurous of his works in any genre, often reaching into remote keys via enharmonic modulations. As such they are challenging essays for both players and listeners.

Nearly fifty years ago, Arthur Loesser noted in *Men, Women, and Pianos* the close association of keyboard instruments (excepting the organ) with the feminine, most especially with young women of the middle classes.[31] The sociology and status of the keyboard sonata in mid- to late-eighteenth-century Vienna was undoubtedly bound up with women, largely amateurs, for whom music making in private and semi-private venues was a suitable display of feminine accomplishment. The association of solo and accompanied sonatas with female keyboard players is suggested by the dedications of Haydn's works in these genres. In fact, apart from the "Esterházy" sonatas of 1774—his first authorized publication, which he dedicated to his prince—all the dedicatees of Haydn's keyboard works were women.

Lest we think that dedications were simply honorific, there were notable talents among the women to whom Haydn dedicated his keyboard works and others who are reported to have played them. Of the sisters Katarina and Marianna Auenbrugger, Haydn wrote that "their way of playing and genuine insight into music equals those of the greatest masters."[32] In his *Jahrbuch* of 1796, Schönfeld recalled Katarina as "sometime ago one of the first female artists on the fortepiano, an instrument which she played not only fluently but also with good taste."[33] In addition to the Auenbrugger sisters, there were Barbara Ployer, student of Mozart and dedicatee of Haydn's F Minor Variations (Hob. XVII:6, 1793); Maria Theresia Paradis, who performed Haydn's G Major Concerto in Paris; and Marianna Theresia Martines, who noted in her autobiography that she began study with Haydn at the age of seven. Reported to be a great favorite of Mozart, one who played his duets with him on the fortepiano, Martines was the daughter of a papal ambassador and during the 1790s presided over a leading music salon in Vienna on Sunday evenings.[34] Magdalene von Kurzböck, to whom Hob. XVI:52 was dedicated upon its publication in Vienna, was described as "the greatest lady pianist of the local musical world."[35] But the English pianist Therese Jansen, later Bartolozzi, was perhaps the most distinguished among Haydn's dedicatees. A successful piano teacher in London, Jansen was named, along with John Field and Johann Cramer, as a favorite among Clementi's students.[36] Haydn honored her with several trios in addition to the late solo sonatas, Hob. xvi:50 in C Major and xvi:52 in E-flat Major. These are works that exploit not only the technical abilities of the player but also the new resources of sound offered by English pianos that Haydn came to know during his visits to London in the 1790s.

Although we do find exceptional women playing concertos in public— Barbara Ployer, for example—most often they performed before semi-private gatherings in the courtly chambers and music salons of Viennese nobility, foreign diplomats, and well-connected music lovers. Here even concertos might be heard; a Fräulein von Hartenstein is reported to have played one of Haydn's at a private concert in Vienna.[37] As we will see, some of Mozart's early concertos served similar functions in aristocratic households.

Rebecca Schröter and Maria Anna von Genzinger, along with the Esterházy princesses and other titled women named in Haydn's dedications, may have been more representative of the vast amateur market served by solo and accompanied sonatas in the late eighteenth century. Iconography of the period confirms the impression that "historically correct" performances of solo sonatas and trios should feature women at the keyboard. The exceptional portraits of men at the keyboard tend to be of composers (see inset on these images in Chapter 5) and players of four-hand music (the famous picture of Mozart and his sister, for example). Apart from their didactic use (as in Haydn's "Il Maestro e lo scolare," Hob. xviia:1), duets might provide a socially sanctioned opportunity for courtship, especially if two bodies were to be seated at a five-octave instrument.

There was surely a range of abilities and training among women keyboard players of both upper and middle classes, and some of Haydn's sonatas are clearly more demanding than others. But Somfai's designation of some of Haydn's works as *Damensonaten*, or "Ladies' Sonatas"—to distinguish them from more demanding "Concert Sonatas"—creates a somewhat false impression. It is historically misleading to suggest that sonatas were gendered male and female, or masculine and feminine, in style. As Brown points out, all sonatas were in some sense *Damensonaten*, just as they were intended for use in the chamber rather than in public concerts.[38]

With this caveat in mind, a better distinction might be made between works that are more intimate and those more public in style. The two late E-flat Major sonatas, Hob. xvi:49 and 52, demonstrate this difference nicely. They also represent Haydn's approach to two very different kinds of pianos, the Viennese and the English, and the schools of playing associated with them. Although it can be assumed that Haydn was acquainted with and responsive to the idiomatic possibilities of the fortepiano in the early 1780s, we have no direct evidence from the composer himself that he intended a given work for this instrument until 1788, when he wrote to his publisher Artaria that he needed a Schanz piano in order to compose the trios Hob. xv:11–13.[39] In 1790, Haydn urged this same instrument on his dear friend Frau von Genzinger, for whom he was writing the E-flat Major Sonata, Hob. xvi:49. Haydn advised her that the Adagio of this sonata is "rather difficult but full of feeling. It's a pity, however, that Your Grace has not one of Schantz's [*sic*] fortepianos, for Your Grace could then produce twice the effect." He specifically noted the unusual lightness and pleasing action of the Schanz instrument.[40] Recalling the comments of our reporter of 1796, Haydn's choice of the Schanz piano for Genzinger suggests that this more sensitive instrument suited her best.

During his London visits, Haydn encountered a very different instrument in the Broadwood piano. The "English" action was more resistant to the touch than the Viennese and produced a much fuller sound; the dampers were raised by pedals rather than knee levers, and a shift pedal allowed the una corda effect, whereby the hammers could be shifted to strike one, two, or all three strings. Only once does Haydn suggest use of the damper pedal, indicating "open pedal" for two of his boldest and most intriguing passages, from the opening movement of the C Major Sonata, Hob. xvi:50. (The second of these is shown in the example here: xvi:50/i, mm. 120–24.) The *pp* marking here might have suggested the shift

Haydn, Sonata, Hob. xvi:50. Allegro, mm. 120–24

pedal as well, whereas Viennese instruments would offer the possibility of the moderator's special effect. This device, unique to Viennese and German pianos, draws a piece of felt between the hammers and strings, producing a somewhat covered, very soft, ethereal timbre. Haydn also took advantage of the English piano's extended range: the high a''' in the finale of this sonata is the only note in all his keyboard works that exceeds the five-octave range typical of Viennese instruments in his day.

With these differences in mind, we might return to the two E-flat Major sonatas. Although they share the same key and were written within five years of each other, it's hard to imagine a greater contrast in style and idiomatic writing for the piano. Of the earlier work, Hob. XVI:49, we learn that Frau von Genzinger was stymied by the crossing of hands required in the Adagio; she writes to Haydn: "I am not used to this, and thus find it hard to do, so please let me know how this could be altered." She doesn't refer to the spots in the first movement that also involve crossed hands, and in neither case is there any evidence that Haydn obliged her request for revision. He did acknowledge that the work was difficult, however, and referred in another letter to Genzinger's "beautiful hands and facility of execution." Still, the technical demands of this work pale in comparison with those of the later sonata.

Perhaps contributing to the graceful and intimate nature of the earlier sonata is the fact that all three movements are in 3/4 meter. The finale is actually marked "Tempo di Minuet," but the first movement has a dancelike lilt as well. The minuet was the most noble of courtly dances and a suitably refined topos for "Her Grace"—though in this particular movement the dance takes some pretty untoward steps. The Adagio, marked "cantabile," is, as Haydn noted, "full of feeling," and shares an improvisatory leisure with the opening variation movements of the D Major Sonata, Hob. XVI:42, and the C Major, Hob. XVI:48, both marked "con espressione." Indeed, the contemporary reviewer of Haydn's D Major Sonata, Hob. XVI:42, might have equally said of this Adagio that it is "so well suited to the instrument, the composer proves to be like a skillful, tasteful singer when she repeats her aria."[41] Such praise must have been gratifying to Haydn, because eighteenth-century writers repeatedly urged composers of instrumental music to emulate the expressive capabilities of vocal music above all else. This same reviewer astutely observed that such a movement is "more difficult to perform than one initially believes, [demanding] the utmost precision and much delicacy in performance."[42] The intimacy of precise and delicate expression characterizes the opening movement as well, as does the playful wit of arrested gestures and repeating snippets that prepare and delay both the returning theme and ultimate closure of the movement. Despite these humorous exaggerations, there is a conversational quality here that perfectly suits music for the chamber and evokes a sense of friends reluctant to give up an amusing subject and one another's company.

The markedly different profile of the "big" E-flat Major Sonata, Hob. XVI:52, is obvious from the grand French-overture-style chords of the opening to the rousing dash of the Presto finale's close. This is a fully theatrical work, public in style if not in performance venue, and its fistfuls of notes don't bring delicate hands to mind. Indeed, this sonata has many earmarks of the London School of virtuoso playing, whose chief exponents were Muzio Clementi, Johann Baptist Cramer, and Jan Ladislav Dussek. All were celebrated pianists who cultivated a public bravura style; in their often symphonic textures, extremes in dynamics, and daunting technical demands, the "professional" sonatas of these composer-performers were closely linked with the more robust sound and greater resonance of English instruments made by the firms of Broadwood, Stodart, and Clementi himself. Many of these features are present in Hob. XVI:50: in brilliant passage-work covering the entire range of the instrument, scale figures in parallel thirds, rumbling broken octaves, rapidly alternating hands, and tutti orchestral textures. We have to believe that Therese Jansen was a powerful player. But in addition to an exceptional pianist, it was the English piano that called forth this remarkable work, as well as the tradition of playing that it promoted. And it is not surprising that this is the sonata today's students and teachers most often turn to when they wish to present a Haydn work in concert.

Mozart's Piano Concertos in Chamber and Concert Settings

In comparison with Haydn's output of sixty-two solo sonatas, Mozart's contribution of eighteen to this genre seems surprisingly small in number. For a composer-performer seeking the favor of potential patrons, sonatas could provide entrée to fashionable circles of music making. They could also serve as teaching pieces, eventually bringing in extra income from publication. But for a composer known in his day primarily as a keyboard virtuoso, the concerto was the genre of choice for self-presentation in public performance. And it was for Vienna, the city he saluted as "the land of the piano," that Mozart produced an astonishing series of concertos for this instrument.[43]

Although Mozart favored the piano concerto as a vehicle for his own appearances, the venues and ensembles for concerto performance were flexible in eighteenth-century practice, and the soloist was not always the composer himself. Several of his concertos, even from the Vienna years, were written for specific women, and of these works some were scored to allow for ad libitum ensembles suited to chamber performance. Among works of the pre-Vienna years, the Concerto in F Major for three pianos, K. 242 (1776), was composed for Countess Antonia Lodron and her daughters, with the third piano part made easy enough for the younger's abilities. (Mozart later transcribed this work for performance on two pianos with his sister, Nannerl.) Also modest in its technical demands is the C Major Concerto, K. 246, written for the Countess Antonia Lützkow, and perhaps intended for performance on two pianos.[44] The Concerto in E-flat Major for Two Pianos, K. 365, which Mozart composed in 1779 and played with his sister, is appropriately more demanding, putting both players on an equal footing in a dialogue that is both intimate and charmingly competitive.[45] The middle movements of three later concertos written for women—K. 449 in E-flat Major and K. 453 in G Major for Barbara Ployer, and K. 456 in B-flat Major for Maria Theresia Paradis—feature the finely nuanced style of *Empfindsamkeit* in intimate exchanges between the piano and orchestral voices. In regard to these works, Robert Levin has suggested that Mozart "may have wished to tailor his music to the personalities of the two women for whom he composed them."[46]

The public style of the E-flat Major Concerto, K. 271 (1777), is in a different league, its theatrical flair and demanding passagework perhaps inspired by the French virtuoso for whom it was written—a young woman about whom little is known but her odd last name, "Jeunehomme" (young man). Here the piano is the full and equal partner of the orchestra in a range of styles that encompass conversational banter and brilliant display, opera seria recitative and aria, and an elegant courtly minuet that interrupts the rollicking romp of the finale. Among the few concertos published during Mozart's lifetime, this work is unusual in having two complete sets of original cadenzas for the first and second movements and three sets of lead-in elaborations for the last movement. Mozart most likely improvised at these moments in his own performances of K. 271, a work that he may have favored to showcase his own virtuosic talents. Although the composer's letters document only one such occasion—in 1777 at an inn in Munich—it is likely that he used K. 271 for his debut performance before Vienna's Tonkünstler-Societät in 1781.[47] Such an appearance would call for the brilliant showing that this E-flat Major Concerto could guarantee.

Once permanently installed in Vienna, Mozart wrote three new concertos (K. 414/386a in A Major; K. 413/387a in F Major; and K. 415/387b in C Major) for his own subscription concerts. In a letter to his father, he described these works as sure to please both connoisseurs and less educated listeners: "a happy medium between what is too easy and too difficult; they are very brilliant, pleasing to the ear, and natural, without being vapid."[48] Perhaps Mozart meant to address a wide market of consumers as well, for these were concertos he published with ad libitum parts for the winds so as to allow performances for piano with string quartet alone, or with oboes and horns as well, or with full orchestra. Similarly versatile chamber scoring is found in the Concerto in E-flat Major, K. 449 (1784), a work commissioned by Barbara Ployer, and again in the "Coronation" concerto, K. 537

in D Major (1788). The trumpets and timpani we are used to hearing in the C Major Concerto of this group, K. 415, may have figured in two public performances that Mozart gave of the work in March 1783, but they do not appear in a printed edition until André's publication of 1802.[49]

In addition to ad libitum scoring, Mozart's carefully voiced figured bass notation in the "Subscription Concertos" indicates a continuo role for the piano—a practice that must have been normative in concerto performances of the day, where the pianist shared with the first violinist the responsibility for keeping the ensemble together.[50] This practice alters somewhat our notion of the keyboard player as simply soloist. The long-anticipated solo entrance, heard not as the piano's first utterance but as a dominant and distinctive voice that emerges from the tutti group, marks a change of role to one of protagonist. First among peers, the pianist may take a leading, an equal, or a subordinate role in the changing contexts of solo and tutti passages.

The two concertos after K. 449 written early in 1784—those in B-flat Major, K. 450, and D Major, K. 451—Mozart called "grosse Concerte," perhaps signaling a change to fully realized symphonic textures as well as increasing technical demands on the pianist. Remarking that these two were "bound to make the performer sweat,"[51] Mozart no doubt relished flexing his own muscles as a pianist much in demand in Vienna. The full-bodied scoring and newly prominent role of the winds in both concertos seem to call for the robust sound of a grand fortepiano by Anton Walter, the instrument that Johann Schönfeld would later report could be counted on "not to snap" under the vigorous fingers of virtuosos. Indeed, one imagines that the qualities of instruments he recounted had much to do with their uses (and players) in private chambers and public concerts.

In the six concertos of 1785–86, Mozart's best known concertos, the voice of the opera composer is especially audible. Ranging from such works as the C Major Concerto, K. 467, which echoes the pacing and diction of buffo intrigues in *Le Nozze di Figaro*, to the ominous world of *Don Giovanni*, previewed in the opening movement of the D Minor Concerto, K. 466, Mozart's handling of both theatrical and intimate gestures is wondrously matched to the versatile persona of the piano and its relation to the varying textures and timbres of orchestral voices. Whereas the opening movement of the A Major Concerto, K. 488, highlights the suave vocal capacity of the piano, that of the C Major Concerto, K. 503, displays the instrument at its most majestic in the confident march of fully "orchestrated" chords and dazzling passagework. In each of the concertos of these years, Mozart's personal voice as composer and performer finds a natural and versatile ally in the Viennese fortepiano, whose idiomatic and expressive range he explored with ever-fresh invention and balanced in perfect partnership with the forces of his orchestra.

Many incomplete spots in the autographs of concertos from 1785 on show evidence of the haste of a busy man who expected to play his own works, filling in such lacunae in performance. In addition to sketchy patches in K. 482, 488, 491, and 537 (in which only the right-hand part is given for the entire second movement as well as for extended passages of the first and last movements), we have original candenzas for only the A Major Concerto, K. 488, and the B-flat Major, K. 595. Perhaps Mozart planned to publish these two, although only K. 595 appeared in print—the first (and last) since K. 453 to be published during his lifetime. He may have written out the cadenza to K. 488 for Barbara Ployer, who must have played the work because we have a highly decorated version of the second movement in her hand.[52] In any case, there would be no need for Mozart to write a cadenza for his own use, for improvisation would be expected at this point. Extended improvisations—as dazzling to eighteenth-century audiences as they are rare today—were featured items in Mozart's public and private concerts, often involving free fantasias and variations on familiar tunes of the day. Although the style of seeming improvisation is captured for others to play in his compositions in these genres, Mozart's appearances as improvising soloist displayed his virtuosity as both performer and composer.[53]

Unable to raise a sufficient number of subscribers to schedule concerts of his own, Mozart played both of his last two concertos on occasions that highlighted others. He performed the first, K. 537 in D Major ("Coronation," 1788), at an unexpected court concert in Dresden during festivities surrounding the coronation of Leopold II, and the second, K. 595 in B-flat Major (1791), at a benefit concert given in Vienna by the clarinetist Joseph Beer.[54] Of these, K. 595 seems especially remote from the virtuosic demands of its predecessors, favoring instead a chamberlike intimacy and a leisurely dialogue among the participants. But even if Mozart's reputation in Vienna as a popular virtuoso had waned, the legacy to future pianists of his achievements in the concerto genre remains unsurpassed, and much can be learned about that legacy from study of the instruments he preferred. From his early enthusiasm for the fortepianos of Johann Andreas Stein to his later affinity for those of Anton Walter, Mozart developed a keyboard style that is inseparably bound to the full expressive range of the piano.

From the first of the Op. 2 sonatas, composed in 1795 and dedicated to Joseph Haydn, to the last, Op. 111 of 1821–22, dedicated to Archduke Rudolf of Austria, Beethoven's bold approach to the medium is audible in a continuous stream of works that reinvent the genre of the solo keyboard sonata. In addition to his innovative formal procedures in these works, his sonatas range more widely in key than those of Haydn and Mozart; nearly one-third are in the minor mode, appropriate for the often passionate and deeply serious affect of his musical discourse in these works. His sonatas press both instrument and player to extremes of tempo—both slow and fast—and to often explosive contrasts of texture and dynamics. Although isolated works, such as the two sonatas of Op. 49 and the Sonata in G Major, Op. 79, are relatively simple and small in scale, the majority of Beethoven's sonatas are uncompromising in their demands for prodigious virtuosity and stamina, and as such part company with the vast majority of amateur players. For listeners, too, the unconventional and provocative gambits thrown down in the opening bars of so many of these works announce challenges to be worked out in large-scale structures of unprecedented length.

The continuous publication of Beethoven's piano sonatas during his lifetime nevertheless suggests a demand for such daunting keyboard music. Departing from the usual practice of offering sonatas in groups of six or three, Beethoven's sonatas from Op. 53 on appeared singly, often after prolonged gestation in sketches and revisions. Equal numbers of men and women appear as dedicatees, the majority being aristocratic patrons among Vienna's nobility. Two of his sonatas are known by their dedications, the "Waldstein" (Op. 53), written for Count Ferdinand von Waldstein of Bonn, and the "Therèse" (Op. 78), for the Countess Therèse von Brunswick. But many acquired nicknames that are suggestive of their reception by listeners and players: the "Moonlight" (Op. 27, no. 2), the "Pastorale" (Op. 28), the "Tempest" (Op. 31, no. 2), the "Appassionata" (Op. 57), and the "Cuckoo" (Op. 79).

Some inscriptions originate with the composer himself, as if to announce the novelty of his approach to the genre, as seen in the two sonatas of Op. 27, each of which he labeled *quasi una fantasia,* and in the descriptive labels for each movement of "Das Lebewohl" (Op. 81a). Op. 26 came to be known as the "Funeral March," after Beethoven's title for the slow movement, "Marcia funebre sulla morte d'un Eroe," which gained sufficient popularity to be issued independently. If this work and the earlier Op. 13, which Beethoven titled "Grande Sonate Pathétique," strike us as incompatible with the option "pour le Clavecin ou Piano-

Forte" printed on the title pages of their first editions, it seems that traditional publishing practices died hard. One would imagine that even harpsichords with swells—hardly commonplace instruments—would seem inadequate for the demands of these works. Beethoven's own title for the "Grosse Sonate für das Hammerklavier" (Op. 106) certainly left no doubt as to the required medium.

If the style and expressive range of Mozart's piano music was perfectly suited to the five-octave instruments of Stein and Walter, Beethoven's compositions made ever increasing demands on a variety of pianos, both Viennese and English. Although all the solo sonatas composed through 1802 stay within the FF–f''' range observed by Mozart, the C Major Sonata, Op. 53 ("Waldstein"), of 1803–4 requires additional keys in the upper register to a''', and the Introduzione movement of this same work strains at the lower limit, reaching for the then generally unavailable low EE (m. 2). The F Minor ("Appassionata") Sonata, Op. 57, of the following year extends the upper register even further, requiring a full five-and-a-half octave range, from FF to c''''. Exploiting the instrument's registral extremes in strikingly voiced spacings and timbres, and often in full-voiced chords of violent dynamic contrasts, Beethoven's orchestration of the piano in these works breaks with that of his Viennese predecessors on nearly every front. In the years that followed, Beethoven continued to push the resources of his instruments to new extremes, culminating in the notoriously difficult "Hammerklavier" Sonata, Op. 106 (1817–18), the only one of his sonatas to require a full six-and-a-half octave range, from CC to f''''. In addition to their unique expressive range of timbre, articulation, and dynamic nuance, period instruments can convey the drama of Beethoven's demands on the registral extremes of the fortepiano in ways that cannot be adequately reproduced on the modern piano.[55]

Various contemporary documents suggest that Beethoven was pushing Viennese builders of pianos as well, and not only in terms of extending the available notes on the keyboard. William S. Newman has provided a valuable summary of evidence regarding Beethoven's response to the various pianos—fourteen, all told—that he played. Some were sent as presents by famous foreign makers (Erard, Broadwood) and those lesser known (Vogel, Kirschbaum); others were sold to him, offered for loan, or given to him by such Viennese makers as Walter, Schanz, Streicher, and Graf. It appears that Beethoven was rarely satisfied for long with many of these and was notoriously hard on them, claiming that "it is my motto either to play on a good instrument or not at all."[56]

Beethoven's own performances of his piano sonatas took place not in public concerts but in chamber settings and private gatherings of Vienna's aristocracy, as was the case generally for this genre. For him as for Mozart, concertos offered public exposure in his early years as a performer in Vienna, and he may have played Mozart's D Minor Concerto, K. 466, at a concert in 1795 to benefit Mozart's widow. We do know that he presented his Quintet for Piano and Winds, Op. 16, in a public benefit concert in 1797, as well as before the Tonkünstler-Societät a year later. In any case, Beethoven's reputation as a virtuoso was sufficiently established to be recorded in Schönfeld's 1796 *Jahrbuch*, where Beethoven is listed as "a musical genius . . . generally admired for his outstanding velocity and the great ease with which he performs extraordinary difficulties."[57] Famous for his improvisations in public concerts, Beethoven continued to improvise before private gatherings of friends well after he discontinued public appearances in 1809. The report of one such occasion, at the home of Baroness von Puthon in 1822, states that "his playing was masterly and showed that he still knows how to handle his instrument with power, enthusiasm, and love."[58]

Many earlier accounts of Beethoven's playing agree that his approach to the instrument, while impressively virtuosic in technique and speed, was sometimes inconsistent and rough. The remarks of Czerny, who studied with Beethoven as a boy, are especially revealing even if they were compiled many years later. With special praise for his teacher's improvisations, Czerny noted that Beethoven's "performance depended on his constantly varying frame of mind," and that "like his compositions, his playing was ahead of its time," whereas "Hummel's sparkling, brilliant playing—well calculated to the taste of the time—was bound to be more intelligible and appealing to the public at large." He reports that Beethoven used "much more pedal than is indicated in his works," and that his "playing of adagio and legato in the sustained style had an almost bewitching effect on everyone who heard it."[59] Although Beethoven adopted certain features characteristic of the London School of pianists, who cultivated a more brilliant virtuosity and the robust sound associated with English pianos of the day, he appears to have favored Viennese pianos, especially those of Streicher. Even so, Beethoven urged this builder to produce "instruments [that] do not wear out so quickly."[60]

Aside from requiring sturdier instruments with more volume to cope with his increasing deafness, Beethoven was especially responsive to the special effects of pedaling. In 1802 he requested a Walter piano with an una corda device. Beethoven's first indication of una corda comes at the close of the Andante movement of his Piano Concerto in G Major, Op. 58 (1805–6), where continuous trills rise from

Ludwig van Beethoven, Sonata, Op. 110 (Paris, M. Schlesinger, 1822). Adagio ma non troppo, mm. 1–16

pp to *ff* and sink back again in a graduated transition of volume accompanied by a magical change of color.[61]

Beethoven's coloristic uses of the damper pedal are everywhere evident in the middle and late period works. The first movement of the "Moonlight" sonata, Op. 27, no. 2, is marked "sempre pianissimo e senza sordino," implying not only that the dampers are raised throughout, but that the moderator might be used as well. Although Beethoven never specifically called for the moderator in his scores, the dreamlike atmosphere of this "quasi una fantasia" welcomes its effect. The dry percussive opening of the "Waldstein" sonata could not be more different, but the extended pedal markings beneath bell-like tones in its finale produce rare colors that are as uniquely idiomatic on Viennese instruments as its pianissimo octave glissandi.

The example here, showing the opening bars of the Adagio movement from the Sonata in A-flat Major, Op. 110 (1821–22), is a telling record of Beethoven's meticulous calculation of expressive effects in the late sonatas. In bar five alone, one finds eight written instructions, along with the dynamic signs, slurs, and *Bebung*-like (trembling) repeated notes that have puzzled later interpreters. In addition to the una corda pedal crescendo here, Beethoven's use of the damper pedal creates effects that are impossible to duplicate on modern instruments. The quick decay of sound after the hammer strikes the string allows for clarity in the recitative and arioso passages, as the top voice sings through a pool of sustained tones. By contrast, the passages without damper pedal speak more directly, but in nuanced and varying inflections of non-legato and portamento as well as in subtly distinguished registral colors. Dynamic changes and fluctuations in tempo are similarly exacting in the remarkably detailed notation of these ten bars. However deficient his hearing, the acuity of Beethoven's inner ear is everywhere evident here, as is his eagerness to communicate that fine-tuning to the player.

In several of the late sonatas, Beethoven's expressive indications appear in German (usually in combination with traditional Italian terms), in what seems to be an attempt to make his intentions more particular: "Mit Lebhaftigkeit und durchaus mit Empfindung und Ausdruck" (With liveliness and with feeling and expression throughout, Op. 90/i); "Geschwind, doch nicht zu sehr, und mit Entschlossenheit/Allegro" (Fast, yet not too much, and with decisiveness, Op. 101/iii). And increasingly his references to the singing voice of the piano exceed what can be indicated by the conventional "cantabile" alone: "Nicht zu geschwind und sehr singbar vorzutragen" (Not too fast and to be performed very singably, Op. 90/ii); "Klagender Gesang/Arioso dolente" (Lamenting song, Op. 110/

iii); "Gesangvoll, mit innigster Empfindung/Andante molto cantabile ed espressivo" (Songful, with the most heartfelt emotion, Op. 109/iii); "Arietta: Adagio molto, semplice e cantabile" (Op. 111/ii). The often-noted lyricism of Beethoven's late style takes its place in these works as simple song in the company of the virtuosic and complex textures of both fugue and variation.

Programmatic intentions motivated inscriptions of another sort in what is arguably Beethoven's most personal and autobiographical work, the Sonata in E-flat Major, Op. 81a, "Das Lebewohl." Dedicated to his pupil, friend, and patron Archduke Rudolf of Austria, the sonata's three movements chart the composer's affective response to the farewell, absence, and return of Rudolf, who left Vienna before the French occupation in the summer of 1809. Although Beethoven explicitly rejected the notion of *Tonmalerei,* or tone-painting, in references to his "Pastoral" symphony, he anticipates in both of these works the evocative and deliberately programmatic intentions of later Romantic composers. Yet rigorous motivic development of materials in extended sonata forms marks Op. 81a as rooted in the classical style. That the expression of its unfolding plot is rooted just as certainly in the sounds of Beethoven's most personal instrument is particularly audible in the transition from the second movement's "Abwesenheit" to the finale's "Wiedersehen." Moving from poignantly wandering chromaticism and diminished harmonies that elude satisfactory resolution to ever darker regions of F minor and B-flat minor, the cantabile theme temporarily gains more confident ground in F major. At the close, memories of the work's despondent opening figure are gradually released and transformed into anticipations of the returning tonic key over an extended pedal. From this pianissimo wash of color, the *Vivacissimamente* "Return" explodes in rushing arpeggios and scales that soar to the upper register of the piano. The highest note of the work, e-flat'''', is reached just before the Poco Andante coda, in which the main theme is extended in repeated eager ascents as both hands participate in intimate greetings, and again at the top of the concluding rush of arpeggios that puts a joyous exclamation point on the scene.

Beethoven's reluctance to be associated with "tone-painters" may have stemmed from the rage for programmatic sonatas that relied on explicit sound effects and heavily annotated scenic depictions. "Battle pieces" of the sort composed by Francis Kotzwara ("The Battle of Prague," 1790) were much in demand, spurring appropriately colorful additions to the piano's resources in stops and pedals that approximated the sounds of bassoon, tambourine, triangle, and drum. Such sonatas, largely addressed to an admiring amateur audience of players and listeners, provided vivid (and noisy) retellings of the victories and defeats of famous generals, complete with bugle calls, cannonades, cries of the wounded, and jubilant signals of victory—all with detailed explanatory notes in the score.[62] One can imagine that Beethoven was eager to distance himself from such boilerplate depictions in composing the deeply personal program of his "Lebewohl" sonata. In any case, the demands of this work would have discouraged all but the most gifted amateurs.

Who, then, were the players of such sonatas? We know that Clara Schumann and Franz Liszt were later champions of Beethoven's late keyboard works, but apart from the composer himself and noted virtuosos of the day, such as Carl Czerny and Ignaz Moscheles, who among his contemporaries in Vienna supplied the demand for Beethoven sonatas that publishers competed to fill? One can only speculate about whether those who purchased his works were actually able to play them. As early as 1801, a reporter in Breslau noted that "pianoforte players gladly venture upon Beethoven and spare neither time nor pains to conquer his difficulties," and another in Paris observed that in addition to those "virtuosi who play only Haydn, Mozart, and Beethoven, . . . in spite of the difficulties offered by their works there are 'quelquefois des Amateurs qui croient les jouer' [sometimes amateurs who believe they can play them]."[63] Among Beethoven's patrons in Vienna, Prince Lichnowsky, dedicatee of the "Pathétique," Op. 13, is reported as "studying Beethoven's works and playing them more or less well"; one wonders what Archduke Rudolf would have made of the "Hammerklavier."[64]

Aside from sonatas inscribed to his male patrons, Beethoven followed the custom of dedicating keyboard works to his students, a practice that could both flatter a wealthy aristocrat and advertise one's status as a piano teacher with connections to the nobility.[65] Among these, the Baroness Dorothea von Ertmann (née Graumann), whom Beethoven dubbed his "Caecilia," had a special place as a devoted performer of his works. Johann Reichardt, who recorded his impressions of musical life during a visit to Vienna in the winter of 1808–9, reported that "as she performed a great Beethoven sonata I was surprised as almost never before. I have never seen such power and innermost tenderness combined even in the greatest virtuosi."[66] Anton Schindler noted that Ertmann gathered about her "a circle of true music-lovers and made the greatest contribution generally among the elite of society to the preservation and cultivation of the purest taste. She was a conservatory all by herself. Without Frau von Ertmann, Beethoven's piano music would have disappeared much earlier from the repertory in Vienna. . . . [She] resisted the pressure of the new direction in composition and playing of Hummel and his followers."[67] If some bought Beethoven's early sonatas because they were the newest compositions of a much-vaunted virtuoso favored in aristocratic households, in time an inner circle of cognoscenti preserved his later works from eclipse by more fashionable composers.

The experience of learning the piano, or even of trying to learn, stays with people all their lives. It affects their posture; physical coordination; relations with parents, siblings, and children; self-discipline and self-confidence; capacity to learn from others and from their own mistakes; capacity to listen, read, process, and think; and ability to speak, move, act—and play—in public. No matter how far they get in learning the piano, the experience affects what happens in their minds and bodies as they listen to Oscar Peterson or Alicia de Larrocha, and in subtler ways as they sing, dance, or listen to music of any sort. Learning the piano gives people from every walk of life and from around the world something in common to talk about. It even gives people today some insight into the lives of Mozart or Liszt, the heroines of Austen novels, or the subjects of Renoir paintings.

Not that everyone who tries to play the piano has the same experience. People become piano students at utterly different ages, with vastly different abilities and ambitions, and they learn on particular pianos from teachers who use particular methods of teaching. In some respects, students are apt to be acutely aware of how different their own experience is from that of others: what piano student has not wished to have been born with Mozart's or Tatum's gift? In general, though, it is all too easy for pianists to assume that the terms under which they learned the piano are universal. In fact none of the institutions or rituals of learning the piano that we take for granted—the figure of the piano teacher in her studio, the weekly piano lesson, the regimen of daily practice, the annual recital—are as fixed as they seem. The way Mozart was taught to play the keyboard is in fact just as remote and incomprehensible to us as is his genius.

Accordingly, this chapter on the experience of learning the piano begins with a section that traces the evolution of piano teaching practices. The subject is as elusive as it is momentous. It is in the teacher's studio and the student's practice room, more than anywhere else, that the piano has shaped a musical culture, yet it is difficult to reconstruct what went on in a piano lesson or practice session a century or two ago. Perhaps the best we can do is to compare piano method books from various times and places—books that tell at least what someone *thought* should go on a lesson or a practice session—and deduce how the experience of taking piano may have changed from one period to another.

Take the figure of the piano teacher, for instance. The term itself bespeaks a degree of specialization that was unheard of in Mozart's day. Mozart's father, the author of a famous method for playing the violin, taught him to play the keyboard along with many other musical skills. How exceptional was that? In an important

Four **The Piano Lesson**

E. Douglas Bomberger, Martha Dennis Burns, James Parakilas, Judith Tick, Marina Tsvetaeva, and Mark Tucker

A lesson as depicted in the frontispiece of a keyboard method book, *New Instructions for Playing the Harpsichord, Piano-Forte, or Spinnet* (London, ca. 1790)

133

keyboard method published when Mozart was an adult, Daniel Gottlob Türk's *Klavierschule* (School of the keyboard) of 1789, we read the following advice: "If the student has progressed to the point where he can play without interruption, then the teacher should accompany him on the violin—for every keyboard teacher should be able to play this instrument adequately—or perhaps the flute."[1]

Mozart was not unusual for his day in being taught keyboard by a musician who was not a keyboard specialist, nor was he unique in being taught by his father. But then, learning from his father meant having his teacher constantly at his shoulder, rather than going for a lesson once a week. In this, too, his experience was not exceptional. Many eighteenth-century music masters called on their students every day to give them lessons. But if lessons were so frequent, practicing must have been different in some corresponding way. And it was. François Couperin, who traveled around Paris in the early eighteenth century giving daily harpsichord lessons to the daughters of aristocrats in their homes, locked the harpsichord at the end of each lesson, presumably to ensure that his students didn't form any bad habits by practicing without his supervision. Admittedly he represents an extreme for that day.

When Mozart had learned all that his father had to teach him—and the two did not agree on when that point was reached—did he go to a conservatory to complete his keyboard training? Hardly, because there were no conservatories then for training professional keyboard players. The history of piano training in conservatories—that is, the evolution of the conservatory system of training that we know today—is a story of its own and the subject of the second section of this chapter.

Then, because the experience of learning the piano has usually hinged on a relationship—sometimes difficult, sometimes loving, often intense—between student and teacher, the concluding section of this chapter features a gallery of teachers and students. Teachers are represented by one group portrait—an account of the women who established piano teaching as a livelihood for women in America—and one individual portrait: of Theodor Leschetizky, who trained some of the greatest pianists of the twentieth century. There are two depictions of piano students who went on to become important musicians—one, Ruth Crawford, exemplifies the relationship of piano student to teacher at its most intense; the other, Duke Ellington, represents the student who learns the piano largely outside formal lessons. Another picture in the gallery shows a writer, Marina Tsvetaeva, who gave up the piano when her mother's death removed the pressure on her to continue, but whose words—because she is one of the great writers of the twentieth century—turn her exceptional childhood experience into a story of universal interest.

Piano lessons were not invented when some enterprising harpsichord teacher switched to the piano one day. Rather, they emerged out of a twofold separation: learning to play keyboard became a distinct branch of learning music, and studying the piano became a distinct form of keyboard study. Taking piano, in other words, became an activity in itself rather than a part of—and means to—a broader achievement. And what about the invention of practicing? Here, too, a distinction evolved: practicing stopped being a continuation of the lesson and started having a function of its own.

These simple-sounding changes, which occurred in the early nineteenth century, continue to affect the way piano is studied. And there is nothing simple about them. Take the separation of piano study from keyboard study in general. Keyboard methods from the very end of the eighteenth century were advertised as usable at either the harpsichord or the piano, but right after the beginning of the nineteenth century, they began to be advertised as solely for the piano. This shift seems easy to explain: not only were harpsichords no longer being made, but there were also hardly any still being played. Yet there is more to this change. Before the piano, keyboard players and teachers had assumed that a good keyboard technique would serve a player on any keyboard. Method writers might have recommended starting on the clavichord before moving to the harpsichord, for instance, but it was understood that players would switch between one instrument and another, adapting their general keyboard technique as needed.[2] When the piano rose to prominence, however, teachers began to develop a technique suitable for that instrument alone. In fact, one of the earliest methods written exclusively for the piano, Johann Peter Milchmeyer's *Die wahre Art das Pianoforte zu spielen* (The correct method of playing the pianoforte) of 1797, contains illustrations comparing a rounded finger position that is good for the piano to various bad finger positions "to which the harpsichord and the clavichord often mislead one, but which one can easily avoid at the piano."[3] Learning to play the piano correctly, in other words, misfitted one to play anything else.

The instrument itself demanded a new and exclusive technique, but students were also swayed by a new concept of what kind of playing they were being prepared for. Keyboard playing had always been a service activity; harpsichord players in particular, whether professional or amateur, were routinely cast in an accompanying role, whether to realize the basso continuo part in an orchestra or other ensemble or to provide the sole accompaniment to a singer. Method books designed for harpsichord players gave considerable space to the skills needed for these services, especially harmony and counterpoint. Because these were also the skills of composition, it could be said that the art of composition was taught at the keyboard. In these methods, solo pieces formed the introductory fare, whereas the skills of accompanying, associated as they were with ensemble directing and composing, were treated as the ultimate goals of keyboard playing.

As soon as methods started to be written for the piano, however, the tables were turned: the earliest piano methods are clearly aimed primarily at preparing students to play solo piano music. The realities of musical life didn't change altogether: pianists, like harpsichordists before them, spent a lot of their time at the keyboard accompanying. But only for a brief time were pianists called on to realize basso continuo parts. Orchestral music, coincidentally, stopped requiring keyboard playing as a regular part of its texture at pretty much the same time that the piano was replacing the harpsichord.[4] In compensation, piano solo repertory almost immediately assumed—and would always retain—a prestige that the solo harpsichord or clavichord literature never had. It is in this sense that learning the piano became separated from learning music in general: playing solo music at the piano wasn't considered a way station on the route to composing or directing an ensemble because it took on a cultural status equal to that of composing or conducting. In Milchmeyer's *Correct Method* of 1797, almost immediately after piano students have learned to round their fingers in that purely pianistic way, they are taught how to finger the passages of parallel thirds, sixths, and octaves that they will need if they are to conquer, for instance, those test pieces of pianistic virtuosity, the Op. 2 sonatas of Clementi. It seems crazy that this instruction in virtuosic technique is given in the second chapter of a work directed—according to its foreword—at "amateurs and beginners." But through this arrangement Milchmeyer suggests that what defines a pianist, even an amateur or beginner, is the ambition, at least, to become a virtuoso.

Few amateurs, however, would seriously have imagined themselves in the public role of virtuoso. Further, the vast majority of beginners, whatever they

Illustration of good *(gut)* and bad *(schlecht)* finger positions for playing the piano, from Johann Peter Milchmeyer's piano method, *Die wahre Art das Pianoforte zu spielen* (Dresden, 1797)

gut　　　　schlecht　　　　schlecht　　　　schlecht

136

imagined, would have known that careers in public performance were not open to them because most beginners at the piano, in Milchmeyer's day and later, were girls, and their parents would not have dreamed of allowing them to pursue such a path. By the end of the eighteenth century, then, many girls were expected to devote their time to learning a form of musical display that originated and in some sense belonged in the public arena—where women were only exceptionally found. They could of course become domestic virtuosos, displaying their pianistic accomplishments at home to their families, friends, and suitors. But as the nineteenth century rolled on, the number of young women taking piano lessons, the degree of virtuosity expected of them, and the amount of time and effort required to meet this expectation rose out of all proportion to the credit they could hope to win by performing to family and guests on their humble parlor pianos. What was going on?

Practicing was becoming a way of life. In the mid–eighteenth century, Friedrich Marpurg had advised keyboard students to refrain from practicing much in the absence of their teacher, so as not to undo in a moment what the teacher had patiently achieved.[5] Even Türk, as late as 1789, in the keyboard method that can be considered the last gasp of pedagogical thought untouched by the piano revolution, distinguished between the practice time advisable for those who are learning to play for pleasure (a handful of hours per week) and the time necessary for those wanting to make a career of the keyboard (three to four hours per day, plus an hour's lesson).[6] During the nineteenth century, that distinction all but disappeared. Piano methods of the period recommend hours of daily practice to young women destined to be amateur players. These students are given endless scales and studies to practice each day before they may begin work on musically interesting pieces. Their practicing no longer simply reinforces—or undermines—what they learned in their lessons; instead it turns them into their own most important audience, because in their hours of daily practicing they are performing their domestic virtuosity, not even to family or suitors, but endlessly to themselves. In the memorable title of Grete Wehmeyer's study of Carl Czerny—who was perhaps the most prolific author of piano studies ever—practicing had become "solitary confinement at the piano."[7]

The piano is a machine. Already when it was invented at the beginning of the eighteenth century, it embodied a more complex mechanism than any earlier stringed keyboard instrument. But it was not until the nineteenth century (which was called the Machine Age even at the time) that the ideal of the machine was

Playing a Machine, Being a Machine

extended to the way the piano was played—or more precisely, to the way people were taught to play it. The new ideal is visible in a pair of drawings that the Boston publishing firm of Oliver Ditson printed in the front of several of its piano methods in the 1840s and 1850s.

In the drawing "Correct Position of the Hands," the keyboard itself embodies the machine ideal of regularity: the black keys form such a relentless row that as your eye moves up the drawing it becomes harder and harder to tell the groups of two from the groups of three. The pianist's hands form correspondingly undifferentiated instruments: the rounding of the fingers eliminates the differences in length among them, and the straightness of the wrists gives the player the means to apply a uniform pressure through the fingers. Nothing quite like this hand position can be seen in representations of or instructions for keyboard playing before the nineteenth century; something like it has been promoted as "correct" ever since. Not coincidentally, the mid–nineteenth century is also when piano manufacturers worked to create a uniform sound quality from the highest to the lowest notes on the instrument. In the drawing "Correct Position of the Body," the human subject is dwarfed by the instrument: her body is barely as big as one leg of the piano—at a time when the grandest of pianos was considerably smaller and lighter than a modern concert grand—and her tiny feet have no hope of reaching the pedals or the floor. "Correctness" for her consists in making her body conform to the machine: her rigid posture on a high stool may give her the best possible chance of keeping her bearings in relation to the huge keyboard, but it also absorbs her into the design of the machine. The piano controls her more than she can possibly control it.

The idea of piano playing as a machinelike activity appeared in piano methods from the very beginning of the nineteenth century. Jérôme-Joseph de Momigny, in his *Première année de leçons de piano-forte* (First year of piano lessons) of 1802–3, already speaks of a law of "economy of movement."[8] By 1830, in a set of "Letters" that Carl Czerny published to an imaginary young woman named Cecilia who is learning the piano, the student is told to aspire to mechanistic ideals of regularity, evenness, and exactness in every aspect of her playing.

In music, nothing is worse than playing wrong notes.

Strike each key perpendicularly; that is, straight downwards, and exactly in the middle.

The scales sound well only when they are played in every respect with the most exact equality. This equality is three-fold; namely—First. Equality of

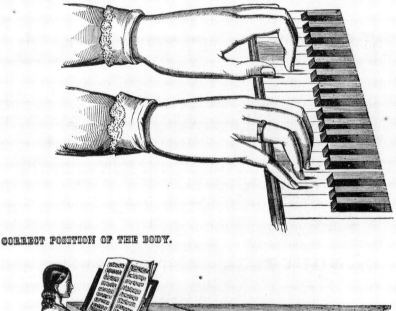

CORRECT POSITION OF THE HANDS.

CORRECT POSITION OF THE BODY.

Illustrations of "Correct Position of the Hands" and "Correct Position of the Body," in an American edition of Franz Hünten's *Celebrated Instructions for the Piano-forte* (Boston, ca. 1850)

strength. . . . Secondly. Equality in point of quickness. . . . Thirdly and lastly. Equality in holding the notes down.

Into the error of accelerating the time, just such young and lively persons as my dear Miss Cecilia are most apt to fall. . . . For the fingers are little disobedient creatures, if they are not kept well-reined in; and they are apt to run off like an unbroken colt as soon as they have gained some degree of fluency.

The same exactitude with which you are obliged to observe the notes, the marks of transposition, the fingering, and the time, you must likewise employ with regard to the marks of expression.[9]

In the guise of describing what is universally "correct" in music, Czerny prescribes a revolutionary musical aesthetic that is at the same time a revolutionary method of child rearing. In the name of perfect evenness—a value hardly mentioned in the musical aesthetics of earlier eras—he requires his student to hold all notes out for their entire written duration, a practice likewise unprecedented.[10] What made his ideology of child rearing equally revolutionary, at least for a work of musical pedagogy, was not its idea of subjecting children, like "unbroken colts," to strict discipline, but its mechanical model of that discipline—the idea that a child could learn by dint of endless repetition to produce something that was perfectly uniform.

From this ideology sprang Czerny's scheme of practicing. Every day Miss Cecilia, at the tender age of twelve, was to practice three hours: "only three hours, of which about half an hour shall be appropriated to the exercises, as much more to playing over the old pieces, and the remaining time to the study of new compositions."[11] The exercises, which needed to be completed first, were to consist of scales and études. It is no coincidence that this was the great age of étude writing; the piano études of Cramer, Clementi, Chopin, and Czerny, all written within a decade or two of Czerny's *Letters to a Young Lady,* are still cornerstones of piano teaching. Even the most musically significant of these, the Chopin études, rest on the idea of repetition, teaching the performer to maintain an even touch while carrying a given figuration through the most awkward dispositions and dramatic transformations on the keyboard. The new pedagogy is revealed at its baldest, however, in sets of evolving finger patterns de-

Carl Czerny, 1791–1857. Lithograph by Engleman; published by Maurice Schlesinger, Paris.

signed to promote evenness of touch through sheer repetition; of these, Hummel's exercises were among the earliest, and a set called *The Virtuoso Pianist* by an obscure French provincial teacher, Charles Louis Hanon, have proved the most enduring.[12]

Machinelike uniformity was promoted in other ways as well. The metronome, invented around 1815 as a means of allowing a composer to set the tempo for a work, was adopted by teachers of the piano and other instruments as a device for a very dif-

ferent purpose: teaching students to hold a tempo for the duration of a piece or passage (see inset). Some teachers, like Friedrich Wieck, encouraged the use of finger-stretching exercises away from the keyboard to strengthen fingers; others, like Johann Bernhard Logier, invented and promoted the use of mechanical devices for the same purpose.[13] In both cases, the idea was to strengthen the supposedly weaker fingers to the level of the stronger ones for a more even touch.

Czerny's ideology did not represent the unanimous opinion of his age. One who led the resistance to it was Robert Schumann, whose hopes for a career as a virtuoso had been ruined by a hand injury perhaps caused by his use of a finger-strengthening device. In opposition to Czerny's approach, Schumann wrote *Album for the Young* (1848), a set of poetic pieces for children to use in learning the piano, along with his "Rules for the Musical Home and Life."[14] These publications, taken together, represent an ideology more old-fashioned than Czerny's in their return to the notion that learning the keyboard should be a general education in musicianship. At the same time, however, they are more progressive in their Romantic insistence that children should not be drilled to become virtuosos so as to impress adults, but should play music that would awaken their own, distinctly childish imaginations. The *Album for the Young,* enormously successful in itself, has inspired to this day many other poetic children's pieces for piano by composers as great as Bartók and Prokofiev.

But Czerny's ideology of piano pedagogy didn't lose out to Schumann's. Rather, an endless jostling between the two ways of thinking can be found in the

Advertisement for two models of the Brotherhood Technicon, from *The Etude,* April 1890. The back pages of such piano magazines were once filled with ads for mechanical exercise devices—some for use at the piano and others, like the Technicon, for use away from it. Most were designed for students' development, but some—more surprisingly—were created for their teachers' use. The appeal of the Technicon, as of much modern body-building equipment, evidently relied in part on the variety of exercises that the buyer could expect to perform with a single machine.

A page of exercise patterns from Johann Nepomuk Hummel's *Complete Theoretical and Practical Instructions for Playing the Pianoforte* (Vienna, 1828)

The Metronome

Marina Tsvetaeva (translated by Jane Costlow, from "Mother and Music")

The click of the metronome. There are in my life a few unshakable joys: not to go to high school; to awake in a place that isn't Moscow in 1918; and not to hear the metronome. How is it that musical ears bear it? (Or are musical ears something different than musical souls?) The metronome I quite loved, until I was four, almost as much as the cuckoo clock, and for the same reason: in it, too, someone was living, but just who—wasn't clear, since it was I who set him back in his house. It was the house where I myself wished to live. (Children always want to live in some impossible place,—like my son, at six, who dreamed of living in a street lamp: it's light and warm, way up high, everything's in sight. "And if they throw stones at your house?"—"Then I'll throw fire at them!") But as soon as I felt the sentence of its methodical click I started to hate it, to fear it, to the point of a thudding heart, of fainting and chills, as now I nightly fear the alarm clock, or any even, nocturnal sound. As though that sound runs down my soul! Someone stands above your soul and urges you on and holds you back, won't let you breathe or swallow, will keep on urging you on and holding you back when you leave—alone in the empty room, above the empty piano stool, above the open piano lid,—because they forgot to close it—until the mechanism winds down. The lifeless—the living; one nonexistent—one who exists. And what if, of a sudden, the mechanism never winds down, and what if I never get up from the stool, never come out from under the tick-tock, tick-tock. . . . It was Death itself, standing above the soul, a living soul, which can die—immortal (dead already) Death. The sound so horrible I even forgot the so-horrible sight: the steel rod, stealing out like a finger, rocking maniacally, stupidly, behind a living back. It was my first encounter with the mechanical world, foreordaining all other encounters, the mechanical world in all its freshness, its steely bouquet, its first steely budding to me. Oh I never fell behind the metronome! It held me—not only to the measure, but physically, it bound me to the stool. The open metronome was the best guarantee of my not looking round at the clock. But mother—fortunately—sometimes forgot, and no Protestant honesty of mine—of hers!—could bring me to remind her, to doom myself to that torment. If I have ever longed to murder anyone—it was the metronome. And that look of sensual vengeance didn't fade from my eyes, as I finished my playing and passed by its bookshelf: over my shoulder—haughtily—I tossed: "I—am leaving; you— can stay!"

subsequent history of piano teaching. Czerny proved to be far from the sternest of the drill sergeants. In some nineteenth-century method books, for example, the exercises—which even in Czerny's scheme occupied just the first sixth of the student's practice time—loom so large and burdensome that the few, shortened examples of real music (by, say, Mozart or Mendelssohn) are presented as a mere concession to the student, described in the books as "Rests from study," "Recreations," or "Amusements."[15] Yet jazz piano teaching in the twentieth century characteristically represents, like Schumann's piano pedagogy in the nineteenth, a new form of eighteenth-century attitudes, especially the attitude that learning the keyboard should be as much about learning to compose, arrange, and accompany as about learning to solo.

Girls, Boys, and Pianos

For the most part, in the two centuries since the characters in *Pride and Prejudice* discoursed on the piano as a female accomplishment, learning the piano has been like learning to cook: girls did it as a matter of course, whereas the relatively few boys who did it got the jobs and the glory. As a result, learning the piano has been a highly gender-specific activity, but specific to each gender in a different way. Czerny, at the very beginning of his *Letters to a Young Lady*, sets out to justify piano playing as a female accomplishment, but keeps acknowledging, seemingly against his will, that it is really a more complex issue:

> You know that pianoforte playing, though suitable to everyone, is yet more particularly one of the most charming and honorable accomplishments for young ladies, and, indeed, for the female sex in general. By it we can command, not only for one's self, but for many others, a dignified and appropriate amusement; and, where great progress has been made, we also ensure a degree of distinction in the world, which is as agreeable to the amateur as to the professional artist.[16]

Without acknowledging that it exists, Czerny's language sets out the terms of a social problem: boys were trespassing into a female realm when they learned to play the piano at all ("though suitable to everyone"), whereas girls were trespassing into a male realm when they got too good at it ("where great progress has been made").

The problem might be said to have begun for a boy when he opened his method book for the first time and saw that the hands and body illustrating the "Correct Positions" at the piano were a girl's—and this in a time before gender-

The first page of Frédéric Chopin, F Minor Etude, Op. 25, no. 2 (Leipzig, 1837). During the nineteenth century, the Chopin études became canonized as studies in piano technique. Consequently, they were not replaced when standards of technique rose, but "improved"—as in the following two examples—in order to set greater challenges. In the Chopin, the "study" is to maintain two continuous lines, in gratingly different rhythms, with the two hands.

The first page of Johannes Brahms, "Etude after Fr. Chopin" from *Studies for the Pianoforte* (Leipzig, 1869). Without altering the rhythmic nature of the étude, Brahms adds to the strain on the pianist's right hand by thickening that part. In the process, he necessarily slows the piece down, while also introducing new harmonic colors.

The first page of Leopold Godowsky, *Studies on Chopin's Etudes* (Berlin, 1914), "Fr. Chopin, Op. 25 No. 2, Fourth Version, For the left hand alone." Among four different variations that Godowsky wrote on this étude, this one is remarkable for the way it challenges the rhythmic basis of the original. By transcribing the Chopin for the left hand alone, he made the piece an exercise in suggesting the overlap of rhythms that a single hand could not literally sustain.

neutral language, a time when masculine pronouns and male examples were uniformly used to cover both sexes. Exactly the same problem was created for him when Czerny addressed his *Letters . . . on the Art of Playing the Piano-Forte* to a young woman. For a girl, the problem might have come to a head when "great progress has been made" and she was told by her teacher and parents, seconded by an authority like Czerny, that being appreciated as an amateur should be as agreeable to her as being applauded as a professional. But it could come up much sooner, as early as she noticed that the models of successful virtuosos placed before her were all male—or for that matter that the word *virtuoso* had masculinity in its root.

Some of this social difficulty might have been avoided if there had been different systems of instruction for girls and boys, if piano playing had been treated as two different activities. Girls might have been taught to provide a "dignified and appropriate amusement" for themselves and their families, boys to thunder away on the public stage. But even in the mid–nineteenth century, when the social segregation of the sexes was extreme—and was justified by the most extreme theories of gender difference—there was a remarkable overlap in the ways girls and boys were taught the piano and what they achieved on it.

The evidence of this overlap lies in the method books that are addressed principally to girls—whether explicitly or through their illustrations of "Correct Position"—and that proceed to provide the volumes of exercises that would be totally unnecessary if the student were being taught just to provide a little accompaniment for singing, dancing, and other simple "amusement." It lies in the concert programs of female seminaries, which show that the students regularly performed the operatic fantasies and bravura variation sets of Thalberg, Herz, Hünten, Gottschalk, and the other great virtuosos of the day.[17] Most tellingly, it lies in the complaints of teachers like Czerny who, having taught young women the skills to play such things, protest that before they are ready, they "have the presumption to attempt *Hummel's concertos or Thalberg's fantasias!*"[18] Girls learned the piano in vastly greater numbers than boys, and many practiced ceaselessly; whatever piano music boys could play, there were far more girls who could and did play just as well.

This distribution of success drove Czerny's complaint: like any man occupying a position of authority in the piano profession, he relied on artificial gender distinctions to maintain the power of men in a field that otherwise would soon have been dominated by women. At the Paris Conservatory, for instance, separate piano competitions were held for men and women throughout the nineteenth cen-

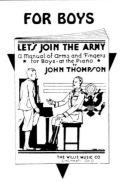

Advertisement for two method books by John Thompson, appearing in Thompson's *World-Known Melodies: Eight Favorite Pieces* (Cincinnati, 1932). In the period between the two world wars, when piano sales slumped worldwide, one way the music industry attempted to broaden its base of sales was to promote piano lessons as a suitable pursuit for boys as well as girls. But how could it attract boys to a traditionally female activity—as the music industry itself had helped make it—without driving away the girls? This advertisement from the period shows the extraordinary lengths to which a music publishing company would go to work both sides of a gender barrier that it was at the same time reinforcing.

Advertisement for the Kinder Adjustable Foot Rest and Pedal Extenders, from *The Etude*, July 1907. As pianos and piano music came more and more to require large performers, inventors found profit in accommodating small ones.

tury, with different assigned competition pieces each year. One year a critic complained that the Kalkbrenner concerto, "which requires a great deal of muscular power," should have been given to the men and the Chopin concerto, "in which grace dominates," to the women, instead of the other way around.[19] But then, a work that was assigned to the men one year might be assigned to the women the next. What really mattered was that there should never be a direct comparison between women and men students, because it was too risky to test the belief that women couldn't play like men.

Why, then, would the male teaching profession, eager to maintain its own power, have taught the two sexes so similarly, given that it was only going to block any comparison of the results the two achieved? To some extent, it has to be assumed, girls who studied the piano must have been inspired by the possibility of playing like the masters and must have plunged on in their practicing, long past the point of being able to provide the "dignified and appropriate amusement" that was expected of them. In many cases, parents of these girls must have been happy for them to spend hours a day practicing ever more challenging exercises and pieces, because doing so kept them fruitfully occupied, indoors and at a suitably feminine activity. But the teachers, too, had their motive: there was much more money to be made teaching girls than boys (because there were so many more girls to be taught) and much more remuneration for training virtuosos than mere amusement-givers (because it took so many more lessons per pupil). Girls, then, were taught to be virtuosos, even though their piano teachers might well have found it necessary, as Czerny did, to warn female students that they were not ready—that they would never be ready—to play pieces of the very sort that they had been trained to play.

Even when girls and boys undertook the same course of study at the piano, they did not necessarily have the same experience of practicing. For one thing, their bodies might well have responded differently, even when the demands made on them appeared to be the same. The stiff posture that was portrayed as the "Correct Position" in the manuals of the 1840s was not so much a musical necessity as a social ideal, one that could be inculcated during the hours spent at the piano. But maintaining this posture for all those hours in the corset that even a young girl at the time wore was not the same as maintaining it in a boy's less constricting clothes.

The size of the piano also affected boys and girls differently. In the eighteenth century the piano had been no bigger than a harpsichord and often smaller. At the beginning of the nineteenth century, though—with pedals appearing at floor level, the keyboard expanding in both directions, and passages in octaves appearing regularly in the newest repertory—the piano suddenly became, for children who learned it, a daunting daily reminder of how far they had to go to measure up in the adult world. Children grow at different rates, and some grow into the piano earlier than others, but many more girls than boys have felt that they would never have the instrument—or the part of the repertory created by big-handed men—within their reach. Since the instrument itself has been unyielding in size, the pianist's seat has been the principal means of helping children, or players of different sizes generally, adapt to it. The piano stool that changes height when spun appeared already at the end of the eighteenth century; it can be considered an important landmark in the ergonomic design of furniture. If anything, it is too well adapted to children, who have always preferred twirling to practicing (see inset).

The same amount of practicing also represented different experiences for girls and boys in the early nineteenth century because for girls, but not for boys, practicing might have been the most strenuous exercise in their day. It was true until well into the nineteenth century, as Arthur Loesser writes of the eighteenth, that "the more money a family had, the less physical work its women were expected to perform, even in the home itself."[20] As the twentieth century approached, piano practicing became increasingly strenuous for girls and boys alike, as exercises and pieces increasingly tested what pianos built with iron frames could withstand—remember Yekaterina in Chekhov's "Ionych" growing "rosy with the exertion" of performing in her home But by then young women were no longer being encouraged to shun physical activity, so that even Yekaterina's exertion at the piano might not have represented the utmost physical effort in her life. The late-nineteenth-century cult of physical education—gymnastics, calisthenics, and sports—extended to women as well as men, and in 1912 a Spanish Jesuit educational reformer could recommend a regimen of sports as healthier for girls than "the prolonged sessions at the piano, so common in Spanish girls."[21]

Thinking of the body as a machine led to attempts to improve its design. In the 1880s, surgeons began performing an operation on pianists in which they severed the tendons between the ring finger and little finger so that the liberated ring finger would be equal in movement to the others.[22] Evidently mutilation for musical purposes didn't end with the castrati. Likewise, treating the body like a machine has made it break down like a machine. Ever since piano students were first set to practicing the piano in machinelike ways, they have been subject to pain and injury, whether they were girls or boys, children or adults, small or large, and whatever their general state of health or fitness. The physical problems have varied from one period to another according to the demands being put on students by the pedagogical systems, the muscle-strengthening devices and exercises, and the performance pressures of the day; the remedies applied to these problems have changed in response to new general theories about the care of the body.

In the late nineteenth century, for instance, when gymnastics was being touted as a cure-all, piano pedagogues devised systems of "hand gymnastics" to be performed before practicing, away from the piano, in order to put the hands and fingers in "a state of perfect development and training" and therefore avoid injury and its consequent "vast waste of time."[23] In the early twentieth century, when psychological stress came to be considered a prime source of physical pain, F. Matthias Alexander developed a training system for promoting "mind-body unity," and his Alexander Technique has since been adapted to the particular needs of pianists as well as other performers.[24] At the end of the twentieth century, "performing arts medicine" has developed as a medical specialty parallel to sports medicine, in some cases adapting remedies similar to those developed for injuries caused by repetitive-motion stress in sports and computing. In piano playing as in sports, the injured often deny their pain and shun help because the cult of the virtuoso, like that of the athlete, allows no room for the admission of weakness.[25] Neither does it allow room for questioning the system by which virtuosos are trained or the need for virtuosos altogether.

The Conservatory and the Piano
E. Douglas Bomberger

The idea of a conservatory where aspiring musicians devote years to learning the skills necessary for a performing career is an old one; such schools existed in sixteenth-century Italy to train singers. But it was not until the nineteenth century that the modern conservatory system took hold, a development that was closely related to the public's growing obsession with virtuoso pianists and the increasing availability of pianos and piano music. Indeed, European conservatories flourished because of the prevalence of the piano, which in turn benefited from the enormous popularity of conservatories.

The Conservatoire National de Musique was the first modern conservatory. Established in Paris in 1795, it was formed by the merger of the Ecole Royale de Chant and the Institut de Musique, neither of which had included piano instruction in its curriculum. The original mandate of the Conservatoire was to direct the music at the *fêtes nationales* so crucial to revolutionary France. But as these occasions lost their prominence, the school shifted its focus to musical instruction, creating a series of textbooks and instrumental methods that became standard throughout France.[26] An entirely state-subsidized institution, the Conservatoire was highly selective and attracted some of France's most prominent teachers and students.

    Almost from the beginning, the piano asserted an important—though not al-

Conservatories in the Nineteenth Century

Le Tabouret (The Piano Stool)

Marina Tsvetaeva (translated by Jane Costlow, from "Mother and Music")

But let us return to the piano stool of my martyrdom. The piano stool was, no doubt, just like any other, but I didn't know that then, what the others were like, didn't even know that there were others; it was the tabouret, *an article without parallel in the house, a magical thing, for it—among all the others—demanded that I sit still, while it—went turning! On its ribbed neck, so reminiscent of a turkey that's been plucked. You turn till it will turn no more and wait—not without anxiety—for the "head" to weaken, to shudder and fall off entirely. But I remember the fall of another head—my own. Holding tight to the seat with my hands, helping it along with my feet, fainting at the thought of sweet nausea to come, not once, not twice, the whole spiral to the top and then down—till your head flies off, tearing from your neck, like a ball from a whirling stick. "Oho! You've gotten all wound up* again!"—*Andriusha, who'd quietly entered and stood watching in silence, looking with malice at my greening face. "—Let's have the penknife, or I'll tell mama how you play your Lebert and Stark when she's not here. (A pause.) Give me the knife?"—"No."—"Then here's Lebert for you!—Here's Stark for you!" And I assure you, the slap was no simple staccato.*

ways welcome—role in the Conservatoire. Between 1822 and 1842, director Luigi Cherubini limited the number of piano students in an effort to stem the growing tide of virtuoso repertoire and techniques.[27] He did not succeed; piano classes remained central to the school throughout the nineteenth century. Chief among the piano faculty was Antoine-François Marmontel (1816–98), whose long tenure at the Conservatoire (1837–87) coincided with both the technological development of the modern piano and the age of the virtuoso pianists.

Conservatories were founded in central Europe early in the century—at Würzburg (1804), Prague (1811), Graz (1815), Vienna (1817), and Innsbruck (1818), among others—but it was the establishment of the Leipzig Conservatory in 1843 that provided the catalyst for an explosion of such institutions in the German-speaking countries. Felix Mendelssohn, the first director of the conservatory, established a three-year curriculum that became the norm for German schools. The curriculum balanced theory with practice: all students were expected to acquire a knowledge of music history and theory as well as basic keyboard and singing skills, the goal being a well-rounded education. Mendelssohn also created the system whereby three to six students of similar advancement took instrumental lessons together. The advantages of this system were twofold: students could learn from their companions, and teachers could earn a higher hourly rate while still keeping tuition costs low. This "conservatory system" of teaching piano and other instruments remained the norm until around the turn of the century, when American schools began to favor private lessons.[28]

The Leipzig Conservatory inspired a host of conservatories that by the end of the century were "shooting out of the earth like mushrooms."[29] A list of only the most important and long-lived includes the Stern Conservatory (1850) and the Neue Akademie der Tonkunst (1855) in Berlin, the Dresden Conservatory (1856), the Stuttgart Conservatory (1857), the Königliche Musikschule in Munich (1867), the

Advertisement for the New England Conservatory of Music, from *Boston Musical Herald,* November 1891. Note the availability of both private and class lessons, an innovation that allowed American conservatories to compete more effectively with private teachers. Note also the emphasis on safety and comfort, which were serious concerns for Victorian parents considering an urban conservatory for their daughters.

THE NEW ENGLAND CONSERVATORY OF MUSIC.

Founded by Dr. E. Tourjeé.—CARL FAELTEN, Director.

COMPLETE IN EQUIPMENT AND SUPERIOR IN THE FACILITIES FOR STUDY.

Thorough and Systematic Instruction in

PIANO; ORGAN; VIOLIN AND OTHER ORCHESTRAL INSTRUMENTS;
VOICE CULTURE, SOLFEGGIO, AND MUSIC IN PUBLIC SCHOOLS;
THEORY, HARMONY, COMPOSITION AND ORCHESTRATION;
TUNING AND REPAIRING PIANOS AND ORGANS;
GENERAL LITERATURE AND MODERN LANGUAGES;
ELOCUTION, ORATORY AND PHYSICAL CULTURE; and
ALL DEPARTMENTS OF THE FINE ARTS.

Both **Class and Private Lessons** by the ablest **American** and **European Artists** and **Teachers.** A large and valuable list of **Free Advantages** including **Concerts, Lectures, Recitals, Orchestral Practice, Chorus Practice,** etc., also the use of a large Musical Library.

A SAFE AND INVITING HOME

For Lady Pupils, under the Supervision of the Director, Preceptress, President, Physician and Lady Assistants. Steam Heat and Electric Light throughout the building. A newly equipped Gymnasium.

Every Comfort and Safeguard Assured.

The advantages offered are not surpassed by those of any similar institution in the world.

TUITION : $5.00 to $30.00 per term of ten weeks. Board and Room $5.50 to $8.50 per week.

Beautifully Illustrated Calendar, giving full information, **sent free** on application to

FRANK W. HALE, General Manager.

Franklin Square, Boston, Mass.

Berlin Hochschule für Musik (1869), the Weimar Orchesterschule (1872), and the Hoch Conservatory in Frankfurt (1878).

The Leipzig model was phenomenally successful, allowing the school to grow very large and attract students from around the world. By 1890, the proportion of foreign students at the Leipzig Conservatory was 54.9 percent, with the majority of those coming from English-speaking countries.[30] Between 1843 and 1918, conservatory records show that 1,644 students from the United States and Canada attended Mendelssohn's school. Musical life in the United States was profoundly influenced by the techniques, repertoire, and tastes acquired at this and other German schools.

Some of these American students founded their own schools when they returned to the United States. In fact, many conservatories were launched in the years following the Civil War. Typical of these institutions was the Oberlin Conservatory, founded in 1867. The first directors of this school were graduates of the Leipzig Conservatory and frankly admitted using the German school as a model. Not only did they adopt its administrative structure and basic curriculum, but they also used the piano method by Leipzig professor Louis Plaidy and the music theory text by E. F. Richter (in translation).[31]

Mendelssohn's laudable goal had been to provide a balanced educational experience for all students, but after his death this ideal was quickly lost.[32] In practice, it turned out to be much easier to assess performance skill than general knowledge. This tendency to focus on performance was furthered by the lack of rigorous enforcement of class attendance as well as the tradition of holding public "examinations," or year-end performances. These concerts, which reached a total of twenty-one in 1884, showcased the talents of the school's best performers and were reviewed in newspapers and music journals. Small wonder that students neglected their academic work in order to spend more time practicing in hope of being chosen to play or sing in one of these prestigious events. In the second half of the nineteenth century, the Leipzig Conservatory and the schools modeled after it became known as virtuoso factories, where, in the words of Hugo Riemann, one could "stick a farm boy with straight fingers and healthy ears in one end, and after a year the finished composer or virtuoso comes out at the other."[33]

Piano Instruction in the Conservatories

In this system of instruction, the piano found a natural home. Not only was it useful for every phase of classroom instruction in music theory and history, but its solo literature also came to dominate the instrumental classes. Under the influence of the touring virtuosos and with the aid of the newly improved piano mechanism, piano students had the means and inspiration to play an important role in the burgeoning conservatory system. In many schools, the piano students far outnumbered those in other areas. The question of what all these pianists would do upon graduation was debated throughout the century, especially as it became painfully obvious that a student trained as a virtuoso soloist would not necessarily be a good accompanist or teacher.[34] In the conservatories themselves, the piano proved its usefulness beyond its function as a solo instrument. Illustrations on the following pages show how integral the piano was to the daily life of the Paris Conservatoire. Even when it is not in use, as in the picture of the trombone rehearsal, its omnipresence is obvious.

Though the Leipzig Conservatory remained devoted to only the most advanced students with professional potential, many schools expanded their offerings to include lower-division classes for children. These preparatory divisions served two functions: they prepared less-advanced students for the entrance requirements of the conservatory proper, and they offered classes for children who lived in the city and were still attending school. Both the Dresden and Stuttgart conservatories had large preparatory divisions, and in fact the students of the *Dilettantenschule* at the Stuttgart Conservatory outnumbered the students in the *Künstlerschule* by ratios of two or three to one throughout the nineteenth century. These lower divisions not only swelled the number of piano students; they also reinforced the notion of the piano as the quintessential instrument for amateur music making in the home.

The role of female students in the conservatories was significant. At many conservatories, they outnumbered their male counterparts. Further, because women were not yet accepted as members of professional orchestras, piano and voice were the overwhelming favorites of female students un-

The home of the Leipzig Conservatory from its founding in 1843 until 1887 (Archive of the Hochschule für Musik, Leipzig)

Das Conservatorium der Musik zu Leipzig.

Einladung und Programm

zur

HAUPT-PRÜFUNG

am

Conservatorium der Musik zu Leipzig.

Mittwoch, den 9. April 1862.

Im Saale des Gewandhauses.

Concert für das Pianoforte von L. van Beethoven (C moll, erster Satz), gespielt von Herrn *Franz Stockhausen* aus Colmar.

Concert für das Violoncell von B. Molique (erster Satz), gespielt von Herrn *Emil Hegar* aus Basel.

Concert für das Pianoforte von J. Moscheles (E dur, Op. 64), gespielt von Fräulein *Doris Böhme* aus Dresden.

„Salve regina" für Chor mit Orchesterbegleitung, componirt von Herrn Karl Munzinger aus Olten in der Schweiz.

Salve Regina, mater misericordiae,
Vita, dulcedo et spes nostra, salve!
Ad te clamamus exules filii Evae,
Ad te suspiramus gementes et flentes in hac lacrymarum valle,
Eia! ergo advocata nostra illos tuos misericordes oculos ad nos converte,
Et Jesum, benedictum fructum ventris tui, nobis post hoc exilium ostende,
O clemens, o pia, o dulcis virgo Maria!

Concert für das Pianoforte von Bennett (F moll, erster Satz), gespielt von Fräulein *Nanette Müller* aus Luzern.

Concerto pathétique für die Violine von *H. W. Ernst* (Fis moll), gespielt von Herrn *August Wilhelmj* aus Wiesbaden.

Program for the second public examination concert, Leipzig Conservatory, 1862. The list of students includes several who later became well known. The program includes piano concertos by Beethoven (No. 3 in C minor, first movement), Moscheles, and Bennett (first movement), as well as a cello concerto, a violin concerto, and a student composition for chorus and orchestra. (Archive of the Hochschule für Musik, Leipzig)

til the last decades of the century. A typical distribution of the student body is found in the records of the Hoch Conservatory for 1883–84. During that year, there were 138 female students and 54 males. Of the young women, seventy-three studied piano, fifty-eight studied voice, while among the other seven were two violinists, one organist, three students of counterpoint, and a lone aspiring composer.[35] Looking again at the New England Conservatory advertisement, it is clear that the institution went out of its way to accommodate female students. Conservatory faculties, however, were typically made up almost exclusively of men.

All these students needed a piano and a place to practice. In Germany, nineteenth-century conservatories did not provide practice facilities; students were responsible for their own pianos. Finding appropriate lodgings and a good piano proved to be one of the principal headaches of being a music student. The American piano student Amy Fay was forced to change apartments in Berlin when her neighbors lost patience with her practicing in the fall of 1870. When she studied in Weimar with Franz Liszt for a summer, she could not find a piano "for love or money" and was forced to have one shipped from Leipzig.[36] City governments passed ordinances limiting the hours when one could practice piano. In 1882 a case came to court in Bamberg involving a young woman who played the same three pieces by an open window from 8:00 P.M. to 10:30 P.M. The neighbors called

A jury for admission into the voice class at the Paris Conservatory, 1903. The piano occupies a central position in this intimidating group—it is not clear whether the pianist is friend or foe. (Bibliothèque Nationale, Paris)

LE JURY DU CONSERVATOIRE

LE JURY DU CONSERVATOIRE NATIONAL DE MUSIQUE
pour l'admission dans les classes de chant.
(Salle du Théâtre)

the police and she was taken to court, where the judge found in favor of the long-suffering residents. Testimony in the trial included ear-witness accounts of her limited repertoire, her "awful" [*furchtbar*] playing, and the acoustical properties of the street where she lived.[37]

The origin of the practice room has not been fully explored. Though there are occasional references to simultaneous practicing by numerous students in the same room, this unproductive practice was obsolete by the early nineteenth century. Individual practice rooms seem to have appeared first in rural schools, where land and building costs were somewhat lower. The 1875 catalog of Dana's Musical Institute in Warren, Ohio, calls special attention to this feature of the facilities, leaving the reader with the impression that practice rooms were still a novelty at this time:

Drawing by Reichan (engraved by Dochy) of a public singing competition at the Paris Conservatory, 1886. Noteworthy are the proximity of the audience to the stage and the position of the singer behind the pianist. (Bibliothèque Nationale, Paris)

> Upon laying this catalogue aside, let it not be with the impression that you have a knowledge of a "Conservatory of Music," where students rent a piano and practice to suit themselves, and take one or two lessons a week; but a "Musical Institute," consisting of a building containing a large number of rooms, each furnished with an instrument where students practice or study. . . . The students of this school have FREE USE OF INSTRUMENTS, the building being furnished with instruments enough to accommodate about one hundred pupils. For every four students that enter the school, it requires two new instruments, which are procured direct from the manufactory. During the summer vacation all instruments out of order are sent to the manufacturers for repairs, being kept in tune during the school year by a competent workman.[38]

In the later nineteenth century, silent keyboards such as the Virgil Practice Clavier made it possible for schools to provide a cheaper alternative to actual pianos and also to avoid the cost of individual practice rooms. By the late twenti-

Drawing by Charles Paul Renouard of Professor Delisse's trombone class at the Paris Conservatory, from *L'Illustration*, July 24, 1886. Though the piano is not being used, it stands ready for checking pitches or providing an arm rest.

eth century, students' dormitory rooms at the Sibelius Academy in Helsinki came with pianos in them. Undoubtedly all this piano practicing fueled the market for pianos. Whether conservatories or their students provided the instruments, makers enjoyed a constant demand so long as the piano remained the most popular instrument for conservatory students.

In addition to the demand for instruments, there was a demand for musical scores. Three categories of "teaching pieces" became a staple of music publishers during their golden age at the end of the nineteenth century. The first consists of books of daily studies and exercises such as the works of Czerny, Hanon, Plaidy, and others. The second category is music written expressly for students. These pieces were short-lived, often capitalizing on the latest fashions either in musical style or programmatic associations. Minor composers produced a seemingly unending flood of polkas, waltzes, and other dances carefully designed to titillate the imagination without overtaxing the fingers of aspiring pianists. Various systems were adopted for grading the difficulty of these pieces to aid students and teachers considering new music. The third category of teaching repertoire consists of works that were not necessarily written for students but which proved to be unusually well suited for pedagogical use. Classic examples are the Mendelssohn concertos, which were played so much by nineteenth-century piano students (particularly at the Leipzig Conservatory) that twentieth-century audiences could no longer bear to hear them.

Among the thousands of piano teachers at conservatories large and small, the most famous were able to create what amounted to a private studio within the conservatory. Teachers like Marmontel at Paris, Leschetizky at Vienna, and Clara Schumann at Frankfurt attracted students who had little interest in the conservatory's general curriculum but sought only to study with the internationally famous teacher. This led to the common practice of hiring assistant teachers who were well versed in the master teacher's methods and who taught all but the most talented of new pupils until they were ready to "graduate" to the master teacher. Schumann taught at the Hoch Conservatory from 1878 to 1891, and by the early 1880s the school had also hired her two daughters, Marie and Eugenie, as piano teachers. Nearly everyone who enrolled as a piano student at this institution studied with one of the daughters for a few semesters before being admitted to the mother's class. That these two were merely teaching assistants is supported by the fact that they both left when their mother retired.[39] Not surprisingly, it was the master teachers—operating virtually as independent teachers within the conservatory—who produced the most distinguished students. The fame of artists like Paderewski, Essipova, Gabrilowitsch, Schnabel, and Vengerova certainly added to the prestige of the Vienna Conservatory, but their success was likely due more to their studies with Leschetizky than to any classes they may have taken at the conservatory.

In addition to prominent master teachers, the conservatory system spawned methods or schools of instruction, the most famous of which was that of the Stuttgart Conservatory. The cofounders of this school, Sigmund Lebert (1822–84) and Ludwig Stark (1831–84), created a system of instruction that not only became the standard at their school but also was used throughout Europe and America. This extremely successful method required students to hold the wrist and arm absolutely still and rely exclusively on finger strength, as illustrated in one student's drawings. Lebert and Stark advocated learning a new piece by playing very slowly, forte throughout, with high fingers. This method produced the initial impression of finger strength and independence, but in the long run it produced arm tension and stiffness in the joints, due to the inability of the fingers alone to cope effectively with the heavy action of the modern piano. The resulting sound was harsh and disconnected, owing to the relentless vertical pounding of the fingers. Many a pianist was ruined by this method, and after the death of both its authors in 1884, attendance at the conservatory declined precipitously.[40]

The popularity of the Stuttgart method illustrates the principal weakness of the conservatories—a tendency to emphasize drill and uniformity at the expense of imagination and individuality. The prevalent atmosphere at the conservatories was described by Fay in a letter to her sister.

Critics of the Conservatories

I don't know that there is much to be told about conservatories of which you are not aware. The one in Stuttgart is considered the best; and there the pupils are put through a regular graded method, beginning with learning to hold the hand, and with the simplest five-finger exercises. There are certain things, studies, etc., which *all* the scholars have to learn. That was also the case in Tausig's conservatory. First we had to go through Cramer, then through the Gradus ad Parnassum, then through Moscheles, then Chopin, Henselt, Liszt and Rubinstein. I haven't got farther than Chopin, myself, but when I went to Kullak I studied Czerny's School of Virtuosen a whole year, which is the book he "swears by." I'm going on with them this winter. It takes years to pass through them all, but when you *have* finished them, you are an artist. . . . However, I suppose it comes to the same thing in the end if one studies Bach, Czerny, or Gradus, only you must *keep at* one of them all the while. The grand thing is to have each of your five fingers go "dum, dum," an equal number of times, which is the principle of all three![41]

Dumb, dumb indeed. The mind-numbing repetition of this sort of practicing pro-

Excerpt of a letter from Edgar Stillman Kelley to his parents, November 12, 1876. Kelley was an American piano student at the Stuttgart Conservatory, where he studied the Lebert-Stark method. His crude drawings illustrate the painful contortions that students were obligated to adopt in an effort to improve finger strength and independence. (Walter Havighurst Special Collections, King Library, Miami University, Oxford, Ohio)

duced generations of pianists whose fingers could surmount incredible difficulties but whose hearts had been closed to the beauties of music. The rigorous curricula that required all but the most talented students to play exactly the same pieces in the same order limited the standard repertoire and discouraged interest in new music. Perhaps most damaging was the notion that completing a book of exercises would make one an "artist." By the last decades of the nineteenth century, critics were calling attention to these drawbacks of conservatory training.

Liszt, the preeminent virtuoso of the century, was vitally interested in the education of young pianists. As a young man he had taught in the Geneva Conservatory for a year, but by his later years he had become a strong opponent of the piano teaching that took place in most conservatories. He recognized that conservatories were by their nature better suited to conservative philosophies and repertoire than to the progressive ideals he espoused. Musicians like Mendelssohn, Clara Schumann, and Joseph Joachim fit very well into the structure of the conservatory, teaching the techniques and aesthetic ideals of the conservative branch of German Romanticism; Liszt and Wagner found few allies for their radical views among conservatory faculties.

During his master classes in Weimar, Liszt used the word "conservatory" as a pejorative to decry anything he considered rigid or unimaginative. He jestingly referred to the students who briefly attended his classes between semesters at the conservatories as *Konservatoriumsvögel* [conservatory birds]. On several occasions he entertained his students with parodies of Clara Schumann, Ignaz Moscheles, and other well-known conservatory teachers. When a student played too mechanically during one master class, Liszt suggested that she probably came from a very stiff conservatory or from a little village this side of it. (Paradoxically, when another student "emoted" too much, he said, "in Leipzig, or Frankfurt, or Cologne, or Berlin at the 'great conservatories,' there you will make a success with that. One can say to you as to Ophelia: 'get thee to a nunnery,' get thee to a conservatory.") In his own teaching, Liszt concentrated exclusively on interpretation, believing that technical training was the duty of the conservatories. Although he recognized the value of technical discipline, he warned against the lack of artistry inherent in finger gymnastics.[42]

For the rest of the century, critics attacked the conservatory system, echoing Liszt's frustration with the rigidity and conservatism of these institutions. Musicologist Hugo Riemann, who had firsthand experience as both a student and a teacher in several conservatories, provided a harrowing picture of the life of a piano teacher in 1895:

Have you, dear reader, ever taken a look behind the scenes of a conservatory? Do you know what it means to make music all day, or even more to hear music all day? . . . Look at this well-preserved man, who is in no condition to keep his chin from sinking to his chest and whose eyelids close, even while a talented girl performs one of the most beautiful spots of the Beethoven G-major concerto. The poor thing is hearing the concerto perhaps for the thousandth time and has already heard six concertos and about a dozen sonatas today. He sat in the same seat at the piano four hours this morning and another two this afternoon. The profession of music teacher and especially of conservatory teacher is a strenuous and quickly exhausting one.[43]

In his discussion of professional music training for the German encyclopedia *Die Musik in Geschichte und Gegenwart*, Christoph Richter refers to "The Age of the Conservatories" as a period that ended in the early twentieth century. Since then, despite the continued prominence of a handful of leading conservatories like the Juilliard School, the trend has been toward more integrated musical education. In Germany the hundreds of private conservatories have been replaced by a system of state-financed *Musikhochschulen* with more government control and uniformity of programs, as has always been the case in France. In the United States, music departments in colleges and universities have become increasingly prominent in training professional musicians, aided by national governing bodies such as the National Association of Schools of Music. A few nineteenth-century conservatories have become affiliated with colleges and universities (Ithaca, Oberlin, and Cincinnati are examples), thereby maintaining a connection to their past status as conservatories while adding the cachet of a college education.

But the conservatories left a powerful mark on the world of the piano. They trained countless piano students—most of them amateurs but a few professionals—instilling in them and in subsequent generations of students certain basic assumptions about the piano and piano teaching that persist to the present day. First, these schools inadvertently encouraged virtuosity as an end in itself, an idea that was in line with concurrent trends in the piano repertoire. The virtuoso works of Liszt, Chopin, and their contemporaries necessitated new methods of teaching the instrument, which in turn encouraged the composition of works with even more demands for virtuoso technique. Second, they introduced a rigorous, systematic approach to learning the instrument, which has continued to be the ideal for many piano teachers. Perhaps more than any other instrument, the piano has inspired analytical thinking about technique and pedagogy. Third, they identified a large body of music as "standard repertoire" (works that every pianist should know), thereby perpetuating the notion of a musical canon. This canon, while incorporating many of the masterworks of Western music, has the drawback of limiting the spread of new and unfamiliar works. Along with the canon has come the perception of the great composer as a hero of almost religious stature.[44] Finally, the conservatories supported the mystique of the piano as the unparalleled vehicle not only for virtuosity but also for home music making, contributing to the growth in sales of pianos and piano music. Despite its weaknesses, the conservatory was inextricably linked to the piano; in their intimate dance through the nineteenth century, it is impossible to imagine one without the other.

In her 1848 novel *Amelia; or, A Young Lady's Vicissitudes*, the domestic writer Eliza Leslie tells of a heroic young woman, who after suffering the loss of her beloved adoptive mother, finds herself barred from an inheritance by her late guardian's greedy and unscrupulous sister, cast out nearly penniless from her childhood home, and spurned by her socially aspiring suitor who, while continuing to worship her privately, disdains marrying a woman bereft of rank. Reduced to making her way on her own, Amelia resolves to earn money by teaching the piano.[45]

As the leading symbol of middle-class domestic life, the piano offered antebellum women the ideal means for bringing in money without surrendering their social standing. Under the mandate of separate spheres, a middle-class woman who abandoned her domestic role to work for a living placed her reputation at stake, laying herself open to isolation and the threat of deepening poverty. But there was little danger of rigid censure in taking on piano pupils. A woman's decision to teach music for pay mostly passed as a harmless adjustment in prescribed social mores.

One reason piano teaching largely eluded middle-class guidelines for female behavior is that women who taught the piano nearly always worked in a family setting, an arrangement which blurred the distinction between genteel amateur music practice and the willful pursuit of pecuniary gain. If a woman had a home of her own, she might offer lessons without ever leaving her family parlor. Some teachers visited their pupils' homes, lending the enterprise an innocent air of female social ritual. A single woman had the option of teaching in a surrogate family by becoming a governess with girls in her charge. Many more found positions

A Gallery of Teachers and Students
The Female Piano Teacher in Antebellum America
Martha Dennis Burns

as piano instructors in female academies, where the daily routine, for both faculty and students, normally followed a family regimen.

Women who gave lessons on their own aimed for discretion in soliciting pupils, attentive to the prevailing standards of female decorum. Some forfeited modesty slightly by placing advertisements in their local newspapers, as often as not, withholding their names. "MUSIC-INSTRUCTION ON THE PIANO FORTE, by a Lady," read one such notice, in a Philadelphia journal from 1850.[46] But most female teachers preferred to seek pupils privately through networks of family relations, neighbors, and friends. Elizabeth Lomax, a widow who taught the harp and piano in the District of Columbia in the 1850s, drew her pupils from a circle of acquaintances that included her late husband's government connections. "Mr. Latham, a member of Congress from California, called to see me today to ask if I would consent to give his wife lessons on the harp," she wrote in her diary in September 1854. "I assented to his request," she went on to say, as if in bartering her talent for pay she were granting a social favor.[47]

Some women combined teaching with other musical employment appropriate to their sex, forming a genteel career out of music. Churches often hired female organists, and many women who taught the piano during the week found additional income on Sundays this way. Some of the most successful female musicians came from prominent musical families, having benefited early from parental encouragement and the support of other established musicians. Faustina Hasse Hodges was the daughter of the musical director for Sydney College, at Cambridge. In 1841, at age eighteen, she followed her father to New York, where he had taken a post as organist for Trinity parish. She began teaching harp and piano at Emma Willard's renowned Troy Female Seminary, near Albany, in 1850, and stayed there three years, choosing eventually to teach on her own, while also assuming her father's vocation as a church organist and choir director. Miss Hodges remained single throughout her life and earned a respectable living in music by teaching and performing, as well as composing parlor music and sacred songs.[48] But women who followed a similar path formed only a small minority among those who taught the piano at some point in life. Most women looked on music teaching as a temporary measure, not as a lifelong means of support.

One of the attractions young women found in taking a post at a female academy was the chance to enjoy a period of independence away from home without putting their marital prospects at risk. Nearly all women who taught the piano in female academies were single, and many traveled great distances in order to teach. "I am about to leave home for a sojourn in the Cherokee Nation," a female

Letter from Ellen Elizabeth Pollard, a pupil at the Leavenworth Female Seminary in Petersburg, Virginia, dated February 15, 1856. She has marked the drawing of the seminary's buildings with an x, noting, "This is the music room." (Pollard Family Papers, Virginia Historical Society, Richmond)

subscriber wrote to the editor of the *New York Musical World and Times* in 1853. "I go partly as a Teacher of Music in the native Female Academy."[49]

Frequently, women turned to piano teaching following a financial reverse in their families. "There is a young lady spending the winter here that I am much pleased with," a Connecticut woman confided in a letter to a New York acquaintance. "She is the daughter of an English gentleman that failures and misfortunes have driven to America." Once in this country, the young foreigner had staved off distress by offering lessons on the piano. "She has as many scholars as she can attend to," her friend noted proudly, "and, as her manner of teaching is much approved, I think she will probably continue a year in this place."[50] Music teaching also offered a practical expedient to widows and older women with families. A woman might take on piano pupils, for instance, to tide her family through difficult times if her husband suddenly lost his income.

Women who studied the piano early in life seldom did so as preparation to teach music for pay. Piano lessons were exceptionally expensive, and most parents well-off enough to afford them could presume that their daughters would never have reason to work. If a woman left home with no means of support, she might invest what she had in learning to play, with the hope of eventually taking on pupils and bringing in extra money that way. But in many more cases, those who taught the piano simply put to good use a skill they had acquired as an embellishment to their schooling in more prosperous times. Mrs. Lomax, the Washington widow, played the harp and guitar as well as the piano years before she began to give lessons. She was "all grace and accomplishments," a source who had known her in the 1840s recalled.[51]

Since anyone able to attract a few pupils could decide to teach music, there were female piano teachers at all levels of skill. Millie Gray, a Virginia teacher, was obviously ill prepared for the job she took on. "I felt very seriously the inconvenience of not hearing," she complained in her diary a year before purchasing her piano in order to teach. "I think my deafness has increased very much lately."[52] Other female piano teachers were exceptionally talented. Girls who attended the Pittsfield Seminary for Young Ladies in 1827 were fortunate in receiving their lessons from Eliza Hewitt and her daughter, Sophia. Although Sophia was only twenty-four at the time, her credits already included several years' service as organist for Boston's much acclaimed Handel and Haydn Society, and a respectable following as a concert pianist.[53] But whatever their grade of musical accomplishment, all female piano teachers negotiated the dominant principles governing female middle-class social conduct.

As Eliza Leslie's novel proceeds, Amelia never actually teaches the piano. Instead, she is wed to a young military officer from a well-to-do family and becomes the envy of all who have previously snubbed her. At the next social gathering, ornamented in diamonds, she takes her place at the keyboard and charms the company with her superior skills. Amelia's good fortune restores the boundary between genteel amateur music practice and working for profit that sudden necessity had briefly obscured, making clear Leslie's view that the dignity a woman preserves in teaching the piano still falls short of the honor she gains by not working at all. The middle-class doctrine of separate spheres did not invite women to market their talents for pay, but other contingencies frequently did. As piano teachers, countless women in antebellum America made the best of opposing goals, earning an income through music while maintaining allegiance to an ideal that promised lasting security and social standing.

In a golden age of piano virtuosos, Theodor Leschetizky (1830–1915)—Teodor Leszetycki in Polish—was the virtuoso teacher of virtuosos. Himself a pupil of Beethoven's student Carl Czerny, he moved from Vienna to St. Petersburg, where he became head of the piano department at the Conservatory in 1862. Soon thereafter, however, in 1878, he moved back to Vienna, where his villa became the headquarters of a piano-teaching operation, connected only nominally to the Vienna Conservatory, that took in hundreds of promising piano students and set them on the road to a career. Among these students were some of the greatest performers of the day, including Anna Essipova (one of a string of pupils whom Leschetizky married), Ignacy Paderewski, Ignacy Friedman, and Artur Schnabel. Remarkably, none of these musicians were musical factory products; all were distinctive artists.

Leschetizky's success as a teacher seems to have rested on contradictions. On one hand, he claimed to have no method, and according to Schnabel "he never spoke, at least I never heard him speak, of technique."[54] Yet students from around the world flocked to Vienna to learn "the Leschetizky method" from him. In fact several of the women who served as "preparers" of new students for the master (teaching them for their first year or so in the studio) issued books on the "Leschetizky method" bearing Leschetizky's endorsement; one of these was even filled with photographs of his hand playing various chords.[55] Accounts suggest that he taught the high-finger technique that was common in the period, yet what Paderewski and others claimed was most important to him was a singing tone—something hardly to be obtained from a high-finger technique.

In the end, Leschetizky's success may have derived in large part from his ability to size up students and help them develop their own particular gifts. Paderewski and Schnabel, for instance, presented utterly different challenges to him. Paderewski arrived at Leschetizky's door when he was twenty-four and already making a name as a composer; Schnabel came to study when he was nine. Leschetizky told Paderewski that it was too late to become a virtuoso because, although he had great musical gifts, he could not hope at his age to teach his fingers the discipline they needed. (To his credit, Paderewski took this verdict as a test, with the result that he later claimed, "I really learned from Leschetizky

Master Teacher,
Master Class:
Theodor Leschetizky
James Parakilas

169

how to work.")[56] Schnabel, on the other hand, impressed Leschetizky as someone who would never become a pianist—that is, a virtuoso—because he was too much of a musician; he was allowed to develop very much on his own.

As important to Leschetizky's students as their individual lessons, apparently, was the experience of his regular master classes. The differences between Paderewski's and Schnabel's accounts of those classes raise more questions about the secrets of his teaching. To some extent the differences might be explained by the fact that Paderewski took part in the classes in the 1880s and Schnabel in the 1890s; that Leschetizky, apparently out of consideration for Paderewski's late start, never asked him to perform in them, whereas Schnabel regularly did; or that Schnabel's account forms part of a tribute he wrote for Leschetizky's eightieth birthday, while Paderewski was writing decades after Leschetizky's death. Paderewski's account is as follows:

> Once a week there was a large gathering of his most advanced pupils who enjoyed private lessons with him, and they played before all the students. It was really a kind of concert but was generally spoken of as the "class." This "class" was greatly dreaded by the pupils as the standard of playing was very high and Leschetizky sat at the piano ready to pour out his wrath and fury

Theodor Leschetizky in his Vienna studio, ca. 1887. The photograph shows the arrangement of side-by-side pianos that fostered, for better or worse, the intense dynamic between teacher and student described by both Paderewski and Schnabel. Compare the illustration in the *New Instructions* (at the beginning of this chapter), which suggests a very different dynamic of a single-keyboard lesson in the eighteenth century. (Österreichische Nationalbibliothek, Vienna)

upon any pupil who failed to measure up to this high standard of his. He showed no mercy. . . . He was kind, good and really very generous at heart. But as a teacher he was implacable.[57]

And here is Schnabel's:

All the students have to be there, and some guests are invited too: patrons of the arts, critics, foreign artists just arrived in Vienna, always an intellectually eminent audience. Several students perform. Leschetizky sits beside them at the second piano, on which he himself always plays the orchestra part and corrects midway through the piece, showing with the liveliest directness how the passage being criticized should sound, how it *must* sound. Each of the students in attendance derives the greatest profit from this, as he develops an ever more intense wish—an ever growing ambition—to be able to feel it and play it the same way. Leschetizky is forever emphasizing that the student should not be capable of playing anything at all, even the slightest finger-exercise, even the stringing together of a few notes, without taste, expression, and beautiful tone. Technique, special effects, passagework as a goal in itself —it's all to be spurned. So is training for any of that. Respect for and joy in the work, in beautiful sound, from the first moment of studying a piece—that's the path to which he introduces one.[58]

In view of Leschetizky's apparent gift for letting students develop in their own ways, what is most puzzling about these accounts is not their difference but their one point of agreement: that he was imperious in imposing his interpretive will on any student who performed in his master class. More than a century later, the question of how Leschetizky taught is far more complex and baffling than whether or not he had a "method."

Like many American families at the turn of the century, Duke Ellington's parents owned a piano. His father, James Edward, or "J. E.," played by ear such popular songs as "Smiles" and "It's a Long Way to Tipperary" as well as operatic arias. When friends gathered at his home, J. E. would lead them in songs like "Sweet Adeline." Apparently he made up the arrangements, hummed the individual parts, and conducted from the piano.[59] Ellington's mother, Daisy Kennedy Ellington, had received some musical training and could read music. She preferred "pretty things" like C. S. Morrison's "Meditation" (1896) and pieces by Carrie Jacobs Bond. The four-year-old Edward is said to have wept at his mother's rendi-

Edward Kennedy "Duke" Ellington, Piano Student
Mark Tucker

171

Oliver "Doc" Perry, whom Duke Ellington called "my piano parent"

tion of "The Rosary" by Ethelbert Nevin. Daisy also liked to play hymns and even ragtime, but she disapproved of the blues.

Ellington's first brush with formal music instruction came when he was about seven years old. His mother decided it was time for piano lessons after he hurt himself playing baseball. His teacher was Marietta (Mrs. M. Harvey) Clinkscales, who introduced the boy to the basics of keyboard technique, hand position, and theory. It is not known how far he advanced; he apparently missed more lessons than he took. At one of Mrs. Clinkscales's pupil recitals in a local church, he was required to play the bass part while his teacher played the treble because he was the one student who had not mastered his piece.

Starting around 1914, years after his instruction from Mrs. Clinkscales, Ellington took a growing interest in music. As a black high-school student he could have pursued training at the Washington Conservatory or with private teachers. But such instruction could not help him learn what he wanted to play: ragtime, popular songs, and dance music. The best way he could master these idioms was to listen carefully to other musicians, practice what he remembered, then entertain at parties and dances for on-the-job experience. His later accounts emphasize how he was dazzled by the musicians he heard: "Those ragtime pianists sounded *so* good to me! And they looked so good! Particularly when they flashed their left hands." Occasionally Ellington also acknowledged the work he did to learn their art: "I could see that the ragtime pianists employed more affected fingering than the concert pianists and that attracted me very much. I hit that fingering very hard and somehow it seemed to come natural to me." A neighbor recalled how Ellington used to practice at night: "Two or three hours of plunking the same chord or a few notes running away from it got to be pretty wearisome."[60]

As an aspiring popular pianist who spurned formal instruction and made little use of written and recorded sources, Ellington had to develop keen ears and a retentive memory. He later reported that he learned to pick songs up quickly by ear when he accompanied contestants in talent shows, "not knowing in advance what song they had chosen."[61] And he developed his skills by listening to other pianists: "I used to spend nights listening to Doc Perry, Louis Brown, Louis Thomas—they were the schooled musicians, they'd been to the conservatory. And I listened to the unschooled, to Lester Dishman, Sticky Mack. There was a fusion of the two right where I was standing, leaning over the piano with both my ears twenty feet high."[62]

Ellington admired Oliver "Doc" Perry, one of the most popular black bandleaders in Washington. Besides being a "schooled" pianist with a "soft . . . touch," he could play the "classics," read the latest popular songs and show tunes from sheet music, and improvise on almost anything. He in turn took an interest in the young Ellington, and in time Ellington began visiting him at his home on U Street, where the older man generously shared his knowledge. Later Ellington recalled these sessions with gratitude: Perry "was absolutely the most perfect combination of assets I could have encountered at that time. He first taught me what I called a system of reading the lead and recognizing the chords, so that I could have a choice in the development of my ornamentation. He was my piano parent and nothing was too good for me to try."[63] Ellington filled in for Perry at Wednesday afternoon dances when the latter had to play for dinner at the Ebbitt House, a fashionable downtown hotel. Perry helped Ellington develop not just musical skills but also a professional attitude toward performing. By the time he left high school in 1917, Ellington had absorbed important lessons about music making, acquired a reputation around Washington as a piano player, and begun to think of pursuing music as a career.

Almost before we realized it the native-born, and in some instances, native-trained, pianist arose in our midst, and we discovered the American woman pianist.

—Harriette Brower, 1918

How Ruth Crawford Became an "American Woman Pianist"
Judith Tick

In 1913, when she was twelve years old, Ruth Crawford began taking piano lessons at the School of Musical Art in Jacksonville, Florida; she began giving them as well a mere five years later. The school's director, Bertha Foster, had invested in her from the start. After Crawford's father died in 1914, Foster waived her weekly $1.50 fee for lessons; in June 1918, upon Crawford's graduation from high school, Foster admitted her to a ten-week music-teacher training course.

As an occupation, music teaching made good sense. The field's enormous growth offered new opportunities to women, who were working outside the home in greater numbers than ever before. Music as an "accomplishment"—for centuries a staple of conventional female education—sheltered women from any hint of impropriety as they dealt with new economic realities. "Music teacher"—an umbrella term that could cover the lady around the corner who gave lessons in her home to the teacher with her own studio—was one thing; "musician" was another. When the census distinguished between them, the distribution clarified the differences between private and public space: the great majority of "musicians" out in the world, on stage as performers, in print as composers, in jobs at conservatories, were men. Female musicians clustered around the lower-status, lower-paying rungs of the professional ladder. Part-time teachers, traveling to pupils' homes or receiving them in their own, had not moved so far from the Victorian parlor. No matter. Women poured into a profession whose supply and demand they controlled.[64]

In 1916 Foster had assigned Crawford the best piano teacher in her school, Madame Valborg Collett, a Norwegian émigré whose credentials included lessons with Agathe Backer-Grøndahl and study at the Leipzig Conservatory. She enters Crawford's diary with Ruth's account of "My First Piano Lesson."

> October 16, 1917: Well, we began about 3:30, no 3:10. We took Loeschorn [sic] premiere, et thrashed him out till the poor fellow was weary until I got it right, and she said, "Good, that's it." Hard worked-for, but mighty delightful when you do get it! During the thrashing, she said I played like a baby, that her pupils did not play like babies, they played like little artists, which hurt my feelings a bit. I am not saying I did not need & deserve this criticism: I am only saying it hurt my feelings a bit, as I think it would anyone's. And I do not feel mad at her, at all.

Crawford turned her humiliation inward. "I remember I wished on the way home, that somehow I could lose consciousness—die or something, to forget the responsibility of having to practise as Mme. Collett had told me to."

But other honesties surfaced in stories she wrote about her musical coming of age. Crawford renamed herself "Mary Marshall" and Madame Collett, "Madame Zielinsky," who was caricatured as the epitome of a snobbish European musician. "From her height of foreign superiority" she pours a torrent of high-toned invective on the head of poor little Miss Marshall: "You have no understanding! no knowletch of piano-blaying! You blay like a baby! Ach!" The woman, whom an adult Crawford would later call "much beloved and much-feared," shrank through narrative into a vaudeville routine.

Madame Collett replaced what she labeled "trash, bash, mush" with such repertory as Mendelssohn's "Songs without Words," études by Moscheles and Heller, an unidentified Beethoven sonata, Brahms waltzes, and Chopin preludes, with his Variations Brillantes in B-flat Major, Op. 12, serving as Crawford's big showpiece. On June 20, 1918, she played it at the annual recital of the School of Musical Art.

"Am scared of recital. . . . I do not know my piece very well," Crawford worried two days earlier. But at Duval Theater, decorated with thousands of shasta daisies and filled with a "large and most enthusiastic audience," success was hers: "Recital over. Everyone says I did splendid. I did not tremble a bit but controlled myself. Almost forgot the audience." A few months later Crawford idealized the moment in another story: "Mary forgot the audience—the lights—everything—absorbed in putting her whole soul and heart into the music. Melody, each note like a pearl, so perfect and so beautiful. The audience was entranced. It listened as one in a dream." The more music empowered her in real life, the more Ruth Crawford polished herself in print, defining herself through musical performance and literary composition.

Crawford was hardly alone. The "American woman pianist" was coming into focus in the early twentieth century both through achievements of actual performers and the cultural discourse surrounding them. Following the trail blazed by Teresa Carreño, pianists such as Augusta Cottlow, Olga Samaroff, and Fanny Bloomfield-Zeisler became role models for the rank and file. Crawford's mother, Clara, proclaimed Cottlow her ideal—a "beautiful finished American lady artist, charming to watch . . . American trained. Nothing bohemian about her . . . I would be proud to have you like her," she told her daughter.

Women like Clara and Ruth formed a national constituency for magazines like *Musical America* and *Etude*, which poured out reams of feature articles about and for women in music. This literature touched on identity (the process of finding a "voice"), professionalization (the socioeconomic choice of occupation), and aesthetics (the relationship between gender and musical performance or composition).

October 12, 1918: "*Etude* came today," Ruth Crawford wrote in her diary. "Read it all morning." Like many other

Ruth Crawford, around 1926–27

young aspiring female artists, she needed *Etude* to open a window into the world of art. She became engrossed by the November 1918 issue devoted to "women's work in music," with articles by the noted composer Amy Beach on "the girl who wants to compose," the great singer Ernestine Schumann-Heink on "the mother's part in musical training of the child," the progressive educator Frances Clarke on "music as a vocation for women," and, for the young American woman pianist, an unsigned article titled "Small Hands and Their Extraordinary Possibilities." When years later she laughed at a woman reading *Etude* in New York, she was attempting to transcend the provincial feminine in her past. "I didn't know anybody outside of Squeehonk read that!" she said.

Crawford slowly made her way into the musical life of Jacksonville. She played at the Woman's Club, the YWCA, the Jacksonville Tourist Club, and perhaps at the important Ladies Friday Musicale, where Madame Collett "praised me up," she wrote. At church lunches for soldiers stationed at the port city during the war, Crawford was "playing piano part time and helping to serve part time."

In 1920 Crawford took a decisive step to widen her musical horizons. She arranged to leave for one year's study with a famous pianist. Europe was out of the question; Mrs. Crawford had read Amy Fay's *Music Study in Germany*. She disapproved of "how lessons were given over there. . . . Mrs. Taylor told me all big foreign musicians are what we would call immoral. . . . No daughter of mine with my consent would ever leave our shores for music."

Instead, Crawford left for the shores of Lake Michigan to take the one-year teacher's certificate program offered by the American Conservatory of Music in Chicago. On September 21, 1921, she boarded a train for the thirty-six-hour ride north. The *Florida Times-Union* took note of her departure the next day in a fancy alliteration: "Miss Ruth Crawford will Perfect herself in Piano Studies under Pedagogue." How eagerly Clara Crawford anticipated her daughter's triumphant return. Then Crawford could list her conservatory certificate and "pupil of" on her business cards and start her own piano studio as that early-twentieth-century model of success and independence—the American woman pianist.

Excerpts from "Mother and Music" (1934) Marina Tsvetaeva, translated by Jane Costlow

But from the beginning I got nowhere with notes. A key you can press, but a note? A key exists, here, right here, black or white, but not the note, the note's on the staff (on which one?). And besides that, you hear a key—but not a note. The key exists; the note doesn't. And why have the note when the key is there? I didn't understand any of it until I had seen—atop a greeting card given me by Avgusta Ivanovna as a *Glückwunsch* for mother—sitting atop the line of notes, not notes—

but little sparrows! Then I understood that notes live on branches, each on its very own, and they jump from there down onto keys, each to its very own. And then—it makes a sound. Some of them, the ones that come late (like the little girl Katya out of *Evening's Repose*: a train waves goodbye as it's leaving, and the tardy Katya and her nurse—are crying . . .)—the ones that come late, I mean, live up above the branches, on some kind of aerial branches, but still they too jump down (and not always on the right place, then it's a mistake). When I stop playing, the notes go back to their branches, and just like birds they sleep, and also like birds they never fall off. My birds fell, nonetheless, twenty-five years later—even leapt off:

All the notes leapt from the page,
All the secrets from my lips . . .

But even though I quickly started to read notes easily (better than faces, where for oh, so long, I read only what was best!)—I could never love them. Notes —got in my way: they kept me from seeing, or kept me really from not-seeing the keyboard, they knocked me off the melody, off of knowing, off the mystery, the way you're knocked off your feet—they knocked me off my hands, kept my hands from knowing their own way, they crept in like an outsider, that "eternal third-party in love" from my poem (that no one understood, because of *its* simplicity, or *my* complexity)—and I never played as confidently as when I played by heart. . . .

But the keyboard—I loved: for its blackness and its whiteness (with the barest hint of yellow!), for its blackness so obvious, for its whiteness (with the barest hint of yellow!) so secretly sorrowful; for the wideness of some, and the narrowness (they're offended!) of others; for the fact that without moving it's as though you're on stairs, and that the stairs—are in your hands!—and right from that stairway flow frozen streams—frozen stairwells of streams along your spine—and fire in your eyes—that very fire from the valley of Daghestan, right out of my brother Andriusha's anthology.

And because the whites, when you press them, are so obviously gay, and the blacks—immediately sorrowful, *truly*—sorrowful, so really and *truly* that if I press —it's as though I'm pressing on my eyes, and tears will burst from them, right away.

And for the pressing itself: for the possibility, at the merest touch, of beginning to drown right away, to drown without end, without hitting bottom, as long as you don't let up—and even when you do!

Because it looks still on top, but beneath the still it's deep—as in water, as in the River Oka, but stiller and deeper than the Oka; because beneath one's hand—

there's a chasm, because that chasm is right in your hands—because without even moving, you fall forever.

Because of the cunning of that keyboard stillness, ready to sound at the slightest touch—and then swallow.

For the passion of pressing, for the terror of pressing: once pressed, to awaken it all. (Just what was felt, in 1918, by every soldier on an estate.)

And because it is—mourning: mother's, in the black-and-white stripes of that summer's-end blouse, when after the telegram: "Grandfather passed on in peace" —she herself appeared, tearstained but still smiling, with the first word for me: "Musia, your grandfather loved you a great deal." . . .

As for musical ardor—it's time it got said—I had none. The guilt for that—or rather the cause of it—was my mother's excessive diligence, she who made demands on me not to my strength and ability, but to the boundlessness, agelessness of a genuine inborn calling. Demanding of me—herself! Of me, a writer already— me, who was never a musician. "Sit out your two hours' worth—and be glad! Me? —when I was four years old, they couldn't drag me away from the piano! 'Noch ein wenig!' [Just a little more!] If only once, just once, you'd ask that of me!" I didn't ask her—ever. I was honest, and none of the predictable delight and praise from her could have forced me to ask for what didn't come by itself to my lips. (Mother tormented me—with music.) But I was also honest about playing, played the two set morning hours, the two evening hours, without cheating (before music school, that is, before I was six!), not even turning too often to look at the lifesaver clock (which, by the way, I understood not a whit till I was ten—I might just as well have turned to look at *The Death of Caesar* over the shelves holding music), but once it had sounded the time—I rejoiced! I played the same in mother's absence as when she was there, played despite the blandishments of the German woman who didn't get on with mother, or of nurse with her bad heart ("you've worn the child completely out!") and even of the handy-man, lighting a fire in the room: "Go on, Musenka, have a run!"—and even sometimes of father himself, who would appear from his study, somewhat shyly: "Surely two hours have gone already? I'm certain I've been listening to you at least three . . ." Poor papa! That was just it, that he *didn't* hear, not us, not our scales, not our Hanon or our gallops, not mother's runs or Valeriia's (she sang) roulades. He didn't hear to such an extent that he didn't even close the study door! Because when I wasn't playing, my sister Asya played; and when Asya didn't play, Valeriia picked things out; and then, drowning and flooding us all—mother—all day and almost all night! But he knew one tune only

—from *Aida*—a keepsake from his first wife, a song bird who had early been silenced. "You don't even know how to sing 'God save the Tsar'!"—mother teased, reproachfully. "What do you mean I can't? I can! (Absolutely ready) God sa-a-a-ve . . . !" But it never got as far as the "tsar," for mother —her face no longer teasing, but sincerely, grimacingly suffering —at once clasped her hands to her ears, and father stopped. He had a strong voice.

Thirteen-year-old Marina Tsvetaeva playing the piano, spring 1906

Later, after her death, he often said to Asya: "What's that Asya, aren't you hitting wrong notes?"—to clear his conscience, in mother's place.

*T*n 1842, Charles Dickens visited the boomtown of the American industrial revolution and was astonished by a piano. In the textile mills of Lowell, Massachusetts, he found that the work was done mostly by young, single women who had been recruited from the farms of northern New England; that in itself was different from the mills that Dickens had visited in England. But he was especially startled when he went to the company boardinghouses where these women lived and discovered how they spent their time after a gruelingly long workday.

> Firstly, there is a joint-stock piano in a great many of the boardinghouses. Secondly, nearly all these young ladies subscribe to circulating libraries. Thirdly, they have got up among themselves a periodical called The Lowell Offering, "A repository of original articles, written exclusively by females actively employed in the mills."[1]

Why might Dickens—and his readers—have been surprised to learn of these activities? Playing the piano, reading books, and writing articles for publication belonged to the list of "accomplishments" that people decades earlier, in Austen's time, had considered appropriate for young women. But all three required a high degree of literacy, an achievement that might have been expected from daughters of wealthy Englishmen who were sent to boarding schools or for whom tutors were hired, but it could hardly have been expected of farm-born factory girls. Dickens had a clear message for his middle- and upper-class British readers: they shouldn't feel that these accomplishments were wasted on factory girls.

But why was Lowell's workforce so well schooled? New England, with its Calvinist heritage, had been an exceptionally literate place for a long while. At the time of Dickens's visit, however, the strong support for universal public schooling there sprang as much from the mentality of industrialization as from religious belief. Mill owners had been persuaded that the best educated workers made the most capable workers, and their workers, as a result, stood to profit from believing the same.[2] In the long run, that belief came to dominate the industrial world, and piano manufacturers were among those who capitalized on the combined spread of literacy and prosperity in the working classes. In 1873 an article in the *Musical Times* of London noted a connection between the spread of literacy and the spread of pianos among English coal miners. According to this report, the secretary of the South Yorkshire Miners' Association had testified to a commission of inquiry that "Fifteen years ago it was scarcely possible to find a collier who could write his name and now every child he had could read and write. A great number owned

Charlotte N. Eyerman and James Parakilas

Advertisement for Chickering & Sons pianos, *Dwight's Journal of Music*, June 15, 1861, displaying the company's factory in Boston even more prominently and proudly than the pianos made there

their own houses as freeholders, and the system was on the increase. Some of them had pianos and harmoniums, and even perambulators. He looked on the piano as a cut above the perambulator."[3]

Thinking Industrially

James Parakilas

Lady's work table, efficiently combining a sewing box, a piano, and a writing desk, made in Germany, mid–nineteenth century (Smithsonian Institution)

To some extent, then, the story of the piano in the middle of the nineteenth century is a continuation of its story during the previous era: the part of society able to afford a piano and learn to play it kept expanding, from the most privileged class to the middle class and, increasingly, to the working class. Industrial-scale production of pianos increased the social role of the piano by enlarging the numbers and classes of people with access to the instrument. But industrialization was more than a means of production; it was also a way of thinking systematically about scale, efficiency, organization, and control in any operation. Above all, it was an inclination to embrace many activities that had previously operated on their own into a single system, operating under a single roof, subject to a central control.

The boardinghouses of Lowell, for instance, represented industrial thinking just as surely as did the mills themselves. Young women recruited from distant farms to work in the mills were cut off from their families; the mill owners built the boardinghouses next to their factories not just to provide housing for these women but also to regulate their lives and thereby maximize their performance at work. The pianos that the owners placed in the boardinghouses allowed the workers to restore their spirits under the company roof and within the hours allotted by the company. As musical instruments these pianos provided either private pleasure for individual residents or social pleasure for groups of them, but as furnishings of the boardinghouses they belonged to the industrialization of human life.

It was not only among factory workers that life in the mid–nineteenth century became industrialized in this broader sense. Even the old notion of female accomplishments—which continued to include piano playing—was turned into a system of education. In fact, the pretension that education in these accomplishments could be ordered and periodically reordered along rational lines, like the production system of a factory, proved all too easy for Nikolai Gogol to mock in the novel *Dead Souls* (1842):

Mrs. Manilov had received a good education. And one gets a good education, as we know, in a boarding school. And in a boarding school, as we know, three main subjects constitute the foundation of human virtue: the French language, indispensable for a happy family life; the pianoforte, to afford a husband agreeable moments; and, finally, the managerial part proper: the crocheting of purses and other surprises. However, various improvements and changes in method occur, especially in our time; all this depends largely on the good sense and ability of the boarding school's headmistress. In some boarding schools it even occurs that the pianoforte comes first, then the French language, and only after that the managerial part. And sometimes it also occurs that the managerial part, that is, the crocheting of surprises, comes first, then the French language, and only after that the pianoforte. Various methods occur.[4]

Even in this caricature it is possible to sense how the cult of industrial-style systems in the middle of the nineteenth century affected everything about the piano, from the manufacture of the instruments to their roles in people's lives. Ironi-

Jacob Marling, *The Crowning of Flora* (detail), 1816. When the pupils at a female seminary, in America or anywhere in the Western world, enacted a performance with music, gentlemen musicians might be called in to play the wind instruments that were not considered proper for ladies. One of the students, however, was sure to be called on to provide whatever music was needed at the piano. (Chrysler Museum of Art, Norfolk, Va.)

cally, the industrial model seems to have made its slowest progress in the piano factory. There were four companies that each made a thousand or more pianos per year by 1850—Broadwood and Collard in London, Pleyel in Paris, and Chickering in Boston. But although the factories of these companies were huge by eighteenth-century standards—Chickering built a new factory in 1853 that was larger than any textile mill in nearby Lowell—efficiencies of scale were introduced more slowly into the production of pianos than into that of textiles (as Chapter 2 relates). In the selling of their products, however, piano manufacturers were quick to seize on new systems of promotion that reached people by the hundreds of thousands. The world's fair, for instance—a phenomenon of the mid–nineteenth century—became a stage on which piano manufacturers competed with one another for prizes and reputation. And although the American manufacturers Chickering and Steinway profited most from the prizes and publicity that their innovative pianos received at the midcentury expositions (especially the Paris Exposition of 1867), these world's fairs gave stature to the piano industry as a whole, making a huge public aware of the importance of piano manufacture to the national and international economies.

By this time, too, piano manufacturers were thinking systematically about another subject: their relationships with performers. These relationships had proven

Engraving of Becker pianos, from St. Petersburg, being demonstrated by pianist-composer D. Magnus at the Paris World's Fair of 1878, in *L'Illustration*, July 27, 1878. The shah of Persia is the privileged listener.

mutually beneficial even when they were informal and unsystematic, as they had been between Clementi and the Broadwood company in 1780 and between Dussek and the Clementi company in 1800. But in 1830 the Pleyel company tried a new, more focused strategy. It opened a concert hall in its Paris headquarters so that the public could hear the great performers of the day perform on Pleyel pianos and then pick out a Pleyel for themselves in the adjoining showroom. Soon Pleyel's local rival, Erard, opened a comparable concert hall, and other ambitious piano makers around the world followed suit.

The solo piano recital didn't develop overnight in the setting of the concert hall, but it is hard to imagine that it would have developed at all if these halls had never been opened for the express purpose of promoting piano sales and if pianists had continued to perform always in theaters, churches, and other multipurpose spaces. These public concerts exerted an influence over the Parisian salons, those exclusive, music-filled parties of the rich, powerful, and artistic that are often contrasted with public concerts in social and musical terms. Within a few years of the opening of Pleyel Hall, nevertheless, the nascent concert system, with its publicity machinery, provided the model for the most famous salon performance in history: in 1837 the Italian princess Christina Belgiojoso took out a newspaper ad to invite the public to her Paris salon, for a fee, to hear the "simultaneous concert of two talents whose rivalry is shaking the musical world right now, with the balance between Rome and Carthage to be decided: Messieurs Liszt and Thalberg will take turns at the piano."[5]

Piano manufacturers had their "house" pianists (Pleyel had Kalkbrenner, Erard had Liszt), but even they needed to go on the road to earn their fame and fortune. The tour itself then became a system. Liszt, for example, became the first pianist to employ an agent, Gaetano Belloni, who for six years in the 1840s served as his advance man, business manager, and secretary on his concert tours across Europe.[6] But here, too, the piano manufacturers got into the act, taking over and systematizing the pianists' tours in order to build the market for their products. The American manufacturers competed with one another by importing pianists from Europe and organizing tours for them around the United States: Anton Rubinstein's tour for Steinway in 1872 was answered by Hans von Bülow's for Chickering in 1875. By the 1890s, the train bearing Paderewski, his Steinway piano, and his staff of publicists, managers, technicians, and others around the country, all paid for by Steinway, was a kind of concert-giving factory in rolling stock.[7]

At midcentury, the industrial ideal of a system that embraces and controls a

Tuning a Cabinet Piano,
engraving in supplement to
Penny Magazine, April
1842

The Piano Tuner

James Parakilas

In the eighteenth century, there were no keyboard tuners as such; keyboard owners and players expected to tune their own instruments or have someone on their premises who did it for them. But during the nineteenth century, piano tuning gradually turned into a profession. The 1827 edition of Gottlieb Graupner's Rudiments of the Art of Playing on the Piano Forte *ends with instructions for tuning the instruments, as piano methods had always done and other keyboard methods before them; but on the title page is a notice that at Graupner's Musical Ware House, where the* Rudiments *was on sale, the public could also find "Piano Fortes Sold, Exchanged, Let & also tuned in Town & Country at the Shortest Notice." The piano tuner had begun paying house calls. Now even the family piano needed a specialist from the piano industry just to stay in working condition.*

Why did this profession suddenly become needed? A great part of the explanation lies with the development of the instrument itself. As the tension of the strings increased, as the fundamentals of the strings grew louder in relation to the upper harmonics, and as tuning pins became trickier to fix in place, it became harder both to hear whether strings were in tune and to achieve a result that would hold. Tuning came to require years of training.

The existence of the profession of piano tuner was marked in England by the publication in 1840 of a textbook, The Tuner's Guide. *By the 1870s, the profession was sufficiently established that it began to be treated as an attractive opportunity for classes of workers with disadvantages in the workplace. The Royal Normal College and Academy of Music for the Blind in England offered training in piano tuning to the blind, as New England Conservatory did to women.*

Because of the dominance of the piano in musical culture, even its tuning affected musical life generally. Edward Quincy Norton produced an equal-tempered piano tuning by 1887, partly in response to the growing difficulty of hearing the upper harmonics of the strings and therefore of achieving any mean-tempered system. This new system of tuning pianos made a difference to the tuning of other instruments, especially when they were used with the piano, and it created an ideal medium for the creation of atonal and twelve-tone music.

whole field of activity was realized at least as perfectly by music publishers. Whereas publishers in earlier periods had balanced musical publications with other products—other printed items in the case of Breitkopf & Härtel in the eighteenth century, other musical products in the case of Clementi & Company in the early nineteenth—now the larger publishers concentrated on music publications alone, but in a systematic way. Their attempt can be seen during this period in the organization not only of their catalogs but even of their music stores. Here, from *Dwight's Journal of Music,* is a description of the store that the publishing firm of Oliver Ditson opened in Boston in 1857:

> There is no music, either in the form of sheet or book, published in this country, that may not here be found, besides a large and well-selected stock of foreign music. . . . The contents of the various compartments are designated by tasteful "letters of gold" above them. On the right we noticed, first "Instrumental Music," followed by "Foreign Music" and "Jobbing Music"—this last being conveniently assorted for supplies to other dealers. On the left, "Vocal Music," "Guitar Music" and "Music Books." Of course these general departments are sub-divided many times, in order to establish a system, without strict adherence to which, a business so multitudinous in its branches could not be carried on.

The building itself was designed for efficiency like a factory in Lowell:

> The building is complete in every particular. Cochituate water is conveyed to every part of it; gas fixtures are arranged in every room: speaking tubes extend to every floor from the first; goods are conveyed through all six floors by means of a powerful wheel, and a huge platform running in grooves, and the rooms being open on two streets are amply provided with air and light.[8]

What can't be detected from reading this description, but only from looking through the major publishers' catalogs of this period, is how deeply this vast system depended on the piano.[9] Original music for solo piano was just the tip of the iceberg. The piano appeared in many other categories that were just as large: songs with original or transcribed piano accompaniments; part-songs and choral music, sacred and secular; dance music, transcribed from stage and dance hall; opera scores and excerpts with the orchestral parts reduced for piano; chamber music with piano; and music of every sort transcribed for piano solo or duet. If we could look under almost any of the "letters of gold" in the Ditson store, we would find music that required a piano.

Advertisement by the music publisher Oliver Ditson in *Dwight's Journal of Music*, January 21, 1860, showing the company's main store in Boston, which had been described in an article in the same journal three years earlier. The ad, like the article, depicts a universe of musical categories to be found in the store.

Indeed, the music publishing industry had been transformed in much the same way as had the rural economy of New England. The farm girls who migrated to the New England mills during the mid–nineteenth century created pressure on others to follow, because their work at the mills, spinning and weaving, replaced similar tasks traditionally performed by women on farms.[10] In the case of music publishing, the popularity of the piano during this period meant that forms of music that did not use the piano fell out of practice. As a result, music that did not include a role for the piano became ever more difficult for customers to find. Music periodicals and other domestic music publications from America at the end of the eighteenth century, for example, are full of hymns and other sacred music in parts, evidently designed for a cappella performance, but by the middle of the nineteenth century almost all comparable publications include keyboard reductions of the vocal parts (playable on harmonium or domestic organ as well as piano). In the earlier period, singers may have used a keyboard or some other instrument to help them learn individual parts, but it would have been difficult for anyone to rehearse all the singers at once by playing everyone's parts together. The new scores with keyboard reduction made that practice easy, and it has been standard ever since. Older methods of learning vocal ensemble music went the way of the spinning wheel and at the same time.

The opera industry in Italy—a scene in which the role of the piano might appear to have been very minor—also illustrates how the spread of the piano transformed musical life. John Rosselli, the leading authority on Italian opera production in the nineteenth century, writes that by the 1870s the "initiative" in operatic theaters "had slipped out of the hands of the impresarios. . . . Publishers decided where operas were to be done, controlled casting, supplied set and costume designs, and often directed the production." The Italian music publishers grew into their position of extraordinary power, he says, "thanks in large part to the spread of the piano."[11] They tended to publish opera scores and excerpts in piano-vocal format (that is, with the orchestral accompaniments transcribed for piano) and sometimes also in arrangements for piano alone (whole operas without words), but seldom in full orchestral score. And on the basis of their profits from the sales of these piano scores (which consequently provided composers like Verdi and Puccini with their basic income), a couple of Italian publishers (Ricordi and Sonzogno) were able, by the end of the century, to dictate which operas were to be performed, and how, in theaters throughout Italy.

In short, the piano in this period took total control of the music industry. Not only did piano makers and music publishers make staggering increases in output

The first page of "Just as I Am" for vocal quartet and keyboard, *Peter's Musical Monthly,* March 1873. This hymn, published in an American family music magazine, seems to be designed primarily to be sung around the piano or other keyboard instrument in the home. The piano part, which largely doubles the voices, can be used to teach the singers their notes and to support them once they have learned them. Charlotte Elliott's hymn text had evidently not yet been identified with the tune that it would eventually make its own, nor had the Bridal Chorus from Wagner's *Lohengrin* yet acquired its cultural function as the standard processional music for weddings.

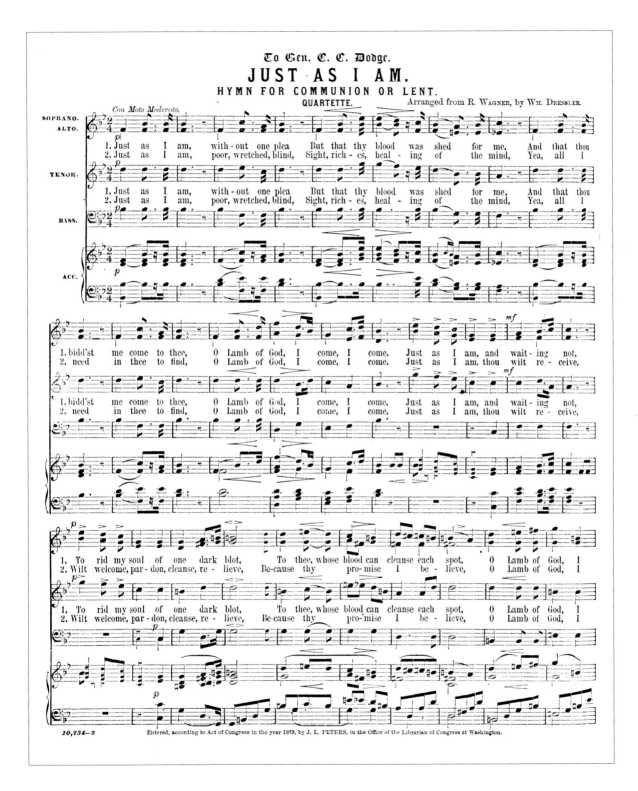

To Gen. C. C. Dodge.

JUST AS I AM.

HYMN FOR COMMUNION OR LENT.

QUARTETTE.

Arranged from R. Wagner, by Wm. Dressler.

10,234—2

and sales, but the new kinds of products they sold and the new systems of marketing they practiced, along with the sheer numbers of new pianos and piano-music publications, affected virtually all the ways people made music. Wherever music was made in the Western world of the mid–nineteenth century, the piano called the tune.

Music to Transport the Listener
James Parakilas

The piano music of this period, from the masterpieces of Schubert, Schumann, Chopin, and Liszt to the humblest transcription or accompaniment, relies heavily on the long-established capacity of the piano to imitate the sounds of other musical instruments or singers. By making listeners imagine that they are hearing something other than the piano in front of them, it makes them half believe that they are somewhere else. When a pianist uses a piano score of Verdi's *Rigoletto* to accompany an opera singer in a rehearsal of "Caro nome," the piano gives her an idea of what it will eventually sound and feel like when she sings the aria onstage with an orchestra. When concertgoers hear a Liszt Hungarian Rhapsody, the piano lifts them out of their seats and carries them off to a Budapest café, into the thrall of a Gypsy violinist and cimbalom player. According to the dominant Romantic ideology of this period, musical masterpieces were expected to perform a poetic act of taking listeners outside themselves—and many masterpieces from this era retain that power.

At the same time, a more mundane form of transportation applied to all the piano music of this period: pianos were to be found in ever multiplying settings, and any one piano piece, of any sort, was likely to be carried from concert hall to parlor to church to classroom and played on a different piano, to a different purpose and audience and effect, in each setting. Any idea we may have of the setting that is proper for a given piece of nineteenth-century piano music is challenged, if not belied, by what is known about performance practice at the time and about the nature of the piano-filled musical world into which that piece was born. The following survey of mid-nineteenth-century music for piano is therefore not categorized by setting ("music for the home," "music for the concert hall"); it is more like a tour of the "letters of gold" categories in Ditson's store, designed to illustrate how this musical repertory allowed its listeners to hear a piano and imagine other musical media and other settings, at the same time as its performers changed the significance of a piece every time they took it to a piano in a new setting.

Consider, for instance, the category of music performed in the competition between Messieurs Thalberg and Liszt in 1837. The contest between them in the

Princess Belgiojoso's salon was actually a rematch: the terms and setting were different, but the same pieces were played. Sigismond Thalberg had made a great effect earlier in the season with a concert in the hall of the Paris Conservatory, to which Franz Liszt had replied by renting the Paris Opera house, a far larger hall, and playing a concert there. At the Princess Belgiojoso's, both pianists repeated their great crowd pleasers from the earlier concerts, Thalberg his Fantasy on Rossini's *Moses in Egypt* and Liszt his Divertissement on the cavatina "I tuoi frequenti palpiti" from Pacini's *Niobe*. Both were piano paraphrases, as they were sometimes called, on favorite melodies from popular operas of the day. The two pianists were competing with each other in their ability to make the piano compete with the sonic glory of voices and orchestra in the opera house. Indeed, in the first round, Liszt had played his "Niobe" in an opera house—a place where Pacini's *Niobe* could have been staged. In effect he was transporting the opera back to its home, after first stealing it away into a piano paraphrase. In fact, Liszt relished direct comparisons with the musical media he was imitating. Once, it seems, he played his transcription of a movement from Berlioz's *Symphonie fantastique* immediately after an orchestral performance of that movement, driving the audience wild.[12]

These face-offs, real or implied, with much larger musical ensembles in the spaces built for those larger ensembles were possible because Liszt and his contemporaries were playing much more powerful pianos than the one that a student had played in the concert hall of the Paris Conservatory only a couple of decades earlier (1809)—an instrument that a critic complained "produces little effect in concerts; it is an instrument exclusively for salons."[13] But the development of more powerful pianos went hand in hand with the development, by pianists like Liszt and Thalberg, of techniques for imitating at the piano the ever louder roar of orchestras, the ever more passionate melody of opera, and the ever more colorful palette of both orchestral and operatic composition in their day. Thalberg's most lasting achievement is a set of operatic arrangements designed to teach pianists the "Art of Song Applied to the Piano," that is, the art of rendering a melody on the piano—and supporting it with accompanying figuration—so that it made the effect of great operatic singing.[14] Liszt specialized in capturing with his two hands the most complex textures of an opera or a symphony, but he also emulated in his transcriptions and his playing of them the single-minded, irresistible force of the nineteenth-century orchestra or operatic cast at full throttle.

Virtuosos like Liszt and Thalberg often held their operatic showstoppers back from publication, at least until they felt they had derived sufficient glory from

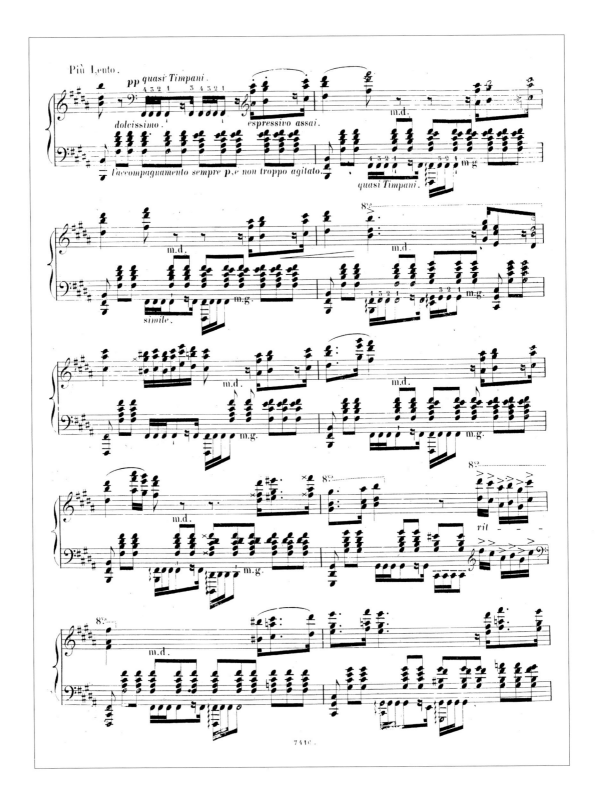

them. But sooner or later these works, which even in their composers' hands migrated from concert hall to opera house to salon, found their way to the practice room and parlor. Thalberg's *Moses* Fantasy, which in the mid-1830s caused listeners to stand and crane their necks to see if the composer had more than two hands, was handled triumphantly by fourteen-year-old Louise Mattmann at her Paris debut in 1840; that and other Thalberg opera fantasies were played—in some version, if not necessarily the original—at student recitals in American girls' seminaries a decade later.[15]

These operatic paraphrases represent the virtuosic and creative extreme of the nineteenth-century piano arrangement. At the other extreme—humble and literal—lie the piano scores of operas, oratorios, concertos, and other genres, scores in which the orchestral parts are transcribed for solo piano. Equally literal, but wholly for piano, are the ubiquitous four-hand transcriptions of every imaginable sort of music. These transcriptions were to nineteenth-century culture what recordings are to twentieth-century culture: they transported music out of the concert hall or opera house or church, so that people could get to hear it, repeat it, and come to know it. For countless musicians, for instance, there were many more opportunities to play a Mozart or Beethoven overture or symphony at home in a four-hand transcription than there were to hear it played by an orchestra. The delights for pianists in getting those works under their fingers are so great and so obvious that four-hand transcriptions of that sort have continued to be republished long after the prevalence of recordings and radio has eliminated the apparent need for them.

But this republication has been extremely selective, leaving most pianists today with no idea how relentlessly systematic the piano transcription industry was in the nineteenth century. Not only was "public" music for orchestra, choir, operatic ensembles, and dance band routinely transcribed for piano, four hands—brought down in scale so that it could be enjoyed in more private settings, presumably—but so was music that was already intimate in scale and nature: string quartets, piano quartets, solo songs (whole Schubert song cycles arranged for piano, four hands!), and works for solo piano. Beethoven's Sonata in F Minor, Op. 57, in fact, derived its epithet "Appassionata" from the title page of a four-hand transcription of the work—and it was only one of several—published more than a decade after his death. Modes of transcription like this one, so unfamiliar today, raise the most acute questions about the act of transcription. When a Beethoven symphony is transcribed for two players at a piano, it is clear what is lost from the experience of hearing the orchestral version in the concert hall, as well as what is

Page from Franz Liszt, *Réminiscences de Norma: Grande Fantaisie* (Mainz, 1844). In this page from the middle of his Norma fantasy, Liszt begins his variations on "Qual cor tradisti," the great ensemble for soprano, tenor, bass, and chorus at the dénouement of Bellini's opera. Liszt derived every element of this complex texture from Bellini's score, but reconstructed and remixed all of them to produce, with just two hands, a magically complete "reminiscence" of an operatically rich moment.

gained by way of hands-on knowledge and sociable pleasure. But when this particular Beethoven piano sonata is shared by two players on the same bench, what becomes of its tempestuous gestures, its supremely self-asserting drama? Likewise, when we turn our attention to other common forms of nineteenth-century piano transcription—the polka arranged for nine pianos (a female seminary specialty), the beginner's version of a classic sonata or concerto (an act of canonization), the arrangement for left hand alone (a tour de force)—we may be able to supply an appropriate occasion for every instance, but we can also detect that an undiscriminating market impulse drove their production as a whole.

In nineteenth-century publishers' catalogs, the piano arrangements are so dominant that it can be hard to spot the listings of original piano music. But no one in that age of Romanticism doubted that originality was important. Indeed, the writing of piano sonatas largely gave way to the writing of works with more original, or at least individual, titles—titles that suggested a particular mood or setting, dance or other activity, or story. This kind of music makes its effect by evocation. Exactly what it evokes may not be expressible in words; whether the title, however vague, has much bearing on the listener's experience may not matter. But the music evokes something beyond itself because it borrows from the languages of music beyond the piano. It transports to the piano the styles, the timbres, the textures, and the forms of song, opera, church music, folk music, music for dance bands and for orchestras. In the great age of piano transcription, even original music was a kind of transcription, but of musical genres, not of specific melodies or works. In programmatic works like Schumann's Fantasy, Chopin's ballades, or Liszt's *Années de pèlerinage*, a complex mixing and switching of generic references gives the work (or a movement within the work) a narrative-like progression. And even in works that assume the conventional titles and movement structures of an earlier age—sonatas, piano trios and quartets, and concertos—making sense of any movement is apt to depend on following the progression of extra-pianistic evocations.

For an example of this mode of musical progression, consider the Largo of Chopin's Sonata in B Minor, Op. 58 (1845). It opens as an austere march in bare octaves, as if played by low brass. After two measures, the character of this march is transformed by a full chord, and a surprising one, suggesting that the full orchestra has taken over; in another two measures the passage is over. It has been less an introduction than a transition, like a passage between scenes of an opera, just long enough to allow one character to go offstage and another to come on, the lighting to be changed, a new episode to begin. The new scene in this case fea-

Chopin, Sonata No. 3, Op. 58 (Paris, 1845), opening page of the Largo

LARGO

Cantabile

J. M. 2187.

tures the soprano, singing a sensuously mournful melody from which we know at once of her longing for her lover. With help from the march rhythms that continue to pulse in the bass and the fluctuations of color that Chopin commands with his extraordinarily effective touches of the damper pedal, this melody sings as no transcription of an actual aria of Bellini or Meyerbeer could.[16] From the pianist's fingers we sense the personality of a singer's voice, the solitary yearning of the character she is playing—a yearning only magnified when the soprano is joined by a mezzo-soprano in the pianissimo fourth phrase of her song.

Everything about this music is typical of a Chopin piano nocturne, here smuggled into a sonata: the slow, plaintive melody in the soprano range, the march rhythm beneath, and now—the clincher—the entrance of the second voice in close harmony with the first. Before the nocturne was a piano piece, it was a salon duet, itself evocative of opera, usually on the subject of love, often for two women's voices with piano. What distinguishes this Chopin nocturne from its vocal model is that after one verse, the composer transports his listener elsewhere. The song, and with it the scene, dissolves into a reverie in endless triplet rhythm, drifting for so long that it seems as if the original song has been left behind forever. It does return, though, through a more convoluted march passage than the opening one, for a second verse. This time the song is transformed into a barcarole—a boat song —because the original march accompaniment is replaced by a continuation of the triplet rhythm from the reverie. It all stays within the realm of the piano nocturne, however; in Chopin's nocturnes, barcarole rhythms are heard even more often than march rhythms. The singer, in other words, returns to her love song, but its import is transformed by her intervening musings.

The wonder of this movement is how complexly it evokes the musical world outside the piano: song melody and march rhythms mixed together; a sonata movement that evokes a piano genre—the nocturne—that itself evokes a song genre that evokes opera; a scene that dissolves into reverie and dissolves back into view; an undercurrent of the march exchanged for that of a boat song. It would be absurd to claim that there is anything typical about the complexity of reference this piece makes; most mid-nineteenth-century piano music, although it draws on the same menu of musical genres that Chopin uses here, works far more simply.

But whether the piece was complex or simple, in Chopin's day the piano it-self, as a medium for transporting listeners from one musical setting to another, added its own complexity to the listeners' impressions, for the simple reason that it was now found in such a variety of settings. A listener in that period, hearing this Chopin Largo in a concert hall, might have imagined the nocturnal scene that the music evoked, including the feel of the sultry night air in which the character was pouring out her love plaint. The same listener, hearing it at home on a summer night, with the chirping of crickets filling the stillnesses of the music—that is, mixing into the experience of the music the kinds of actual sensation that the concert hall excludes—might instead have imagined the perfumed air of the opera house in which that imaginary scene was being enacted, or of the salon in which the operatic enactment was being imagined. The richness of poetic impressions that music like this was capable of stirring in its day—and has been capable of stirring ever since—was created in part by the very prosaic spread of pianos by the midcentury piano industry to every imaginable site for musical listening.

Because it was so adept at creating poetic impressions, the piano was the preferred instrument for accompanying songs. In the nineteenth century one of the main reasons people had pianos, or learned to play them, was to accompany singing, their own and that of others. In 1827 the preface to a piano method published in Boston by Gottlieb Graupner urged customers to take up the piano with the argument that "of all instruments as yet known, the Piano Forte claims precedence as an accompaniment to the human voice; and its use has become so universal, that the education of a young lady is hardly thought to be complete without it."[17] Today certain repertories of song for solo voice and piano from this period—particularly the German repertory of Schubert, Schumann, and their successors—stand in such high esteem as concert music that it is hard to connect them with music making in the parlor, or with the presumably simpler fare that people sang and played there.

But the relationship of concert performance to domestic performance in that period was utterly different from what it is now. First, song recitals hardly existed. Singers performed all the time in concerts; in fact, it was exceptional for pianists or other instrumentalists or composers or concert societies to put on concerts without including singers on the program; but there were few concerts consisting entirely of songs.[18] What singers sang when they appeared in concerts varied tremendously, but prominent in most programs were opera arias and ensembles, usually with piano accompaniment, and if the singers alternated those arias with songs written for voice with piano, the songs themselves might well alternate between material we would consider serious and that which we would deem sentimental—"Home, Sweet Home" next to "Der Erlkönig." Nor was there any simple distinction between what opera singers sang and what amateurs or students sang on the concert stage. Acclaimed singers made many of their appearances on con-

certs given by acclaimed pianists, and a famous pianist —whether Liszt, Chopin, or Rubinstein—was never too proud to accompany a famous singer. There was little need for professional accompanists until the twentieth century.

Not that a virtuoso pianist was needed to perform the accompaniments. Composers—whether Schubert or Schumann, Liszt or Chopin—seldom made song accompaniments as technically challenging as piano solos. But they did regularly ask of the piano something that eighteenth-century composers almost never did in songs: that it play a distinct role in dramatizing the song's poetry. In nineteenth-century songs, the piano part not only sets the song's emotional tone; it then may manage its emotional course, in part by projecting some aspect of the action that the poem depicts: for example, the galloping of the horse and the stops and starts of the spinning wheel in Schubert's two famous early songs "Der Erlkönig" and "Gretchen am Spinnrade." The piano transports the listener into the scene that the words specify. But even in the song cycles of Schumann, famous for their rich accompaniments and for long piano codas at the ends of songs, the piano parts show consideration as much for the singer as for the player: a good part of the time, the accompaniment reassuringly doubles the singer's notes.

Why did composers restrict themselves in this way? In the first place, because they were writing for publication, and song publications were aimed at all the places where there were pianos, especially homes. That meant that they were aimed at both professional and amateur performers—although it should not be assumed that only amateurs performed in homes, or that only professionals performed in public. And there was another consideration, which modern performance practice lets us forget: singers often accompanied themselves, and songwriters expected them to. They therefore reserved the most complicated piano passages for the moments—like the Schumann codas—when the singer-player was not doing two things at once. Young ladies like those whose education Gottlieb Graupner was so eager to complete were expected to be able to play to their own singing. What they sang and played depended on their accomplishment at

Drawing by Ferdinand Georg Waldmüller, made in 1827, of Franz Schubert and Josephine Fröhlich at the piano, with Johann Michael Vogl standing behind them. The pianists as well as the "singer" are evidently singing. (Graphische Sammlung Albertina, Vienna)

both skills. Given that many young ladies studied both voice and piano for many years, it is not implausible to read in Goncharov's novel *Oblomov* (1859) that the title character loses his heart to Olga Ilyinskaya when she sings him the aria "Casta diva" from Bellini's *Norma*—already a considerable feat for an amateur singer—accompanying herself at the piano.

For that matter, the first performance of Schubert's immense and emotionally demanding song cycle *Winterreise* (1828) was given by the composer himself, singing to his own playing. That was a private performance for friends, but another singer-composer, Carl Loewe, gave public recitals of his songs—dramatic ballads

Anton von Werner, sketchbook drawing labeled "AvW Brunoy 24. Oktober 1870." As a soldier in the Prussian army during the Franco-Prussian War, von Werner made this sketch of a scene in a house outside Paris where he and his comrades were billeted; almost a quarter century later he developed the sketch into the monumental oil painting *Im Etappenquartier vor Paris*. The image, though sketched quickly at the time, makes a complex point about competing and yet compatible national cultures: the Prussian soldiers, invading a private French home, find a use for the owners' piano, turning it into a vehicle for imposing a sublime product of German musical culture, Schubert's song "Das Meer erglänzte weit hinaus," on their hosts. In the later painting, the upright piano is incongruously transformed into a shiny black grand. (Kupferstichkabinett, Staatliche Museen, Berlin)

—from the piano bench. The size of the audience had to be limited to one or two hundred, but compared with twentieth-century singer-pianists, who often rely on a microphone even in small clubs, he was still reaching a remarkable number of listeners.[19]

In the nineteenth century, then, songs were performed in as many different settings as were piano solos. The mode of performance varied—that is, the singer could double as pianist or have a separate pianist. Furthermore, site and mode of performance did not altogether depend on each other. Nineteenth-century listeners, as a result, had a bewildering variety of performance experiences of song, due to the wide availability of the piano and the widespread skill in playing it. We can readily imagine the difference it made to their impressions of a song whether they heard it sung in a parlor or a concert hall, but it is harder for us to say what difference it made whether the performance was a dialogue between a singer and a pianist or a soliloquy by a musician absorbed in singing and playing at once. Unlike nineteenth-century listeners, we hear Schubert songs performed only as a dialogue. Would it help us imagine their varied experience of the nineteenth-century repertory if we compared it with our own experience of listening to contemporary songs, sung sometimes by a singer who stands holding a microphone and sometimes by a miked singer sitting at the keyboard?

The performance of dance music at the piano introduced another option: to dance or not to dance. The piano may have been involved only marginally in public dancing in this period—seldom playing in performances of ballet or other stage dancing and taking at most a background role in bands that played for social dancing. The main site for the performance of dance music at the piano was undoubtedly the home. Huge quantities of dance music for piano were published for domestic use. Some consists of transcriptions of ballet scores, some of music transcribed from the repertories of popular dance bands, and some is original or derived from popular music of other kinds; every operatic melody of the day seems to have been reworked into a waltz or a quadrille. All of it would have transported listeners in their imaginations from their parlors or salons to more public dance floors of the ballroom and the stage. Dancing was very much a social spectacle, an act of self-display, and the social dances of the time, no less than the choreographed movements of ballet ensembles, were organized in patterns that required fairly large groups to realize. Dancing in the parlor may have had its own pleasure, but even that derived from transferring dance steps devised for a crowd to a more intimate setting.

It is possible to be transported to a dance floor in one's imagination without taking a step, and sometimes there is no way to tell which pieces of dance music for the piano were intended—or used—for dancing. One obvious test would be whether the phrases of the music fit with the steps of the dance, but Chopin's dance pieces for piano—many waltzes, polonaises, and mazurkas, with a scattering of other forms—often conform quite strictly to the dance patterns and yet are quite regularly said to be "idealized" dance pieces: not for dancing. The term "idealized" may simply be a way of saying that it is music for the concert hall (where dancing was restricted to the mind's body) rather than for the parlor (where anything went); but how can we know? If any dance music was idealized, it was surely the ballet music of the period, because the steps and groupings of a waltz, say, as danced in a ballet were unlikely to have been quite like those of a ballroom waltz. But that idealization raises still another question about a Chopin waltz or any original dance music for piano: how can we judge whether it was meant to evoke—or accompany—the dancing of the ballet stage or the ballroom?

In any case, if the Chopin waltzes were equally suitable for concert hall and parlor, most of the dance music published for piano in the nineteenth century was not so adaptable and therefore did not raise the same questions. Because this dance music presents itself in long sequences of short segments, many in the same meter and phrase length and most in the same key or closely related ones, ready for the pianist to repeat, skip, and rearrange at will, it is distinctly more suitable for parlor dancing than for concert listening. Schubert's waltzes, rather than Chopin's, represent this type. Some of this music is even published with dance instructions in the score, so that customers could practice at home those dances that they might find themselves performing at a ball. People had many reasons for dancing at home, and those who owned a piano had one overriding reason for using it to accompany their dancing: a single person at a piano could supply enough sound, harmony, and rhythmic oomph to send a single couple or a parlor full of dancers swirling.

The piano was also a means of transporting listeners back in time, of helping them explore the music of the past. More precisely, the piano was both vehicle and subject in the mid-nineteenth-century evolution of historical consciousness about music. It was a vehicle in that musicians who took an interest in music written for harpsichord or other older stringed keyboard instruments usually performed it on the piano. Those interested in reviving early music at this time focused on works, not instruments. It was exceptional for a harpsichord to be brought back into service, as it was in a concert given by Ignaz Moscheles in London in 1837; it was then only a few decades since harpsichords had been dis-

Quadrilles.

ORPHEUS WALTZ QUADRILLE.

STRAUSS.

No. 1. Orpheus Waltz.

Figures by J. S. Knight.

8 (or 16 *ad lib*) bars prelude before commencing each figure.

First Figure. First 4 balance, (4 bars.) Turn partners, (4 bars.) Forward, (4 bars.) Half right and left, (4 bars.) Balance, (4 bars.) Turn partners, (4 bars.) Waltz to places. (8 bars.) All waltz round, (16 bars.) Sides the same.
End the figure with all balance to partners, (4 bars.) Turn to places, (4 bars.)

carded as obsolete. The piano became a historical subject, rather than a vehicle, when pianists began to retain the piano music of the past, such as that of Haydn and Mozart, as classics in their repertories, instead of discarding it as previous generations had generally discarded the music of their predecessors.

Likewise, the piano became a historical subject when musicians not only began to keep playing works by composers of the previous generation, but also resolved to preserve and hand down the performance style of those composers and their day. An early instance of this resolve was the attention that former Beethoven associates like Anton Schindler and Carl Czerny gave, after his death, to describing the way that Beethoven had performed his own piano works.[20] Here again, the focus was on works rather than on instruments, even though piano design and construction had changed enormously in the few decades between the time that Beethoven was performing and the time that his followers were publishing their accounts of his performances.

The piano was both vehicle and subject when musicians began sweeping the music of the older keyboard instruments and that of the piano together to create a single keyboard history, tradition, and repertory, in which the earlier instruments figured as prototypes and the piano as the historical culmination. This sort of historicism manifested itself in the "warmup" role given to Bach and Mozart in conservatory training and conservatory piano programs. It was also a driving force behind such monumental publishing series as *Le Trésor des pianistes* (1861–74), which was started by the musician and publisher Aristide Farrenc and completed by his widow, Louise Farrenc, a composer and professor of piano at the Paris Conservatory, and which covered keyboard music from the sixteenth century to the middle of the nineteenth. These publications in turn provided inspiration and material for piano concert series surveying the history of keyboard music (Anton Rubinstein's famous historical series, performed in the 1870s and 1880s, occupied seven lengthy concerts), as well as for historicist music by composers from Brahms and Saint-Saëns to Ravel.

In all these historical activities a novel excitement manifested itself: that of delving into the past with one's hands at the keyboard. At the same time, the characteristic nineteenth-century habit of controlling by systematizing was in operation: works written for different instruments were combined in a single classification system, like the pieces of music in Ditson's store; they were played together on the same instrument, the way separate trades were combined under the single roof of a nineteenth-century factory; and the concept of "the history of the piano" brought earlier histories under its flag, the way Western powers in this period

First page of "Orpheus Waltz Quadrille," based on music by Johann Strauss, from *The Home Circle*, vol. 2 (Boston, 1863)

were bringing ancient civilizations in the rest of the world under their imperial control.

The Workhorse of Musical Life
James Parakilas

The pianoforte is the most important of all musical instruments: its invention was to music what the invention of printing was to poetry.

—George Bernard Shaw, "The Religion of the Pianoforte"

The analogy that Shaw asks us to consider in "The Religion of the Pianoforte" is between getting to know Shakespeare by reading his texts (rather than seeing the plays in the theater) and getting to know operas by playing and singing them at the piano (rather than seeing them staged). In both cases, he goes on to argue, it is the experience of reading through the text for oneself—an experience that saves it from the travesties visited on even the greatest works by theatrical producers—that brings it alive, allowing one to understand and feel and remember it. When he calls the piano "the most important of all musical instruments," then, he is not thinking about the importance of the piano in the performance of its own repertory, but about its importance as a stand-in for an orchestra, in situations where no orchestra is available, where individuals need to study a work for themselves, and where the piano is valued for helping someone read a musical text and imagine

Jakob Götzenburger, drawing of an early-music performance at the home of Professor Anton Friedrich Justus Thibaut of the University of Heidelberg, early nineteenth century. The piano had by then become the customary guide for trying out vocal music, even music from before the era of the piano. (Kurpfälzisches Museum, Heidelberg)

its sounds. By Shaw's day, the piano had transformed the way people learned music of all sorts, and he was right to look behind the scenes, as it were, and notice what a difference it made that a piano was there.[21]

The piano made a difference literally behind the scenes, during rehearsals. It is difficult to reconstruct how operas, ballets, oratorios, orchestral works,

Drawing of a rehearsal at the Paris Opera, in *Le Monde illustré*, April 10, 1875. The opera is *Hamlet* by Ambroise Thomas. Perched on a rehearsal platform built over the pit, the piano—joined by the concert-master's violin—literally takes the place of the orchestra.

masses, and other large-scale works were rehearsed before the advent of the piano. The most telling evidence is of a negative kind: there is little sign that musicians made or used special scores just for rehearsal. That changed when the piano arrived, and the appearance of printed rehearsal scores for piano in itself suggests that new kinds of rehearsal practice developed. These scores had the parts for all or some of the participating forces reduced to a form playable on the piano. With a "rehearsal-only" score of an unaccompanied choral work, a pianist could help the singers to learn their notes and to put them together; with a piano-vocal score of an opera or oratorio, a pianist could give the singers an idea of how their parts would fit with the orchestral part; and with a reduced score of a concerto, a rehearsal pianist could provide the same service to an instrumental soloist.

With so little known of prior rehearsal practices, it is hard to say how the piano and the rehearsal score changed rehearsing. In opera rehearsals, for instance, the harpsichord seems to have been used, sometimes in conjunction with bass or other instruments, since the invention of opera at the beginning of the seventeenth century. But the harpsichord played in the staged performance too, and its player may have played pretty much the same notes in rehearsal as in performance. By contrast, the piano, which took no role in the performance, stood in for the whole orchestra during rehearsal. Even if no reduced score was available, pianists were expected, at least from the beginning of the nineteenth century, to play the essential parts of an orchestral score at sight. In fact, in Adam's important *Méthode de piano* of 1804, instructions on the art of reading a score at the piano appear at the end, exactly where the instructions for basso-continuo realization would have been in a harpsichord method.[22]

What difference did it make to have a rehearsal instrument that could substitute for the whole orchestra? Opera rehearsals with full orchestra have always been extraordinarily expensive, and a great many rehearsals with piano could be held for the price of a few orchestral ones; in that way all the elements of the production other than the orchestra could be more generously rehearsed. It can be imagined, for instance, that the elaborate staging for which the Paris Opera was famous in the nineteenth century—its huge chorus directed to move dramatically around the stage rather than stand in place all the time—developed because the rehearsal pianist made it affordable to have sufficient numbers of blocking rehearsals.[23]

By contrast, ballet rehearsing stuck to a pre-piano tradition. Well into the nineteenth century, ballet rehearsals were accompanied by the violin at the Paris Opera, which set the pace in production methods as well as repertory for ballet companies across Europe. The white-haired violinist who appears in many of Degas's paintings of ballet rehearsals was a real fixture there. Like the harpsichordist in the opera rehearsals of previous centuries, the ballet violinist presumably played the same part, more or less, in rehearsal as in performance. Because the violins had the predominant voice in the orchestra, and because the dancers needed to follow the music but did not—like opera singers—need to pick notes out of the full orchestral texture, they could learn their steps to the tune of a violin and then move into orchestral rehearsal without confusion. But in the twentieth century, that system broke down. Perhaps as ballet scores became more rhythmically complicated, the violin was found incapable of supplying what the dancers needed in rehearsal. Or perhaps maintaining this anomalous practice in a musical system dominated by the piano simply came to seem like spinning your own thread in a world of factory-made textiles. In any case, Degas's violinist was replaced by pianists specializing in ballet rehearsing. Today these pianists develop a rhythmic rapport with dancers, the way choral and opera and Broadway pianists develop a breath rapport with singers, and in many cases that rapport helps keep ballet pianists in business even now that the alternative—the tape recorder—costs a lot less per rehearsal than they do.

In the music classroom, the piano has figured much as it has in the rehearsal room. When the history and appreciation of music became a classroom subject,

Edgar Degas, *The Dancing Class*, ca. 1871. Even though the ballet rehearsal room at the Paris Opera had a piano, rehearsals there were accompanied by solo violin. (Metropolitan Museum of Art, New York)

Dancers of the New York City Ballet "listening to the music before starting to rehearse," photograph by Alfred Eisenstaedt in *Life* magazine, December 28, 1936. Whereas Degas composed his painting as a "snapshot" of unposed rehearsing, Eisenstaedt posed his dancers in a painterly composition that emphasizes their dependence on the piano and its player. The music is *Mozartiana*—piano pieces by Mozart orchestrated by Tchaikovsky, but restored to the piano in rehearsal.

Page showing keyboard arrangements of Asian melodies, from William Crotch, *Specimens of Various Styles of Music, Referred to in a Course of Lectures,* vol. 3 (London, 1808)

the piano was there to illustrate it. A remarkable early instance was the course of lectures on the history of music that William Crotch gave as professor of music at Oxford University, starting in 1800; these lectures were illustrated in part by the Music Room orchestra, in part by Crotch himself at the piano. Furthermore, he published three volumes of music examples from these lectures a few years later (1808), more than two decades before he published the lectures themselves. The examples, or *Specimens of Various Styles of Music*, as he called them, were therefore meant to serve an educational purpose of their own. "The intention of this Work," he wrote in his preface, "is to bring into one point of view Specimens (adapted for keyed instruments) of the various Styles of Music, beginning with the written music of the ancients, and the unwritten, or national, music of many different countries; and proceeding through the works of the most eminent masters of every age down to the present time."[24]

If the main purpose of Crotch's work was to instill in the public an awareness of the vast musical treasury of human history, a secondary purpose was to provide keyboard players with "good subjects for practice, calculated for all stages of their progress." Here was yet another instance of the nineteenth-century inclination to comprehend and systematize a whole world of music at the piano. Some corners of that world lent themselves to translation to the piano more readily than others. In transcribing traditional melodies of many cultures—Irish songs, a "Hottentot tune" and a "Bedouin air" from Africa, melodies of Asian and North American peoples—for the piano, all harmonized in piano styles, Crotch introduced the dilemma that has bedeviled the study and appreciation of folk or traditional or "national" song ever since: how to transfer music from its cultural home to another setting without denaturing it. The piano defines the problem: its fixed scale, its abrupt attack, its dying tone, and its need for chords to bring a melody to life—all of which create difficulties even when the piano represents the sounds of a modern Western orchestra or vocal group—make for greater distortion still when it represents the music of the distant past and distant cultures.

Yet the piano, with these shortcomings, is the instrument that Western music educators chose in the nineteenth century for the all-purpose representation of music to students and to the public. When James Ivory turned E. M. Forster's novel *Howards End* into a movie in 1991, he hit upon a brilliantly appropriate economy in transforming Forster's famous scene at a concert performance of Beethoven's Fifth Symphony into a scene at a public lecture in which the music is analyzed at the piano. If the piano was a fixture of music education for the masses

The Image of the Composer at the Piano

James Parakilas

Vasily Shkafer as Mozart and Fyodor Shalyapin as Salieri in the original production of Rimsky-Korsakov's *Mozart and Salieri*, Savva Mamontov's Private Russian Opera, Moscow, 1898. The singer sat at what was evidently meant to suggest an eighteenth-century instrument, but the audience heard a modern piano played offstage.

Louis Boilly, *Portrait of Citizen Boieldieu, Composer*, 1800 (Musée des Beaux-Arts, Rouen)

In Mozart and Salieri, *Pushkin's "little tragedy" of 1830, Mozart demonstrates his superiority to Salieri as a composer by improvising at the piano. It seems a natural way to bring the act of composition alive in a play, quite aside from the fact that the historical Mozart was a legendary keyboard improviser and the historical Salieri was not. The effect is no less striking in Rimsky-Korsakov's operatic setting of the play (1897), in which the sound of Mozart's piano playing (provided in the original production by an offstage Sergei Rachmaninoff) is as much of an intrusion into the ambience of orchestral sound—and therefore as clear a marker of the act of musical creation—as it is an intrusion into the ambience of speaking voices in Pushkin's play.*

But by then the visual arts had already adopted the piano as a necessary fixture in the image of the composer. The stance is almost invariable: the composer is at the piano, but not playing it. The piano assures us that the composer is thinking in notes; seeing the composer in an awkward position for playing assures us that he or she is engaged in creating, not mere playing. François-Adrien Boieldieu, the composer of La Dame blanche *and many other opéras comiques, is standing rather than sitting at the piano in Boilly's portrait of 1800. Loïsa Puget, who not only composed romances but also sang and played them to great acclaim, is even more tenuously connected to her piano in Dantan's statuette of 1834; evidently she must be turned completely around from*

the piano to convince us that she is composing rather than performing and therefore that she is the composer of her own songs.

An identifying keyboard was even used to represent composers of earlier eras. A mid-nine-

Engraving after a painting by Edouard Hamman, *Mass by Adrian Willaert*, in *L'Illustration*, September 2, 1854

Lower right: Jean-Pierre Dantan (Dantan jeune), sculpture of Loïsa Puget, 1834 (Musée Carnavalet, Paris)

Lower left: Michael Okoniewski, photograph of Christopher Rouse, *New York Times*, August 10, 1997

teenth-century painting depicts the sixteenth-century composer Adrian Willaert surrounded by his musicians, as he would have been in a painting done in his lifetime. But they are not standing before a choirbook singing, as they would have been represented then; he is sitting at the keyboard.

This tradition of representation never lost its grip. In 1997, when the composer Christopher Rouse was photographed for an article in the New York Times, *he protested that he didn't want to be photographed at the piano, that he didn't play, didn't use it to compose. But the photographer knew the conventions of his trade: he made the composer sit on the bench and turn away from the keyboard, toward the public lens of the camera.*

at the turn of the century (when Forster's novel was set as well as written), it has always been a fixture in the music classroom of universities and conservatories as well. Music history teachers have expounded the Renaissance motet on it. And music theory teachers have built their curricula on keyboard repertory, centering the study of counterpoint on the Bach keyboard fugues and the study of analysis on the Beethoven piano sonatas. They could demonstrate works like these at the piano, pull out strands and fragments for inspection, and then reassemble them. Even in the twentieth century, when recordings have transformed the teaching of music in the classroom, the piano has kept its place there, in part because it permits the teacher to perform musical dissections with ease.

If music history and theory teachers have been expected to know how to play the piano, so have trained musicians in general. In the 1927 music encyclopedia of the Paris Conservatory, it is described as

> practically indispensable to know how to play the piano, even if one wants to learn any other instrument or devote oneself to vocal studies. Having to read two staves, two clefs, and a number of notes and chords simultaneously is an excellent means of achieving perfection in ear-training and sight-reading, it could even be said in *hearing integrally*, for one hears music better when one knows how to read it well.[25]

And what about composers? Louis Adam—to return to his *Méthode* of 1804—encouraged piano students with the thought that "practically all the great composers developed their genius on the instrument that you are cultivating."[26] That is an astonishing claim to have made at a time when composers were still at work who had grown up before the piano was widespread. Perhaps it should be read more as a prophecy that has been largely fulfilled, at least in the Western classical tradition, or rather has become self-fulfilled, because piano training was made an "indispensable" part of the education of composition students, as it was of other music students. Actual practice by composers is another matter. Some composers use the piano all the time, some occasionally, and some hardly at all. Ravel once scolded his English composition student for working in a Paris hotel room with no piano, saying: "Without the piano one cannot invent new harmonies." But the student was Vaughan Williams, and apparently he could.[27] It is only the popular image of the composer that requires a piano as a professional attribute. However composers produce their music today or ever did, the nineteenth-century musical system continues to define their career for them as one more function within the imaginary factory of the piano.

Henri Matisse, *Piano Lesson*, 1916, oil on canvas, 8' ½" × 6' ¾" (The Museum of Modern Art, New York, Mrs. Simon Guggenheim Fund. Photograph © 1998 The Museum of Modern Art, New York.)

214

Piano Playing in Nineteenth-Century French Visual Culture

Charlotte N. Eyerman

Henri Matisse's *Piano Lesson* (1916) was painted at a moment when France was war torn and war weary. Rather than portray the tumultuous world outside, the artist focuses on the hermetic atmosphere of the home. Furthermore, his treatment of this subject during World War I can be considered a nostalgic move, for "piano paintings" constituted an important tradition in nineteenth-century French art. Matisse was reviving but also transforming that tradition, not least in that the traditional piano paintings overwhelmingly depicted women, rather than boys, at the piano. And it was not just in paintings that this visual theme appeared: images of piano playing saturated all levels of nineteenth-century French art, from "high art" paintings (both academic and avant-garde) produced for exhibition or for commercial or interpersonal exchange to inexpensive, mass-produced prints (typically lithographs and engravings), ranging from sarcastic to celebratory in tone, intended for a popular (though literate and largely middle class) audience. The Matisse painting connects in different ways to every part of this tradition.

Visual artists concerned with contemporary life often depicted the subject of the woman at the piano as part of "everyday life" imagery in nineteenth-century French visual culture.[28] The motif abounds in nineteenth-century French popular prints that illustrated sheet music, advertisements, novels, popular literature, and magazines—from satirical journals like *Le Charivari* to conventional women's magazines like the *Journal des demoiselles* to the most prestigious "high cultural" music publication, the *Revue et gazette musicale*. The image was so pervasive that it became cliché: cartoonists lampooned piano-playing women for their musical mediocrity, social climbing, and erotic dalliances—themes that were echoed in textual sources ranging from popular novels to *physiologies* (taxonomies of social types). Subsequently, the woman at the piano became an increasingly popular theme in avant-garde painting (notably in the work of artists we think of as Impressionists: Paul Cézanne, Edouard Manet, Edgar Degas, Gustave Caillebotte, Auguste Renoir). These representations—lithographs, engravings, and high-art paintings—vary widely in terms of tone, function, and level of aesthetic quality.

An 1845 illustrated advertisement for music lessons, for example, attests to the centrality of piano lessons in feminine education, as well as to the cultural currency of the "woman at the piano" motif. The image employs conventional iconographic features: a young woman plays an upright piano in a well-appointed bourgeois home, replete with framed pictures that convey material well-being and refined taste. The advertisement's logic assumes that the viewer will recognize herself and her home in the depiction.[29] It promises that musical ability is attainable and reassures the potential pianist that "all persons having absolutely no

Advertisement for
Musique en 30 leçons
(Music in thirty lessons),
1845

216

MUSIQUE
EN 30 LEÇONS

Au moyen de sa Méthode, Mme Eugénie Lafond enseigne (par principes) à toute personne n'ayant aucune notion de musique , à s'accompagner le Chant et à jouer le Quadrille sur le piano.

PRIX DES COURS
de Piano de Solfège de Vocalisation et de Chant .

15 FR. PAR MOIS, trois leçons par semaine

Pour les Dames, les Mardi, Jeudi et Samedi de 1ʰ à 3ʰ   Pour les Messieurs, les Lundi, Mercredi et Vendredi, de 3 à 5ʰ

LE PRIX DES LEÇONS PARTICULIÈRES SE TRAITE DE GRÉ A GRÉ

35 , RUE RICHELIEU

Nota. Après les leçons, Mme Lafond met pour l'étude des pianos à la disposition de ses élèves .

Imp Lemercier à Paris.

notion of music can learn how to accompany singers and to play dance music on the piano." The advertisement intently sells piano training to prospective pupils for its social benefits. Furthermore, the visual information suggests that the young piano student will learn poise along with music, judging from the player's straight, dignified posture.[30]

The function of piano lessons went beyond learning to read or play music. In their quest to become musical adepts and entertainers, young women garnered the skills to become both socially and physically "upright." The visual language

Achille Devéria, *Prélude,* in *Journal des femmes,* May 1832

of the advertisement articulates the cultural weight that piano playing held as an arena of feminine activity and accomplishment. In this context, the motif of the woman at the piano itself is commodified by its use to sell music lessons.

Similarly, the feminine press promoted piano playing to its readers, primarily in the form of fashion-plate images, sheet music for the piano, and information about the music industry and musical culture in Paris. Achille Devéria's fashion-plate drawing *Prélude*, for example, was intended to be mass reproduced, to be consumed by a magazine-reading audience of (presumably) middle-class, fashion- and culture-conscious, literate women.[31] Published in the first issue of the *Journal des femmes* in May 1832, *Prélude* conjures an idealized image of grace and sorority. Devéria represents two socially intimate female figures at an upright piano, one seated, the other standing. His image embraces the notion of the piano as a literal site of harmony. The women are fancily dressed, engaged in a culturally and aesthetically appropriate activity, and occupying a lovely domestic space. The well-appointed interior is decorated with the requisite items: upright piano, framed artwork, generous curtains, vase of flowers. The image suggests plenitude and ease, a model to be emulated, ideally to be obtained, or at the very least, simply to be desired.

Many illustrators in the 1840s depicted girls from the lower echelons of the socioeconomic ladder as piano players. An untitled lithograph by Paul Gavarni published in *Le Charivari*, September 1843, illustrates the perception that the piano was becoming democratized. The image functions as a visual corollary to ideas voiced by social commentators, such as the *Charivari* columnist who observed in 1844: "As the piano has become an indispensable piece of furniture, and that is found today in practically every salon, in every attic apartment, and in every porter's *loge*, manufacturers see themselves as obligated to whip up these instruments in such a manner that they will fit into the tiniest little corners."[32] The lithograph visually confirms the perception that young women who inhabit a decidedly un-middle-class world were playing the piano. In the foreground of Gavarni's image, the viewer apprehends an inelegantly dressed man standing over a stove, bellows in hand as he supervises a heating kettle. In the hazy background, we discern a young woman seated at a compact upright piano, the outlines of sheet music visible as she plays, hands poised over the keyboard. The domestic space represented here—a dark, cramped kitchen—marks a departure from the middle-class homes featured in the advertisement and the fashion plate. The proliferation of images that depict both middle-class and working-class women playing the piano confirmed the widespread cultural belief that "the in-

Paul Gavarni, untitled
lithograph, in *Le Charivari*,
September 1843

Opposite: Honoré Daumier,
*Les Musiciens de Paris, no.
6, Le Charivari,* 1843

evitable piano begins to penetrate everywhere."[33] And the perception that women
from every social stratum were playing the
piano suggests that in the decades following
the French Revolution—particularly during
the economic boom years of the 1830s and
1840s—the practice was no longer the exclusive province of the upper classes.

Piano playing also served as a social and
sometimes sexual mediator. On one hand, it
was regarded as an artistic accomplishment
(rather than a professional pursuit) that allowed young women to display themselves
appropriately. Musical ability was perceived
to enhance marriage prospects. In many
cases, however, the piano facilitated not only
romance but social mobility, for the talents
of the young woman were frequently employed to improve her status by marrying
well. In addition to providing a means for social climbing, piano playing often allowed
for contact between men and women. Many
images of women at the piano exploit the
music lesson scenario as a courtship arena, to depict either innocent or erotic
interaction. The novelist Honoré de Balzac literalizes the idea of woman as an
instrument to be played by men: "Woman is a delicious instrument of pleasure,
but one must be familiar with the quivering cords; study the pose, the timid keyboard, the changing and capricious fingering."[34]

In a lithograph published in *Le Charivari* in 1843, the caricaturist and keen
social observer Honoré Daumier employs the piano as a site of seduction. Here,
the male piano teacher's body language reveals decidedly nonmusical intentions
as he leans suggestively toward the young woman.[35] In the background, an oblivious chaperon attends to her needlepoint. The pianist's physical comportment suggests that she is engaged in her playing. A caption puts into the teacher's mouth
lines containing solfège syllables that we are to imagine him emphasizing to keep
the chaperon from becoming suspicious: "If you only knew how pretty you are!
pretend you're playing DOn't talk.—You don't like me SO—I hope you'll always

Chez Bauger & Cie Edit, R. du Croissant, 16.   Chez Aubert, Pl. de la Bourse .   Imp d'Aubert & Cie

Si vous saviez comme vous êtes jolie ; faites semblant de jouer. –Taisez-vous **do**. Vous ne
m'aimez pas **si** –Et je serai toujours! **la mi** .

like MI."[36] In this case, piano playing operates as a pretense for romantic dalliance.[37] The print invokes the long-standing stereotype that male music teachers generally attempted to rob female pupils of their virtue.

The prints illustrated here are typical woman at the piano images from the vernacular visual traditions of nineteenth-century France. Although the motif was employed variously by popular illustrators, these prints suggest the ubiquity of the theme and its accessibility to the general public and painters alike. But nineteenth-century painters who painted the subject were also informed by the tradition of seventeenth-century Dutch paintings (and prints that reproduced them).

Indeed, Dutch painting was on the minds of French art critics and theorists during the 1860s, and painters would have been aware of these ideas and conversant with the tradition. As a subject in the history of art, the music lesson has a long and venerable history. It was a popular theme in seventeenth-century Dutch art, especially because the paintings were read both literally and allegorically. Pictures served a moralizing function for seventeenth-century Dutch viewers, particularly regarding sexual comportment.[38]

A typical picture of this genre is Gabriel Metsu's *The Music Lesson (Lesson at the Virginal)* from the 1660s. The woman is seated at the keyboard with one hand on the keys while a man—her teacher? her lover?—stands over her. The man represents the outside world, for he still wears his cloak and carries his hat in hand. Visually, the position of his body embraces hers, as if in a split second he could wrap his arms around her body. Will they sing together, or will the music stop in favor of bodily harmonies?

Dutch painters did not always explicitly identify the keyboard instrument as a site of seduction. Vermeer, for instance, in *A Young Woman Standing at a Virginal*, circa 1670, implies that the woman's playing is a metaphor for love, or perhaps literally a prelude to it. The woman's warm, welcoming gaze implies amorousness, while the Cupid figure in the painting directly behind her presides over the domestic space as he strikes a victorious pose. Furthermore, in the narrative logic of the picture, the empty chair in the right foreground will soon be occupied, undoubtedly by a male visitor. Her attention, we sense, will not long remain on her music.

Seventeenth-century Dutch genre painting (depictions of everyday life) enjoyed a revival in nineteenth-century France, particularly in the 1860s. In large measure, the renewed interest in Vermeer and his peers was fueled by the art critic Théophile Thoré-Bürger.[39] The critic owned the Vermeer and used an engraved reproduction of it to illustrate one in a series of articles he wrote for the

Gabriel Metsu, *The Music Lesson (Lesson at the Virginal)*, 1660s (Musée du Louvre, Paris)

Gazette des Beaux-Arts in 1866.[40] Reproductions of Dutch paintings therefore joined the stream of popular imagery already saturated with representations of women at the piano.

The young, and at the time experimental, painters (Cézanne, Degas, Manet, Caillebotte, and Renoir) who took up this theme thus had access to two significant touchstones for these images: recent French prints and seventeenth-century Dutch paintings and their reproductions. Nineteenth-century French genre paintings that depict the theme of a woman at a keyboard instrument are indebted to and visually update these two precedents. Furthermore, we cannot overlook the enduring ubiquity of the woman at the piano in the popular press, nor the prominence of piano playing in the social and familial milieu experienced by this group of young artists. Each artist's treatment of the theme indexes a different note in modern life and painting: Cézanne's somewhat sardonic portrayal of his sister, Degas's and Manet's social intimacy and tension, Caillebotte's backdrop of sexual drama, and Renoir's commercial and historical ambitions.

During the 1860s, Cézanne painted the woman at the piano theme three times, yet only one version survives: his *Young Girl at the Piano (Overture to Tannhäuser)*, circa 1869–70.[41] The painting depicts two women in a somewhat cramped domestic space that does not resonate with the seventeenth-century Dutch pictures. It does, however, utilize the compositional conventions and the sardonic tone seen in popular images. Furthermore, the colors, patterns, composition, and angularity of the figures emphasize a decidedly modernist pictorial agenda. As a young woman dressed in white plays the upright piano, an older woman sits, focused on her needlework and, presumably, listening to her daughter play. Although she looks like a chaperon from the tradition of popular lithographs, in this case there is no threat of seduction; the male gaze is held by the viewer (and the painter) outside the picture space.[42] Cézanne casts his unmarried sister as trapped by family life and literally anchored by the piano.

The title implies that she is playing a transcription of the Overture to *Tannhäuser:* domesticated Wagner. It is quite possible that amateur pianists such as Cézanne's sister would have played a transcription from the *Tannhäuser* score in the late 1860s. The opera famously bombed in Paris in 1861. As early as 1860, however, the music and art critic Champfleury commented that "the Overture to *Tannhäuser* was already known in Paris to those who heard it in a one franc concert between a polka and a quadrille, insofar as it allowed for delightful conversations between coulissiers [stagehands] and the girls."[43] His reference to a one-franc concert suggests that one piece of Wagner's music at least was reaching a

Jan Vermeer, *A Young Woman Standing at a Virginal*, ca. 1670 (National Gallery, London)

popular audience in Paris even before it reached the stage of the elite Opéra. Cézanne's painting testifies to another path of popularization: domesticated Wagner was democratized Wagner.

The group we think of as Impressionists socialized together at events that centered on musical experience in public and private spaces. In addition to attending opera, ballets, and concerts, many of these young painters attended musical soirées hosted by Edouard Manet and his wife, Suzanne, a talented pianist. Suzanne's playing was admired by the painters and music lovers Edgar Degas and Henri Fantin-Latour and so respected by the composer Emmanuel Chabrier that he dedicated his 1873 *Impromptu* for piano to her.[44] Apparently, too, Suzanne played Wagner on the piano for Charles Baudelaire as he lay on his deathbed.[45] Manet's friends were effusive in their praise for Suzanne's playing: Fantin wrote rhapsodic letters about Madame Manet's performance of Schumann and Beethoven, while Degas expressed his appreciation for the Manets' musical evenings in paint. In the late 1860s, Degas painted a dual portrait: Suzanne at the piano, Manet as listener.

This painting, *Edouard Manet and Madame Manet* (circa 1868), amounts to a kind of double homage to musical amateurism. As a portrait of Suzanne at the piano, it is a pictorial tribute to her talent in a nonvisual realm of artistry. It functions, too, as a portrait of Manet as listener, for his pose, gesture, and facial expression signal a state of reverie. Degas's painting celebrates the engagement of player and listener rapt in the production and consumption of invisible, immaterial sound. The picture is intimate in subject matter, setting, and the circumstances of its production, for Degas offered it to Manet both as a token of friendship and as material proof of his own status as a music lover. Manet received the picture with disastrous results. As Degas reported to the picture dealer Ambroise Vollard, Manet was so displeased with the portrayal of Suzanne that he reacted by cutting off the

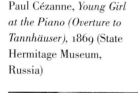

Paul Cézanne, *Young Girl at the Piano (Overture to Tannhäuser),* 1869 (State Hermitage Museum, Russia)

right side of the picture. Upon seeing the disfigured canvas, Degas removed it and departed abruptly, "without even saying goodbye."[46]

Later that year, in a gesture that seems equally competitive and proprietary, Manet undertook his own version of his wife at the piano. Thus, his *Madame Manet at the Piano* (1868) acts as a corrective to the earlier conception in that it compensates for the cut-off right side of Degas's double portrait. This time Manet excises his own body from the scene and focuses exclusively on his wife playing the piano. This work asserts that his status as a listening amateur is a given—literally built into the painter-sitter and husband-wife relationship. This small work, painted of his wife, for his wife, was intimate in every regard: subject, scale, function. It was, for all intents and purposes, a testament of Manet's love for his wife, for it was exhibited only once, in 1884, and remained in her possession until her death in 1906. The painting remained Manet's only treatment of the theme.

Significantly, both Degas's and Manet's portrayals of Suzanne at the piano were conceived as private works. Thus, they express social intimacy and noncommercial intentions. Degas hung the violated painting in his home until his death in 1917, and the work was never exhibited in public. But Degas returned to the woman at the piano theme in 1869 with more public aspirations in mind. He submitted his *Madame Camus au piano* (1869) to the Salon of 1869, an official art exhibition. It was rejected by the conservative exhibition jury (though a subsequent portrait, *Madame Camus en rouge*—not at the piano—was accepted by the Salon in 1870). In the 1869 work, Madame Camus faces the viewer frontally as she touches the keyboard with her right hand, and in this sense the work adheres to the conventions of portraiture, not the subgenre of the woman at the piano. The piano in the portrait functions as an attribute of Madame Camus's identity rather

Edgar Degas, *Edouard Manet and Madame Manet*, ca. 1868 (Kitakyushu Municipal Museum of Art, Japan)

than as a site of activity. Her formal pose and direct acknowledgment of the viewer underscore that the work is a portrait in the grand tradition. Apparently, Degas was very proud of his accurate, legible rendition of the Beethoven score.[47] Perhaps it was the same music that he had heard Suzanne play so many times at the Manets' musical parties.

In contrast to the tension between Manet and Degas, paintings of women at the piano seem to have nourished the friendship between Gustave Caillebotte and Auguste

Edouard Manet, *Madame Manet at the Piano*, 1868 (Musée d'Orsay, Paris)

Renoir. At the second Impressionist exhibition in 1876, both painters exhibited piano pictures. Whereas Renoir's painting *Femme au piano* (1875; presently in the Art Institute of Chicago, Ryerson Collection) depicts the more typical theme, Caillebotte's work presents his brother Martial playing a grand piano in a domestic interior. Caillebotte's work, *Jeune homme jouant du piano* (reproduced in the Introduction), was received especially well by the critics because of the perceived seriousness of his male player.

In his essay on the works in the 1876 exhibition, Edmond Duranty noted—and celebrated—dramatic changes registering in the artistic production of his contemporaries.[48] Duranty advocated that artists dispense with "formulaic" approaches (such as emulating past traditions) and instead depict figures in the contexts of their everyday lives, bathed in the light of the contemporary moment, in the context of real surroundings that "indicate [their] financial position, class, and profession. The individual will be at a piano, examining a sample of cotton in an office, or waiting in the wings for the moment to go on stage, or ironing on a makeshift table."[49] Duranty's admonition must have resonated with painters: his words fit neatly with the pictures in the 1876 exhibition, and artists continued to follow his critical directive.

In 1881 Caillebotte painted *The Piano Lesson*, a work that depicts two women

Edgar Degas, *Madame Camus at the Piano*, 1869 (Foundation E. G. Bührle Collection, Zurich)

seated together at the keyboard, intently gazing at the sheet music before them. This piano lesson is not the site of erotic exchange, but the painting itself is implicated in a complicated sexual drama. Although the identities of the women have not been firmly established, it has been suggested that the one on the left is the visiting student, for she still wears her hat. Interestingly, Caillebotte gave this work to his friend the painter Claude Monet. It was never exhibited and remained in the Monet family until 1966. Monet's link to the subject may be the woman on the right, who was perhaps meant to be his then-mistress (and future wife). At the time she was married to Monet's dealer Ernest Hoschedé—who in soap-operatic fashion was paying for one of Monet's apartments while Caillebotte paid for the other.[50]

An overt visual connection to Monet's work registers in the passage above the piano—either a mirror or a Monet painting. Though ambiguously rendered, the painted surface approximates Monet's brushwork and palette; it seems not to reflect the vase that occupies the space between the sheet music and the wall. Additionally, the fact that Monet hung the painting in his bedroom until his death in 1906 points to the intimate resonance the subject and the painting must have held for him.[51] Although the identity of the female figure remains mysterious, the circumstances of the painting suggest that Monet, the Hoschedés, and Caillebotte were involved in thematically—and practically—complex webs of personal and financial ties that crystallized around paintings of women at the piano.

Significantly, in 1892, Caillebotte received one such painting as a gift from Auguste Renoir (inscribed "To my friend G. Caillebotte, Renoir"). It stands as a reminder of Renoir's appreciation for Caillebotte, of the reciprocal nature of friendship between the artists, and it also acknowledges the painters' shared love of music, because they often attended concerts and soirées together.[52] This work is one of a series of six that depict the same scene with slight pictorial, compositional, and narrative variations.

The woman at the piano subject had implications for Renoir's artistic identity that went far beyond his friendship with Caillebotte. Indeed, he was the most prolific painter of this theme in nineteenth-century French painting. Renoir's treatment of the motif throughout his career suggests that the subject served his artistic ambitions extremely well. For a complex set of reasons, the most intriguing group of paintings that depict this subject is the series Renoir produced in 1892: six variations that represent a pair of adolescent girls at an upright piano.[53] Significantly, this serial project culminated in a state purchase—the first of Renoir's career and the only direct purchase from the artist as opposed to works that would

Gustave Caillebotte, *The Piano Lesson*, 1881 (Musée Marmottan–Claude Monet, Paris)

later be bequeathed to the state's collection.[54] The work—probably the last of the six in the series—was purchased "off the rack" in Renoir's studio by Henri Rou-jon, minister of fine arts.[55]

Renoir's serial treatment of the six *Jeunes filles au piano* paintings varies in color, tonality, surface, and composition. Each painting depicts a seated young blonde woman as she touches the keys of an upright piano with her right hand and grasps sheet music with her left, as if she has just turned the page or is about to do so. A brunette companion stands at her side and leans inward in a gesture that bespeaks casual intimacy. Both girls consistently focus on the sheet music, their partially open mouths suggesting either song or rapt attention. Musical notations are implied in Renoir's depictions of the sheet music, yet they remain illegible in all six versions.

Renoir's serial practice resembles the project of his friend and Impressionist compatriot Monet, who painted and exhibited at least twenty multiples of the *Grainstacks* of 1889–91.[56] Whereas Monet focuses on the chromatic and tonal variations germane to the study and representation of landscape, Renoir brings the changeable pictorial weather indoors and domesticates it within the fictional confines of the bourgeois salon. Renoir's translation of the serial form from land-scape to figural painting reveals an ambitious artistic agenda that was at once pictorially innovative and commercially savvy.

Musicality within the work is expressed at the level of the painter's chro-matic, compositional, and iconographic choices. The harmony of color reinforces that of theme: soft greens, peaches, and pinks permeate the domestic space and envelop the girls. Renoir wishes to saturate our visual, aural, and physical senses, and the vehicle for this multifaceted sensory experience is the *jeunes filles:* one produces sound from the instrument; the other leans over her, both as participant in the musical act and as audience.

Most of Renoir's piano pictures were intended for consumption by a diverse public. For example, the coincidence of the state's purchase of the recently painted final installment of the *Jeunes filles au piano* series and a May 1892 Renoir show at the Durand-Ruel gallery was a brilliant marketing move, for it united his artistic ambitions and his commercial success. Apparently at Renoir's request, the fine arts minister permitted the recently acquired painting to be in-cluded in the Renoir exhibition at Durand-Ruel's gallery. The move is significant because the Musée du Luxembourg (France's official museum of contemporary art) was closed for reorganization until late in the year. The state's picture was displayed at a commercial gallery *before* it was displayed for the public in the

noncommercial, official space of the contemporary art museum. Thus, the presence of the state's version within the commercial space of the gallery lent authority to Renoir's and his dealer's enterprise. The work effectively was guaranteed heightened publicity and a high-profile spot in the Parisian art world. Indeed, the moment this last picture in the *Jeunes filles au piano* series was publicly displayed in the museum, the painting, the painter—and, arguably, the subject matter—garnered the high-profile stamp of official artistic legitimacy.

While the state purchase in 1892 represents the highest public achievement an artist could hope for, Renoir continued to paint the "woman at the piano" for private purposes. In 1897, for example, he returned to the motif for his portrait of Yvonne and Christine Lerolle, the daughters of Henri Lerolle, a friend of Renoir who was a fellow painter, collector, and musical amateur.[57] The portrait was initiated at Renoir's behest, and the Lerolle family did not buy the painting, though they did acquire some preparatory drawings of the work. The painting remained in the artist's possession until his death. Whereas the sisterly pair in the 1892 series are models who perform a fictional role in the studio, Yvonne and Christine Lerolle are depicted within the confines of their home. Seated at a grand piano and framed by Degas paintings (jockeys and horses; dancers) that hang on the wall, the Lerolle sisters occupy "real" time and space as opposed to the domestic fictions proposed by the 1892 series.

The 1897 Lerolle portrait, however, bears direct pictorial and compositional links to the 1892 series. In both works the piano-playing figure and the companion figure wear similar garb and share similar gestures. The Lerolles are clearly in their late teens or early twenties, whereas the *jeunes filles* of the 1892 series are clearly in

Pierre Auguste Renoir, *Yvonne and Christine Lerolle at the Piano,* 1897 (Musée de l'Orangerie, Paris)

early adolescence. It is as if, in Renoir's pictorial imagination, those young girls matured into Yvonne and Christine: they pinned up their hair and graduated to a grand piano. The artist clearly had an attachment to both subjects, for the *Portrait of Yvonne and Christine Lerolle* was hanging in his salon in 1899 and remained in his personal collection until his death, as did an unfinished version of the *Jeunes filles au piano*.[58] While the state purchase secured a place for the "woman at the piano" on the walls of the Musée du Luxembourg, the 1897 portrait reclaimed the subject as an intimate expression of the Lerolles' private life and an index of Renoir's friendship with them.

The recurrence of the motif in Renoir's practice suggests that it held substantial interest for him. Although other major Impressionist-era artists depicted the subject, Renoir's approach to it was sustained across twenty-three years. The 1892 series reveals the depth of his engagement. By treating the woman at the piano subject as a series and by targeting the pictures to several different audiences, Renoir managed to be simultaneously traditional and innovative. In its purchase of *Jeunes filles au piano*, the French state endorsed Renoir's pastoral vision of late-nineteenth-century femininity whether it represents fact or fiction, reality or myth. In the process the woman at the piano, originally the subject of fashion plates and caricatures, was elevated to a level commensurate with the most exalted subjects of the French visual tradition, and the place of feminine, domestic musical culture in nineteenth-century French history was secured.

Pyotr Kulinich, cartoon from the collection *A kak u Vas s . . . yumorom?/Have you a sense of . . . humour?* (Krasnodar, Russia, 1990)

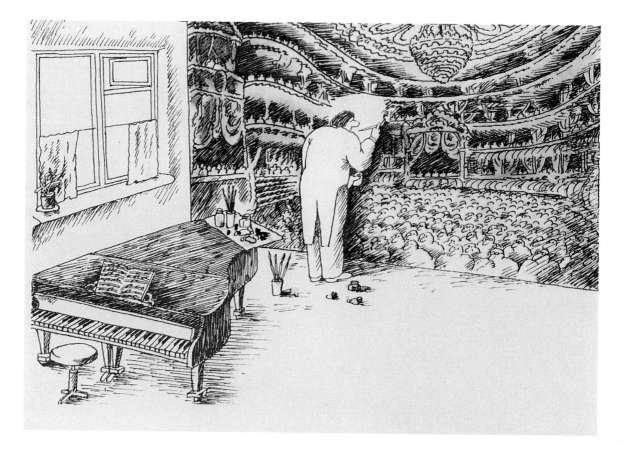

As to the gentlemen who turn over the leaves for the pianists at St James's Hall, is there a great *virtuoso* with whom they are not familiar? What exciting tales they could tell of their breathless efforts to follow incredibly swift *prestos;* and what pleasant reminiscences they must enjoy of delicious naps stolen in the midst of dreamy *adagios* with a nice long repeat included within one open folio. For they sleep, these men: I have seen one of them do it at the elbow of a great artist, and have forgotten the music in contemplating the unfathomable satiety of the slumberer, and in speculating on the chances of his waking up in time for the *volte subito.* The eyes did not fail to open punctually; and their expression, unmistakeably that of the sleeper awakened, relieved me of the last doubt as to whether he had not been ecstatically drinking in the music with his eyes shut. What are Liszt's experiences compared to those of a man so prodigiously *blasé* that not Madame Schumann herself can fix his attention for the brief space of two pages?

—George Bernard Shaw, in *Dramatic Review,* April 10, 1886

Six **The Concert and the Virtuoso**
Richard Leppert and Stephen Zank

*W*hat were piano concerts or "recitals" like in the past? It is difficult to know exactly, because histories of keyboard instruments and music do not always describe these performances, and it remains tempting to assume that such musical events were "variations upon a theme" of late-twentieth-century performing practice—that is, variants of the contemporary piano recital that audiences so often hear today. But the history of piano concerts is much richer than a simple comparison to today's concert practices suggests. Although varying traditions developed within different national boundaries, the piano evolved the same set of performing roles—supportive, collaborative, competitive, and solo—wherever it was heard in public.

Present-day notions of the concert presume the existence of a concert repertory. But much of the music played in public on the piano, for much of its history, was not specifically for concerts, or even specifically for the piano. Instead, the piano acquired—along with its ever expanding usefulness to everyday musical life—an indispensable "imparting" role in communicating to new audiences vast repertories beyond its own. As the conveyer of other repertories for more than two centuries, the piano gained vitality and prestige. Indeed, it is the decline of this role that threatens the piano's relevance today.

The role of audiences was also surely of paramount importance in defining past concerts, perhaps even more so than the potential monetary or societal reward for the performer. Concert audiences are an unusual community, one created

The Piano in the Concert Hall
Stephen Zank

solely for the experience of listening to music—earlier performances in homes and at court didn't require a willingness to sit with strangers for such a singular purpose. Moreover, audiences did more than just enjoy the music; they were active listening participants. The French verb *assister* (which implies testimony to an event) captures this meaning better than does the more familiar English *attend*. Such "assisting" participants were a feature of Renaissance academies in Italy, the sixteenth- and seventeenth-century *collegia musica* of the German-speaking lands, and the tavern concerts of seventeenth- and eighteenth-century England, where the story of the piano in the concert hall begins.

Finally, a "concert" is about the space in which the performance occurs. According to Thurston Dart, musical acoustics may be essentially categorized as "resonant," "room," or "outdoor." A single composer might compose differently for the acoustics of a highly resonant cathedral, the "completely 'dead' surroundings" of a theatrical "room," or an open-air setting.[1] In order to understand the changes in piano music and in concert programming for the piano, we need to appreciate not only the ways the instrument itself developed but also how and why halls were designed for public performances of music.

London

Our debt to the musical life of the United Kingdom is great. The idea of "public pub" concerts (publicly advertised concerts in taverns) may at first seem unremarkable or unrefined, but the sharing of musical events outside the sphere of one's own intellectual or artistic fellow travelers was novel and important. For a variety of reasons, London manifested a restless, flourishing public concert life by the late seventeenth century, and roots of the "canons" of musical repertories—so crucial to the success of the piano in the eighteenth and nineteenth centuries—may be traced nearly this far back.[2]

Differences between the performance practice in London tavern concerts and those associated with some of Schubert's Lieder in Vienna more than a hundred years later are less striking if we keep in mind Dart's distinctions concerning the exigencies of live music. Because the early piano and its forerunners were plainly instruments designed for "rooms," this is precisely where we find the child Mozart and Johann Christian Bach, the "London" son of J. S. Bach, performing in the 1760s. In 1765 the *Public Advertiser* in London announced a "concert" by the Mozart children at the Swan and Hoope Tavern, mentioning in particular the harpsichord, four-hand playing, and Papa Mozart's famous trick of placing a handkerchief so that his children could not see their hands as they played (betraying at an early date a "circus" role associated with keyboard playing).[3] J. C.

Bach had appeared the year before in a "Great Room" appropriated from a church, but his use of a pianoforte cannot be documented until 1767.

Bach's concerts (in conjunction with Karl Friedrich Abel) gained an enthusiastic public large enough within the decade to justify the construction of "greater rooms." These rooms, the elegant Hanover Square Rooms, were opened in 1775 and remained the site of the series until Bach's death in 1782; later Haydn was to write his "London Symphonies" expressly for these rooms, and the great touring keyboard virtuosos of the next century would perform in them. This hall joined a number of other concert halls, referred to as "rooms," "taverns," or the like, in London and elsewhere in the country. After the Hanover Square Rooms, the most important music hall was "Mr. Johnston's Great Room" in Dublin, built as early as 1731.[4]

Although such rooms were clearly aimed at select segments of society, more resonant London spaces—accommodating larger and more diverse audiences—provide us with another arresting image of the future circus role of the piano in concert. In 1742—three decades before the construction of the Hanover Square Rooms—an enormous rotunda was opened at the Public Pleasure Gardens of Lord Ranelagh, in what is today Chelsea. As Canaletto's painting of this rotunda shows, a proscenium of sorts was constructed in the middle of the structure to include both an organ and a fireplace, giving a nod (in an almost Janus-like way) to both

Canaletto (Giovanni Antonio Canal), *London: Ranelagh, Interior of the Rotunda,* 1754 (© National Gallery, London)

church and state (that is, public but controlled space), as well as home and hearth. Here, where Handel had premiered some of his organ concertos, the child Mozart played both the organ and—more surprisingly, given the size of the space —the harpsichord. Whatever the frailties of this instrument in such an arena, a glimmer of the piano's future roles in the service of mass public amusements is unmistakable.

A Zumpe square piano (the piano that was available for performance in London in the late 1760s) would have sounded even feebler in such a space than a harpsichord. But in the 1780s and 1790s, English makers like Broadwood made great strides in the design of grand pianos: the increased stability and reliability, along with the extended ranges, of the Broadwood grands appealed greatly to the (mostly foreign) keyboard virtuosos of the London Pianoforte School and made it possible for them to challenge seriously the violin's supremacy as solo instrument.[5] Nevertheless, these pianists, having secured the enviable role of performing "alone" before their listeners, in fact appeared on the concert platform playing almost exclusively concertos and chamber works for varying media (including voice); in England as elsewhere until 1830, solo works were more often heard in the home.[6]

Vienna

In Vienna, public concert life evolved in its own peculiar and (at least in terms of piano playing) slower fashion. The less-young Mozart ("mature" being plainly inadequate here) made his third trip to Vienna in the early 1780s and settled there, playing to small groups in the interior rooms of the aristocracy. In 1784 alone, he performed fourteen times at the mansions of the Esterházy and Galitzin families, but Mozart had learned from his travels in England and elsewhere: the following year he set up a series of six public concerts in a converted flour warehouse.[7] If the ambiance of these concerts did not quite match that of the Bach-Abel concerts in the stylish Hanover Square Rooms, Mozart's paying public (for once) was more than adequate, and from subsequent "subscription" concerts flowed his extraordinary series of piano concertos, without which our keyboard repertories would be profoundly different, perhaps unthinkable.

That Mozart had to cart a pianoforte around to his performances in 1784 indicates that the instrument had yet to be fully accepted in Vienna, despite the fact that the best pianos by then were the English and the Viennese.[8] That he looked to converted buildings for what he hoped would be fruitful future concerts indicates that Vienna had yet to provide for the kind of public musical life that London had long enjoyed. Life for a keyboard musician in Vienna was precarious at best. The third largest city in Europe (after London and Paris), Vienna had become a center of empire only recently, in the eighteenth century; its society remained unstable well into the next. Vienna's population declined precipitously after the occupations of 1804 and 1809, and the general economic recovery, though swift, was not well under way until the 1820s.[9] The structures of musical life developed fitfully: Charles Burney claimed that in 1772 there were no music shops at all in the city; Carlo Artaria began to publish music there in 1780 only as a sideline.[10]

Moreover, the social life of the city, especially after the Congress of 1814–15, revolved around the theater (musical as well as spoken), and it is unlikely that more than a handful of concert events during this period could have challenged its predominance in everyday life. As Beethoven withdrew from public life, lamenting the decreasing interest in his music, Schubert struggled to make ends meet by writing (among much else) music intended for the theater. With Paganini's appearances in 1828, a concert instrumental repertory—albeit one whose flashiness Beethoven and Schubert disdained—was finally enshrined. Vienna's own keyboard players, among them Mozart's pupil Johann Hummel as well as Carl Czerny, Sigismond Thalberg, and Ignaz Moscheles, were thereby presented with a new and startling set of challenges.

But concert opportunities for pianists were not plentiful: apart from official court, church, or theater appointments—and possibilities of performing in private settings—serious musicians were left mostly to their own devices. The complexities of procuring rooms for any kind of public musical performance at the time were formidable: concert halls as such did not yet serve the public as in London or, for that matter, in smaller cities like Leipzig, where the Gewandhaus—an entirely satisfactory facility to nineteenth- and twentieth-century understandings of a recital hall—had been completed in 1784. Until the two halls of the Musikverein were opened in Vienna in 1870, those of the Redoutensaal in the Hofburg (the Hapsburg palace) were the principal alternatives: the larger of these was essentially an opera house dating from the seventeenth century and refurbished in 1700, whereas the smaller was used more often as a ballroom.[11] The imperial theaters were expensive, booked far in advance, and often too large; even if they could be reserved, it was usually difficult to assemble enough musicians not already engaged elsewhere to mount the expected program of mixed orchestral and chamber works.[12]

The showrooms of individual piano manufacturers—which were highly successful venues in England, France, and the United States—appear not to have been such important performance spaces in Vienna, although makers of pianos were plentiful.[13] The principal manufacturers like Stein, Graf, Bösendorfer, and Streicher made their showrooms available to not-yet-established artists at no charge, but much of this music making in the first part of the century in Vienna appears to have suffered from a lack of adequate publicity and journal attention. Traces of it survive, however: a notice in the Viennese press in 1820 offering piano and violin instruction suggested that the instructor's professional and personal credentials might be examined at the Stein showrooms.[14]

To make matters worse, self-managed concert endeavors (generally called "benefit concerts," or "charity concerts" when the proceeds were dedicated to charitable causes) presumed a degree of instrumental virtuosity and showmanship, a condition that didn't suit every pianist or composer who might want to put on a concert. Schubert, for instance, lived long enough to hear his music performed at some of the evening concerts of the Vienna Gesellschaft der Musikfreunde, but these performances transpired in rooms "more like a musical salon than a public concert."[15] One solution, in the absence of virtuosity, was noted by the critic Eduard Hanslick: a performance of Czerny's arrangement of the overture to Rossini's *Semiramis* for eight pianos and sixteen "upper-class" hands.[16] On the other hand, the Viennese public warmly welcomed the virtuosity of the nineteen-year-old Frédéric Chopin when he gave two concerts in the imperial Kärntnerthor theater in 1829. His success, however, depended not so much on his playing as on a familiar program format that made use of mixed accompanimental and orchestral forces and included such light original fare by the composer as the Variations on "Là ci darem" and the "Rondo à la krakowiak"; ballets were featured in the second halves of both concerts.[17] This success, however, hardly foretells the course of Chopin's future, which was soon to unfold on very different terms in the very different musical world of Paris.

Paris

During the revolutionary decades, the concert life of Paris was chaotic at best. Even the city's most distinguished and long-lived series, the Concert Spirituel (where in 1768 Mlle Le Chantre had played a sonata and other works on that novelty, the "clavecin piano-forte"), succumbed to the turmoil after 1790. Yet musical life, though severely affected and in some cases stunted, hobbled along.[18] In 1791, in the midst of the Revolution, the Paris *Affiches, annonces et avis divers* announced an orchestral concert for the National Circus in the inner courtyard of the Palais Royal, where a young woman was to "perform a pianoforte concerto"; a ball was to follow the concert.[19] A few years later the violinist Pierre Baillot, who was to found the first public chamber music concerts in Paris, drew attention to the piano's place in a changing concert scene that disturbed him: "The epidemic of musicoragicomania is spreading. . . . Every tiny circle has turned into a concert society, every table into a piano, every woman into a musician. . . . A quarter of an hour is ample time to hear three Gluck operas, a few Italian finales, a few ponts-neufs, potpourris, romances, and a grand sonata by Steibelt may be thrown in."[20] If the piano in Paris in the 1790s had not yet replaced the violin as the preferred solo instrument (as was the case in London), it had obviously made substantial gains.

By 1827, the critic François-Joseph Fétis was complaining in his new music journal that the piano was displacing orchestral and chamber music.[21] By this he did not mean that the solo piano concert had yet arrived. He belonged to a long line of critics who believed that concert programming, because it "offers no plot interest like a tragedy, a comedy, or a tableau," relied on sheer variety to attract audiences: "A concert including only vocal numbers might just be tolerated if there is artful variety, but if only symphonies or concertos are heard, such uniformity would only create total boredom."[22] The particular formula that Chopin availed himself of in Vienna, however—"alternating symphonic excerpts, solo concertos requiring brilliant virtuoso feats, and vocal excerpts from operas"—was no longer uniformly followed in Paris after about 1815.[23] Instead of appearing mainly as the solo instrument in a concerto, the piano was beginning to be heard in ever-changing roles that might keep it occupied—or might keep more than one piano occupied—almost incessantly throughout a concert.

In a benefit concert for a poor family in 1835, Liszt performed among other works a rather bizarre version of Beethoven's "Moonlight" Sonata: the first movement was presented in an orchestral version by one M. Girard, and Liszt performed the final two movements at the piano.[24] And in performances of piano concertos, the orchestral part might be taken—"imparted"—by one or two pianos. A review of a concerto performance given in 1830 explained this practice as an improvement over orchestral performance, on the grounds that orchestras seldom rehearsed the parts sufficiently.[25] A second piano might be used within the orchestra, as John Field did in his Fifth Piano Concerto "to sharpen the edge of the orchestral tone."[26] Or a concerto for more than one piano might be played, like J. S. Bach's concerto for three keyboard instruments, which was performed by Ferdinand Hiller, Liszt, and Chopin at a concert that Hiller put on in March 1833.

Concerts that featured such concerto performances also included all sorts of chamber music in which the piano participated with other instruments and with singers. In his autobiography, the American George F. Root recalled a performance at the Paris rooms of Henri Herz in 1851 that would be surprising to our contemporary notions of concert making: "Madame Viardot [the great singer Pauline Viardot-García] played a difficult waltz by Chopin, to which had been added, in a most musianly manner, a melody which she sang. It was a curious and wonderful performance."[27] A group of pianos might be played together, with one or two players per piano, as in Vienna. When Chopin arrived in Paris in 1831, the reigning pianist of the moment, Friedrich Kalkbrenner, struck a deal with him by which Chopin could perform his own Piano Concerto in F Minor and his "Là ci darem" variations if on the same program he assisted in Kalkbrenner's Grande Polonaise for six pianos, twelve hands.[28] Yet in the midst of such multiplayer works that included piano, there was also increasing room on concert programs for piano solos.

That piano solos—modest pieces like the waltzes of Chopin as well as the overwhelming opera fantasies of Thalberg and Liszt—were able to hold their own within such mixed programs is partly a tribute to the improvements that were being made to the strength and sonority of French pianos (especially in the singing middle ranges). Such major French manufacturers as Erard and Pleyel had learned a great deal from the British trade during their extended "sabbaticals" in London during the Revolution. Returning to Paris, Erard reopened his factory in 1796 and Pleyel opened his in 1807; both eventually turned out pianos that virtuosos preferred to any English or Viennese instruments. For virtuosos—refugees like John Field from the London School and Chopin from Poland, stars like Herz, Liszt, Thalberg, and Clara Wieck from all across the continent—Paris was the place to make a name in the 1830s and 1840s, the center of European musical life from which reputations and repertories radiated to the rest of the Western world.

Engraving of a piano concerto performance at the English Opera House, London, 1843, from *Illustrated London News*, December 23, 1843. Orchestral performances in the middle of the nineteenth century were frequently given by raising a stand for the orchestra on the stage of a theater.

Whereas in Vienna during the first half of the nineteenth century a keyboard player made his or her way primarily in the salons and private concert rooms of the upper classes (or, on an occasion of great luck, in one of the grand theaters), in Paris a greater range of facilities became available earlier on. Not that facilities in themselves made the route to success for a pianist any less arduous. On her first visit to Paris in 1832, Clara Wieck (later Clara Schumann) faced the quandary of how to move up as a performer from the rooms of the privileged classes to those of the manufacturers, and then (if possible) to one of the grand theaters. "In Paris," according to Nancy Reich's description, "it was customary to play at soirées in the lavish homes of aristocrats or wealthy music lovers, await a newspaper mention, and then, at the right moment, schedule a public concert."[29] But by then several rooms had at least been constructed in Paris expressly for public concerts, whereas a decade earlier the pianist Ignaz Moscheles had resorted to arranging public performances in an opera house, the Salle Favart, after having duly made the rounds of other rooms.[30]

Not the least important of the new rooms was the elegant concert hall of the Paris Conservatory, opened in 1811, which owed its existence in no small measure to public enthusiasm over the institution's first student concerts. Statutes of the revolutionary government required regular public performances by students from 1796, and in the following year student "exercises" began at the Odéon, then moved to the theater of the Société Olympique before returning to the Conservatoire. A significant degree of continuity was attained in these concerts by 1800, and from then until 1815 the public student concerts of the Paris Conservatory constituted the most serious and stable series of concerts since the demise of the Concert Spirituel.[31] By 1809, however, a correspondent from the *Allgemeine musikalische Zeitung* (among others) had noted that the hall of the "Exercise" concerts (the "Old Hall" of the Conservatoire, rue Bergère since 1802), which accommodated at most three hundred, would no longer do.[32] Hence 1811 saw the opening of the "new" hall of the "old" Conservatoire, where an extraordinary series of concerts under the direction of the violinist and conductor François Habeneck unfolded from 1828. Habeneck, though resolutely opposed to engaging foreign "stars" as soloists, allowed Kalkbrenner (inspector at the conservatory) to play his own concertos and over the years engaged some twenty-two pianists to play with his orchestra, among them Mendelssohn, Franck, and—for his two final programs of the eighth season—Liszt (playing a concerto by Weber) and Chopin (performing his own Introduction and Polonaise).[33]

More significant for the development of piano-centered concerts, perhaps, was the inauguration by leading Parisian piano manufacturers of their own rooms for public performances: smaller than the hall of the Conservatoire, these concert halls, attached to the manufacturers' factories and showrooms, quickly counted among the more desirable places for keyboard players to be heard in Paris. Pleyel's hall was opened in 1830 with a long concert of varying media, featuring most centrally Kalkbrenner in another of his piano concertos; Fétis, by now more sanguine about the piano (perhaps because of the varied repertory), praised the instrument, the concerto, and the event. Pleyel opened a second hall in 1839, and within a few years the two halls featured as many as two hundred concerts in a season.[34] Henri Herz, a pianist who like Clementi doubled as a piano manufacturer, followed suit with a slightly larger concert hall. This hall occasionally welcomed orchestras, but for the most part, like those of Erard, Pleyel, and other piano makers, it was used primarily for chamber music concerts featuring pianists, singers accompanied by pianists, and other instrumentalists in conjunction with pianists. In concert spaces built and run by piano manufacturers, the piano could never have been pushed offstage for very long.

The Solo Recital In 1837–38, while on tour away from his Parisian home base in such cities as Milan, Rome, and Vienna, Liszt hit upon the plan of reducing the number and prominence of assisting musicians in his concerts; on occasion he went so far as to play a concert entirely by himself. Liszt's strategy may be explained in part as a self-protective device, a response to the strains of enlisting and working with different musical collaborators wherever his tours took him. The term *recital* began to be applied to solo piano performances very soon after, although at first it was used to describe the pianist's performance of a single work rather than the entire concert; notices for a concert by Liszt in London's Hanover Square Rooms on June 9, 1840, announce that "M. Liszt will give . . . Recitals on the pianoforte" and that he will "give a recital of one of his great fantasies." As the practice of giving solo concerts was taken up by other pianists—by Charles Hallé in London in the 1850s, for example—the term *recital* began to be applied to the event as a whole, at first in English, later in French and other languages.[35]

The solo recital was not instituted without resistance, however. Audiences nearly everywhere were accustomed to an established format, to a certain kind of "show." Sterndale Bennett had warned Clara Schumann of this in 1855: "In England, they must always have so many expensive singers at concerts that they will not always give Pianistes as much as they deserve."[36] Pianists risked failure, in other words, if they were not willing to perpetuate a system from which they could usually expect to derive little profit for themselves. In the end, it was not until the 1870s that Clara Schumann felt secure enough to attempt what Liszt had tried—also in the face of resistance—more than thirty years before: to break free of the perpetual gaggle of assisting artists and perform by herself.

The rise of the solo recital coincided with a general recentering of concert programming away from the fashionably new toward the classic. By the late nineteenth century, the formulas of the classical piano recital as we know it today were all being explored, from the single-composer program (all Beethoven sonatas, say, or all Chopin in various genres) to the conservatory model (a roughly chronological program proceeding from Bach preludes and fugues to a Beethoven sonata through works of Chopin or Liszt or Schumann to whatever counted as new).[37] In the collected reviews of music critics of the day like Eduard Hanslick in Vienna and George Bernard Shaw in London, these formulas can be seen emerging. But the older model of the mixed program with assisting artists can also be seen persisting and blending with the new. Shaw, for instance, accepted grudgingly a performance of the Brahms B-flat Concerto on three instruments (one solo, two for the orchestral parts) at "Messrs. Broadwood's rooms." "The ensemble of the three Broadwood grands was not so dreadful as might have been expected, and the pretty finales pleased everybody," he wrote. But the continued vitality of the multiple-piano tradition drove Shaw to a "frenzy of exasperation"—as it would many listeners today—when it touched a classic of the solo piano repertory, the Mozart C Minor Fantasy:

> Imagine my feelings when Madame Backer-Grøndahl, instead of playing this fantasia (which she would have done beautifully), set Madame Haas to play it, and then sat down beside her and struck up "an original part for a second piano," in which every interpolation was an impertinence and every addition a blemish. Shocked and pained as everyone who knew and loved the fantasia must have been, there was a certain grim ironic interest in the fact that the man who has had the unspeakable presumption to offer us his improvements on Mozart is the infinitesimal Grieg.[38]

New York and Beyond

The alacrity with which repertories and performance practices were transferred from London, Paris, and Vienna to the New World is astounding. Of the first great wave of touring pianists to come to the United States (in the 1850s), Louis Moreau Gottschalk—returning to America after years in Europe—and Sigismond Thalberg won the largest share of public recognition, certainly in New York. Their programs

Drawing of a concert with Pablo Sarasate as violin soloist in the Salle Pleyel, Paris, late nineteenth century. The pianist appears to be playing not as soloist but as a member of the orchestra—something that pianists did with surprising persistence in the history of the orchestra.

resembled those popular across Europe at the time, a miscellany of operatic solos and duets, occasional overtures and concertos, and various solo works for piano or violin. The American pianist William Mason made a somewhat less sensational impact than Gottschalk or Thalberg, perhaps because he promoted more serious concert fare than they did—solo repertory by Beethoven, Chopin, Schumann, and Schubert.[39] Only a handful of New York programs between 1849 and 1865, however, resembled solo piano "recitals"; the first recorded of these was offered by "Mr. Morgan" in January 1856. The following year Thalberg performed a series of solo matinee concerts, but he included selections on the organ as well.[40] Carl Wolfsohn's concerts perhaps more closely resembled a recital series. Wolfsohn, who had arrived in 1854, performed all of the Beethoven piano sonatas in Philadelphia in 1863. He repeated the series in New York twice at Steinway Hall, then played the entire works of Schumann and Chopin for audiences in New York before removing to Chicago in 1873. Later he planned a series of historical concerts numbering about one hundred, but carried out only a few of them.[41]

Steinway Hall opened in New York in 1867, but the hall built by the firm of George Steck (like Henry Steinway a German immigrant) had preceded it by two years. In 1875 the sons of Jonas Chickering built a formidable hall on Fifth Avenue with a capacity of two thousand. Here performed the pianists Hans von Bülow, Rafael Joseffy, and Vladimir de Pachmann, and even orchestras like the Boston Symphony. In Boston and Chicago the company maintained small rooms, comparable in capacity to the concert rooms of Pleyel and Erard in Paris, but Chickering Hall in New York was an early example of the larger kind of hall constructed worldwide since the third quarter of the nineteenth century to accommodate larger audiences and performing ensembles. In 1911 Alfred Dolge noticed that "the erection of concert halls by piano manufacturers is entirely due to the influence of the virtuosos."[42] The (European) virtuosos kept coming, and the Americans continued to build halls for them. Von Bülow premiered Tchaikovsky's First Piano Concerto during a Chickering-sponsored visit to Boston. American piano manufacturers also brought Anton Rubinstein, Teresa Carreño, Anna Essipova (Leschetizky's student and wife), Ignacy Paderewski, Leopold Godowsky, and many others. The piano firm of William Knabe, one of the most prestigious in the country, brought Tchaikovsky himself to New York for the opening of Carnegie Hall in 1891, as well as to its home city of Baltimore, not as a pianist but as a conductor and composer.

The Chicago piano maker Kimball, by contrast, engaged Fannie Bloomfield Zeisler, a pianist whose family had settled in Chicago when she was five, to inaugurate its hall there in 1884. And the enlightened Chicago publisher Clayton Summy, following the tradition of European piano builders, provided a recital hall (and publicity) free of charge to aspiring artists from the 1880s.[43] American pianists like Bloomfield Zeisler, following the examples of Gottschalk and William Mason and Amy Fay, continued to go to Europe for advanced training, in part because of a relative lack of organized conservatory-level training in the United

Exterior view of Chickering Hall, New York, probably at the time of its opening in 1875

States, but also because most of the successful models for aspiring pianists in the New World were European. Even early in the twentieth century, when some of the most successful performers on the international circuit, like Godowsky, had settled in the United States as piano teachers and when a few American pianists, like Bloomfield Zeisler, had established themselves on the European performing circuit, American piano students by the thousands continued to flock to Europe for study and for concert debuts to launch their careers. Civic pride might lead institutions and companies in places like Chicago to promote the talents of "their own," but they could not break the prestige of international exchange that had dominated the business of piano concerts since the days when the German-born and German-educated Johann Christian Bach, fresh from triumphs as a performer and composer in Italy, introduced the piano to audiences in London.

Two-piano concert by Béla Bartók and Ditta Pásztory, Budapest, March 24, 1939. Photographs of great piano performers live in concert are rare. In this one can be seen a twentieth-century couple who embody a tradition of duo-piano couples stretching back at least to the Dusseks in the eighteenth century. Nevertheless, duo-piano performance in the twentieth century is not quite chamber music, as in the eighteenth century, nor a substitute for piano with orchestra, as it often was in the nineteenth, but an expansion of the concept of solo piano performance.

During the twentieth century, the trend of building halls "bigger and better" has continued, creating the kind of settings presaged in Mozart's childhood appearance at the Ranelagh Pleasure Gardens in London, an exterior interiority aptly described by Michael Forsyth: "Nearly all North American auditoria built between 1925 and 1940 were based on a philosophy that few would agree with today, which likened the ideal concert hall to the outdoor music pavilion." Celebrated alternatives exist, to be sure, but such renowned public spaces as Severance Hall (1930), the home of the Cleveland Orchestra, and teaching facilities such as the Music Hall at Indiana University (1941) were designed with precisely this "outdoors" sound in mind.[44] In the design of these huge halls no particular accommodation was made to the needs of the piano, despite the prominence of that instrument in the concert life for which they were built, nor was the design of the piano adapted in any serious way for the halls.

But in certain concert halls built in the middle of the century, accommodations of both sorts can be found. In the asymmetrically fan-shaped concert halls of the Finnish architect Alvar Aalto, and even in his one design for an opera house (Essen, 1959), more space and seating is provided on the "keyboard side" of the hall—the side from which the audience can see the pianist's hands on the keyboard—than on the opposite side. It is the piano that accommodated the architect, however, in the first of many "centralized" concert halls, the Philharmonie (1956) in Berlin. Here the centering of the stage made peculiar acoustic demands on the piano, whose lid would have cut off sound to listeners sitting "behind" the stage. The solution was to create a multidirectional "butterfly" lid for the piano.[45]

At the end of the twentieth century, rooms for piano performance remain; indeed they have proliferated in number and kind, but the place of the piano in them is unclear. The architectural metaphor of the outdoors, for instance, has been exchanged for the reality of the sheds and shells of public parks and music festivals around the world. But the adaptiveness that has been shown in the creation of spaces for piano performance has not been matched in programming ideas or in the attitudes of audiences, with the result that the place of the piano in such spaces is unclear. It is most secure in the prevailing "Pops" or "Prom" format of concerts in Boston, London, and virtually everywhere else: piano with orchestra, soon after the overture. In concerts of contemporary music, the piano is least secure. In rooms that have been designed expressly for the performance of that music (like the Espace de Projection at IRCAM, the musical institute of the Pompidou Center in Paris), what has long been the most basic division of concert hall space—a stage for the performers and seating throughout the rest of the room for the auditors—is apt to be lacking. A piano is often lacking in such a room as well. It may even look out of place there. Yet paradoxically, it may be the one object whose presence can still persuade us to think of that room as a concert hall. A similar absence of stage and seating marks what may be the most important kind of performance room to be created in the twentieth century: the broadcast or recording studio. In settings like these, where the traditional interplay of room, instrument, player, audience, and sounds is overthrown, what does it take to bring all into accord?

Cultural Contradiction, Idolatry, and the Piano Virtuoso: Franz Liszt
Richard Leppert

Audience fascination with virtuoso performers at concerts and solo recitals in the nineteenth century closely paralleled, and even exceeded, that accorded popular music performers today. Niccolò Paganini on the violin and Franz Liszt on the piano set the standard: praised and damned, worshipped and ridiculed, both claimed a public attention that bordered on fetishism, a phenomenon in which an object or person becomes a locus of displaced desire. This intense public interest in these and other virtuosos was fed by the bourgeois social and cultural revolution swirling around them—a revolution in which the performers took an active, though at times contradictory, role.

During the middle decades of the century throughout most of Western Europe, especially the industrial north, the economy and the social fabric increasingly reflected bourgeois interest and control. At the same time, this newly triumphant middle class was self-consciously—and obsessively—working to define the parameters of its own identity on an ideological base defined by various conceptions of individuality. ("The nineteenth century was intensely preoccupied with the self, to the point of neurosis.")[46] But the broad terms that were to define bourgeois virtuoso superstars like Liszt represented both a hyperbolic form of bourgeois culture and, paradoxically, an alien, perhaps alienated, opposite. Stated simply, Liszt and Liszt's music represented an aesthetic correlative of the emerging middle class (although he was much the darling of the aristocracy as well), and also its radical opposite, however difficult it was then and now to pin down precisely what this opposite was. Not least, the cultural confusion about virtuoso performers hinged on debates about the nature of Art and the Artist (both newly spelled, literally or figuratively, in upper case) in the first age of the bottom line —debates that remain unsettled to this day (note the level of raw politics in the U.S. Congress over funding of the National Endowments for the Arts and Humanities).[47]

The definition of what might constitute art, and the nature of art's social function in the emerging cultural economies of individualism and capitalism, were critical issues of broad concern as virtuoso pianists like Liszt emerged on the European scene. Liszt's career as an international virtuoso soloist occurred between the revolutions in France of 1830 and 1848, class struggles that were organized around the future of the bourgeoisie. Not accidentally, Liszt's career, like that of a number of other early piano virtuosos, got its jump start in Paris, the cultural and political epicenter of these events.

Liszt performed during a period when aesthetics as a field of philosophical inquiry was first defined and, so far as music is concerned, widely discussed in journals published throughout Western Europe. No small matter: for the first time in Western history, the cultural pecking order of the arts was rearranged so that music, formerly judged lesser than the textual and visual arts, was considered preeminent. Music was the sonorous sign of inner life, and inner life was the sign of the bourgeois subject, the much heralded, newly invented, and highly idealized "individual." The European gold standard of the sonorous inner life was quickly and generally established as Beethoven—a composer whom Liszt determinedly championed and whose music he regularly played.

Liszt himself was a focus of attention for a variety of reasons. His technical facility on the piano was by myriad accounts staggering; his artistic sensibility, to say the least, provoked in most audiences a strong reaction either pro or con. In his music and performance alike, Liszt encapsulated concerns about music and the social role of art. Specifically, Liszt—and others like him—helped to focus concern over the complicated, perhaps contradictory relationship of music to artistic practice on one hand and (mere) entertainment on the other. Bourgeois identity, gradually consolidated first against the entrenched aristocracy and later against what came to be understood as the working class, was distinctly anxious about popular appeal: popularity was politically suspect, due to a cultural fear of "the mob"; popularity likewise was culturally suspect to the extent that mass appeal risked blurring the lines between those values that defined and divided the social classes.

Liszt's virtuoso career was very brief in relation to his long life (1811–86); it lasted just over a decade from about 1835 to 1847, ending when he was only thirty-five. But these were years of such volatility in matters aesthetic and political that the effect that he and others like him created continued unabated even after his death. Liszt set the stage for the contradictions of cultural modernity; he enacted these contradictions in his compositions and his life (ranging from indulging in public love affairs, some with married women, to taking minor holy orders; from a life at the edge of secular propriety, and sometimes well beyond its boundaries, to espousing devout religiosity during the later nineteenth century's most rampant period of social Darwinism and religious indifference). Most of all, he enacted these contradictions in his performances, manner, mannerisms, and personal "style."

Liszt, who effectively invented the solo recital, understood its personal and political stakes. In 1839 he writes from Italy to Princess Christina Belgiojoso: "I have ventured to give [in Rome] a series of concerts all by myself, affecting the Louis XIV. style, and saying cavalierly to the public, 'The concert is—myself.'" In one telescoped utterance, Liszt concatenates Art with self, and brags of personal agency at the very heart of middle-class identity (ironically by invoking the words of Europe's aristocratic archetype). More to the point, Liszt makes clear that he comprehended performance as a form of highly personal communication (in which he literally "recites" on the piano), precisely mirroring the fundamentals of bourgeois subjectivity. In the same letter, he struggles to name the recital as *musical soliloquies* (I do not know what other name to give to this invention of mine)."[48]

To be sure, a significant quantity of the truly staggering amount of piano music by Liszt occupies a middle ground between original composition and what we might call cover versions, for example, his numerous arrangements—better, fantasies—on popular operatic arias, or his more straightforward piano transcriptions of Beethoven symphonies. Liszt's "covers," which by definition are not truly original, nonetheless provided him with a perfect opportunity to mark his singularity by other means. Put simply, he made these well-known musical nuggets his own, either by "expanding" an opera tune into a kind of rhapsodic symphony of solo instrumental embroidery, or, conversely, by "reducing" a composition for a full orchestra to a solo that strikingly preserved the texture and general effects of the original. Music publisher Pietro Mechetti noted that "many passages in his works suggest that one of his immediate objects seems to be to turn the piano as much as possible into an orchestra."[49] This same impression is acknowledged by Ernest Legouvé, in the *Revue et gazette musicale* in 1837: "Liszt's whole career has been a challenge hurled at the word impossible." Legouvé registers his own disbelief that Liszt had announced a performance at the Opéra: how could he hope to "transport the thin and puny sounds of a single instrument into that vast space, into the hall still resounding with the overwhelming effects of the *Huguenots* and accustomed to the whole gamut of dramatic emotions, and which even the most powerful tones of the human voice can barely manage to fill"? Legouvé need not have worried. The performance included a concerto, during which Liszt "victoriously dominated" the orchestra.[50]

Modernity as Looking

The nineteenth century marks the establishment of one of modernity's defining principles: it was the age of the visual, the time when we acquired our "common sense" that a picture is worth a thousand words, and that seeing is believing.[51] The exponential increase in the availability of images during the nineteenth century—in both black and white and color—is difficult to comprehend from the standpoint of our own image-dominated place in history. Suffice to say that the impact of images came to define the entire culture, shaping identity itself in ways that could not have been imagined only a couple of generations earlier. Images, available through cheap reproductive technologies from color lithography to photography, spawned the rapid growth of the advertising industry and the publication of hundreds of popular magazines and newspapers. Images did not so much satisfy a craving as whet an appetite that to this day remains insatiable, and to such a degree that sight quickly gained precedence over the other human senses as the principal means of knowing.[52]

The sight of music has always been central to music's social functions and meanings.[53] But sight's relation to musical semiotics was cemented in the course of the nineteenth century with the full-bore development of absolute music, that is, instrumental music—from solo sonatas to symphonies and concertos—without the "explanatory" narrative of song literature, opera, and oratorio, or of textual programs that accompanied some other forms of instrumental music and guided musical reception. More than ever before, performers' bodies, in the act of realizing music, also helped to transliterate musical sound into musical meaning by means of the sight—and sometimes spectacle—of their gestures, facial expressions, and general physicality. Liszt, who cultivated and exploited a "look," is the premier performer in this sense. Implicitly, he understood that music was at once a sonoric and visual discourse, and he communicated to his audiences by both means.

Liszt was heard; Liszt—as he himself clearly recognized—was also very much "looked at." Liszt's playing, like Paganini's, fueled by technique that seemed metaphorically or even literally demonic, was matched by visually dramatic physical movements, of which both performers were fully conscious. Their performances were sometimes described as being watched, not simply heard.[54] The most prestigious form of visual representation at the time, however, the formal portrait, by definition did not permit visual reference to the dramatic physicality that marked Liszt's playing. Indeed, among the many oil paintings of Liszt, few actually show him at the piano, and those that do preserve portraiture's generic decorum by representing him as a kind of dreamer in quiet, if privately passionate, reverie at his instrument.

The best known portrait of Liszt, by Josef Danhauser, shows him seated at a Graf piano. However idealized, the 1840 painting captures in aestheticized form the flavor of Liszt's impact on his audiences. Marie d'Agoult, Liszt's longtime lover, is seated literally at his feet, with her back to the viewer. Opposite her, in a chair and smoking a cigar, is George Sand. The men listening are, from left to right, Alexandre Dumas *père*, Victor Hugo, Niccolò Paganini (looking improbably fit in this the year of his death after years of very ill health), and Gioacchino Rossini. The women are represented as emotionally undone by their response to

Josef Danhauser, *Liszt at the Piano*, 1840 (Staatliche Museen, Berlin)

the music. Sand's gentlemanly top hat lies on the floor, as if tossed aside in distraction. Although she is cross-dressed, her face is that of a woman in thrall, as if Liszt's playing has remade her into a "typical" woman. Overcome by the music, Sand employs her right hand to press closed the covers of a book held by Dumas: heart overwhelms mind, reason surrenders to feeling.

Marie d'Agoult's hat, with its fulsome black veil, also lies on its side, as if put down in a hurry as she arranged herself for Liszt's performance; her gloves and handkerchief lie atop the piano, in a small heap, as though hastily discarded. The hat's removal bares Marie's back and allows us to see her hair, in long, loose curls: cascading hair was a then-standard visual metaphor for women's sexuality.[55] In other words, Marie, as well as Sand, serve as overdetermined metaphors for awakened desire. Herein is a paradox; in nineteenth-century novels, the situation is commonly reversed: "Hair down, face illuminated by candles, eyes vacant, the female pianist was depicted as a prey to *male* desire."[56] Not the least source of excitement for audiences with male virtuosos resides in the fact that their performances often contradict, or at least challenge, the increasingly rigid boundaries organizing male and female subjectivity defined by gender difference. Performers like Liszt excited their audiences by staging a violation of a cultural taboo.

Danhauser's Liszt stares intently at the looming, oversized bust of Beethoven on the piano, looking up at the sculpture as if playing for a god, and oblivious—so it is made to appear—of the effect of his playing. Paganini and Rossini appear transfixed, both staring straight ahead, Rossini with his arm supporting Paganini, whose own arms are tightly folded against his chest, absented from his violin, as though he were silenced by a still greater master. (There are few images of Paganini without his violin, but in this instance his own virtuosity is of no importance except as a visual footnote.) The French writers, Dumas and Hugo, both hold books, but the activity appropriate to their craft, reading, is interrupted: Liszt, as it were, overtakes them. Danhauser, leaving little to chance, equates Liszt with Beethoven himself and, equally significant, Lord Byron, Romanticism's ideal of the heroic (read masculine) artist, via the portrait-within-the-portrait on the wall at the rear center.

Emma Siegmund (1817–1901) gave this account of an 1841 concert in Hamburg: *Enthusiasm*

> Pale and fragile like an adolescent, features stamped with great nobility, he gives the impression of a spirit whose wings have already knocked often at death's doors, but one that is destined to go on vibrating for some time before

its swansong. There is nothing terrestrial in the playing of this artist; I thought I saw open up before me the whole of infinite space.[57]

Similar was the recollection of Kurd von Schlözer (1822–94) of Liszt performing in Göttingen the same year: "With it all you had to *see* him at the piano! Everything he did on the keys was mirrored in his features, flashed in his eyes and electrified all his movements. . . . It was divine!"[58] These two typical reactions to Liszt in performance specifically recognize his physical body as a text to be read. As a result, the music produced was doubly scripted, not only as a sonoric event defined by formal musical processes but also as a spectacle: the language of the soul, speaking through the language of the body. Trouble is, both "languages" are subject to ambiguity, paradox, contradiction, and—inevitably—depend for their meaning on a complicated cultural hermeneutics.

The cultural semiotics of musical virtuosity were inscribed onto performers' bodies; the abstract quality of artistry and the paradoxical immateriality of sonority itself were experienced and made concrete by the presence of performers creating sound. In *Those Who Are Carried Away*, Gustave Doré's acid caricature, otherwise-sober gentlemen are shown to have surrendered to irrational musical enthusiasms; the act of looking is transformed into a form of obsession, mesmerization, extreme emotional release, and, most important of all, desire. In many ways, music and the emotional life it sanctioned were a release for nineteenth-century audiences, who had become constrained by strict social codes. As Richard Sennett points out, the Romantic artist played an increasingly compensatory role in the eyes of his audience, as a "person who really can express himself and be free. Spontaneous expression is idealized in ordinary life but [only] realized in the domain of art."[59] Musicians literally played out, visually and with sound, the exotic, sensual, and dramatic fantasies of those seated before them, as it were, the return of the repressed.

As Friedrich Schlegel, the early-Romantic aesthetician, revealed, "The consciousness of the infinite in the indi-

Gustave Doré, *Those Who Are Carried Away*, from *Grotesques*, 1849

vidual is the *feeling of the sublime*. This is present completely unrefined in the individual. And *this feeling of the sublime is enthusiasm*."[60] By the prevailing terms of Romantic aesthetics, music was the ideal site of the sublime precisely because, as an abstract, immeasurable art, it exceeded then-emerging tendencies to measure (and hence ultimately control) everything. Art, in other words, was an imagined (only imagined) refuge from capitalism's impact on culture generally, the prevailing "rationalism" that we now recognize in the bar graph and the annual report. Nevertheless, the virtuoso, a kind of superman who performed music in ways exceeding the capacity of ordinary musicians, ironically embodied a defining principle of the Bourgeois Ideal: Individualism—but at a cost and as a threat.

The virtuoso was a troublesome paradox: he was the literal embodiment of extreme individuality, but one that ran risk of exceeding the demands of bourgeois decorum, reserve, and respectability. Put differently, the extreme individuality of the virtuoso might as easily be read as the self-serving and solipsistic excesses of the old aristocracy—except that virtuosos were performing for money in a new market economy of the arts (as opposed to aristocratic forms of private patronage): they were putting on a show that respectable people paid money to watch. For some—those carried away—the sublime was experienced vicariously; others were convinced that they were simply being taken to the cleaners. Either way, the virtuoso's performance at once realized art while staging personal identity as a spectacle.

No general agreement prevailed regarding the spectacle of Liszt. A critic for *The Musical World*, writing at length about a Liszt recital in 1840, opens with a comment that alludes to vision and looking, and also with deep irony removes the art of music itself from critical judgment: "Viewed, then, as a display of pianoforte-playing, and putting music out of the question, it was little short of a miracle." In the body of the review, Liszt is presented as a false musician who leads listeners astray, with a distinct moral imperative underscored by reference to uncontrolled sensuality and illicit sexuality: "The feeling he excites is what we should call *animal* astonishment." Liszt's playing is "wonderful and exquisite," but lays "snares for the affections of the musically-unwary. He is prostituting his great powers to the worst of ends. He is playing the wanton with a noble and beautiful art, and stirring up a passion for error in those who have appetite enough to prove all things, but lack discernment to hold fast by that which is good."[61] Liszt, in other words, is a threat to female virtue, a topic that I shall revisit later.

Yet in the same journal a few years later, Liszt's effect on the audience, though perhaps still more profound, is found wholly elevating. His recital performance is equated with the rising of the sun, no less; he is described as gradually enlightening his audience from the opening bars of the first warm-up piece. Liszt's "rays" at first reach barely above the horizon, but by the heart of the program his star reaches its noontime zenith. His "exertions" are defined as "outpourings of mind" and, in a second breath, named a universalistic *"mind of man!"* Liszt is equated with the conquering military leader who produces "a revolution of feelings in our breast"; that is, his performance effectively bridges the increasingly troublesome dualism of mind and body, the bugaboo of modernity that constitutes at its core the paradox of identity. Liszt, a secular god, reforms the listener into an ideal. The listener, attending the performance for mere pleasure and amusement, is taken over by him. He "breaks us up to the very core of our soul, and upharrows the very subsoil and fundaments of our mind." Liszt, in other words, makes us (once again, or perhaps for the first time) truly human. The language is both fully informed by the dark language of possession, whereby the New Man is in fact Liszt's puppet, and provided a distinctly positive spin: "Our feelings have been unripped, torn, and *decomposed* as it were; but it is not disorganization which follows, but reconstruction, *regeneration!*"[62]

In other accounts from the same period, Liszt is not only deemed a natural wonder, in language borrowed directly from early Romanticism's love affair with untamed nature, among the most common sites for experiencing the sublime ("the Niagara of thundering harmonies"), but also a creature of prehistory and myth ("the Polyphemus of the pianoforte"), and even of the extraterrestrial ("the Aurora Borealis of musical effulgence").[63] Liszt is established as the Nietzschean Superman *avant la lettre.* Yet the hero's impact on his adroit viewers is replicated in his own being. Heinrich Adami, in 1838, noted that *"of all his listeners he is himself perhaps the most carried away."*[64]

Liszt's self-absorption does not detract from the thrall that overtakes his audience, as suggested by the frontispiece to an 1842 pamphlet (part of a series published under the title *Berliner Witze*), *Das Liszt-ge Berlin,* a satirical response to Liszt's effect on Berliners, women especially.[65] Liszt takes up the second of three vignettes, seated at the piano in profile, grandly gesturing with very long fingers and surrounded by a laurel-wreath frame. Above him and looking down from two crowded boxes, nearly two dozen women, and a very few men, gawk (one holds a lorgnette, another a spyglass), gasp, weep, and even collapse. One man holds a woman aloft for a better look over those standing in front of her as she prepares to toss a laurel wreath toward Liszt; another woman wipes her eyes while leaning on

Last. Liszt. Lust. (Burden. Liszt. Enjoyment.) Frontispiece to *Das Liszt-ge Berlin,* in the series *Berliner Witze* (Berlin, 1842)

Last.

Liszt.

Lust.

a man for support. And so on. The real point is that such strong and various emotions are produced that normal decorum is abandoned, social proscriptions are violated. At the bottom of the image ("Lust" = Enjoyment), men and women carouse with beer and wine. A woman front and center, her face displaying stupefaction, appears to clutch a laurel wreath with one hand and her bosom with the other. Another woman, just to the left, looks adoringly at a glove, presumably Liszt's, which she has presumably pilfered.

The image, for all its formal simplicity, is nonetheless cleverly organized around a visual and, equally important, linguistic progression that forms at once a visual sentence and a punlike declension (Last—Liszt—Lust). The meanings that accrue are ambiguous to a degree, but this much is certain: Liszt is the verb-agent controlling the visual and word texts. The "Enjoyment" (Lust) of the drinkers centers on the physiological effects of alcohol; the "Burden" (Last) of the theater audience at the top of the frontispiece is the equally decentering emotional-spiritual impact of the heavy weight (the Burden or Demand) of artistic experience on the new bourgeoisie (what in our own century would be named the "culture vulture"). In the middle of the emotional (Last) and physiological (Lust) turmoil sits Liszt: that is—in German—"List," in a play on words often exploited with regard to his name, the sound of which (though not the spelling) in German duplicates that of the word that means "cunning." The words are alliterative and arranged in alphabetical order: Last—Liszt—Lust; they demonstrate a degenerative social progression that the pianist activates and for which he is held responsible. The visual joke is funny, but like most jokes it marks a point of cultural anxiety.

Active-Passive

Concert halls and opera houses were at once public spaces and, paradoxically, privileged ones. Who was who depended on and helped determine where one sat within the circle of theatrical spectacle, part of which involved the performance on stage, part of which involved the performance by the audience of its claim to privilege. The musical experience was not just a matter of hearing; it was also a matter of seeing the social order enacted within an architectural, sonoric, and aesthetic frame. The lorgnette was a standard accoutrement of dress, used as much to surveil fellow spectators as to watch the action on the stage.[66] Musical performance sites in the nineteenth century were lavishly decorated, literally replacing both palaces and churches as the arena for framing new versions of human self-idealization. In the theater, social order was not a matter of the moment; it repeated itself night after night via spatial, temporal, spectacular, and sonoric paradigms all acting in consort.

Honoré Daumier, *The Public Gallery*

During the nineteenth century, musical performance space became increasingly disciplined. As virtuoso display (aural and visual) reigned on stage, listening became more its opposite—in Peter Gay's words, a "worshipful silence."[67] Social standing was demonstrated by emotional restraint; for bourgeois men in particular, listening meant showing no reaction. To behave differently, as Honoré Daumier showed in his caricature *The Public Gallery*, invited rebuke.

To sneer at people who showed their emotions at a play or concert became de rigueur by the mid-19th Century. Restraint of emotion in the theater became a way for middle-class audiences to mark the line between themselves and the working class. A "respectable" audience by the 1850's was an audience that could control its feelings through silence; the old spontaneity was called "primitive."[68]

James Johnson reiterates the point: "Policing manners . . . became an act of self-reassurance. It confirmed one's social identity by noticing those who didn't measure up, whether through (choose your label) ignorance, laziness, bad upbringing, insensitivity, or overall dullness."[69] Not the least contributor to the discipline of quiescent listening was fear: "To not show any reaction, to cover up your feelings, means you are invulnerable, immune to being gauche. In its dark aspect, as a mark of self-doubt, silence was a correlative of 19th Century ethology."[70] An audience's ability to achieve the ideal of physical impassivity was challenged by the fact that some seating commonly included backless benches or unpadded wood chairs; standing at recitals also occurred.[71] Thereby discomfort was raised to a principle of metaphoric honor, as part and parcel of disciplined attention, in stark contrast to the spectacle of frenetic physical heroics on the raised stage. But however completely the ethic of silence gradually defined concert behavior during the nineteenth century, sanctioned release from this self-discipline came in the form of wild applause when the music stopped. The audience could reward itself for its focused concentration—the *work* of attentive listening—by releasing energy in the earned "leisure" of adulation.

Still, compensation was available in the form of transference, whether by witnessing virtuosos or listening to the music they performed. Not surprisingly, such virtuosity became codified in the concerto, nothing if not the metaphor of the isolated and individualized hero against the collective identity of the orchestra, itself led by a titan with whom one sometimes worked in concert, at others times seemingly against. The height of this struggle occurs during the cadenza, when the soloist momentarily and triumphantly breaks free from the orchestra in a moment that metaphorically acknowledges the victory of steady hard work. While the exhausted (orchestral) masses/minions catch their collective breath, the hero marches on, his energies at full force.

Looking at Liszt　　Like no other musician before him, except perhaps Beethoven, Liszt was the subject of a staggering number of images from the time he was a child prodigy, within a decade or so of his birth in 1811, to his death (and after) in 1886. These images employed all the major visual media of the nineteenth century: photography, oil painting, oil miniature, pastel, drawing (in pencil, charcoal, and colored chalk), watercolor, silhouette, wood engraving, steel plate engraving, lithography, sculpture, relief (especially medallions of bronze and marble), plaster casting (life and death masks, hand casts), and caricature.[72] In an age obsessed with the visual, Liszt's body was an object of almost fetishized fascination, whether in a form that idealized him as an artistic genius or mocked him as a freak of nature or tasteless circus performer. The Liszt iconography runs the gamut from elaborate single and group oil portraits, unique objects, to multicopy lithographs (widely available, eminently affordable, yet—to use modern parlance—suitable for framing), to cheaply produced ephemera appearing in magazines. By nineteenth-century standards, "Liszt" was very visible for a very long time throughout Eastern and Western Europe. This fact helps underscore the degree to which Liszt—and other virtuoso musicians—served as cultural barometers: they outline the social construction of Art and the Artist, and the degree to which both were constituted by crossing the boundary protecting bourgeois identity.

Liszt was more than a man or a performer; he was also a psychological projection created by his audience—"ordinary"-bourgeois and aristocratic publics, and published critics alike. Liszt was a consumer product in the early history of modern consumption, and he was much consumed, thereby convincingly demonstrating virtuosity's cultural utility. And true to the necessity of capitalist production driven by the requirements of the consumer economy, he repeatedly reinvented himself—and was by others reinvented—throughout his long professional life. And this reinvention received its public due: Liszt the virtuoso, the composer, and indeed the man, for decades was continually reevaluated in musical journals in an exercise that represents the aesthetic correlative of new-model product reviews in *Consumer Reports*.

Further, much of the nineteenth century's cultural imagery was extreme. Demonic—even satanic—iconography was fairly standard fare for Liszt, as earlier was true for Paganini, and was often linked to his sexual impact on women. Via demonism the artist is linked to irrationality and superstition, a kind of pre-Enlightenment survival. But such pigeonholing is not quite so neat, not least because virtuosos like Liszt were also recognized as resolutely modern to the degree that they served as an aesthetic correlative to the industrial age.

The virtuoso, despite his strangeness, was nonetheless firmly anchored to the *Working Stiff* paradigms governing bourgeois systems of knowledge. Schumann, writing about Liszt's études, clarifies as much: "One ought also to see their composer play them; for just as the sight of any virtuosity elevates and strengthens, so much more does the immediate sight of the composer himself, *struggling with his instrument, taming it, making it obey*."[73] Schumann smartly defines musical virtuosity as opposite of what we might expect.

Open display—performance bravura—was often regarded by music critics as

an appeal to popular (read vulgar) taste, reflecting the establishment of the high-low distinction between Art and popular culture. Thus in the *Allgemeine musika-lische Zeitung* (August 31, 1841) Liszt's playing is described as "astonishing rather than satisfying, [and] more deified by the mob than received with the quieter, more contemplative applause of connoisseurs."[74] But Schumann recognized the other side of virtuosity's coin: namely, that it was a hyperbolic manifestation of the self-disciplining bourgeois. The performer wrests the chaos of infinite sonoric possibility into the shape he demands—and the result of such work is the Work. Not for nothing is the étude the perfect metaphor for the complicated links between nineteenth-century Romanticism and the governing precept of industrial capitalism, defined by what Max Weber famously named the Protestant work ethic. Frenetic performers, and equally frenetic conductors and their disciplined orchestras, constituted via sight the aesthetic transformation of human mass labor, and via sound the aesthetic manifestation of the results of work: namely, artistic production. The cartoon of Hans von Bülow conducting reminds us of things to come: the high-speed motion of modernity as captured in early industrial films celebrating ever more efficient Taylorist technologies of material manufacture. The comedy reflects not just derision but in equal measure the disquieting awe demanded by supermen, in which actions speak much louder than words. Indeed, the viewer-listener's thrall is evident in the faces of "those who are carried away."[75]

Opposite: Hans Schliess-mann, *Hans von Bülow Conducting,* in *Le Figaro,* 1884

Anonymous caricature of Liszt conducting: "Forte" *(left),* and "Piano," ca. 1851 (Liszt Museum of the Liszt Academy of Music, Budapest)

Liszt's own highly physical conducting style, in an age when men were expected to behave always with decorum, also drew attention—whether awe or contempt. But it also underlined the bourgeois ideal of industry's ceaseless energy. And as with Liszt's piano playing, his body visually "read out" the music's semiotics to the audience, as enthusiastically noted in the *Allgemeine musikalische Zeitung* in 1844, again using the image of the sun.

> He possesses the chief gift of the genuine conductor, that of being able to cause the *spirit* of a work to be illuminated in its full splendour. . . . The joys and sorrows of the music are shown by his mobile features, which reflect everything he is feeling: and his eyes, which flash with great energy, would inspire any orchestra to unaccustomed activity. Liszt is the soul of music personified. He radiates as brightly as the sun, and whoever comes into proximity with him feels warmed and illumined.[76]

Inspiration and Business

In 1841 Ignaz Moscheles, fellow piano virtuoso, composer, and conductor, confided in his journal that Liszt's "tossing about of his hands, which he seems to think a mark of inspiration, I still regard as an eccentricity, although it is no doubt remarkable that he accomplishes the most perilous leaps with scarcely a single mishap."[77] Two points are worth teasing from this remark: First, Liszt's entire body reads the music to the audience at the same time as his fingers, so to speak, realize the notes. Liszt's "inspiration," more than aurally evident, is available in two complementary ways, one sonoric, the other visual, which together over-determine the preferred reading of the performance. Second, Moscheles suggests that Liszt's gestures are not spontaneous (as Mendelssohn had once read them) but self-conscious, well rehearsed, and altogether very much part and parcel of the artistic business. Art and commodity sneak a less than hidden embrace.

Liszt's bodily movements are visually recorded almost exclusively in caricatures—as was the case for many other nineteenth-century piano virtuosos. Liszt's public career coincided with the very beginnings of photography, and was well in advance of motion picture technology. The sole technological means by which to capture his physical freneticism was this then-dominant form of pictorial exaggeration. That is, the generally recognized exaggeration of his performance style was captured by a parallel hyperbolic form of visual representation. Among the most striking is János Jankó's eight-frame caricature (p. 270) in 1873 of a Liszt performance that provides an explanation (originally in Hungarian) for each of the pianist's gestures:

[1] Liszt appears, his cassock tempering the arrogance of his smile.
   —Thunderous applause

[2] Opening chords. He turns his head to be certain of his audience . . .

[3] closes his eyes and seems to play for himself alone

[4] Pianissimo: Saint Francis of Assisi speaking to the birds. His face is radiant.

[5] Hamlet-like broodings, Faustian despair. The keys exhale sighs.

[6] Reminiscences: Chopin, George Sand, tender youth, moonlight, and love.

[7] Dante: the Inferno; the damned and the piano tremble. Feverish agitation. The hurricane breaks down the gates of Hell. Boom!

[8] He played just for us—while trifling with us. Applause, shouts and hurrahs![78]

The text implies that Liszt is well aware of how he is manipulating his audience. First, the caricatures take aim at precisely what is visually commanding about Liszt: the extreme range of movement accorded his body in front of an audience whose own movements are confined by the social decorum increasingly associated with public performances. Second, the textual commentary, deeply ironic, presents a jumble of association and mixed metaphor, as though Liszt's performance and physical presence together derationalize his audience's response to the music. History is set in turmoil, chronology disestablished in favor of free association: Saint Francis, Dante, Hamlet, Faust, Chopin, and George Sand occupy the same terrain and chronology, and these figures are linked in free association to youth, love, sighs, thunderstorm, and moonlight. The center does not hold; rational gravity gives way to sensual chaos: the reverie, the decentered dream, the Rorschach blot. The experience of decentering is made visible in the body of the artist-pianist (who performs in every respect), and decentering is

Anonymous, *Inspiration: Liszt*, ca. 1836 (Hungarian Historical Museum, Budapest)

269

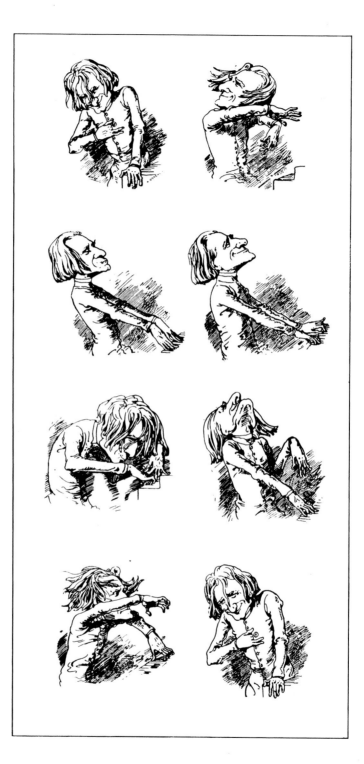

János Jankó, *Franz Liszt at the Piano*, in *Borsszem Jankó*, April 6, 1873

experienced by an audience out of control—it is experiencing the "mystical ec-stasy" of Liszt's 1840s concerts.[79]

Often Liszt's reviewers read the performance situation differently; in keeping with Romantic idealist sensibilities, many presumed Liszt's artistic integrity and his sincerity, while agreeing with Liszt's critics that his effect on the audience was profound:

> But the joy which seizes possession of Liszt, inspiring him to ever greater enthusiasm, reveals that this way of playing, far from straining for empty ef-fect, is but the expression of his innermost being and of the sentiment that dominates him. . . . I am convinced that at the moment he sits down at the piano he has forgotten the audience packed closely around him and is so pre-occupied with his performance that he no longer has eyes or ears for anything besides. It is this that marks out the genuine artist, and those who maintain that at his concerts Liszt performs for his public alone, and not for himself as well, have never understood or apprehended him![80]

Heinrich Adami, who wrote these words about an 1839 performance in Vi-enna, introduces two key components of Romantic artistic authenticity: domina-tion of the artist by the art he brings to life—replicating the terms of spiritual possession—and sincerity. Yet Adami recognizes that authenticity, dependent on these two qualities, cannot be objectively determined. The artist's claim to authen-ticity is willed onto the artist by the auditor-believer. Nonetheless, a crucial com-ponent of modernity is anchored in Romantic authenticity. Seeing is believing.

Later in the same review, Adami comments on Liszt's physical stamina and his apparent exhaustion, which together both underscore the critic's point and raise Liszt's artistic credentials by alluding to his suffering. Liszt's own Fantasy, *Réminiscences des "Puritains"* (S. 390), after Bellini's *I Puritani*, is, to quote Adami,

> performed with a power and stamina that would have been a source of aston-ishment in any other player, but not in Liszt who, when carried away by his own inspiration, appears to forget all physical suffering and not to notice any weariness until the final chord has died away beneath his hands. Experience has long since shown that artists never play better than in an agitated, ailing condition, and thus it seemed to me and many others that never had we heard Liszt play better than he did on this occasion!

The editor of the *Edinburgh Review*, Henry Reeve, left what has become a famous account of an 1835 Liszt performance in Paris. Although it is impossible to know the precise accuracy of Reeve's memoir, what matters most is the evident expectation that both Liszt himself and his audience will experience an emotional release triggered by Liszt's playing.

> As the closing strains began [from one of the Venetian boat songs in Mendelssohn's *Songs without Words*], I saw Liszt's countenance assume that agony of expression, mingled with radiant smiles of joy, which I never saw in any other human face, except in the paintings of our Saviour by some of the early masters; his hands rushed over the keys, the floor on which I sat shook like a wire, and the whole audience were wrapped in sound, when the hand and frame of the artist gave way; he fainted in the arms of the friend who was turning over [the pages] for him, and we bore him out in a strong fit of hysterics. The effect of this scene was really dreadful. The whole room sat breathless with fear, till Hiller came forward and announced that Liszt was already restored to consciousness and was comparatively well again.[81]

Liszt transfixes his audience, while Reeve deifies him. Liszt's playing seemingly embraces the entire audience and virtually ravishes them with its physical prowess. Thus captivated, the onlookers experience—and to a degree witness—a musical and physical climax that shakes the room, followed by an equally dramatic physical collapse and loss of consciousness. This total decentering of the self before an audience is described in explicitly postcoital terms: Reeve ends his account by remarking that both he and his female companion "trembled like poplar leaves," held as they were in Liszt's thrall. In the instant of his collapse, the hyperphallic pianist-artist is literally transformed into his extreme opposite, the fainting woman who nonetheless conveniently revives to become hysterical.[82] The instability of assigned gender norms in Liszt's condition—*hysteria* in the nineteenth century named a psychosexual condition ascribed to women—defines no small part of Reeve's fascination. Libidinal audience excitement was stimulated by male virtuosos, who publicly leapt back and forth across the increasingly higher walls of gender boundaries under construction during this period.

Identification with the Machine

Romantic artistic identity depends on bridging cultural gaps, on establishing a relation between opposites and holding them in productive tension. Thus the rationalized mechanization of the new Industrial Age, of which the piano itself was a perfect example, is connected to its extreme opposite, the freewheeling, seemingly unpredictable, improviser-composer virtuoso.[83]

Whereas the movements of the steam engine's pistons and the factory gears driven by these engines are fully planned, the pianist performing on the machinery of the piano, itself the direct result of factory production, apparently escapes the instrumental rationality of the Machine Age. At the same time, the staggering numbers of performances (of increasingly difficult pieces) given by virtuosos like Liszt do exaggerated honor to the bourgeois work ethic on which the Industrial Age depended for its success, the effect increased proportionally by the cultural value assigned to the difficulty of the music played. Virtuoso performance constituted an aesthetic transformation of bourgeois male heroics. In the course of Liszt's most active years as a virtuoso performer (1839–47), he gave more than one thousand performances, one concert every three days on average.[84] Liszt's mystique in this regard continued long after his career as a frenetic traveling virtuoso ended. A published caricature from 1876 shows an intent and somewhat demonic Liszt seated at the keyboard of his "musical steam engine," a veritable one-man brass and percussion band, replete with a steam whistle and bell, reminiscent of factory signaling devices, and the odd woodwind. Ludwig Bösendorfer fires the furnace chamber of Liszt's instrument, while the steamy spirit of Wagner rises from the bell of a French horn that does double duty as a smokestack.

Not only does the history of piano design, manufacture, and distribution in the nineteenth century serve as a perfect metaphor of capitalist economic principles in operation; the piano itself has been an agent of capitalism's political, economic, and ideological success. Robert Winter has pointed out that "the nineteenth-century piano was a self-sufficient, all-conquering machine. . . . On no other instrument except the organ (where issues of portability and repertoire limited the possibilities) could one person impose his or her will more completely on the music."[85] Winter's point may be pushed further: the virtuoso pianist was himself likened to a machine, and thereby rendered at once superhuman and not human at all. Just as the technical "rationality" of machines remained outside the scope of common knowledge, much like the computer or the automobile engine today, so also was the virtuosic capacity of performers like Liszt beyond the scope of ordinary understanding. The mystery of machines, and of virtuosos performing on a musical machine, fed from contemporaneous fascinations with and anxieties over the brave new industrial world. The saving grace of musicians in this respect was that they demonstrated a magical ability to out-machine the machinery. Music in general, and the performances of piano virtuosos in particular, served as an

Karl Klič, *The Bayreuth Musical Steam Engine*, in *Humoristische Blätter*, August 20, 1876

aesthetic analog to economic, political, technological, and cultural modernity. Indeed, Liszt experienced the most direct interface of his own playing with the archetypal sign of modernity, the railroad. His account, from 1838, is in a letter written from Milan:

> A gentleman preoccupied with the progress being made by industrialism, and struck by the advantage there would be in having oneself transported from Milan to Venice in six hours, gave me for a theme: La strada di ferro [the railway]. A theme like this I saw no way of dealing with other than by an uninterrupted series of glissandi from the top of the piano to the bottom; and, fearing to break my wrists in this contest of speed with a locomotive, I hastened to open the final note.[86]

A French engraving of pianist Sigismond Thalberg produced around the time of his triumphant arrival in Paris (where he was soon to be locked in direct competition with Liszt) assigns the performer eight arms with forty digits that, judging from his placid visage, appear to work independently and dependably, in perfect synchronization.[87] The pianist's right arms appear to rotate like a sprocket, bringing each of its multiple hands into use at a predetermined point, a musical machine par excellence. And following basic principles of industrial planning, there is a parts supply in the form of spare left and right arms kept in Thalberg's pockets. (In fact, during a performance, very little of Thalberg's body moved, apart from his hands, thereby producing a quite uncanny visual effect, very much the opposite of Liszt.)[88] The late-twentieth-century fascination with multitasking and multifaceted corporate executives preserves the trope and demonstrates its still current centrality to modern identity. The front page of a recent *Toronto Globe and Mail* arts section reads: "The Player: Michael Levine makes culture deals the way other people make coffee. If you've never heard of him, that's because he likes it that way."

Anonymous, *Sigismond Thalberg*, ca. 1835–40 (Bibliothèque Nationale, Paris)

Laurence Acland, *The Player*, photo-illustration of Michael Levine, *Toronto Globe and Mail*, October 25, 1997

Opposite: Anonymous, *Liszt-Fantasy*, in *La Vie Parisienne*, April 3, 1886

In a satiric magazine illustration published in Paris in 1886, the year Liszt died at seventy-four, the composer-performer's musical prowess is directly and unambiguously linked to sexual potency, evident in the hyperphallic ceremonial "sword of honor" slung from his waist. Liszt's eight arms and multiple long fingers only reinforce the phallocentrism of the image, and not coincidentally equate him with the insect world, the arms and fingers in abundance also resonating with another popular image of the time, the sexually rapacious Medusa. Celebrated for her commanding, captivating, and ultimately castrating look, Medusa is ultimately "castrated" herself by Perseus, who cuts off her head, thereby restoring patriarchal order to its "rightful" place.

Liszt's hands were prominently featured in the many paintings and prints of him produced throughout his life. His hands were also the subject of a marble sculpture and several times were cast in plaster.[89] Not least, they generated quite a bit of prose. Anne Hampton Brewster wrote about them at length, framed by a question asked of her by Liszt himself: "What can you make of my hand?" Brewster then projects onto his hand the confirmation of his biography and her own emotional transference:

LISZT ET LA MESSE DE GRAN. — *Dominus robiscum.....* avec trompettes, canons et fusillades. Étrange que cette messe, composée par un abbé, soit sans contredit la moins religieuse que nous ayons jamais entendue.

LISZT ET TOUTES SES CROIX. — Pourrait s'en faire un complet, qui la chevelure aidant, serait tout à fait decent. Sans compter qu'au moindre mouvement tout cela rendrait un son argentin, préférable encore aux coups de grosse caisse donnés par Mme Hunyadi.

LISZT, SA MUSE ET SA MAIN. — L'une assez agréable, ma foi, tant qu'elle se contente de porter son costume national hongrois. L'autre, main fatale, terrible exemple de prédestination. Où mettre de pareilles mains, si ce n'est sur un piano ?

LISZT ET SON SABRE — Y a renonce aujourd'hui, après avoir reconnu qu'il faisait plus de mal au piano avec ses seules mains. Spécimen étrange de la race des tentaculifères. Huit mains à quatre octaves chacune, trente-deux octaves !!!

LISZT ET SES CZARDAS. — En cheuxique dans l'intervalle nous ayons entendu les Tziganes, dont le moindre coup d'archet ou de czimbalum vaut toutes les rapsodies du monde. Et puis, depuis le fameux voyage à Pesth, je me defie de la Hongrie. Si tout cela n'était qu'une blague !

LISZT A ROME. — Désesperant de le faire renoncer au piano, à ses pompes et à ses œuvres, le pape — ceci est peu connu — le destina à faire faire aux huit mains leur purgatoire sur la terre. Ceci explique bien des choses, surtout les defiles dans l'église avec toutes les patronesses, les entrées dans le monde au bras de Mme Hunyadi, et ces ovations sans motifs et sans fin, que nous acceptons comme une épreuve d'en haut.

The palm is covered with rays, betraying that his life has been an agitated, eventful one, full of passion and emotion, [here Brewster defined the singular Artist Genius]—but the philosophic and material noeuds, or knots, on the Apollo and Mercury fingers, the logic and will on that wonderful long thumb, which extends beyond the middle joint of the fore-finger, shows how this remarkable man has been able to conquer instincts and govern temperament [and here she first acknowledges more than a hint of sexual excitement, only to underscore the degree to which Liszt himself has conquered his instincts]. According to palmistry, this self-control is shown in the palm lines, which are a little defaced. [A respectable lady, Brewster firmly relocates Liszt as the bourgeois gentleman, self-disciplined and self-controlled, and a hard worker to boot:] Serious, severe work, and study of a high and noble character, have effaced the impressions of a stormy youth, and placed him in an old age on a lofty plane where he enjoys serenity and peace.[90]

And so continues the discussion, finger by finger, even knuckle by knuckle. Brewster finds the fingers "remarkable"; she discovers in one the sign of "ambition," in another "iron," and in still another "great renown"—adapting the then common practices of physiognomy and phrenology, which assessed character and mental capacity based on measurements of the face and skull, respectively, to a reading of the hands.

The Virtuoso as Embattled Hero: The Recovery of Masculinity

The analogy of virtuoso pianists to machines is tempered by an opposing metaphor of extreme individualism constructed on a foundation of the hero. In 1839 for example, Liszt was called by a critic "this musical Byron," and virtuoso pianists and their concerts were commonly linked, respectively, to warriors and warfare.[91] No less a critic than Robert Schumann was caught up in this metaphor:

> And how Liszt went at the piece, with a strength and grandeur as if it concerned a battlefield manoeuvre. . . . At this moment he seemed, indeed, that field commander to whom, in outward appearance, at least, we have previously compared him [Napoléon], and the applause was mighty enough to have been a *Vive l'Empereur!*[92]

In perfect keeping with these military associations, Wilhelm Friedrich IV of Prussia awarded Liszt the *Ordre pour le Mérite,* a military distinction "normally gained on the field of battle."[93] The accompanying increase in masculinity is likewise anchored by the Hungarian Sword of Honor, given Liszt in 1840 when he was twenty-eight. For a time thereafter the sword became part of his performance attire, although it cut both ways, notably in Paris, where great hilarity was had at Liszt's expense in the press.[94]

At times, this military imagery strayed into allusions to a form of masculinity linked to violence, where audience admiration is tinged with fear. In 1855 a writer in *The Musical World* referred to Liszt sarcastically as "the most violent and vigorous of improvisators [*sic*], [who] murders, it is well known, every piano he touches. He is decorated with various crosses and swords for this kind of prowess."[95]

Liszt's playing overwhelmed the commonplace associations and uncertainties revolving around the piano and masculinity. His success benefited directly from exploiting the tensions evident in bourgeois concern. During the eighteenth and nineteenth centuries, musical instruments were commonly appropriated to one or the other gender, and keyboard instruments were commonly, if not universally, deemed feminine.[96] The association of music in general with femininity and the assignment of masculine or feminine traits to specific instruments underscore not only the uneasiness about music's role in the promotion of masculinity but also the extremely uncertain ground on which masculinity itself was built during this period.[97]

Just as writers often noted Paganini's breaking of violin strings, and his amazing ability to continue without hesitation or mistake on the remaining strings, so also they noted Liszt's breaking of piano strings and shattering of the instrument's hammers, while lamenting the inability of the modern piano to stand up to his assault. After hearing Liszt perform in 1838, Friedrich Wieck, father of Clara Wieck Schumann, wrote:

> Who could describe his appearance as a concert artist? After he had destroyed Thalberg's Erhard [Erard piano] in the first piece, he played the Fantasie on a Conrad Graff [Graf], broke two middle strings, went and fetched the second Graff from the corner, and played his Etude. After he broke two strings again, he played it once more, but not before he had loudly proclaimed to the audience that he had not succeeded, and would play it again.[98]

Liszt commonly performed on more than one piano in his recitals, switching instruments between pieces. The practice was a response to the physical instability of the instruments of the time. Virtuosos typically broke piano strings and destroyed hammers, especially when performing on pre-iron wooden frame instruments, which in general were more lightly built than the full-iron frame models.[99] Liszt's broken pianos bear an obvious similarity to the purposeful smashing of electric guitars that accompanied 1960s concerts of The Who, Jimi Hendrix, and others, preceded in performance by the prominent use of these instruments as visual metaphors of the phallus.

Heinrich Heine, commenting sarcastically on Liszt's playing, remarked that "the keys seemed to bleed," which resonates with comments by a reviewer of a concert given by Liszt at Darmstadt in 1845 who likened Liszt's fingers to "ten steel hammers."[100] And Moritz Gottlieb Saphir, who admired Liszt's performances in Vienna, lavishes praise on him by transposing the piano into a woman whom the pianist seduces with a fervor that conflates with the imagery of rape:

> Liszt . . . is an amiable fiend who treats his mistress—the piano—now tenderly, now tyrannically, devours her with kisses, lacerates her with lustful bites, embraces her, caresses her, sulks with her, scolds her, rebukes her, grabs her by the hair, clasps her then all the more delicately, more affectionately, more passionately, more flamingly, more meltingly. . . . After the concert Liszt stands there like a victor on a battlefield. . . . Daunted pianos lie around him; torn strings wave like flags of truce; frightened instruments flee into distant corners; the listeners look at each other as after a cataclysm of nature that has just passed by. . . . And he stands there leaning melancholically on his chair, smiling strangely, like an exclamation point after the outbreak of general admiration. Thus is Franz Liszt.[101]

This tale of sexual violation dovetails with widespread—indeed clichéd—accounts of Liszt's famous effect on women, especially at the height of what Heine sarcastically named "Lisztomania," by which he meant mass hysteria surrounding Liszt in the 1840s. General male resentment is little disguised in these accounts and satires. Women sought cuttings of his hair; as Henry F. Chorley reported in his musical memoirs, "dear, sentimental German girls wore bracelets made of the pianoforte strings which he broke in his frenzy!"; and some females "even carried glass phials about their persons into which they poured his coffee dregs. Others collected his cigar butts, which they hid in their cleavages."[102] Liszt's student Anne Hampton Brewster, writing in *Dwight's Journal of Music* in 1870, claimed that aristocratic women "used to steal Liszt's gloves, cut them up into strips, and with the cherry-stones they took from his plate after a supper or dinner, make necklaces and armlets, which they would wear on their handsome throats and arms with more pride and exultation than they did their family diamonds."[103]

In these instances, all pretense to bourgeois decorum is overwhelmed, overcome by emotion that spills beyond the concert hall. Men who admired Liszt found in him a mirror of their idealized selves: extreme accomplishment, individual—indeed unique—talent, and more problematically, worship by women. Women responded to attributes that they were rather less likely to find in their men: the qualities just mentioned, but also more. These included especially an artistic temperament, demonstrated in sound and spectacle, and marked by emotions otherwise culturally suppressed, the same emotions that the other arts—poetry, novels, paintings, and the like—commonly described and often lionized.

Recall Schopenhauer on the question of musical affect: "The inexpressible inner essence of all music, by virtue of which it flows past us so utterly comprehensible and yet so inexplicable, like a familiar but eternally distant paradise, is rooted in the fact that it reproduces all the movements of our innermost being but quite divorced from phenomenal life and remote from its misery."[104] *In Closing*

What Schopenhauer acknowledges is that the "condition" of music is less an aspiration of art and more a desire for an embodied happiness that resides only in the imagination. Schopenhauer's notion of "the inexpressible inner essence of all music" involves the decentering of the self, a letting go of mind. But it also requires joining a social group—an audience—that is disciplined and immobilized. Desire is cultivated, but it is simultaneously transferred onto the spectacle of the Other; a projection of the self is cast into and onto the sight and sound of the performer, especially the virtuoso, who enacts the desires imagined—and stage manages them as well. As Robert Schumann correctly understood: "If Liszt played behind a screen, a great deal of poetry would be lost."[105]

The virtuoso anchored a broad range of paradoxical, often contradictory meanings: artist and businessman; inspired superhuman and machine; utterly sincere in character and calculatingly manipulative; authentic and fake; masculine and feminine; Byronic hero possessing militaristic stamina and strength, but ironically in the body of a pale, thin, and sometimes fainting aesthete. These polarities not only define people's obsessive fascination with the virtuoso in the nineteenth century but also mark the virtuoso at the epicenter of the cultural and social issues that characterize modernity itself.

The 1870s to the 1920s were the heyday of the piano in Western musical culture. By 1870 production of pianos had grown to about 85,000 instruments a year in the four leading piano-producing nations—in order, Britain, the United States, France, and Germany. From then the number increased relentlessly, until by 1910 it had reached almost 600,000 a year in those four countries alone. Given that pianos are long-lasting products, this growth represents an astonishingly steady rise in the number of first-time buyers during this fifty-year period. The music business in general—music publishing, concert giving, and music education—prospered alongside the piano industry.

World War I and its aftermath brought disruption and decline to the piano industry and related enterprises in Europe, but it was business as usual in the United States, which already by the beginning of the war was producing more pianos than the rest of the world. After 1923, though, piano sales plummeted in the United States as well (in part because sales of player pianos, which had accounted for more than half of the piano production there in the years around 1910, were wiped out by the advent of radio and recordings). By 1930 worldwide piano production was barely a third of what it had been in 1910. The figure did not return to that high-water mark until the late 1960s, but that was hardly a comparable level of production, because the world was then far more populous and prosperous than it had been fifty years earlier.[1] And by the 1960s the piano was much more of a specialty instrument than it had been at the beginning of the century. It was still central to the Western classical repertory and a few newer repertories, like jazz, but it hardly mattered to other repertories of popular music. Further, the piano steadily yielded its functions as an educational tool and a medium of home entertainment to the phonograph, radio, and television.

Production in a capitalist system expands in order to survive, and the enormous expansion of world piano production from the 1870s to the 1920s indicates that the piano industry did not simply rely on the growth of its existing market—the European and American middle class—but found scope for expansion in new directions: social, geographical, and institutional. Social expansion meant marketing pianos (and the culture of the piano) to the working classes, such as those York-

Expanding Markets
James Parakilas

Nakamura Daizaburō, *The Piano*, silk screen, 1926. The pianist, who is the painter's fiancée, is playing Schumann's "Träumerei" on a piano built by the Czech firm of Antonín Petrof and donated to the Meirin primary school in Kyoto by residents of the school district. (Kyoto Municipal Museum of Art, Japan)

shire coal miners who as of the 1870s were said to be buying pianos along with perambulators. Geographical expansion meant selling pianos throughout the world and building a system to transport, sell, and service them there, not just packing an occasional instrument from England off to India, as had been done in the eighteenth century. And institutional expansion meant that pianos were installed and played as never before in places of work, business, and leisure, in churches and schools—even in hospitals, asylums, and prisons.

Each of these expansions was facilitated by conditions of the times. It became possible to sell pianos to working-class families because in this period of unprecedented prosperity workers, especially urban workers, had far more purchasing power than did their predecessors. It became possible to sell pianos around the world because Western imperialism in its all-encompassing phase was leaving barely a piece of the non-Western world unclaimed; anywhere in that world, the administrators, soldiers, business people, and missionaries of the occupying power were sure to want pianos for their own use, and the presence of pianos in their lives influenced the people whose country they occupied. In the Western countries the institutions of civil society became home to pianos because the working day was being regulated to produce regular periods of leisure for workers to enjoy in stores, restaurants, bars, music halls, theaters, and clubs, and because institutions of confinement were now being expected to reform and educate those consigned to them.

But piano manufacturers (along with those in related businesses) also had to adapt their marketing to take advantage of these conditions. Manufacturers produced significantly cheaper pianos and offered monthly payment schemes, putting pianos within the reach of working-class buyers.[2] Western musicians created musical textbooks, for use with a piano or other keyboard instrument, to teach the Western musical system to non-Western schoolchildren, and soon Western conservatories were training piano students from non-Western countries. In addition, music publishers poured out piano and piano-vocal scores designed to be used not in the concert hall or the home but in the school, the church, the synagogue, the place of business, and—by the first decades of the twentieth century—the movie theater. In fact, the piano itself was redesigned for the movie theater, tricked out with devices to provide special effects. In their marketing strategies, in other words, the piano-related industries took account of differences in class, in geography, and in the places where music was made. The world seemed to be the limit for their products, so long as they learned what it took to cross the world's boundaries.

For their customers, however, the situation was more complicated. To a working-class family in Europe or the Americas, owning a piano might seem to represent a step into middle-class respectability; but if many working-class families owned pianos, was that advantage extended or diluted? Could respectability include everyone, or could one group of people claim to be respectable only if another group was not?

The more places the piano went, the more it tested the nature, value, and durability of cultural identities. The piano was used in this period to promote middle-class Western music and cultural values among people who were not middle class or not Western—and to demote their own musics and cultures. Does that mean that it served to reduce the world's cultural diversity? Yes, but at the same time the piano was used by people who were not middle class, not Western, or not white to adapt their own musical traditions for survival in the modern world. Did that mean that these groups were defining themselves culturally by means of the piano? Again, the question cannot be answered simply. As soon as these groups devised new piano styles, the groups they defined themselves against started appropriating those styles as their own: white middle-class Americans and Europeans, for example, began learning to play and dance the rags of African-Americans and the tangos of working-class Argentinians.

The roles of the piano in this period raise questions of cultural identity that have not lost their urgency a century later. And the piano music of this era that retains the most power is that in which a cross-fertilization of cultural identities plays a large part: concert music from the Western centers of power that enshrines a longing for other places and times, and popular music of the Americas so cosmopolitan, so sophisticated, that it has since become classic.

Probably the most famous African-American pianist in this period, the ex-slave known as "Blind Tom" (Thomas Greene Wiggins, or Bethune, to use the name of his former masters), is not in fact representative of the way the piano was now extending its social reach. He was more of a throwback to the eighteenth century, the age of piano prodigies like Maria Theresia Paradis, whose genius was likewise associated with her blindness and other attributes that set her apart from most of the people who paid to hear her. Blind Tom was unusual in having had access to a piano while a slave, but the piano can hardly be said to have lifted him out of servitude, let alone to have represented much advance in his social status: for almost a half century after Emancipation, his genius continued to be exploited by the white family that had once owned him.[3]

For a picture of the people of this period to whom owning a piano and playing it represented a real social achievement, it would be better to return to Duke Ellington's parents, whose musical lives are sketched in the portrait of their famous son as a piano student (see Chapter 4). Within the community of African-Americans in their city—a whole community that was denied the social status of the white middle class by virtue of race—J. E. and Daisy Ellington belonged to the most socially ambitious sector, as we can tell from the musical repertory they played on their piano (hymns and ragtime to sentimental songs and opera). J. E. Ellington's work defined him and his family as belonging to the working class, but it was precisely among literate and advancing working-class families like the Ellingtons—no matter what their race—that the piano was making the greatest inroads at the turn of the century.

Both Ellingtons were literate; in fact, it continued to be almost a cultural law—unsupported by any musical necessity—that the piano belonged to the literate class of society. But in musical literacy they differed: J. E. played the piano by ear, whereas Daisy played from notes. Each of these skills, a considerable achievement to acquire, enables a person to perform complex music. Yet there was then and continues to be a difference between them in social prestige. Note reading, associated as it is with expensive lessons, classical music, and verbal literacy, was and is considered the higher-class method, especially among those living in the border between poverty and prosperity. Daisy Ellington, who herself most clearly embodied the social aspirations of her family in the musical realm, was the one who decided that her son Edward should have piano lessons; but Mrs. Clinkscales's teaching was not the primary means by which he eventually realized those aspirations.

A couple of decades earlier, in the little Southern town of Texarkana rather than the nation's capital, Scott Joplin's study of the piano represented similar familial social dreams. He, too, learned from various sources and by various methods, although in his case the formal lessons in classical music seem to have been a more serious part of the mix. Those lessons are said to have been given to him by a German immigrant musician and scholar named Julius Weiss. From the mid-nineteenth century to the mid-twentieth, German immigrant musicians—many of them products of the biggest conservatory system in the world—played an immeasurable role in the musical (and especially pianistic) development of the Americas; and conversely music (and especially the piano) provided them with the means to advance their social ambitions in their new home. But although Germans were the immigrants most likely to come to the New World already equipped to make their livelihood from the piano, members of other immigrant groups were apt to develop relationships with the piano once they arrived. The fifty years around the turn of the century was a period of unprecedented global displacement of populations, and it is no coincidence that between 1900 and 1920 the most booming markets for pianos were in countries like the United States, Australia, and Argentina, which were absorbing the largest numbers of European immigrants.

What the piano meant to these immigrants was as complex—and variable—as what it meant to them to be immigrants. An immigrant's ethnic identity was in effect a negotiating position within an evolving new identity, and the piano could be a tool in that negotiation. Many European immigrants to the New World came with musical traditions and abilities that had no connection to the piano; the piano represented their aspirations to be successful in their new land. But because it was itself a part of European culture, the piano could also remind them of the land they left behind; and that identification with their past could in turn help them find their place in their new home. In *Mount Allegro* (1943), Jerre Mangione's lightly fictionalized account of growing up as the child of Sicilian immigrants in Rochester, New York, the family player piano is a symbol of American modernity and American opportunity—his family, like the Ellingtons, belong to the most aspiring part of their community—but it is nevertheless used to maintain emotional bonds with the old country. He grew up, he writes, in

> the neurotic years following the First World War when Sicilian parents considered it a social disgrace if there was not a player piano in the house with a complete set of Verdi operas to pump out on it, and a piano teacher making weekly trips to instruct the children. . . . For my relatives it was the miracle invention of the twentieth century. It gave them a medium for reviving their musical memories of Italy and it was a perfect excuse for forcing a musical education on all their children, something that only the rich had been able to afford in Sicily.[4]

According to Nicholas Tawa's study of musical acculturation among ethnic Americans in this period, Mangione's family was unusual in giving piano lessons to sons as well as daughters. Among immigrants to the United States from a variety of European countries, sons were more likely to be taught the violin and daughters the piano, and for remarkably consistent reasons: the violin was both a more likely source of livelihood for a son and a more "authentic" instrument for expressing the music of their native land, whereas a daughter who played the piano was helping her family cross a boundary that was both national and social. Tawa quotes a Jewish mother from Poland who told her daughter: "In America, to be a gentlewoman, I hear, you must know how to play the piano. So you go take lessons."[5] And when Mangione explains why his relatives considered it appropriate to give piano lessons to a daughter, you would think they had been reading Jane Austen:

> It was fine if you could afford piano lessons for her; that was something of a luxury but it made sense, for a girl who knew some music was bound to be more *simpatica* than a girl who did not and, of course, everyone knew that when a man wanted to marry he tried to choose a girl who was *simpatica*.[6]

Mangione's claim that the player piano gave his relatives "a medium for reviving their musical memories of Italy" bears examining. The piano rolls that he specifies as representing their ethnic self-respect are "a complete set of Verdi operas." If the Mangiones arrived in America knowing more than a few Verdi arias, among other songs of all sorts in Italian or dialect, they would have been ahead of most of their compatriots, and they probably were: having Verdi on their piano stand was very likely not so much their way of keeping up with the Rossis as of keeping ahead of them. But whatever piano rolls of Italian music they owned and pumped out, "reviving their musical memories of Italy" did not have to mean simply replaying, in this modern form, music they knew from the old country. In fact, that country meant something different to them once they had left it. It had to be reinvented to be remembered, and the reinvention was apt to include a discovery of cultural monuments like Verdi who defined a nation they had had little consciousness of when they lived in it (note that he refers to his family as Sicilians, but their musical memories are of a place called Italy). The immigrants' piano, whether or not it came with a player mechanism, was the "miracle invention" that could turn unremembered songs into "musical memories," just as it could turn remembered songs into something suitably modern.

The Steinway grand in the concert hall could have a similar effect when Paderewski played Chopin on it in cities like Chicago and Milwaukee, places where his audiences typically included hundreds or even thousands of Polish immigrants. The fact that many of those immigrants had never heard a piano, let alone Chopin, before they left Poland did not stop his concertgoers from "reviving their musical memories" of Poland. He made them want their children to learn to play Chopin. Furthermore, the presence of non-Poles in the audience was a crucial part of the effect. It was the lionizing of Paderewski within American culture as a whole that made him such a source of pride to Polish immigrants. And that pride, not just in Polish culture, but also in America's recognition of that culture, meant that through Paderewski's piano playing, Polish immigrants and their children not only could have memories of a musical Poland that they didn't

Cover sheet to Will A. Heelan and H. B. Blanke, "In the Good Old Irish Way: A Celtic Waltz Song" (New York, 1907). The lyrics invite Irish-Americans to maintain their Irish character by making merry: "Never mind how much innocent noise we make, / If you don't make enough, sure they'll think it 'twas a wake." But Irish-Americans who needed to work at maintaining the "good old Irish way" and who played the piano and dressed in high style to dance were clearly settled into a "prosperous new American way" of being "Irish."

remember; they could also turn their Polishness into a way of feeling at home in America.

The aspiration of new classes of people to join in the culture of the piano prompted conflicting responses from those already in possession of that culture. The music industry, which possessed the product itself and was driven to sell it on the widest possible scale, promoted the spread of pianos as if it were a form of democratization. "Every American Citizen," ran an ad by Droop's Music House of Washington, D.C., in 1907, "should have a piano in his home: years ago, this was a luxury; now it is almost a necessity."[7] And as in Clementi's day, when method books offered shortcuts to learning the piano, the music industry now offered a radically simpler way to make music on the piano: the player piano. To that industry, the difficulty of learning the piano was simply an obstacle to sales, whether to rich or poor, black or white, immigrant or native, and the technology of the player piano could obliterate that obstacle, eliminating even the choice between learning to read notes and learning to play by ear.

But the music education profession, another of the possessors of piano culture, saw a different opportunity. Although interest in the piano may have risen across all social classes in considerable part because the piano industry had found ways to dumb down piano playing, music educators believed that they could capitalize on the interest without yielding to the dumbing-down. For many—from the organizers of school music programs to George Bernard Shaw, in his campaigns for "Music for the People" as a newspaper music critic in the 1890s—this meant not only teaching people of every class how to listen to music and how to make it for themselves; it also meant teaching them that the music they learned to love and to make should be the highest-class music, Western classical music—and by implication that they should forget about other kinds.

Behind the campaigns of these music educators lay motives not free of contradictions: a genuinely democratic commitment to extending the blessings of musical culture to all people and a no less genuine fear that in a society where the same means of music making—notably the piano—were becoming available to all people, bad musical influences were apt to spread from the lower classes to the upper if good ones were not spread from the upper classes down. The virulence of response to the fashion of ragtime by the guardians of musical culture in the United States—Edward MacDowell, professor of music at Columbia and the most famous composer in America, described it as "nigger whorehouse music"—can hardly be explained without considering that this was the first important repertory of African-American music written and published for the piano and therefore the

"Music Builds Citizenship in Chicago Schools," *Musical America*, January 8, 1916. Here the energies of turn-of-the-century populism are turned to the cause of universal music education. The author of the article praises the Chicago school system for its standardized program of assembly singing, in which the children of the rich and the children of immigrants learned songs "of the worth-while sort—little classics." These songs included folk songs of the countries from which most of Chicago's immigrant population came. Every school in the city, it seems, had a piano, though the children of the rich learned from a grand and the children of the "Ghetto" learned from an upright.

MUSIC BUILDS CITIZENSHIP IN CHICAGO SCHOOLS

Good Effects of Musical Training Extend to the Home and Community—Improve Physical and Mental Condition of Children—A Movement That Meets the Musical Requirements of 300,000 Students

CHICAGO, ILL., Jan. 3—Music is one of the most important factors in the school life of Chicago. Not only is it working wonders as a socializing influence and in laying the foundations of true musical education, but it is proving an agency of reform for unruly and backward pupils. Nor does its influence cease with the schools.

Through the music department of the public school system music has become a potent factor in hundreds of Chicago homes where the training given at school has been imparted to parents, brothers and sisters. Pianos and other musical instruments have found their way to many of the humbler homes of the city because of the musical training given the little children in the public schools.

In these homes music, which was once practically an unknown quantity, is now a necessity. The benefits of the musical course in the public schools cannot be overestimated. They accrue, not only to the children, but to the schools as a whole and to the community.

"Répertoire" Increased Monthly

Every month the child in the Chicago public schools adds a new selection to his répertoire. And these songs are all of the worth-while sort—little classics. The music of every nation is drawn upon, especial attention being given to the folk-songs of the various nations. For instance, during the present year the list included: Brahms's "Cradle Song," "Men of Harlech," "Still, Still with Thee," Grieg's "Patriotic Prayer," "Killarney," "Hark, Hark, the Lark!" "Sweet and Low," "Loch Lomond," "Bohemian National Hymn," "Star-Spangled Banner," "Finiculi, Finicula."

Mrs. A. C. Heath, who for years has supervised the musical courses in the Chicago public schools, has not only perfected a graded system of work through which the children begin in the first grade to learn one-part and folk-songs and progress to three-part songs, sight reading and the writing of simple chords and melodies, but she is responsible for the system of "assembly singing."

The assembly singing is especially adapted to a city of the size and character of Chicago, where children of different nationalities and races meet in the public schools and where they are frequently transferred from school to school as their parents move from one locality to another. The assembly idea is simply the training of the various classes in the various schools by the grade teachers in a selected number of songs.

Teach Classes Team Work

The same song is taught in all of the schools the same month. Then the various classes meet in the assembly room of the school and sing together. The result of this is exceptional team work, and, when occasion demands it, the pupils of a number of schools will sing in chorus any of the songs taught in the classrooms, and do it in splendid fashion.

When the National Educational Association met here in 1912 a chorus of 1500 voices sang before the convention, under Mrs. Heath's direction. No hall could be obtained large enough for rehearsals, and the 1500 children, drawn from various schools, met for the first time on the Auditorium stage the minute before they began their first number. But the program was gone through without a hitch.

As a step toward educational training the method of teaching music in the Chicago schools is notable. Music is a

Above: Pupils of the Swift School, Chicago, at Their Musical Exercises. This School Is Attended by the Children of the Richer Chicagoans. In Center: 800 Children of the Jackson School at Morning Singing Exercises. This School Is in the Heart of the "Ghetto," and the Pupils Are Children of People of Many Nationalities. Below: Selected Chorus Singing at the Swift School, with the Other Pupils as Audience and Critics

vocation, Mrs. Heath argues, just as much as carpentry or bricklaying, or any of the other trades. The general value of the training begins with the child's first lesson, in the first grade. He is first taught to assume a correct position, and he is then given a breathing exercise. These and the simple note sounding which follows act as a physical culture exercise and at the same time teach voice control and proper production of tones.

And as the child advances in school, so his musical training advances. When he graduates from the public school he has an excellent foundation laid for carrying on his vocal work with a view to making a profession of it. The music taught all the way through is good. In the more advanced books the classical works are drawn upon.

It is taken for granted in the Chicago schools that every child is "musical." Mrs. Heath believes that singing is a

natural function of childhood and the pleasure the children derive from the "singing lesson" proves that her belief is correct. Many excellent voices have been discovered by means of the public-school music lessons, and in the city to-day are a number of excellent glee clubs which had their beginning in the lower grades of the public schools. But whether or not the pupils have the making of great

[Continued on page 20]

The Alma-Tadema Stein-
way, an art-case piano
built in New York in 1883
for Henry Marquand, sent
to London to be decorated
by a team of artists and
craftsmen under the direction of Sir Lawrence Alma-
Tadema, and delivered to
Marquand, a businessman
and the second president
of the Metropolitan Mu-
seum of Art, in 1887. The
painted panel above the
keyboard, *The Wandering
Minstrels,* is by Sir Edward
J. Poynter, who was president of the Royal Acad-
emy. The piano now be-
longs to the Sterling and
Francine Clark Art Insti-
tute, Williamstown,
Massachusetts.

first that could be played by great numbers of respectable white girls on their parlor pianos.[8]

If music educators were made nervous by the prospect of newcomers to the piano who lacked a knowledge of the classics, a final group of traditional possess-ors of piano culture—the rich—were made nervous by the idea that people of classes, races, and origins other than their own had pianos at all. The piano, which had once distinguished the rich from everyone else, and then the rich and the middle class from the laboring class, now belonged to almost everyone. The great virtuosos, who once had graced the salons of the rich and famous, were now playing to crowds of thousands. How, then, could the rich still derive any social distinction from the piano? One answer was to lavish money on its decoration, so that a rich family's piano looked altogether different from anyone else's piano. It was in this period that the most prestigious piano makers created art-case depart-ments, hiring distinguished artists—Kate Faulkner at Broadwood, Thomas Dew-ing at Steinway—to fulfill commissions from the rich and powerful for unique pi-ano cases incorporating expensive materials, elaborate carving, and ambitious paintings.[9]

But as soon as the rich and powerful tried to make their pianos distinctive, the rest set about emulating them. Fancifully decorated pianos began to appear on the Broadway stage, in nightclubs, in the Hollywood revue, and eventually in Liberace's Las Vegas act. These pianos were typically white, reversing—or mocking —the sober black of the concert-hall piano. The mockery was double-edged, because through these stage pianos, ordinary people could fantasize about living the life of the rich at the same time that they could snicker at the pretension of that life. But in a photograph taken in 1947 of the Lewiston Orphéon, a chorus of French-Canadian immigrant men in a Maine mill town, we can see the same kind of piano embodying a different spirit. Standing around that piano, dressed in their tuxedos, the men in the photograph—mostly workers in shoe and textile mills by day—are not emulating anyone else's life so much as they are asserting the richness of their own, a richness compounded of their French and Roman Catholic musical heritage, their communal solidarity, and their increasing prosperity. In show business, the decorated piano became a way of playing with, not worshipping, the idea of wealth; in a factory town it embodied a cultural dignity achieved, not just aspired to, by immigrant workers. But if it served those purposes, it evidently could no longer serve as a social marker for the rich themselves. And so, although the grand piano continues to represent "class" in advertising and popular culture, piano makers' art-case departments have long since gone out of business.

L'Orphéon of Lewiston, Maine, 1947–48. Fifty years after this photograph was taken, surviving members of the group were still performing together. (Jean Byers Sampson Center for Diversity, Lewiston-Auburn College, University of Southern Maine)

Negotiations over social class are as plainly written into the piano music of this period as into the cases of its pianos. It is ironic, for instance, to find that in an era when music educators were busy teaching high-art music to the masses (and calling that process Music *for* the People), composers of high-art music were busy making their compositions out of folk music, domestic or foreign (the Music *of* the People). To be fair, composers had been doing this for a century already. But the nature of the negotiation was changing. Edvard Grieg, for instance, had given his Piano Concerto, premiered in 1869, a Norwegian identity by introducing into the finale a theme that might have been borrowed from the Norwegian Hardanger fiddle tradition. In a work calculated to put Norway on the high-cultural map, it is understandable that he would have created a theme that was just Norwegian enough to be noticed and would have presented it—like any other kind of theme—so as to display the full resources of the piano and of its tuxedoed performer to urbane audiences in Norway or anywhere in Europe. The concerto did what it was calculated to do and has remained hugely successful.

Three decades later, however, Grieg made free arrangements for solo piano of seventeen authentic Hardanger fiddle tunes that had been carefully transcribed by a violinist of his acquaintance, publishing them in 1903 as his *Slåtter*, Op. 72. By then his purpose was considerably different. He had the transcriptions themselves published separately, and in his preface to his arrangements he made allowance for the difficulty that concertgoers might have in appreciating music of a character so different from what they were used to. "Those who can appreciate such music," he wrote, "will be delighted at the originality, the blending of fine, soft gracefulness with sturdy almost uncouth power and untamed wildness as regards melody and more particularly rhythm, contained in them."[10] To say that the national character of Norway, or any country, came from the "uncouth power and untamed wildness" of its rural folk was by then cliché. To appropriate folk music from that folk, tame it into concert music, and hand it to urban audiences in that form was also a long-established practice.

Grieg went on to write that his purpose was "to raise these works of the people to an artistic level, by giving them what I might call a style of musical concord, or bringing them under a system of harmony." But the "style of musical concord" he adopted here admits of neither virtuosity nor much charm. Instead of surrendering the fiddle tunes to the figurations most comfortable on the piano and the sonorities most resonant on it, he engages in a tug-of-war between what suits the folk fiddle and what suits the modern piano. In the beginning of the piece called "Gangar," for instance, he gives the pianist's right hand the awkward task of play-

First page of "Gangar (efter 'Möllargutten')" (Step dance, from the repertory of "the Miller"), from Edvard Grieg, *Slåtter* (Norwegian peasant dances), Op. 72 (Leipzig, 1903)

ing both the ornamented melody and the drone on the A below it, creating dissonances of considerably less "concord" on the piano than are produced on the Hardanger fiddle. At the same time, even the left-hand part stays in the fiddle range, eschewing the resonance of the piano's lower strings. Gradually those lower strings are brought into play: the variety of sonority within the piece—a concession to the resources of the modern instrument—is evidently needed to "raise these works of the people to an artistic level." Yet this is never an easy marriage between fiddle and piano. As a result, the *Slåtter*, received unenthusiastically when Grieg premiered them, have continued to be only a specialist's pleasure.[11] Most urban concertgoers don't like to be shown how awkward it is to enshrine the "wildness" of their country cousins.

What Grieg did for and to the fiddle music of his rural compatriots, W. C. Handy did for and to the blues of his fellow African-Americans a few years later. His first publication, in 1912, was a piano piece he called "The Memphis Blues," derived from a band piece, "Mr. Crump," that he had composed for a political campaign. Three decades later, in his autobiography, *Father of the Blues*, Handy described how he had drawn on the practices of less-educated blues musicians to create this piece (and in the process explained and qualified the title of his book).

> The melody of Mr. Crump was mine throughout. On the other hand, the twelve-bar, three-line form of the first and last strains, with its three-chord basic harmonic structure (tonic, subdominant, dominant seventh) was that already used by Negro roustabouts, honky-tonk piano players, wanderers and others of their underprivileged but undaunted class from Missouri to the Gulf, and had become a common medium through which any such individual might express his personal feelings in a sort of musical soliloquy. My part in their history was to introduce this, the "blues" form to the general public, as the medium for my own feelings and my own musical ideas. And the transitional flat thirds and sevenths in my melody, by which I was attempting to suggest the typical slurs of the Negro voice, were what have since become known as "blue notes."[12]

In that final strain of "The Memphis Blues" the "transitional flat thirds" that Handy describes are the C-sharps; the "sevenths" are the A-flats. But the piano can't "slur" pitches like a singer; that is, it can't shade a pitch between the notes of two adjacent keys, so Handy worries obsessively at how to make the piano "suggest" what it can't do. Melodically, he tries slurring the C-sharp into the D over and over in different rhythmic positions (as in the passage for left hand, marked *legato*); elsewhere he "suggests" the unplayable pitch through the harmonic dissonance created by posing the C-sharp in the right hand against a left-hand chord that includes the D (every time the C-sharp is played in the first four measures of the example). At almost exactly the same date, Béla Bartók was using exactly the same technique (in his music it is sometimes called the Bartók Chord) for exactly the same purpose, in piano arrangements of eastern European folk music.

In 1963 LeRoi Jones (later Amiri Baraka) was to write, in *Blues People*, his cultural history of "negro music in white America": "W. C. Handy, with the publication of his various 'blues compositions,' *invented* it for a great many Americans and also showed that there was some money to be made from it. . . . There was even what could be called a 'blues craze' (of which Handy's compositions were an important part) just after the ragtime craze went on the skids. But the music that resulted from this craze had little, if anything, to do with legitimate blues."[13]

Final strain of W. C. Handy, " The Memphis Blues" (New York, 1912)

Whenever musicians from a respectable class decide to take up the musical language of a disadvantaged class and "suggest" its distinctive character in their own musical medium, there is room for a charge like Baraka's that the "legitimacy" of the original is being lost. Grieg himself wrote, when he first saw the transcriptions of the Hardanger fiddle tunes: "At the moment it seems to me that it would be a sin to arrange the dance tunes for piano. But that sin I probably will commit sooner or later. It is too tempting."[14]

Grieg, Handy, and others in their position knew that they missed something and destroyed something by transferring such music to that medium of respectability, the piano. Handy had learned about musical respectability as a child when he had brought home a guitar that he had saved up the money to buy, only to be told by his parents—a preacher and a preacher's wife—"Whatever possessed you to bring a sinful thing like that into our Christian home?" That was how he had become a pianist.[15]

The tunes played by Hardanger fiddlers or the blues of "Negro roustabouts, honky-tonk piano players, wanderers and others" are called "legitimate," "authentic," or "pure" by people on the outside—people of another class—who nevertheless want to connect themselves to that music, want to claim it as part of their cultural roots. In order to do that, they need to have it conveyed to them and their class somehow, for their enjoyment, inspection, and possession. In the days of Grieg, Handy, and Bartók, that meant that "sooner or later," and with whatever loss in musical character, it had to be arranged for the piano. What allowed Baraka to take his stand against such arrangements, or inventions, was not a new level of consciousness about musical appropriation. It was the appearance of a new means of conveyance, a new technology that was less musically distorting, perhaps, but no less deracinating than the piano: the recording.

In a sense, Grieg's fiddle arrangements and Handy's piano blues represented nothing more than an extension across social boundaries of the mid-nineteenth-century practice of committing music of every medium to piano arrangement. And although it is possible to object that the piano was sometimes an unsuitable medium of transmission or to accuse a higher social class of using it to make an unearned profit, musical and monetary, from the music of a lower class, it is hard to ignore the vitality and richness that music in this period derived from the endless musical crossings of social boundaries, a process that had the piano at its hub. For one thing, the movement did not all go in one direction. While Debussy was invoking the ragtime craze in his suites of concert piano pieces, Joplin was breaking into the market for elite dance music with his elegant waltzes and two-steps. And while Ives was making the sturdy hymn and march tunes of his youth the themes of his avant-garde sonatas and songs, Gershwin was bringing the harmonic sophistication of the concert music of his day to the songs of Tin Pan Alley. The cross-fertilization of musical styles in this period makes audible the social fluidity of the age; it is the fruit of the massive migrations across social and geographical boundaries that had previously kept people and their music segregated. In this sense Irving Berlin's "I Love a Piano," the work of a Russian cantor's son whose parents, fleeing anti-Semitism, brought him to New York when he was five, can be heard as an immigrant's hymn to the social openness of America, where he could be equally content stopping "right beside an Upright, Or a high-toned Baby Grand."

Throughout the twentieth century, in fact, the Americas proved to be the most fertile breeding ground for developments in popular music because musics and musicians could more easily cross paths and learn from one another there than in the Old World. As early as 1868, a cartoon in the Brazilian magazine *A Vida Fluminense* put its finger on the crucial difference in musical conditions, by way of mocking the practices of amateur singers in Italy, Germany, France, and Brazil. The crucial contrast is not that the Brazilian dilettante sings to a guitar, while the Europeans sing to the piano or without instruments at all; whatever attitude to the guitar is being expressed here, it is not that of W. C. Handy's parents. No, the

EM ITALIANO.

OS DILETTANTI, OU COMO SE CANTA

EM ALLEMÃO.

EM FRANCEZ.

EM BRASILEIRO.

Anonymous, *Os Dilettanti* (The dilettantes), in *A Vida Fluminense*, April 15, 1868 (Library of Congress)

crucial detail in the picture of the Brazilian singer is the piano that he shuns in order to accompany himself on the guitar, a piano that nevertheless stands at the ready, music on its stand. It is a picture of a culture in which the same musician is allowed to move around among different instruments, each with its own social history and class associations.

In the first decades of the twentieth century, the Brazilian pianist-composer Ernesto Nazareth produced a body of piano music that represented just such a crossing of social boundaries, drawing on music from Chopin to the popular Brazilian dance, the maxixe, and influencing composers of both popular and concert music in turn. His many "Brazilian tangos" are to Brazilians what Joplin's rags are to Americans, their popular and their classical music at the same time. Earlier composers had already used the generic title "Brazilian tango," which in itself reveals that the tango originated outside Brazil, but Brazilians from Villa-Lobos to the present have claimed that it is Nazareth's tangos that truly express the character of Brazil and especially the urbanity of Rio de Janeiro. Listening to the opening of Nazareth's famous "Odeon," it is hard to avoid the impression that its distinctive character comes from a certain marriage of the popular and the

First page of Ernesto Nazareth, "Odeon: Tango brasileiro" (Rio de Janeiro, ca. 1910)

classic: the opening phrase, consisting of nothing but a rhythmicized bass line punctuated by chords, could be the lead-in to a tango by a popular dance band; the classical touch is the sly extension of that texture into further phrases, so that the lead-in becomes the main theme of the dance. Even the title "Odeon" points to a meeting place of the classes of Rio society. Although Nazareth occasionally performed piano recitals in exclusive social clubs and concert halls, he made his living for many years accompanying silent films at the Cinema Odeon in Rio. And it was there, listening to Nazareth and an orchestra that included Villa-Lobos expound Brazilian popular styles as background music to movies, that Darius Milhaud made his discovery of those styles, which he later took back to France and introduced, in his own transmutations, to concert audiences in Europe and the rest of the world.[16]

Piano Imperialism

The English soldiers and businessmen who brought pianos to India in the 1790s and the German physician who brought one to Japan in the 1820s had no idea what they were starting. They wanted to be able to keep music, as they knew it, in their lives while they were living on the other side of the world. They weren't thinking about interesting Indians or Japanese in the piano or its music. They couldn't have imagined that by the end of the nineteenth century their successors —soldiers, government officials, missionaries, businessmen, and educators from all of the most powerful Western nations—would have established a dominating presence there and throughout the globe. And they certainly didn't suspect that one of the spoils of that imperialism would be supplies of ebony and ivory for piano manufacturers. By 1900 people in the non-Western world who earlier had no reason to be interested in the piano had been given reasons by the force of Western imperialism.

But not everyone in India or Japan or any other non-Western land had heard a piano or taken an interest in it by 1900. Nor did everyone who heard one respond alike. In every country where the piano was introduced, there was some combination of hostility to it as alien and attraction to it as modern. For that matter, individuals had their own mixtures of responses, which must have reflected in some ways their feelings about Westernization in general. In Satyajit Ray's 1984 film *The Home and the World* (*Ghare-Baire*, based on a novel of Tagore), the struggle within an upper-class Bengali family in 1908 over whether to cultivate the piano or the traditional Indian instruments reflects, on the level of private life and personal identity, the terms of the family's conflict over whether to adapt to British rule or fight against it.

A Steinway grand being delivered for a concert by Helena Morsztyn (who appears on the far right), Nagpur, India, 1923. The Western imperial powers liked to represent Western culture as a blessing that they were bringing to the rest of the world; here the blessing—embodied in a piano—is shown in the most literal way to be nothing but a burden. (La Guardia and Wagner Archives, La Guardia Community College, City University of New York)

Between resisting the piano and embracing it—which is to say, between holding fast to native musical tradition and rejecting it—sometimes lay the path of musical accommodation. The accommodation sometimes involved an attempt at conciliation between the piano and a native keyed or stringed instrument. In Burma, for instance, the piano, introduced in the royal court in the late nineteenth century, was at first tuned to the scale of the royal Burmese xylophone, the pattala, and when used to perform courtly music was played with two fingers in a manner much like the pattala's two-mallet technique. In the early twentieth century, the piano accompanied Burmese silent films; later it was used in movie soundtracks; today it is a naturalized Burmese instrument playing both the court repertory (a nationalized repertory, now that the royal house no longer rules) and popular pieces, and its use in films keeps it associated with Western technology.[17]

In Iran, early in the twentieth century, musicians in the Persian classical tradition under the leadership of Ali-Naqi Vaziri effected a mutual accommodation between the piano and their own seventy-two-string dulcimer, the santour, retuning the piano like the santour while rebuilding the santour along the lines of the piano. They also adapted playing techniques from each to the other. All these accommodations served the politically charged purpose of modernizing the Persian tradition so that it could survive in a changing world. As Steven Whiting describes this situation, the piano exerted its influence in Iran even where it wasn't played, because the comparison to the piano boosted the prestige of the santour over that of the softer Persian lutes as the classical repertory began to be performed in larger, more public places.

In each country touched by Western imperialism in the nineteenth and early twentieth centuries, the piano meant something different. It represented the West differently because the West touched each of those countries in a unique way. The piano and the music that Westerners used it to introduce corresponded in different ways to the instruments and music that were already performed in each country, and thus they presented a unique challenge to each musical culture. Each culture, in turn, responded with a different balance of resistance, welcome, and adaptation.

Although it would be impossible in this book to tell each of the histories that the piano created in different countries, what follows is a case history of a single country, Japan, that turned to the piano in the 1870s—right at the beginning of the period under consideration in this chapter—and has since developed an important role in the world history of the piano. This case study raises many of the issues that could be raised about other countries in the same period, yet it tells of experiences and attitudes that are by no means typical of other countries.

In 1871, in the face of debilitating Western imperialist pressures, the government of the Meiji Emperor sent to the West a historic embassy of nearly fifty officials and as many students headed by Prince Iwakura Tomomi.[18] The original purpose of the so-called Iwakura Embassy was to negotiate revisions of the unequal treaties that Japan had concluded at gunpoint with the Western powers. But after its first stop in the United States, its members realized that this was an impossible goal. In fact, it became clear that Japan's liberation from these treaties depended on how "civilized" it could become in the eyes of the West.

For the remainder of its tour, therefore, the mission refocused its attention on unlocking the secret of the West's wealth and power so that Japan might one day make them its own. It was during this pilgrimage that modern Japan's founding fathers discovered the usefulness of the piano not only in demonstrating a country's cultural accomplishment for diplomatic gains, but also in molding a people to suit domestic political agendas.

Government by Piano: An Early History of the Piano in Japan
Atsuko Hirai

In the United States, members of the Iwakura Embassy were treated to formal receptions and banquets, at which, to the dismay of the Japanese, American dignitaries were accompanied by their wives, daughters, and nieces. Once they had eaten and heard speeches, moreover, the men and women invariably took to the floor in each other's arms and danced the evening away to what the Japanese at the time called "Western strings," that is, the piano. Even in proverbially staid Salt Lake City, "folks facilely shed solemnity" and treated their visitors to music and dancing until the wee hours.[19]

When they visited American grammar schools, the Japanese found the same instrument put to more seemly use: it accompanied the pupils' singing. Singing taught boys and girls to "worship God and respect proper relationships among

The Piano for Japan

people"; it "stimulated the mind and cultivated the disposition, like the musical training at the Imperial Court of China's Golden Age."[20] These children were to grow up and become patriots who loved family, community, and country. For this noble mission, the piano seemed an essential ingredient.

The Iwakura Embassy was not the first to introduce the piano to Japan. The oldest extant piano in Japan, a square pianoforte made by William Rolfe of London, was brought there in 1823 by a German physician, Philipp Franz von Siebold.[21] But it was the Iwakura Embassy that helped the piano gain official recognition as the musical instrument of the new age. Having been entertained royally at the world's best concert halls and opera houses, the embassy's members became personal patrons of Western music in Japan. Nagai Shigeko, for example, a girl who went to the United States with the embassy, studied at Vassar College and, upon returning home, became one of the first piano teachers in the country.

After more than twenty months abroad, the Iwakura Embassy returned to Japan in September 1873. Having seen the West's colonization of the Middle East and Asia, the embassy was determined to marshal the country's resources toward industrialization. Struggle, sometimes armed, ensued. But amid conflicts over modernization, the sights and sounds of culture and national civility persevered.

In 1874, the protocol department of the Imperial Household Ministry became the first in the country to train civilian musicians in Western music.[22] The students were court musicians who entertained foreign dignitaries. But finding pianos proved difficult when no more than a dozen were owned by Japanese. In the court's studio, the musicians practiced on the piano the government had bought from the Belgian consulate general. At home, they practiced on a keyboard drawn on cardboard. And practice they did, for the honor of the country.

Western Scale,
Japanese Soul

In 1875, the year after the court musicians began their study of Western music, the government founded the Tokyo Normal School for Women. A teachers' college, the Tokyo Women's Normal had schools for children attached to it. The government recognized the need to teach music at such an institution and bought the school a piano even before providing one for the protocol department of the Imperial Court. But the piano came without the kind of music that would advance the noble goal of improving students' health, cultivating their moral sensibility, and stirring patriotic fervor. The school at first drafted court musicians to supply just such music, but they wrote songs in modes best sung with traditional accompaniment.

The person slated to fill the gap was Luther W. Mason, an American who came to Japan as an employee of the ministry of education. A native of Maine, Mason studied at the Boston Conservatory of Music and made his name in America teaching and writing about music education in the schools. His sojourn in Japan was arranged by Izawa Shūji, a Japanese student whom he had befriended in Boston and who, upon his return to Japan, became the president of the Tokyo Normal School (for men). The collaboration between Mason and Izawa laid the foundation for school music programs.[23]

For personal use Mason took to Japan a piano, two organs, and a violin. In addition, he ordered for his school in Tokyo ten pianos, four violins, two violas, two cellos, two double basses, one clarinet, one flute, and many books of, and about, music. He also sent for parts to a reed organ, which he used to teach a Japanese technician how to build the instrument.[24] He was to be at once composer, arranger, musicologist, music teacher and performer at large (like a band teacher at an American high school), piano tuner, and piano builder.

Officially, Mason was the chief instructor at the newly established Ongaku Torishirabe-gakari, the education ministry's music department or school that later became the Tokyo School of Music and, eventually, today's Tokyo University of Music. Here he trained the school's first class of about thirty future teachers and performers of Western music. The primary qualification for application to the school was a prior musical background. Age and gender were not considered. Partly because of this rule, the majority of the students were women from former samurai families or of equivalent standing.[25]

Mason's success as a teacher of applied music there, and later also at the Tokyo Women's Normal, may be seen from the perspective of Edward Morse, who taught zoology at the Tokyo Imperial University. Some two years before Mason arrived in Japan, Morse heard a concert that the teachers from the Tokyo Women's Normal and Kindergarten also attended. The instruments were the usual assortment: two koto, a shō, and a flute. An old man played the shō, which, to Morse's ear, "had an extraordinary sound." While a young man sang, the shō kept up "an accompaniment in one or two tones sounding not unlike a bagpipe." The music was "by no means unpleasant," and yet "the question constantly arose, 'Is this music in our sense of the word?'" Its merits escaped Morse.[26]

In 1882, two years after Mason began teaching at the Tokyo Women's Normal, Morse attended a public exhibition of Mason's classes. He discovered then that "the Japanese could be taught to sing in our way." There was piano playing, too, and "a little boy of five years, scarcely large enough to reach the keys, played some simple thing on the piano with remarkable skill." The boy also wrote music on a blackboard as Mason played it on the violin, prompting the teacher to call him "a Japanese Mozart!"[27]

Mason's work as a composer and arranger resulted in a textbook of songs titled *Shōgaku shōkashū* (Songs for primary schools).[28] Most of the thirty-three songs collected in this volume were famous tunes from various parts of the world, to which Japanese words were set. Others were simple, short exercises in the diatonic scale. Although Mason was the book's chief creator, only one of his songs was included.[29]

Many of the songs in the book praised the natural beauty of Japan—Mount Fuji, the River Sumida, cherry blossoms, autumn leaves—in the same vein as "America the Beautiful." Others taught the cardinal virtues, especially filial piety, in the Confucian mold. In fact, Mason's sole compositional contribution, "Gorin no uta" (The song of five proper human relationships), took its subject straight from a Confucian text.[30] Still others exalted loyalty to the emperor and love of country over love between parent and child or man and woman. These are precisely the kind of moral sentiments that the Meiji government wanted to foster in its people through school songs.

The Japanese "translation" of "The Blue Bells of Scotland" epitomized the convergence of the Japanese soul and the Western scale. Here are some of the lyrics of the Scottish folk song:

Hashimoto Chikanobu, *Picture of a Musical Ensemble of European Winds and Strings,* May 1889. The song being performed is "Iwama no shimizu" (A spring issuing from the rocks), from the song collection *Meiji shōka* (Meiji songs), compiled by Owada Takeki and Oku Yoshiisa (Tokyo, 1889). Oku was a pupil of Mason. (Metropolitan Museum of Art, New York)

Oh where, tell me where, is your Highland laddie gone?

He's gone wi' streaming banners where noble deeds are done

And it's oh, in my heart I wish him safe at home.

Note how this Scottish love song was turned into a litany of Imperial loyalism in the Japanese version, "The Beautiful":

Where are my beautiful sons?

My beautiful eldest son

Took a bow and left, spirited,

To be in front of the Emperor.

Where are my beautiful sons?

My beautiful middle son

Took a sword and left, spirited,

To be by the side of the Emperor.

Where are my beautiful sons?

My beautiful youngest son

Took a shield and left, spirited,

To be behind the Emperor.[31]

The Japanese mother who surrendered her three sons to the emperor did not utter a word of complaint that they might not return home. The Meiji government later selected a verse from the same book for Japan's national anthem, "Kimigayo" (Your Majesty's reign). Set to an original tune, the anthem proclaimed that the imperial reign "will last thousands of years until pebbles grow into a rock and gather moss."[32]

Judging from "The Song of Five Proper Human Relationships," Mason was not an inspired composer. And although he was a versatile performer, he does not seem to have been a virtuoso on any instrument. In the school's concerts, he played the piano, organ, and violin for choirs but left solo piano performances to his teaching assistants, such as Nagai Shigeko, the Vassar graduate. Mason nevertheless made one lasting and unmistakable impression on Japanese piano education: he introduced to the Japanese the piano exercise book written by the German composer Ferdinand Beyer (1803–63). Known simply as Beyer, it remains the standard exercise book for piano study in Japan.

The Rokumeikan, or Deer Cry Pavilion, was a semi-official social club built in Tokyo in 1883 and used by the men and women of Japan's charmed circles to entertain foreign visitors as well as themselves. Until its closing in 1889, it offered

Scherzo at the Rokumeikan

performances of serious music. But its main attractions were nightly cocktail parties, bazaars, masked balls, and amorous encounters. These events showcased prominent Japanese in morning coats and Victorian full skirts in hot pursuit of what the Iwakura Embassy had glimpsed as the elegant pastime of Europe's and America's high societies. Under the glittering surface, the whole affair was the desperate attempt of Foreign Minister Inoue Kaoru to persuade Western powers to revise the unequal treaties with Japan.

Contrary to the minister's hope, extravagance at the Rokumeikan gained neither admiration abroad nor public approval at home. Yet it offered one more avenue through which the piano could enter Japanese society: amusement. Dances required music and, at the Rokumeikan, the piano rose to the occasion, especially during the weekly dance lessons. Anna Lohr, the pavilion's German artist-in-residence and the music teacher to the Japanese navy's band, not only made music on the piano, but also gave dance lessons. Some days she pounded out the polka, waltz, and mazurka; other days, the quadrille and lancers.[33]

These steps and tunes were not without followers outside the Rokumeikan, despite the notoriety and contempt that they earned as a means to attain foreign policy goals. While schoolchildren learned Western-scale songs so upright and patriotic, grownups acquired a taste in Western entertainment that may have been decadent in form but was patriotic still in claim. In 1887, even before the Roku-

Hashimoto Chikanobu, *Simplified Picture of Dignitaries Dancing*, February 8, 1888. According to Julia Meech-Pekarik, this print may show a dance hall at the Rokumeikan.

308

Le Japon en l'An 188..-

Le père   la fille   et le futur.

Georges Bigot, *Japan in the Year 188-: The Father, the Daughter, and the Future*, in *Toba-e*, July 1887

meikan lightheadedness was over, the visiting French cartoonist Georges Bigot published a drawing that shows the piano assuming a role in a more "respectable" scene of courtship: a daughter sings to her own piano accompaniment as her father peers down upon her hands and her prospective husband sits at attention behind her.[34]

Koeber, Junker, and Company

In the summer of 1893, the history of the piano in Japan turned over a new leaf with the arrival of Raphael Gustav von Koeber as a professor of philosophy at the Tokyo Imperial University. Koeber, then forty-five, had been born in Russia and distinguished himself as a piano student of Nicholas Rubinstein at the Moscow Conservatory. But instead of becoming a concert artist, he entered the German academic world after studying literature and philosophy at the universities of Jena and Heidelberg. His career in Germany included teaching the history of music and aesthetics at the Karlsruhe School of Music.[35]

Koeber was unquestionably the most cultivated European to accept employment by the Japanese government. It is little wonder, then, that he had a profound influence on a whole generation of educated Japanese. More significantly for this study, music and piano beckoned Koeber again once he was settled in Tokyo. He gave the first of his known public performances ten months after arriving in Tokyo. By the end of the same year, Koeber had become the most sought-after artist in town. In 1898, he was made an instructor in piano at the Tokyo School of Music.

One of Koeber's most generous gifts to Japan's musical world was Gluck's opera *Orfeo,* which the Tokyo School of Music produced in 1903. This was the first time an entire Western opera had been performed in Japan, and Koeber at the piano played the one-person orchestra from start to finish.[36] The production was also memorable because it launched the career of Shibata Tamaki, who sang the part of Euridice. Later, as Tamaki Miura, she became the first Japanese to sing the title role in *Madama Butterfly,* opposite Caruso, at the Metropolitan Opera House.[37]

Koeber's important collaborator was another musician from Europe, August Junker. Trained by the legendary violinist Joseph Joachim while at the Staatliche Hochschule für Musik in Cologne, Junker came to Japan after playing with the symphony orchestras of Boston and Chicago and joined the faculty of the Tokyo School of Music in 1899.[38] Although his bohemian personality was not as easily accepted as Koeber's serene respectability, Junker came to be known as "the father of orchestral music" in Japan.[39]

For more than ten years, Koeber and Junker premiered for Japanese audiences a number of works by European masters from the Baroque to the Romantic periods. The most celebrated was Koeber's performance of Mendelssohn's Piano Concerto in G Minor, accompanied by the Tokyo School's symphony orchestra under Junker's direction.[40] According to a local newspaper, "the concert compared favorably with those in Berlin or London."[41]

The Piano and Japan's Coming of Age

Around this time, the Japanese made a quantum leap in other areas of Western music as well. It had not been the custom, for example, for performers to play works in their entirety or according to the original scores. Short pieces, such as sonatinas, escaped cuts, but longer sonatas and concertos were usually reduced to one movement. In Koeber's day, by contrast, this practice declined quickly.[42]

Programming was another area of change. The standard practice had been cafeteria-style performances of different instruments and genres of performing arts from all over the world. In one concert, an audience might hear vocal music from lieder to a nagauta (long song), instruments from solo violin and solo piano to Chinese harps, Japanese noh and kyōgen, duets of viola and zither, and, if performers could be found, a piano trio or a string quartet. During Koeber's and Junker's time, Western music began to fill entire programs, although at times Western and Japanese music still shared the stage.

About the same time, the Japanese perspective on piano literature also shifted toward works that required new levels of technical virtuosity. When Japanese musicians first started studying the piano, their public performances commonly included pieces straight out of exercise books by Beyer, Czerny, or Clementi. Two popular exceptions were Weber's "Aufforderung zum Tanz" (Invitation to the dance) and Mendelssohn's "Rondo capriccioso." In the first decade of the twentieth century, however, many attempted advanced concert works, such as Beethoven sonatas, Schubert impromptus, and Chopin ballades.[43]

Finally, there was an exponential increase in the number of music students, graduates, and performers as more Japanese studying abroad returned home to teach and as better-trained European artists found employment at Japanese music schools. The majority played instruments other than the piano, usually the violin, which was more affordable and more pleasing to Japanese ears. Still, with assistance from visiting Europeans, Japanese pianists and other instrumentalists were able to fill concert programs.

Not all the changes at the turn of the century can be attributed to particular individuals. These changes were part and parcel of the history of Japan's effort to reclaim its national autonomy. The cherished goal of the Iwakura Embassy, to abrogate the unequal treaties with the West, began to be achieved on the eve of the Sino-Japanese War of 1894–95, when England agreed in principle. After the Japanese military victory against Russia a decade later, all the powers concurred. The growth of Western music in Japan coincided with its becoming a fully sovereign nation again.

The Japanese did not gain international standing by military prowess alone. Japanese manufacture of keyboard instruments took off in the first decade of the twentieth century. Companies such as Yamaha, Nishikawa, and Matsumoto competed not only with one another but against foreign firms as well. Yamaha

The chorus and orchestra of the Ueno Academy of Music, under the direction of August Junker, 1905. The phenonemal Kōda Nobu, appearing here as a violinist, is seated just to the right of Junker with her instrument tucked under her arm; her stand partner is her sister.

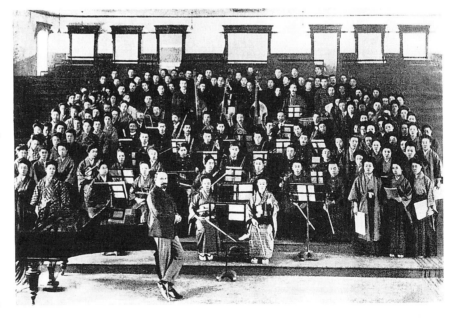

pianos were awarded honorary grand prizes at world expositions in St. Louis and Seattle in 1904 and 1909, respectively.[44] Even so, it was primarily Japan's military might, not cultural accomplishments, that won it the recognition of the West.

The Piano and Japan's New Middle Class

Although Western music became more established in some quarters of Japan in the early twentieth century, pianos still belonged in general to public arenas such as government offices, schools, churches, theaters, concert halls, hotels, and department stores. Even in these places, one did not always find a piano. According to an unofficial count of 1910, most large primary schools in Tokyo owned a grand piano. Of the three hundred middle schools in the entire country, however, only forty could boast such good fortune.[45] Outside Tokyo, it was unrealistic to expect to see even an upright at a primary school.

In the early twentieth century, however, private ownership of pianos expanded beyond the elite of the early Meiji period. Although the upper class held on to its advantages, a new middle class was born with bureaucrats, professionals, and entrepreneurs at its core. This new group was both interested in Western culture and capable of purchasing pianos.

Some literary works of the time captured the sounds of the piano from these quarters. The great writer Natsume Sōseki (1867–1916) is of special interest. He created many characters at the center of the rising middle class: government officials, university men—professors, researchers, students—businessmen, journalists, urban landlords, along with their sons and daughters who did not toil for a living. They paid attention to Western music because they were the educated Japanese of the new century. Natsume's novels, taken in chronological order, register the steadily increasing place of the piano in the life of this class, as well as the toll it took on members of this class to adjust to the cultural change that the piano represented.

In his first novel, *I Am a Cat*, published in the daily *Asahi* from January 1905 to August 1906, the characters play and discuss the violin, but not the piano. In *Nowaki* (An autumn storm), written five months later, Natsume introduced the piano into his fiction. A student goes to hear a concert of Western music that includes a piano trio, a violin and piano sonata by Beethoven (he at least recognizes the composer's name), and an adagio by . . . but then the student—who is very much a stand-in for the author himself—looks out the window and becomes lost in the sight of the birds that seem to dance to the music.

In the same year, Natsume depicted a female character who, having been brought up in Kyoto, cannot keep pace with the fast-changing world of Tokyo. On a rainy day, she listens to the koto a neighbor plays at home and remembers "the Kyoto of spring, of rain, of koto. Koto . . . becomes Kyoto. I love koto." Her regrets intensify: "I wish I had learned to play the piano. I wish I had kept up my English." She knows that "the world I have known will not last much longer."[46]

A year later, in 1908, Natsume created a strikingly modern woman, Mineko, in *Sanshirō*. Mineko is well educated for a young woman of the day. She speaks English, dresses smartly, and mingles freely with men. Most important, she goes to concerts and plays the piano. She captivates Sanshirō, a university student from the provinces, but marries a man in a frock coat and a silk hat. Sanshirō thereupon becomes interested in a friend of Mineko's who also plans to take piano lessons.

For Natsume's mostly female characters, piano playing was only a polite accomplishment, as it had long been for Western women. In Japan, though, it joined a somewhat different list of female accomplishments: performing the tea ceremony, arranging flowers, painting with watercolors, and cooking.[47] If Natsume tried to give the piano a deeper meaning for his characters, he lacked both the love of music and the expertise in it to succeed. Still, he insisted on putting pianos in his novels as though his writing would be incomplete without them.

Six months after publishing *Sanshirō*, Natsume paid a price for endowing one of his most alluring female characters with a piano. He was forced, "at long, nagging last," to buy a piano for his daughters. His wife announced that, to pay for it, she planned to use the royalty of four hundred yen from the first two thousand copies of the novel. He "agreed willy-nilly," wondering "how children can possibly appreciate playing the piano." On the day the piano arrived, Natsume's house "went upside down"; he did not write a single line of his next novel that day.[48]

World War I left a clear mark on the Japanese piano market. As soon as the war broke out, Western countries ceased to export pianos to Japan and other Asian countries. Japanese piano makers responded by increasing production to claim the domestic market and the markets in China, Korea, and Australia. The momentum continued even after the war, when imports from the West resumed. But the domestic market failed to expand, partly because pianos remained prohibitively expensive. In the early 1920s, a new domestically produced upright piano cost six to eight times the average monthly income of a middle-class worker.[49]

Although installment payments may have eased the pain of piano buyers, one problem persisted: urban Japanese houses were not built to accommodate pianos.

The Limit of the Piano's Reach

313

Pianos were as much a punishment to soft tatami-matted floors as dirt floors would be to them. But a room with a wood floor, more fitting to a piano, was a luxury that ordinary city dwellers could ill afford; it required other exotic and expensive household items like chairs, tables, desks, and carpets. Besides, a Western-style room did not serve multiple purposes—dining room, family room, even bedroom —the way a tatami room did. A room that could house a piano had to be an addition to the usual Japanese living space.

Against this background, in the early 1920s, urban residents were presented with an architectural dream: "the cultural house." It was to be a five-hundred-square-foot structure that had a Western-style room, complete with a piano. Developers translated the dream into "cultural villages" in Tokyo's suburbs. These houses were not cheap. Their buyer-occupants were university graduates with incomes far above average. Some of them no doubt bought a piano.[50] But both cultural houses and pianos remained beyond the reach of most Japanese.

In addition, schools never became an unfailing market for pianos nationwide. Obviously, the economic boom in Japan during World War I benefited schools in some parts of the country. In 1917, for example, the prosperous city of Osaka boasted sixty-one pianos among more than 120 primary schools and kindergartens, and the city expected all those schools to have a piano in a few years. Five years later, though, the northernmost prefecture of Aomori could claim only seven pianos among all its educational institutions, from primary to normal schools.[51]

As the nationalist zeal of both the government and the people abated after Japan's victory against Russia in 1905, pressure eased on schools to bear the musical flags of national pride. Besides, pianos were not absolute necessities at schools so long as teachers had organs to help them teach patriotic songs to children. Although statistics are unavailable, probably few Japanese schools lacked an organ in those days. In other words, the limited educational role assigned to the piano by the government also restricted its reach in pre–World War I Japan.

Japanese Women and the Piano

According to Natsume Sōseki, Koeber believed that there was but one true musician in Japan: Kōda Nobu (1870–1946). Kōda was the first graduate of the Tokyo School of Music, and in 1889 she became the first student of music sent abroad by the government. Kōda studied first at the New England Conservatory of Music, then continued her training in Vienna, where she studied piano, violin, viola, voice (lieder), harmony, and composition. Her teachers included violinist Joseph Hellmesberger (1855–1905).

Upon returning to Japan six years later, Kōda became a full professor at the

Tokyo School of Music, where she taught classes and gave public performances. Her repertories included not only European music for piano, violin, viola, and voice but also music for traditional Japanese instruments, which she had learned to play as a child. One year, a music magazine voted her the most popular Japanese female musician.[52]

Less phenomenal perhaps but proficient still were Koeber's and Kōda's own students, including Tachibana Itoe, Kanbe Aya, Kuno Hisa, and Ogura Sue. Like Kōda, many of these women studied in Europe as well as Japan. The best became professors of piano at the Tokyo School of Music. Tachibana attained the highest professional rank of chokuninkan, the emperor's personal appointee at a government school. She and Kōda were also named to the venerable Japanese Academy of the Arts. Kuno Hisa's life ended tragically in Germany with her suicide. Ogura Sue, who attended the Hochschule für Musik in Berlin until the outbreak of World War I, gave a debut recital in New York to critical acclaim and taught piano at a conservatory in Chicago. In male-dominated Japanese society, these women's accomplishments were eye opening.

Below these stellar achievers was a layer of competent female piano players. Almost every year since its founding, the Tokyo School of Music had graduated more female piano majors than men. By 1912, the last year of the Meiji Emperor's reign, the ratio of women to men who had played the piano in a concert during their school years or after graduation was nearly three to two.[53]

The Meiji government's objective in training women in the piano was to foster piano-playing schoolteachers, not professional performers. In addition to accepting the piano as a vocation for women, the government advanced an educational philosophy that embraced it as a nonprofessional, middle-class value. Watanabe Tatsukiyo, the president of the Tokyo School of Music, believed that women should stay home and "hold the fort." Yet he knew that women, especially urban homemakers, could develop psychological problems from being in a house all day. So Watanabe prescribed piano to these women in much the same way that psychiatrists might prescribe medication to depressed patients. "Music will cheer up women who stay home," he said. He also advised women to learn to play the piano so that they could enliven Japanese parties, which, in his opinion, were "too stiff and formal."[54] It was this type of semi-official encouragement that colored Natsume Sōseki's female characters' interests and helps explain the popularity of the piano among middle-class men and women.

The achievements of the female pianists of pre–World War I Japan is a significant lesson in women's empowerment. They played a vital role in their government's policy to make the country sufficiently rich and strong to survive Western imperialism. They carried not only the burden of the incipient art but also, it seemed, the fate of the national community of the Japanese. No matter how begrudging men were in recognizing these artists' accomplishments, what counted in the end was not their gender but their work that was believed to contribute to the survival of Japan.

The Piano Institutionalized
James Parakilas

By the end of the nineteenth century, pianos could be found not just in people's homes and in musical institutions, but almost anywhere that people gathered. Places of business, educational and religious institutions, and residential institutions (such as hospitals, orphanages, nursing homes, asylums, and prisons) were providing music to a large public in situations where only the privileged might earlier have had it. Pianists began to make their livings accompanying the activities of daily life and providing solace to those who were judged unfit for ordinary life. The piano became institutionalized in the institutions of civil society.

A simple change at the music store represents one side of this shift. In a music store and lending library in early-nineteenth-century London, as we saw in the advertisement for Domenico Corri's establishment in Chapter 3, a patron might be accommodated with "Apartments, and Instruments of every Description, for the Purpose of trying Music." In the early twentieth century, there was still apt to be a piano in the store for trying music, but now the store might also provide a "song plugger," a pianist who would demonstrate to the patrons the songs and other items that were for sale. Song plugging represented a new stage in the promotion of music; department stores as well as music stores provided pianists and pianos to promote sales of sheet music, and in New York the song pluggers who worked in piano cubicles in the music stores of Tin Pan Alley by day would move to the theater district by night, to plug the same songs in theatrical revues and the intermissions of movie showings. Song plugging represented a new form of livelihood for musicians; George Gershwin was making a living at it when he was fifteen. And it represented a step into what Craig Roell has described as an age of musical consumerism; instead of having to work a new song out for themselves on the piano, patrons could now have it realized for them before they bought it.[55]

Pianos turned up in other kinds of stores, for purposes other than selling music. In an engraving of a photographer's studio in Cincinnati as early as 1854, we see a piano provided in a space that doubles as a waiting room for those about to sit for their photographs and a showroom for those who might buy the studio's work; presumably this piano—true to a long tradition of music in artists' studios

—might have been heard in the rooms where the sittings were held as well. This one image, then, brings up the history of background music in waiting rooms, where it helps pass the time; in artistic sittings, where it helps both the sitter and the artist stay relaxed and composed; and in showrooms, where background music helps put customers in a favorable frame of mind. For that matter, how can we—accustomed as we are to canned music in such situations—tell whether the piano in this image is being played by a musician hired by the studio or by a customer amusing herself and others?

Because travel can seem like an endless stay in a waiting room, pianos were placed in the lounges of steamships and in other kinds of conveyances. Captain Scott's ship carried a player piano to Antarctica; the dirigible *Hindenburg* carried a piano specially made of aluminum for lightness. In each case tedium turned out not to be the problem, and the piano couldn't help. It did on the *Titanic,* though, where those left behind by the lifeboats at least had musical accompaniment during their last hours on the ship.

If music could help artists or photographers and their subjects during sittings, it could have a similar effect on people's concentration as they engaged in other kinds of work. Early in the history of filmmaking, for instance, music was played on the set, in the words of the director Abel Gance, "not only to give the mood, but to keep everyone quiet." The actress Lillian Gish, however, felt that "the music

Engraving of the showroom of Ball's Great Daguerrian Gallery of the West, Cincinnati, Ohio, in *Gleason's Pictorial Drawing-Room Companion,* April 1, 1854

was fine, of course, when I wasn't trying to concentrate on a scene." The music was provided by anything from a single piano to the thirty-piece Palm Court orchestra used during the shooting of Cecil B. DeMille's *Ten Commandments* (1923).[56]

If background music could dispose customers to buy photographs, it presumably did that by making shopping seem like a form of entertainment; in fact, to say that a consumer society was being created at the begin-

ning of the twentieth century is to say that for the first time it was being made possible for a considerable part of a society to find shopping entertaining. Eating in a restaurant—another luxury that was being extended socially—was already something of an entertainment, especially for anyone who was saved from cooking and serving at home by it, and it was doubly entertaining when the establishment installed a piano, to be played alone or with other instruments and song. In still other places that served food and drink, the defining business was entertainment, and here—in music halls, dance halls, cabarets, café concerts, and saloons—a piano was the basic musical equipment, to which other instruments might be added, for accompanying singing and dancing of all sorts. Toulouse-Lautrec's *Moorish Dance (La Danse mauresque, ou les almées)* of 1895 shows this sort of entertainment, although it was painted for an outdoor site: a Paris fair. It is one of two panels that the artist painted to adorn the front of the fair booth devoted to performances by the famous Moulin Rouge dancer La Goulue. At the same time that the panel divided the performance area from the public, the image painted on it brings together the dancer, her admirers, and that necessary sideline figure, the dance-hall pianist.

Music and drink had always been companions of prostitution, but in the late nineteenth century prostitution was moving more and more from establishments where the "typical visit" was "usually short, quiet, and veiled in secrecy," in the words of Timothy J. Gilfoyle, to places of public entertainment where "the sex of the brothel was available, but so were the intoxication and camaraderie of the saloon and the entertainment of the theater." Pianos provided much of the music for that scene, contributing to a reorganization of prostitution in which "proprietors at once gained greater control over the workplace of the prostitute and created a more profitable form of commercial sex."[57] Another extension of the factory model, it seems.

The roles of the piano in religious institutions have in large part been defined by the similarities and differences between the piano and the pipe organ, the tradi-

Filming of the silent movie *Monsieur Beaucaire* (directed by Sidney Olcott) in 1924. A piano is among the instruments that can be seen in front of the set, providing background music to the acting.

tional instrument of worship in Western Christianity. Because the piano could substitute for the organ in preluding, postluding, and hymn accompanying, it was used in churches too remote or too poor to have an organ. When the Mormon community made its trek to Utah in the 1840s, for instance, its members endured the considerable difficulty of dragging a piano (and a melodeon) across the continent in order to keep their faith alive with music. But the piano could also give worship a character different from what the organ gave it. In James Baldwin's *Go Tell It on the Mountain* (1953), the group ecstasy that the Harlem congregation reaches as Brother Elisha leads them in song from the piano would seem quite different if he were playing a pipe organ instead. And as gospel music has developed in African-American churches, the piano and the electronic organ have come to be played

Henri de Toulouse-Lautrec, *La Danse mauresque* (The moorish dance), 1895 (Musée d'Orsay, Paris)

319

Front parlor of Mary Humphrey's brothel, Cheyenne, Wyoming, ca. 1900 (Amon Carter Museum, Fort Worth, Texas)

Below: Susa Young Gates, daughter of Brigham Young, on the importance of music—and the piano—in Mormon history and family life, *Musical America*, November 20, 1915

How Utah's Pioneers Carried Music Across "The Rockies"

Musical Study and Performance Encouraged as an Uplifting Influence Among People of Latter Day Saints' Church—Brigham Young's Love for Music and the Universal Talents of His Children and Grandchildren—Oratorio Performances in the Seventies—Hauled Piano with an Ox Team in 1848

By SUSA YOUNG GATES

[Mrs. Susa Young Gates is a daughter of Brigham Young and the mother of Lucy Gates, the noted American soprano.]

ALL of my brothers and sisters were musicians of a sort. And there were thirty or forty of us, you know. Father was a natural musician. His mother, Abigail Howe, one of the famous Massachusetts Howe family, was one of five sisters, who were locally quite famous as singers in Northboro and Hopkinton, Mass. My grandmother, Abigail, who died about 1821, bequeathed her love of beauty, music and refinement to her family of eleven; five brothers and six sisters. Grandfather, John Young, fought four engagements under General Washington. I have seen his war papers in the Boston State House. His sons, John, Joseph, Brigham and Lorenzo, formed a male quartet as boys and were, I thought when I heard them as elderly men, marvelously beautiful singers.

Early Music Makers

Father fostered and encouraged the

Members of a Deeply Musical Family: Ten Older Daughters of President Brigham Young. Photographed in 1865. Five Are Now Living

Brigham Young (Second from Left) and Four of His Brothers. John, Joseph, Brigham and Lorenzo Formed a Male Quartet as Boys

Susa Young Gates, Daughter of Brigham Young and Mother of Lucy Gates

Piano Brought Across "The Plains" by Ox Teams in 1848 by President Heber C. Kimball. The Piano Is Now in the Bureau of Information, Salt Lake City

Melodeon Brought Across "The Plains" by Brigham Young in 1848. It Is Now in the Relic Room of the Bureau of Information

together, taking distinct musical roles.

D. H. Lawrence's poem "Piano" reminds us that Sunday evenings were set aside in many Christian homes for "hymns in the cozy parlour, the tinkling piano our guide." By the end of the nineteenth century, instrument manufacturers were offering small organs for the home as well as harmoniums and other domestic keyboard instruments that would recall the sound of the organ better than the piano did—and that therefore might prejudice their

owners to use them more for hymn singing than, say, dancing. But countless families like the Lawrences might dance to their adaptable pianos on Saturday night without supposing for an instant that its "tinkling" was less than a suitable "guide" for their hymn singing on Sunday evening.

In schools as in church, the piano served in good measure as a guide to singing, at least through the nineteenth century. From the beginning of that century, private seminaries for girls regularly offered piano lessons to their students, but in public schools from England and America to Japan, it took most of the nineteenth century just to establish the moral and intellectual need for instruction in music, the best method to teach children singing and sight-singing, and the best selection of songs for them to sing. By the latter part of the century, the training of music teachers for the schools was beginning to include piano instruction, so that the teachers could accompany singing groups as well as give examples in music appreciation classes. But teaching students to sing particular songs was also a form of appreciation—a way of teaching them to revere the values expressed in the songs. Wherever schools were creatures of the government, school songs became an exercise in nationalism, whether the songs were patriotic or "folk." And the teacher's piano supplied not only the notes to be sung but also an arranger's idea of the character of the students' national music.[58]

In a turn-of-the-century photograph of the Athens (Ohio) Lunatic Asylum, built in 1874, a piano is being played in the ballroom. Given that the facility was built with a ballroom, it goes without saying that it would have had a piano. Why there should have been a ballroom and a piano in a nineteenth-century lunatic asylum is perhaps not so important a question as what they were used for once they were there. Singing and dancing were recognized as mental-health therapies in the nineteenth century. But the ballroom sometimes served as a concert hall as well as a dance floor for the patients: listening is therapeutic, too. It served as a chapel, where hymns were sung to the piano. The staff and even community groups used the space and instrument for their own banquets and other gatherings. The presence of the piano did not define the function of the room as social or therapeutic, as a place for patients or for others; it broke down those distinctions.[59]

In any institution of confinement there may be a piano. The piano may be used to reach past patients' ailments or handicaps, to bring their bodies and spirits alive. It may be used to create social bonds among children with no parents, aged adults who have survived their spouses and even their children, people of all ages whose disabilities cut them off from some kinds of social interaction. In the vast, cold hall of a prison where thousands of inmates sit in rows to hear a concert —or did before canned entertainment made prison officials forget what a difference live music can make—the piano turns the prison fleetingly into a home; the

The ballroom, or parlor, at the Athens Lunatic Asylum, now the Southeast Psychiatric Hospital, Athens, Ohio, early 1900s

A class in Dalcroze Eurhythmics, Institute for the Education of the Blind, New York, 1935

Below: Prisoners assembled for a concert, San Quentin Prison, California, before 1937

sound of the piano has always been the sound of home. Even where it is not intended to, a piano in an institution of confinement can provide a reminder, a link,

a passport to the outside world; in the 1960s an inmate in a British prison taught himself to play on the chapel piano, and on being released he got a job as pianist on a cruise ship.[60] Whatever the problem is that the institution was founded to deal with, the piano is there to contribute to the cure. But to recognize that is to recognize that putting a piano in an institution of confinement is simply treating the residents as human beings. We all use music as a cure for what ails us.

Preview: Silent Movies with Piano

Michael Chanan

As Kurt Weill once said, the silent movie needed music the way dry cereal needs cream. Unable to provide it by mechanical means, the cinema gave the piano a great boost, at least as long as the screen was mute. We know that piano improvisation on popular tunes accompanied projection from the debut of the Lumière Cinématographe in Paris in 1895 onward (at the London debut it was a harmonium), and that the use of the phonograph to provide music was also an intermittent early practice (technically unsatisfactory, but people kept trying). In the music halls and the large purpose-built cinemas that began to appear in the years before World War I, there were bands and even whole orchestras ready to provide lavish accompaniments, but as film shows spread rapidly, it was pianists for whom there was greatest demand. One account reports that in Britain in 1924 cinemas were said to employ half the members of the musicians' union, which had doubled the size of its prewar membership, and four years later, they provided more than three-quarters of paid musical employment.[1] The music publishers benefited from a corresponding increase in demand for sheet music.

From the outset, music did more than mask the sound of the projector—it helped to tame the uncanny nature of the new invention, the unsettling magic that was part of its original attraction, and in due course it became another way of setting the scene.[2] At first there was little attempt to match the music to the image. Kurt London's book on film music dating from 1936 describes the early accompanists: their repertory remained a matter of complete indifference, they played anything they liked.[3] Such indifference could only pass "unnoticed" as long as the music had to answer to no more than the short, disconnected scenes that made up the

A 1924 film showing, with a piano at the center of the small ensemble that provides the musical accompaniment. This is a staged photograph (given the lighting problems, it could hardly be otherwise) in which a movie still has been superimposed on the screen.

early film show. But as film began to evolve its narrative capacities, finding music to correspond to the moods and scenes placed new demands on accompanying musicians to help make the dramatic shape of these films more intelligible, and indeed, as pianists became more adept at reading the screen, they developed a repertoire of techniques that not only assisted in concentrating the audience's attention but helped to tell them where they were in the flow of the drama. Prestigious productions would commission arrangers to provide appropriate scores, but the majority of accompanists would have to rely on a kind of folk wisdom that quickly grew up to cope, in which tremolos expressed passion, pounding chords signified menace, and different stock pieces were linked by tricks of rapid modulation and improvised chords.

We might speculate for a moment on the way that silent cinema might have stimulated the rebirth of the art of musical improvisation—an art still very much alive in the age of the great Romantic virtuosos, and which was being reborn, in the quite separate context of the emergence of jazz. But in a world where the commercialization of music hall and vaudeville had already produced the standardization of popular music according to the dictates of the publisher, such a possibility is hardly expectable. It was in the same decade as the invention of cinema that a newspaper columnist dubbed the street in New York where the publishers gravitated with the name Tin Pan Alley. A significant part of their business after the turn of the century came from the sale of sheet music for picture house pianists, and by 1910 a small industry had began to supply special cue sheets to go with the latest releases: an Irish melody for an Irish story, sentimental ballads for Florence Turner films, marches for war pictures, and so forth.

According to an account by one of those involved in the business, "The piano players who received the Ennis system of Vitagraph Music Cues probably felt after a while that there were only a limited number of musical compositions in the world and that Remick and his fellow publishers had the exclusive rights to these compositions," adding that "We showed our class by injecting at times the classical and standard numbers—a few of them, anyhow."[4] The system quickly spread, institutionalizing what was already an established informal practice that now perpetrated an authorized classification of music according to the crudest possible categories. A manual for the movie pianist published by one of the leading music publishers, Schirmer, in 1924, had a quick reference index with fifty-three categories, from Aeroplane to Western. Under "Sinister" we find only the Coriolan Overture by Beethoven. Under "Religioso," Handel's "Largo," "The Old Hundredth" by Bourgeois, "Onward Christian Soldiers" by Sullivan, and the unaccredited

"Agitato No. 3" (unnamed piece by Otto Langey), from Erno Rapée, *Motion Picture Moods for Pianists and Organists: A Rapid-Reference Collection of Selected Pieces* (New York, 1924). The rapid-reference index can be seen along the side of the page. The music is so blatantly derived from Schubert's song "Der Erlkönig," it is no wonder Rapée labeled it "suitable for gruesome or infernal scenes, witches, etc."

hymn "Lead Kindly Light." Under "Sadness" are fourteen pieces by such compos-
ers as Beethoven, Chopin, Grieg, Anton Rubinstein, Tchaikovsky, and Massenet.

The use of classics was favored by cinema managers because it helped avoid
the risk of copyright infringement at a time when its enforcement was becoming
stronger. There were those who argued that it also helped increase the musical
sophistication of a growing audience, but cultural critics demur. In the view of
T. W. Adorno, for example, music in this situation develops a liability to decompose
into a series of aural tidbits, highlights, and icons, and the result is a process of
fetishization that detaches the music from any meaningful context. The effect
reaches far beyond the cinema: it creates a way of hearing that insists on associat-
ing music forever with pictures, whether appropriate or not, reducing it to a kind
of mnemonic of the image. It is indicative that the cue-sheet system introduced by
Vitagraph was devised by a press agent. Music, in other words, was not regarded
as an aesthetically integral part of the viewing of a film but as a sales device.

As such, of course, it works both ways, and after the coming of the talkies,
when music became integrated into the production process, there are countless
cases of films functioning as advertisements for pieces of music that become best-
sellers as a result, from regular pop tunes to the classics. The opportunities that
cinema provides here range from the specially composed theme tune to the un-
planned result of a choice of soundtrack music. It is a critical question, however,
what kind of shifts and realignments of cultural meaning are produced when a
Mozart piano concerto, for example, becomes a best-seller and acquires a new
nickname as a result of an arbitrary association with a tale of elopement by a
*tightrope walker and a soldier in nineteenth-century Sweden (*Elvira Madigan,
directed by Bo Widerberg, 1967). If this is precisely the kind of dislocation of
meaning, or dissociated transference of affect, said to typify the culture of post-
modernism, then there is also the case of the Paul Newman and Robert Redford
*gangster movie a few years later (*The Sting, *directed by George Roy Hill, 1973)*
that sparked a revival of Scott Joplin's ragtime that lodged itself in industry leg-
end; according to a senior music industry executive speaking in 1997, the ragtime
craze the film awakened was in large part responsible for the great upsurge in
piano sales in the 1970s.[5]

On a snug evening I shall watch her fingers,
Cleverly ringed, declining to clever pink,
Beg glory from the willing keys. Old hungers
Will break their coffins, rise to eat and thank.
And music, warily, like the golden rose
That sometimes after sunset warms the west,
Will warm that room, persuasively suffuse
That room and me, rejuvenate a past.
But suddenly, across my climbing fever
Of proud delight—a multiplying cry.
A cry of bitter dead men who will never
Attend a gentle maker of musical joy.
Then my thawed eye will go again to ice.
And stone will shove the softness from my face.
      —Gwendolyn Brooks, "Piano after War"

Eight **Hollywood's Embattled Icon**

Ivan Raykoff

"After war," the piano was ruined. By 1945, the year Brooks's poem was first published, the devastation of two world wars had severely shaken twentieth-century civilization: entrenched empires had fallen, genocide of unprecedented proportions had been committed, and new weapons of mass destruction had annihilated entire cities. Amid such monumental events, the piano might seem like an insignificant and irrelevant piece of musical furniture, but in the course of these upheavals, and in their aftermath, the instrument came to represent something much greater than itself. It had become a nostalgic symbol of the Western cultural traditions threatened, damaged, or even destroyed in these battles. Brooks's sonnet invokes a number of these nostalgic connotations surrounding the piano: its capacity to convey tradition and trigger memory ("rejuvenate a past"), its power to elicit emotional response and feeling ("old hungers"), and its association with femininity ("her fingers, cleverly ringed"). But the impact of war and suffering has disabled the piano's musical powers. Where the pianist could once "beg glory from the willing keys," and the listener could unguardedly allow feverish musical feeling to work its charms, that "proud delight" is now suddenly interrupted. War—which threatens tradition and traumatizes memory—here becomes a catalyst for a cold, hard despair supplanting nostalgic warmth. The piano's musical spell had become tentative ("warily . . . will warm that room") and is finally rendered impotent for the grieving listener.[1]

The piano at war: sanctuary of love and battlefield of the sexes in *Casablanca*, 1942

329

The piano was not only a symbol of culture, it was a symptom of cultural change. Seeing a piano, one imagined classical music, inspired artistic creativity, bourgeois domesticity, noble aristocracy, the grand spectacle of public performance, and the intimacy of private expression. Seeing a ruined and wrecked piano, one could infer the destruction and loss of those threatened attributes; one could imagine humanity, culture, and art facing the aftermath of war, or Eurocentric civilization struggling, and failing, to maintain cherished ideals in the face of senseless savagery. The piano thus became a nostalgic representation of a vulnerable—and perhaps redeemable—past.

Cinema, the most popular and persuasive of all twentieth-century art forms, appreciates the communicative power of this widely recognized cultural icon. In film, such images can relay multivalent connotative meanings to provide context, tell stories, and invoke myths in a single passing glance. During and after the 1940s, the image of the destroyed piano became a recurrent cinematic icon—in both Hollywood and foreign films—to represent a wide range of nostalgic ideals associated with the cultural life of a previous era.

In this light we see why it was useful, perhaps necessary, for the makers of the blockbuster hit *Titanic* (1997) to show a ruined and broken piano in the ship's submerged stateroom. As an underwater camera scans the interior of the sunken ship near the beginning of the film, it travels alongside the skeletal remains of a decaying, waterlogged grand piano. This brief image is a crucial component in the broader symbolism of the doomed ocean liner, which sank on its maiden voyage in 1912: both ship and piano signify past glory, opulence, elegance, and "the good life" gone awry.

But where the *Titanic*'s tragic fate invokes a morality tale on the dangers of hubristic technology, this image of the silenced piano is infused with a nostalgic sense of humanity. In that same stateroom, the two protagonists discover their deep physical and emotional yearnings for each other—to the soundtrack accompaniment of a solo piano. Their coming-of-age story is set in stark opposition to the demands of society and propriety, and the piano is a significant musical component in this struggle to love. Although the young lovers win their battle against the inflexible demands of family and class, their fate, like the piano's, is sealed by the larger, uncontainable struggle between civilization/ship and nature/ocean.

In Jane Campion's 1993 film *The Piano,* the instrument again endures the conflicts of primordial nature versus European civilization and romantic love versus familial duty; it is first abandoned on a deserted beachhead, later attacked and dismembered, and finally drowned in the course of its "psychological" battles. Here the piano echoes a woman's inner life, and thus signifies, by the climax of the film, the apparent silencing of her emotions and desires. Although one might imagine that the jettisoned piano sinking in the sea provides narrative closure on issues of colonialism, female repression, and sexual frustration, in fact another piano takes its place in the story's somewhat bourgeois dénouement. Campion's piano-themed story of vulnerability in battle has been tempered with a form of redemption.

In *Titanic, The Piano,* and countless other Hollywood and foreign films, the piano, an emblem of the "Romantic"—that is, both the historical era and the emotion—accompanies and enacts narratives of idealized love and unattainable desire. These eroticized, often nostalgic associations are the mainstay of the piano's repertoire as a cinematic icon. An object of the warm and cozy past, the piano appears frequently as a safe sanctuary of love, but one threatened or doomed as change looms in the future. Add to this notion the political expediencies of a culture at war, and these associations take on a loaded significance: the piano becomes an embattled Romantic icon, threatened just as love (humanity), freedom (desire), tradition (history), and democracy (or whatever applicable political ideal) come under attack.

Such embattled pianos are sites of explosive tensions, or waiting traps, or even musical coffins. In *Schindler's List* (1993), a few clattering tones from an upright piano murderously betray the Jews hiding within to attacking Nazi soldiers. In *The English Patient* (1996), a toppled grand piano in a ruined Italian villa has been mined by invading Germans, set to explode if certain keys are touched. In *Saving Private Ryan* (1998), an American soldier is wounded by sniper fire as he tries to rescue a young child (the hope for the future); he collapses onto an abandoned upright piano amid the rubble of the bombarded French village (which, like the ruined piano, is part of a European past now destroyed).

Perhaps no cinematic portrayal captures these two motifs of piano connotation (the sanctuary of love, the battleground of conflict) as perfectly as that most famous Hollywood piano scene of all, Sam (Dooley Wilson) playing "As Time Goes By" for estranged lovers Rick and Ilsa in *Casablanca* (1942). Humphrey Bogart and Ingrid Bergman enact their cinematic affair "with" the piano in two distinct senses: the instrument accompanies, as an indispensable soundtrack device, their inopportune Parisian romance with an appropriately nostalgic song (much as piano music does in the *Titanic* seduction scene), and it provides an important plot device as the hiding place for the valuable "letters of transit" that enable Ilsa and her husband to begin a new life together in America. Sam's upright piano is even more secure than Rick's office safe, for it protects through its apparently innocent aura of culture—a quality regarded as sacrosanct even (or perhaps particularly) by the German "bad guys" of the story.

The Classics Politicized

As the representative solo instrument of nineteenth-century Romanticism, the piano of Beethoven, Chopin, Liszt, and Brahms was a symbol for the practices and ideals of that era, including the "high art" tradition of "classical" music and the various musical, social, and philosophical attitudes surrounding it. With World War I and the advent of the modernist aesthetic, tastes and trends in culture—including musical culture—began to change significantly, and the emblematic Romantic piano weathered these shifting winds with difficulty. Arthur Loesser writes of this period, "Skepticism of the piano went with skepticism of the way of life that had nurtured it. The low point of both was reached in 1933, the year of the bank failures and of Hitler's rise. The idol had been tottering for a quarter of a century; now it fell from its little pedestal, its halo shattered."[2] Significantly, Loesser invokes probably the single most important—and usually overlooked—factor for the piano's eventual ruin: its connection to world politics.

In the cinema of the 1930s and early 1940s, the piano was still a symbol of antebellum elegance; during this period, Hollywood musicals frequently employed the instrument for its innocent and classy connotations of refined, "cultured" entertainment. *King of Jazz* (1930), Universal Studios' first feature-length all-Technicolor musical, presented an elaborate setting for George Gershwin's *Rhapsody in Blue*—five pianists "play" an immense grand piano keyboard while Paul Whiteman's orchestra accompanies from beneath the raised lid (see illustration in the Introduction). The classic 1933 musical *Flying Down to Rio* introduced the soon immortalized dance team of Fred Astaire and Ginger Rogers, featuring the pair dancing atop seven white grand pianos. Perhaps the most famous and extravagant of such production numbers is Busby Berkeley's grand piano "ballet" in *Gold Diggers of 1935*, in which fifty-six smiling beauties play fifty-six gently spinning white pianos choreographed in curving and symmetrical formations, and a solo dancer twirls atop the piano lids in a billowing white dress that seems to defy gravity. (White-piano dance routines receive a spoofing in the 1981 musical *Pennies from Heaven*, when Bernadette Peters's grammar school class erupts into a tap-dance routine on their grand-piano desktops.)

The emotional impact of classical music, particularly the late German Romanticism that had so heavily influenced film scores of classic Hollywood com-

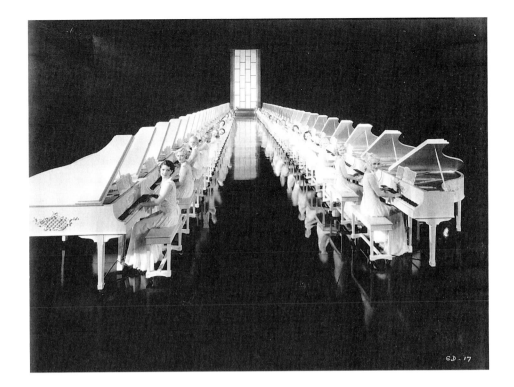

Point of convergence between public entertainment and private domesticity, the piano nurtured an appreciation for musical culture—not only the classics, but emergent popular forms such as jazz as well. Grand pianos create grand spectacle in *Gold Diggers of 1935* (above). At left, Al Jolson plays and sings for his appreciative mother in *The Jazz Singer* (1927), Hollywood's first "talking picture."

Soldierly camaraderie at the piano. In *Anchors Aweigh* (1945), Gene Kelly and Frank Sinatra try out the grands at the Hollywood Bowl. *Opposite*, Carl Raddatz and Otto Ernst Hasse play a Chopin Polonaise and Wagner opera excerpts in *Stukas*, a 1941 German battle-action film about Luftwaffe flyers.

posers in the 1930s and 1940s, was now also pressed into service to stimulate patriotic feeling. Political systems of all persuasions embraced high culture artifacts like classical music as being among the war's lofty causes, while cinematic productions harnessed the classics—and the piano—to remind war-weary audiences of the moral justifications for battle.

In his book on British film music, John Huntley considers a number of productions in the 1940s that utilized classical music "to bring the best to as many people as possible to cheer them on to better times." The work of Britain's Council for the Encouragement of Music and the Arts was portrayed in the 1942 short *C.E.M.A.*, the final sequence of which features Tchaikovsky's B-flat Minor Piano Concerto accompanying views of a canteen audience and a munitions factory in production. *Battle for Music* (1943) depicts the wartime struggles of the London Philharmonic Orchestra, with pianists Eileen Joyce and Benno Moiseiwitsch performing at a benefit after German bombings destroy the orchestra's instruments and concert hall. *Listen to Britain* (1942), described by Huntley as "the music of a people at war," includes a sequence at the National Gallery in which Myra Hess, later knighted for her morale-inspiring concerts through the Blitz, performs a Mozart piano concerto.[3] (Hess may also have been the inspiration for the opening scene of *Love Story* in 1944, starring Margaret Lockwood as a concert pianist whose recital at the National Gallery features, symbolically enough, Chopin's "Revolutionary" Etude.)

In Hollywood, too, concert pianists dedicated themselves to the war effort via the movies. José Iturbi appeared as himself in a half dozen MGM musicals during the 1940s; the first of these was *Thousands Cheer* (1943), in which he conducts a multinational chorus in the "United Nations" march by Dmitri Shostakovich. In *Follow the Boys* (1944), Artur Rubinstein does his part for the soldiers overseas, joining such show-business stars as Marlene Dietrich, Orson Welles, W. C. Fields, the Andrews Sisters, and Sophie Tucker to provide "real living entertainment" for the boys away from home. Rubinstein performs Franz Liszt's famous "Liebestraum," while superimposed behind him is a spinning globe and images of soldiers, nurses, and other service members listening appreciatively amid their duties.

The Germans had their own version of the patriotic musical variety film. *Wunschkonzert* (Request concert, 1940) was based on a popular Sunday afternoon radio show broadcasting favorite songs, announcements of births, and dedications to loved ones. Like *Follow the Boys*, the film enacts a broadcast show that unites the front to the homeland through music. In addition to popular singing acts and Eugen Jochum conducting Mozart's "Marriage of Figaro" Overture, *Wunschkonzert* also portrays a young German soldier playing Beethoven's music on the piano at his home. After he is killed in a heroic effort to save his fellow soldiers, his mother requests that her son's favorite song be played once more on the broadcast, as she weeps near the now vacant piano. (Even the Soviets could appropriate Beethoven: in the short film *Appassionata* of 1963, the actor playing Vladimir Lenin listens for the first time to the eponymous Beethoven sonata, exclaiming, "I have never heard anything better . . . I could listen to it every day. It is marvelous, superhuman music.")[4]

As Nazi Germany continued its political and ideological conquests during the early 1940s, the music of German composers (Wagner in particular) became associated with the extremes of German nationalism. Even today, the notion of German, and thus politicized, classical music still informs certain film narratives, and the piano is often called upon to represent the combative carrier of these still potent associations. In *The English Patient*, a grand piano has been rigged with Nazi explosives, but Juliette Binoche's character plays a portion of J. S. Bach's "Goldberg Variations" without setting them off; warned of the danger, she jokes weakly that if the Germans placed the bomb, playing Bach should be safe. This same "loaded" power could be transferred to another sort of war, but Mozart's music serves as only a temporary talisman to fend off Indian attack in the 1960 western *The Unforgiven*. When the tribe plays its preparatory flute war dance, which they believe will make them bulletproof, Burt Lancaster's character vows to "give them some magic of our own!" The matriarch of the family (Lillian Gish) races through the opening of the C Minor Fantasia on a grand piano stationed outdoors, but the spell soon fades, and in a striking scene Indian warriors attack the piano with spears and tomahawks, shattering it to pieces as they themselves are shot down.

Piano concertos proved to be a favorite "politicized" musical genre in 1940s Hollywood features. Perhaps the image of the piano soloist pitted against orchestra and conductor lends something of a battle mystique to these works; in the hands of evil culprits, however, they could prove fatal. In the 1943 remake of *The Phantom of the Opera*, Claude Rains (just after his portrayal in *Casablanca* of the corrupt but compassionate police captain Renault) stars as the pitiable madman-monster driven by frustrated love. In the climactic rescue scene, a performance of the Phantom's new piano concerto (performed on screen by a character portraying Franz Liszt, no less) brings the police to the door of his subterranean hideaway, and their gunshots cause the crumbling walls to crash down upon the unlucky, misunderstood pianist-Phantom as he plays for his captive girlfriend.

Above Suspicion is another 1943 Hollywood production, a spy story from MGM set in Germany and Austria, with Joan Crawford and Fred MacMurray as Anglo-American newlyweds who spend their honeymoon in 1939 doing an undercover search for a missing British agent. One dramatic climax occurs at a Salzburg concert hall: a shot fired during a loud timpani attack in Liszt's E-flat Major Concerto kills a high-ranking Nazi official in charge of the Dachau concentration camp. Pure Hollywood invention, this dramatic piano moment is absent from the original 1941 novel by Helen MacInnes, but given the accumulated mythology of the piano as a politicized "weapon," its iconic derivation seems clear.

In the hands of the good guys, however, the concerto could end in (usually romantic) victory. In *Dangerous Moonlight* (1941), exploding bombs throw an American woman into the arms of Polish pianist Stefan Radetzky (Anton Walbrook), as they kiss to the love theme of his newly composed "Warsaw Concerto." In *Rhapsody* (1954), John Ericson plays a G.I. who is also a concert pianist, studying in Munich and doing musical battle with a dashing Italian violin virtuoso for the love of Elizabeth Taylor's character. Hollywood frequently revised literary portrayals to fit the image of the conquering pianist-hero. *Rhapsody*'s Hollywood script, based on the 1908 novel *Maurice Guest* by Australian writer Ethel Florence Lindesay Richardson (who published under the name Henry Handel Richardson), altered the story's ending to ensure a victory for the pianist-protagonist. Instead of his suicide as in the novel, the film closes with his triumphant performance of Rachmaninoff's Second Piano Concerto, a musical metaphor for his conquest over the obstacles to love.

Romanticism aflame: Bernard Herrmann *(Psycho, Citizen Kane)* wrote the "Concerto Macabre" performed in *Hangover Square* (1945). A pianist-composer (Laird Cregar), afflicted by a Jekyll/Hyde-type schizophrenia, suffers homicidal blackouts whenever he hears a discordant noise. The climactic premiere of his new concerto occurs just as the police catch up with him. In trying to escape, he sets off a conflagration, but the concerto must go on!

Song of Russia, yet another 1943 production from MGM, features Tchaikovsky's B-flat Minor Concerto as the music of Allied heroism, accompanying a story of Russian resistance against invading Nazis. Robert Taylor plays an American symphony conductor who visits the Soviet Union and falls in love with, and marries, Nadya Stepanova (Susan Peters), a young peasant woman who is somewhat paradoxically a talented concert pianist as well as a model Communist farm maid. ("It is a privilege to drive the tractor," she asserts solemnly.) When the Blitzkrieg descends, she fights valiantly alongside her countrymen, and a fair amount of melodramatic plot is thus generated for the Tchaikovsky background. In an early version of the script, Nadya is fatally injured and dies in her husband's arms, whereupon he returns to America to conduct "her" concerto for the Russian war relief effort. In a later version, they both flee to America, where they battle together for peace via the signifying concerto.

Because MGM had made two anti-Soviet comedies *(Ninotchka* and *Comrade X)* before the war, Franklin Delano Roosevelt himself encouraged this pro-Soviet portrayal to strengthen American sentiment toward the Communist allies.[5] *Song of Russia*'s political sympathies are clear, and the film even includes a rousing speech by Stalin. Soon after its premiere, *Motion Picture Herald* printed a cable attributed to Soviet composer Aram Khachaturian: "I must say I liked the film," he writes. "There was a certain noble and idyllic quality about it that spoke for the warm feeling that is drawing the American and Russian people together. . . . Music helps to promote friendship among nations. *Song of Russia* is a tribute to the cultural collaboration of the American and Russian people."[6] In one of the fickle twists of politics, this same film was later cited by the infamous House Un-American Activities Committee as evidence of pro-Communist sympathies in the Hollywood film industry.

Chopin Drafted!   Like classical music and piano concertos, the stories of the great pianists' lives were also subjected to particular political applications during and after the 1940s. The historical moment required mythic heroes to represent patriotism and determination, and the virtuoso concert pianist was often drafted for this cause. Musical history was easily revised—not to mention invented—by movie scriptwriters to apply certain already highly mythologized struggles of these pianist-heroes to the particular revolution at hand. From a musicological perspective, classic Hollywood pianist films such as *A Song to Remember* (on the "battles" of Frédéric Chopin) are historical travesties that perpetuate misconceptions about these artists' lives and creativity, but as political propaganda they deserve close critical examination for their impact on the image of the embattled piano.

The most consistently politicized pianist-hero in film has undoubtedly been Chopin, and *A Song to Remember* of 1945 was the Hollywood hit that catapulted him, his music, and the myth of his patriotic passion into the American imagination. Portrayed as a Polish revolutionary who harnesses his musical talents to help battle the czarist forces controlling his homeland, Chopin provided for American viewers of the 1940s an allegorical figure of resistance to Nazi aggression in the overrun nations of Europe, and a model of selfless sacrifice in the cause of freedom.

Cornel Wilde plays the role of Chopin, bringing to the character a masculine, almost athletic personification at odds with the usual notion of Chopin as weakly or effeminate. As depicted in the film, Chopin's brief life was torn between fierce loyalty to his rebellious country and romantic submission to a controversial aristocratic woman, George Sand (Merle Oberon); out of this struggle between patriotism and love came Chopin's inspired music. (American viewers at the time may

"Art is our consolation, and our duty." Hilde Krahl, as a persevering Clara Schumann in the Nazi-era film *Träumerei* (Germany, 1944), posed with severe grandeur not unlike the emblematic eagle in the lower right-hand corner. A cinematic role model for war-weary Germans, Clara supported her husband through his battles of career and health and championed his music and his memory after he died. The 1947 Hollywood version of the story, *Song of Love*, likewise emphasizes Clara's devotion to Robert (Katharine Hepburn and Paul Henreid, *below*), but portrays her as an angelic "reigning saint" of music and a dedicated, domesticated mother of eight.

A genealogy of the pianist's candelabra. *Above,* Wolfgang Liebeneiner, seated at the piano, as Frédéric Chopin, Sybille Schmitz as George Sand, and Hans Schlenk as Franz Liszt in *Abschiedswalzer* (Germany, 1934). *Right,* Cornel Wilde as Chopin and Merle Oberon as Sand, in *A Song to Remember* (1945). *Opposite,* Liberace, with two candelabras, as Liberace, posing for a Valentine's Day television special in 1979.

have felt particularly ambivalent about the figure of Madame Sand, who connotes aristocracy or perhaps even Vichy France.)

A third major player in *A Song to Remember* is Chopin's early teacher, Professor Elsner (Paul Muni), an aged mentor and father figure who provides the moral weight of the story, encouraging and sustaining Chopin's patriotic fervor. When a young, teary-eyed Chopin pounds the piano angrily because czarist soldiers are taking Polish political prisoners to Siberia, Elsner understands the boy's sentiments, exhorting him to remember that "Music and freedom are like one! They both belong to the world. A real artist wants freedom in every country."

Later, Chopin's father is upset about his son's attending secret revolutionary meetings. "Hands like Frédéric's were not meant to carry guns!" he insists. "The best way for him to serve his people would be to become great in his own profession!" (The notion of war service through music is a theme frequently invoked with regard to other cinematic pianist-heroes as well.) In another scene, Chopin joins the underground revolutionary Polish patriots, who listen to a Russian rebel expounding the familiar American ideals of "life, liberty, and the pursuit of happiness"—not an anachronism in 1945, when the United States and the Soviet Union were still allies. "You want those rights," he preaches. "So do my people! We have that one hope in common. Yet they tell us that the Polish people and the Russian people are enemies!" When Chopin must flee Poland after a patriotic outburst ("I do not play for czarist butchers!"), his boat slips across a foggy river, an image perhaps reminiscent of Emanuel Gottlieb Leutze's famous painting, *George Washington Crossing the Delaware*.

As Chopin falls under the feminine temptations of George Sand and her luxurious aristocratic life, he gradually forgets his patriotic cause and composes "trivial" music (mazurkas and waltzes) instead of finishing his great patriotic polonaise (the so-called "Heroic" Polonaise in A-flat Major, Op. 53). But Elsner recalls the prodigal son to patriotic duty: "Genius is a rare gift! So many ordinary people seem to be robbed to make one such man. And the man worthy of the gift should draw closer to those people as he becomes more great, fight harder for them with that same genius!" When Chopin determines to play a concert tour across Europe to raise money for his country's rebellion, Sand tries to dissuade him on account of his health, but the pianist-hero's bravery and selfless patriotism win out. The famous blood-on-the-keys scene highlights his strenuous concert tour and marks his ultimate sacrifice for the cause of freedom.

At Chopin's deathbed, Elsner intones, "It is not merely music Chopin composed. It is music with a meaning for the world." How international that world actually was can be appreciated when one learns that the script for *A Song to Remember* was originally written by Ernst Marischka for the 1934 German film *Abschiedswalzer* (Farewell waltz), starring Wolfgang Liebeneiner in the role of Chopin. Thanks to the success of *A Song to Remember*, Marischka's script was even nominated for an Academy Award in 1946 for best writing in an original story. *Abschiedswalzer* relates the story of Chopin's life up to the early 1830s, when he rose to fame as a Parisian virtuoso. Like *A Song to Remember*, it is set against the backdrop of Poland's anti-czarist uprising, but its portrayal of political strife seems intended more to mirror the romantic discord in Chopin's personal life. Unlike *Song*, in which an anti-czarist remark drives Chopin from Poland, in *Abschiedswalzer* it is girlfriend Constantia's pretended betrayal—encouraged by revolutionary friends who want to spare Chopin the dangers of the impending rebellion—that precipitates his flight to Paris.

As *Abschiedswalzer* tells it, Chopin's Paris debut turns out to be the same day as the Polish uprising. His performance of the passionate A Minor Etude (Op. 25, no. 11) calls forth images of the struggle of courageous Polish freedom fighters, the retreat of the Cossacks, and the fluttering of the victorious Polish flag. Significantly, *Abschiedswalzer* was among those biographical films favored by the Nazi regime for its ideological and nationalistic connotations. In it, Chopin proclaims, "Ich liebe mein Vaterland mehr als mein Leben!" (I love my Fatherland more than my life!), and Elsner, his German teacher, declares, "Dein Reich ist die Musik!" Of the movie, the *National-Socialist Courier* exulted, "All deserve a leaf of the laurel wreath crowning this masterwork, which represents a highpoint of German film production—the fame of which is carried forth into the world simultaneously with the glory of Chopin."[7] Where *Song* glorifies Chopin's death in its tragically heroic ending, *Abschiedswalzer* leaves off romantically, with Chopin and Sand departing for Mallorca while Constantia and Professor Elsner return to Poland, "having given Chopin to the world."

Not long after the end of World War II, the Poles themselves produced yet

Poster for *Chopins Jugend*. "What Beethoven means to the German *Volk*, what Tchaikovsky and Glinka mean to the Russian people and the Soviet citizens of today—that is what Chopin means to the Poles: the central stature of a national poet of sound, in whose creations a highly musical and music-loving people recognizes its most treasured feelings and noblest sentiments, and in whom they see the radiant hero of their nationalist dreams and fantasies as well as the artistic representative of their populace carrying forth a mighty portion of cultural value before the entire world." From an East German film brochure ("Progress Filmillustrierte") promoting the release of *Chopins Jugend* (the German dubbing of the 1952 Polish film *Młodość Chopina*).

another ideology-laden telling of the Chopin story. *Młodość Chopina* (Chopin's youth) is a 1952 film starring Czesław Wollejko in the title role. Like *Abschiedswalzer*, this film covers the composer's early years amid the revolutionary movements in Europe, but it adds a heavy dose of Communist ideology: Chopin is portrayed as "the great revolutionary musician of the Polish people," a resolute patriot firmly on the side of the oppressed against (in this case) the power of the Polish aristocracy, the church, and right-wing reactionaries. Even Chopin's music gets a Marxist spin: composing "for the people and from the music of the people . . . Chopin absorbs with joyous delight the folk-songs and village songs sung to him by the maid Suska, and from these musical inspirations his creativity blossoms."[8] (His muse is now appropriately unaristocratic, as befits a Socialist hero.)

In America, the box-office success of *A Song to Remember* ensured that Chopin's "Heroic" Polonaise became a lucrative musical commodity. Sales of the recording by José Iturbi (who played on the film's soundtrack) reached a record one million copies, and Lawrence Morton, discussing in a 1945 article the "unprecedented" interest in Chopin generated by this popular film, noted that "a West Los

Ignacy Jan Paderewski, Polish pianist-statesman, was immortalized on the silver screen in 1938. At the age of seventy-six, he starred as himself in the British film *Moonlight Sonata*, a boy-meets-girl love story enhanced by the maestro's performances of Beethoven and Liszt and his own celebrated "Menuet."

344

Angeles shop reported as many requests for Chopin as there had been for the Andrews Sisters' 'Rum and Coca-Cola,'" and that bobby-soxers "listen to the A-flat Polonaise as enthusiastically as they listen to 'Laura.'"[9] The same music generated a million-selling "Chopin's Polonaise" for bandleader Carmen Cavallaro. In addition, "Till the End of Time," a love song based on the polonaise theme, spent nineteen weeks on the 1945 *Your Hit Parade* and proved a hit for Perry Como and other crooners of the era. "Mark my words," Elsner remarks to the music publisher Pleyel in *A Song to Remember*, "sooner or later they're going to steal those melodies!"

Making pop music out of the polonaise cleverly tapped into the reservoir of politicized connotation and wartime nostalgia that was generated by the piece. "Till the End of Time" was so popular, in fact, that Hollywood made a movie out of it in 1946. The love story of a lonely war widow (Dorothy McGuire) and a young, cocky ex-G.I. (Guy Madison), *Till the End of Time* utilizes the reconstituted Chopin theme as soundtrack music to accompany their romance, but it also admits the polonaise's militaristic connections immediately after the opening credits, when the theme segues into the U.S. Marines anthem. In the final scene (a standard Hollywood run-into-each-others'-arms moment), the tune returns, full volume, to connote the victory of love over postwar disaffection and the romantic conquest of the again-heroic ex-soldier.

If Chopin became the fictionalized Hollywood representative for overrun Poland during World War II, and the polonaise the musical anthem for patriotic freedom fighters, then the internationally acclaimed Polish concert pianist Ignacy Jan Paderewski provided a real-life manifestation of this mythology. After the outbreak of World War I, Paderewski devoted himself to concertizing for the benefit of the Polish war effort, raised substantial money for his country's cause, and spoke publicly on its behalf. He was a leading figure in organizing the Polish Republic and served as its foreign secretary and prime minister, representing his newly liberated nation at the signing of the Treaty of Versailles and at the League of Nations in 1921.

Paderewski and the allegorized Chopin also provide the probable models for yet another Polish pianist-cum-patriot of the movies. The 1941 British film *Dangerous Moonlight* concerns a pianist-fighter (à la Chopin) who plays for Poland (à la Paderewski) and believes that there is "no art not worth fighting for." He is accompanied by his devoted, at times self-centered, wife and muse (à la Sand), who loses him to the resistance effort but then rouses him from a shellshocked stupor after his suicide crash into an enemy plane. Like Chopin in *A Song to Re-*

member, Stefan Radetzky is valued for his musical talents over his patriotic desire to fight; he is sent on a safe mission far from the embattled homeland. Like Paderewski, he serves his country musically, in exile, on a three-month American concert tour to support the Polish war relief effort. Stefan offers thanks "for what the people of your country have been doing for the people of mine. I speak for them when I say that we are very grateful." When his audience demands an encore, he announces, "I'll play one more piece: the last music to come out of free Warsaw. The music that taught the world that Poland was still alive. And tonight it still is!" (He plays not the "Heroic" Polonaise but Chopin's equally famous "Military" Polonaise in A Major, Op. 40, no. 1.)

Just as *A Song to Remember* helped sell the "Heroic" Polonaise to an eager public, *Dangerous Moonlight* introduced Richard Addinsell's immensely popular "Warsaw Concerto." Such lucrative business around Chopin- and Paderewski-type virtuosos proved profitable for another Polish virtuoso wannabe, Wladziu Valentino Liberace. Throughout his early career in the 1950s, Liberace, the self-styled "Chopin of TV," repeatedly invoked the dubious tale that Paderewski himself ("a friend of my mother's") had encouraged him as a child. Liberace also made frequent references to his Polish ancestry (from his mother's side of the family). In liner notes to a recording of the "Warsaw Concerto," he declares, "I would like to dedicate to my Polish mother and to all Polish people the composition that expresses the wonderful faith, hope, and great courage of these peace-loving people during the merciless bombing of their capital city during World War II."[10]

Broken Heroes

Not all pianists achieved glorious patriotic victories, or survived the war unscathed. The pianist traumatized or injured by military conflict is yet another Hollywood metaphor for the brave soldier-hero (or, in the case of *Song of Russia*, heroine) who endures, but also suffers, the consequences of war.

In the 1942 British thriller *The Night Has Eyes*, James Mason plays a reclusive, mysterious former pianist shellshocked by the Spanish Civil War. "I gave up music for war," his character explains bitterly. "I had an idiotic notion that civilization was worth fighting for—that nothing that really mattered, not even music, could exist under slavery." Not unlike the pianist-killer in *Hangover Square*, Mason's character is tormented by psychotic murderous impulses, but a determined and attractive young schoolteacher (Joyce Howard) cures him with her love. (Mason later starred as the even more demonic Uncle Nicholas in *The Seventh Veil* in 1945, limping about with his menacing cane and demanding the love of Ann Todd's character, a disturbed concert pianist eventually "cured" by psychoanalysis.)

Blinded virtuosos struggled against their handicaps in two postwar films. *Musik i Mörker* (1948, available with English subtitles as *Night Is My Future*), an early work by famed Swedish director Ingmar Bergman, tells a poignant story of tragedy redeemed by love. After a handsome young soldier (played by Birger Malmsten) is blinded by a firing range accident, he is depressed and suicidal (performing Chopin's anguished D Minor Prelude, for example), until a young woman helps him find new hope to conquer his disability. And even if the pianist in Hollywood's *Night Song* (1947) is not blinded through war service per se (instead, it is the consequence of a drunk driver smashing through a cafe window), his handicap still serves to represent a physical tragedy of the kind faced by the disabled ex-soldier. Dana Andrews and Merle Oberon star in this sentimental love story (she, a wealthy socialite, feigns poverty and blindness to help him complete his piano concerto, which wins a competition of her devising, which pays for an operation to restore his sight, and so forth), and Artur Rubinstein, as "a very good friend" of Miss Oberon's character, provides another Hollywood cameo, performing the concerto's premiere with the New York Philharmonic under Eugene Ormandy.

In many postwar movies, the pianist-hero becomes an "innocent" artist trapped by a tragic and debilitating fatalism—unless saved by the nurturing love of a female muse. Although his war service is required as part of the fight for politicized music, after enduring these cultural battles the veteran-virtuoso finds his instrument and career in shambles. But whereas postwar Hollywood piano romances such as *Rhapsody* and *Night Song* could draw their narratives of salvation from the romantic Chopin-Sand mythology, a darker view of the situation was evident in noir films. Here the role of nurturing muse is typically usurped by a dangerous femme fatale, and a sense of hopeless circumstance afflicts the now disempowered pianist-hero.

This bleak impotence is famously portrayed in the B-grade noir classic *Detour* (1945). Early in the story, Al (Tom Neal) enjoys a relatively uncomplicated, if frustrated, career as a New York nightclub pianist, playing Chopin waltzes after hours in the empty club, but a bleak noirish underside surfaces in the pulp dialogue with his girlfriend, who listens to his rhapsodizing:

Sue: "Mr. Paderoowski, I presume? It's beautiful—you're going to make Carnegie Hall yet, Al."

Al: "Yeah, as a janitor. I'll make my debut in the basement!"[11]

Sue: "I don't blame you for being bitter, darling, but you mustn't give up hope! Why some day—"

Al: "Yeah, someday! If I don't get arthritis first!"

But far more serious matters arise for this cynical antihero. Like Chopin under Sand's sway in *A Song to Remember*, Al loses his virtuous Constantia-like girlfriend and suffers under a dominating femme fatale—only now the impotent (or sickly, Chopinesque) pianist-hero has no further will to fight and allows himself to be blackmailed into obeying her commands. Al chooses passivity over action, submission over heroic resistance, and captivity over freedom fighting. When his tormentor asks, "You don't like me, do you?" he whines, "Like you? I love you! My favorite sport is being kept prisoner!"—but Al does achieve a problematic victory in this "war" when he inadvertently strangles his captor. (Significantly, Martin M. Goldsmith's original novel, published in 1939, presents Al as a violinist. Goldsmith also wrote the screenplay adaptation, but changed Al into a pianist, perhaps to invoke the popularized pianist-hero mythology. Still, the reluctant criminality remains the same: as the novel's protagonist claims, "I'm a musician, not a thug. The few dishonorable things I did, I didn't *want* to do, I *had* to do.")[12]

The war veteran as wrecked virtuoso. In *Detour* (1945), Tom Neal plays an ex-pianist who turns inadvertent killer in his battle for freedom.

On a musical level, too, *Detour* is haunted by references to frustration and failure. When Al's girlfriend sings "I Can't Believe That You're in Love with Me" at the club, it is "their" song, but Al continues to hear the refrain long after losing her, and it becomes an unavoidable echo that taunts him for his helpless defeats. "Did you ever want to forget anything?" he complains, hearing the tune again on a restaurant jukebox. "Did you ever want to cut away a piece of your memory, or blot it out? You can't, you know, no matter how hard you try. Sooner or later you'll get a whiff of perfume, or somebody will . . . maybe hum something—then you're licked again!"

Leo Erdody's score to *Detour* does "hum something" significant throughout the film, accompanying the image of the failed pianist with ironic quotations of another Chopin reference, the 1940s hit song "I'm Always Chasing Rainbows." Based on the slow middle section of Chopin's well-known Fantasy-Impromptu, Op. 66, "I'm Always Chasing Rainbows" (lyrics by Joseph McCarthy and music by Harry Carroll) was originally written for a 1918 Broadway show. In 1946, spurred by the success of *A Song to Remember,* Perry Como revived the song; his recording spent twelve weeks on *Your Hit Parade* and was subsequently covered by numerous other artists of the time. Like Hollywood drawing on popular classics for politicized representations, *Detour* exploits the currency and meanings around this Chopin song, but with a dark irony. The Chopin motif echoes throughout the film as a sign of hopeful possibilities (when Al and Sue head home from the Break o' Dawn Club, when Al decides to hitchhike to Los Angeles, and so forth), but its promise is never fulfilled. As the song's lyrics lament, "I'm always chasing rainbows, watching clouds drifting by. My schemes are just like all my dreams, ending in the sky."[13]

The defunct pianist-hero, a casualty of the collapse of the piano's political utility after the end of World War II, continues to haunt the Hollywood imagination. As a victim of the unpopular and rather unheroic American wars in Korea and Vietnam, this figure became an antihero, a disillusioned and disenfranchised musical misfit. Jack Nicholson personifies this loss of cultural status and heroic power in his role as Bobby Eroica Dupea in the 1970 classic *Five Easy Pieces.* A drifter caught between opposing worlds of blue-collar tedium and "the good life" of cultured upper-class sophistication, Dupea has rejected his "auspicious beginnings" as a concert pianist for an oil-rigging job and a life of bars, motels, and bowling alleys; without his pianistic potential, however, he has also lost his purposeful identity. In a famous scene, he spots an upright piano on the back of a truck in a traffic jam and hops on to play Liszt's Second Hungarian Rhapsody to his captive audience—but when the truck unexpectedly exits the freeway, he ends up "lost" again.

An analogous but more conscious frustration persecutes Harvey Keitel's hitman-pianist in *Fingers* (1978). The character of Jimmy "Fingers" Angelelli is another disaffected concert pianist frustrated in his career because of the demands of his aging father, a Mafia kingpin who gets his son to do the dirty work. (The promoting paternal role of a Professor Elsner is long past, it seems.) Here the pianist-antihero is again impotent and undirected, another "inadvertent" killer torn between good art and unsavory duty.

Significantly, the women of the piano did not suffer the same postwar musical malaise or loss of purpose and courage as their male counterparts. Bobby Dupea's sister in *Five Easy Pieces* is still a concert pianist, struggling with Bach in a re-

The war photograph *Tchaikovsky, Germany* (1945), by Dmitri Baltermants, captures a scene of Russian soldiers playing an upright piano in a bombed-out German home (J. Paul Getty Museum, Los Angeles). The photograph is of a piece with the exceptionally beautiful 1957 Soviet film *Letyat zhuravli* (The cranes are flying), in which a young man plays his concerto amid the German bombings of Moscow: "If not for this war," he laments to his beloved, "I'd be playing this in the Tchaikovsky Hall—for you!" Amidst a more recent war, in Chechnya *(below)*, another Russian soldier plays an abandoned piano in a wrecked park in Grozny (*New York Times*, February 10, 1995).

cording studio. Joan Crawford's character in *Johnny Guitar* (1954) turns to the piano as a temporary sanctuary against the inflamed emotions of the townspeople who have come to demand her cooperation in hunting down a fugitive. She remains aloof and nonaligned: "I'm not taking sides with anyone!" a defiant Vienna tells them as she plays. "I'm sitting here in my own house, minding my own business, playing my own piano. I don't think you can make a crime out of that!"

During World War II, the piano fought for Poland; today, it struggles on in the Balkans. The images of the piano as sanctuary for women and of the wrecked piano as a casualty of war continue to circulate amid the recent battles afflicting the former Yugoslavia. In a *New York Times* article from 1994 examining the effects of the Bosnian civil war on activities at the Sarajevo conservatory of music, Roger Cohen reported that the school remained in operation despite the ravages of war on its facilities and the psychological toll of the ethnic conflict on its teachers and students. He portrayed the school as an enclave of cultural stability, its music creating a peaceful oasis in the midst of destruction: "Among the scarred streets and alleys of Sarajevo there is one comforting crossroads, where the sound of a Beethoven sonata or a Chopin waltz may be heard. The music, sometimes flowing, sometimes betraying a student's faltering hand, cascades from the Sarajevo conservatory. In its lightness and otherworldliness, it offers solace in a city still raw with suffering."[14]

Battles of Today

Cohen constructs an opposition between modern-day brutality and the comforts of the musical past. He invokes the nostalgic associations of classical music, drawing on images of nineteenth-century Hapsburg grandeur (elegant concerts, wealthy patronage) and Biedermeier stability (musical home life, diligent piano lessons). The invasion by the present into the past is enacted quite literally in a later part of the article: "Last year, two Serbian shells came through the ceiling of the concert room, which with its chandeliers and chairs upholstered in blue velvet contrives nonetheless to retain vestiges of a Viennese plushness. The concert piano, ruined by the shell blasts, is propped unused on a metal leg."[15]

So the piano appears, not unlike an injured soldier on a crutch or prosthetic limb. The traditional centerpiece of the concert stage, the grand piano seems situated at ground zero of the hall's destruction, and its damage bespeaks a mortal blow to the world of culture. As an icon, the image of this teetering, unplayable piano parallels the handicapping of both the conservatory's mission and the musical life of Sarajevo. (The city itself ramifies iconically as the site of the assassination of Archduke Francis Ferdinand of Austria, an event that sparked World War I and, by extension, the end of imperial culture.)

Cohen goes on to interview a number of students and teachers at the conservatory. All those quoted are women (understandably, as most of the male population has been involved in fighting, not music making), and nearly all are pianists.

> "I play to defend myself," said Ivana Velican, 14, a piano student. "I mean, I am not—I cannot be—free. But I can sit at the piano. And I can hope that everyone learns to feel the love that I feel."

> "I became very different in the war," said Jasmina Kapic, a pale and slight 16-year-old who resumed playing the piano at the beginning of the war, because, she explained, it was a means to survive.

> Seated at her piano, Inas [Mursed] looks out—just 80 yards away—on apartment blocks where the Serbian flag flies. Bullet holes in the wall of her living room show how close the war has come. After playing a Chopin waltz she said music was her "journey to the sea." It is a means to forget, to think positively of the future.

> Mrs. [Angelina] Papp, a Serb from Belgrade who came to Sarajevo 25 years ago, has chosen to stay in the Bosnian capital because she feels her life is contained in the two old pianos in her room in the conservatory.[16]

The piano is presented as an instrument of women—indeed, Mrs. Papp's identity is intimately connected with her instruments, and her studio seems more her home (where "her life is contained") than merely a place to teach. The piano is also portrayed as a site of safety and spiritual reinvigoration for these female survivors. As savior and as salve, the instrument provides a defensive shield, a mode of escape, and a tool for emotional catharsis.

The cinematic narrative of the piano as survivor amid the destruction of Hapsburg culture is told in the rather obscure 1948 Austrian film *Der Engel mit der Posaune*, remade in England the following year as *The Angel with the Trumpet*. Based on a novel by Ernst Lothar, the story traces the history of the Alt family, owners of Vienna's foremost piano-building firm, through the tortured Austrian history of Crown Prince Rudolf's suicide, Kaiser Franz Josef's death, World War I, the Nazi Anschluss, and the destruction of World War II.[17] In the English movie, as the first new piano is built after the war, elderly Hans Alt tells his children that for two centuries the Alts "have gone on making pianos in spite of everything—in spite of war, and poverty, and hunger—simply because they believed that what they were doing was more important, more lasting than those things. That's why this piano is here today." The film's moral seems to be that culture will go on, so long as pianos can be built.

But more commonly, the ravages of these Balkan and Slavic battles are mirrored in the image of a ruined grand piano. A 1947 Hungarian film, *Valahol Európában* (Somewhere in Europe), is set at the close of World War II, when orphaned youngsters loot a ruined castle and imprison its elderly caretaker, a former conductor who wins them over with his playing. In *Kanat* (1956), Polish director Andrzej Wajda's story of the anti-Nazi Warsaw uprising, a troubled composer plays for his besieged comrades, and a broken grand piano lies amid the rubble in the streets. *Vukovar: The Way Home* (1994), a damning depiction of the Serbo-Croatian Civil War, likewise shows an embattled instrument left to the abuses of winter weather, vandalism, and enemy fire; a bourgeois family's upright piano is looted as war spoils, and a Mozart piano concerto echoes throughout the film's soundtrack with nostalgic, romantic poignancy (perhaps a reference to another soldier's tragic love story, the popular 1967 Swedish film *Elvira Madigan*).

Neither has Hollywood neglected the iconic piano in its portrayals of the Balkan wars. In *The Peacemaker* (1997), the debut release of the much-touted Spielberg-Katzenberg-Geffen production company DreamWorks, Marcel Iures plays the sympathetic role of a noble bad guy (à la *Detour*), a Bosnian terrorist who is also a classical pianist ("I am not a monster. I am a human man—just like you, whether you like it or not"). Early scenes show him giving lessons on an out-of-tune grand in his Sarajevo apartment, explaining that a Chopin nocturne can have many moods ("Changing a single note can turn joy to sorrow"). In his final scene, held at gunpoint as the timer on his stolen nuclear warhead threatens to destroy the United Nations and all of Manhattan, his single demand is a poignant, if not pathetic, plea of nostalgia: "I want it to be like it was."

Comic Destructions

The piano may have been "wrecked" in the course of past and recent wars, but the cinematic resonances of this embattled icon need not always be grim and tragic. Since the early days of cinema and well into our own time, the piano has provided a comic chopping block for spoofs and parodies of the dramatic cultural and political destructions it has endured.

If the piano suffered any adverse handling in early films, it was probably in the context of slapstick comedy routines, such as Harpo Marx's hilarious grand piano destruction—caused by fortissimo poundings on Rachmaninoff's C-sharp Minor Prelude—in *A Day at the Races* (1937). Grand pianos crashing down from

Luis Buñuel drew on Salvador Dali's eccentric imagination for this classic scene in *Un Chien andalou* (1928): a man dragging bloody donkey corpses in two Bechstein grands. One year later, Laurel and Hardy spoofed the horse-and-piano connection in their short film *Wrong Again.* When a millionaire instructs Laurel and Hardy to put "Blue Boy" on the piano, he means the famous painting, not a race horse of the same name!

high-rise lifts provided a favorite visual gag in numerous animated cartoons, and piano-moving skits provided plenty of opportunities to chuckle over smashing, crushing, even drowning pianos. In an early Charlie Chaplin short, *His Musical Career* (1914), a steep flight of stairs and a mixed-up repossession order occasion a chase involving an indignant millionaire, Chaplin, and his moving partner, during which the piano in question rolls into a lake. Finally sinking with the piano, Chaplin manages to pound out a few last chords.

Laurel and Hardy had their hilarious moments with piano moving, too. In *Swiss Miss* (1938), a flimsy bridge across a treacherously deep canyon—and an unexpected gorilla—present precarious obstacles. In *The Music Box* (which won an Academy Award in 1932 for best short subject), another flight of stairs provides frustrations similar to Chaplin's, but the piano—in a crate labeled "Fragile"—miraculously survives. Its destruction comes instead at the hands of an irate professor who wasn't expecting the delivery and who happens to hate that "mechanical blunderbuss." Soon after he chops the instrument to pieces with an axe, his wife comes home and expresses great dismay over what has happened to her surprise birthday present.

The culturally ingrained pianist-hero image is ripe for parody as well, as Charlie Chaplin proved in spoofing Hitler as an occasional virtuoso in *The Great Dictator* (1940). Amid the daily routine of world conquest and portrait posing, Chaplin as Adenoid Hynkel, dictator of Tomania, plays chromatic riffs on the piano, which leave a bad taste in his mouth; later, while the Jewish ghetto is burning, he plays a parodic version of Paderewski's "Menuet." In the 1944 musical *Two Girls and a Sailor*, Gracie Allen performs her hilarious "Concerto for Index Finger," explaining that her other nine fingers must keep busy knitting for the war effort. And Dr. Seuss enters the fray, as well, with his 1952 film *The 5,000 Fingers of Dr. T.* In this wry and eccentric film, a demented goose-stepping piano teacher (Hans Conreid) terrorizes captive boys in the dungeons of his piano prison camp in a way that blends Orwellian nightmare, Cold War angst, and Fascist megalomania.

François Truffaut's *Tirez sur le pianiste* (Shoot the piano player, 1960) is the classic send-up of the pianist-hero character now rendered impotent—at times laughably, at times disturbingly so. Charlie/Edouard (played by Charles Aznavour) is a down-and-out barroom pianist who is inadvertently drawn into an absurd world of violence (again, shades of *Detour*). During a brawl between the bar owner and a spirited, angry waitress, the apathetic pianist-hero walks away, muttering to himself, "You're out of it. Let them fight it out. Just go and take your seat at the piano. You can't do anything . . . for anybody. You don't care anyway. You don't care one way or another." Later, when he does grapple with the barman,

Franz Liszt armed with flame-shooting grand piano in *Lisztomania* (1975)

their duel with sharp knife and detached telephone receiver captures the comic impotence of the fighter-pianist role.

The movies, it seems, have long exploited the mythologized connotations of the embattled piano and the pianist-(anti)hero. *Song without End* (1960), which dramatizes the thwarted love affair between Franz Liszt (played by Dirk Bogarde) and Princess Caroline Sayn-Wittgenstein (played by Capucine), tries to insert a few political touches to the tale: revolution in Vienna provides a dramatic backdrop for Liszt's passionate search for Caroline, and later, in Russia, when he stands up to her powerful husband, a friend warns him to "Be careful, Franz, and don't forget—Russia defeated even the great Napoléon!" Liszt retorts, "Napoléon couldn't play the piano!" But by 1960, perhaps the notion of the revolutionary pianist-hero was no longer so marketable, and a different type of "war"—an inner conflict—needed to be fought. *Song without End* transposes an outward battle into one concerning religious conflict in Liszt's life: "It's difficult to be either good or bad," he laments. "I'm part gypsy, part priest. When I'm alone, I want the world—when I have the world, I want the peace and seclusion of a monastery. I'm at war with myself!"

Because discussions of the heroic pianist inevitably come around to Franz Liszt, the last word on the matter can go to Ken Russell and his outlandish *Lisztomania* (1975). British rock star Roger Daltrey plays Liszt, not only a teen idol and seducer of courtly women (an enraged Count d'Agoult catches his wife in bed with Liszt at the beginning of the film and puts them into a coffinlike piano case on railroad tracks, where a rushing locomotive smashes them to pieces), but also a triumphant pianist-hero who does battle with the personification of evil: Richard Wagner as Dracula, Hitler, Satan, and the Antichrist. "Your work is a creation of the Devil," Liszt screams as he attacks Wagner by playing a spinning piano shooting flares of fires (the ultimate cinematic piano-weapon), "but my music will drive him out!" Not unlike Claude Rains's Phantom, Wagner dies amid this concerto as his castle crashes down upon him.

But it takes more than a performance of "Totentanz" to exorcise the legacy of the piano at war. From a spaceship built of huge organ pipes and angel wings, surrounded by all the women of his earthly life, the ultimate pianist-hero-lover attacks the Wagnerian Nazi demon and finally saves the world. As Liszt flies off victoriously into outer space, he sings to the tune of his famous "Liebestraum,"

Now love, sweet love,
Oh, now that love has won!

Oh, now that love has won!
Now love, our love,
Our love has ended war!
He'll torture man no more!

Perhaps the world has once again been made safe for pianos.

The piano has always been an adaptable instrument: from the start, it has been used to adapt music from one setting to another, and its design has been continually updated to accommodate new musical tasks and styles. But at the end of World War I, a moment of cataclysmic suffering and disorienting social upheaval throughout the industrial world, things changed. For the first time in the history of the instrument, not only did sales of pianos begin a long-term decline; piano manufacturers stopped experimenting with their product and even discontinued recent innovations. For example, after sales of player pianos plummeted in the late twenties, manufacturers dropped them from production. In general, only conventional pianos in something very close to their turn-of-the-century forms were produced right on through the twentieth century.

This ossification in the design of the piano was matched in its concert repertory. By the beginning of the twentieth century, piano recitals—like most classical-music programs—consisted overwhelmingly of music of the past (Bach through Brahms), and by the end of the century, even with a slight extension up to Bartók, the repertory came to represent an ever more distant past. Although only the very latest of that music had been written for an instrument like the twentieth-century grand (the Steinway Model D is the instrument of John Cage and Ray Charles, not of Brahms and Debussy), playing that mostly fixed repertory on a largely unchanging instrument helped keep the music frozen in a perpetual present.

This lack of novelty in instrument and repertory was itself new to concert culture, and composers, performers, and audiences had to accommodate themselves to it. As in previous centuries, some of the finest pianists of the twentieth century were also important composers, but Ferruccio Busoni, Sergei Rachmaninoff, Béla Bartók, and Benjamin Britten—unlike Mozart, Beethoven, Chopin, and Liszt—made their mark as pianists by performing the classics as much as by playing their own and their contemporaries' music. For them, unlike their predecessors, composing for their own instrument became an exercise in getting the music of the past out of their systems, out of their fingers; and unlike their predecessors, they could expect no innovations in piano design to open up new sound possibilities. At the same time, composers' customers had changed radically. Audiences at concerts of new piano music might still be full of pianists, but now far fewer of them were amateur women pianists who had practiced their whole youths away. Sergei Prokofiev and Pierre Boulez, then, could not write sonatas for amateurs and professionals alike (or for the home and the concert hall alike), as Schumann

Nine **1920s to 2000: New Voices from the Old Impersonator**

Michael Chanan,
James Parakilas,
and Mark Tucker

Romare Bearden, *The Piano Lesson*, 1983, watercolor and collage

359

and even Ravel had written piano works large and small; instead, they wrote them almost exclusively to be played in concerts by professional performers—and increasingly by contemporary-music specialists. This change mirrored a movement in the art world: nineteenth-century painters made portraits and landscapes for private buyers, hoping that some of those works might eventually wind up in museums, whereas twentieth-century painters expected their dealers to sell some at least of their works directly to museums.

One composer, Erik Satie, responded to (or perhaps even anticipated) this split between the music of the home and of the concert hall by envisioning piano music as a private conversation between himself and the performer. He filled his piano scores with jokes—teasing performance directions and visually amusing notation—that, as he made clear, the player was by no means to share with any audience. A great many more composers responded by making their piano music fearsomely difficult, to listen to as well as to play. And though the piano retained its adaptability of setting (it could still be heard in homes, thanks to recordings), audiences lost the idea that new concert music was music to take to their own pianos and learn.

This unpromising situation provoked composers into making innovative uses of the unchanging instrument. Much of the magic of twentieth-century concert music for the piano, in fact, comes from the ways that composers have confronted the traditional concepts of how a piano is played and what sounds it can produce. Pianists specializing in popular music have also treated the instrument in new ways, but for very different reasons. They, too, used unchanging pianos, unless they switched to electronic keyboards, but everything else about their circumstances was new in the twentieth century: the repertories and styles they played; the size and makeup of the ensembles in which their pianos were placed; the amplification of the sound not only of their pianos but of the singers and the other instruments with which they played; and the behavior expected of them on stage. Playing the piano in public is, after all, a form of dramatic display, and any public display of pianos or piano playing reveals something about attitudes toward the piano in the culture where that display is made.

Take, for instance, the Broadway singer Helen Morgan, pictured sitting atop a piano as she appeared in the role of Julie in Jerome Kern's *Showboat* in 1927. A hundred years earlier the piano might not have borne her weight. Fifty years earlier her pose, exposing her ankles, would have been scandalous. But by the 1920s, when tiny Morgan was appearing in nightclubs, it was a sign of a new social and sexual freedom for women that she could climb up on the piano to be seen when

"Le Water Chute," from *Sports & Divertissements*, music by Erik Satie, drawings by Charles Martin (1914; published Paris, ca. 1925)

she sang. In *Showboat* she didn't even need any help to be in view; she was perched there only for effect while she sang "Bill." Her accompanist isn't to be seen in this studio photograph, but he was part of the effect. Not just her musical collaborator, he represented a sympathetic listener, propping her up with his attentiveness and his piano as she—from her precarious and immobilizing, if commanding, perch—poured out her longing in song. A singer didn't need to sit on the piano to invoke these symbolic relationships; in a classical concert he or she could create a similar effect by standing in the curve of the grand piano. And the collaboration of singer and accompanist could be used to dramatize many other relationships; in Nina Berberova's story *The Accompanist* (1936), a young woman hired as accompanist to an opera singer becomes like an eighteenth-century servant, spying on her employer, tracking her infidelities, which lead to the husband's suicide. For that matter, women sitting on pianos have not always presented a persona like Helen Morgan's, but they are always making more of a display of their sexuality than they—let alone an Austen heroine—would do sitting *at* the piano.

Jerry Lee Lewis, standing on the piano, was also displaying his sexuality, but not in the form of longing. His aggression was as evident in his playing of the piano as in his standing on it: he once promoted himself as "Jerry Lee Lewis and His Pumping Piano." When he attacked his instrument by leaping onto it, he was acting out a persona of rebelliousness exactly the way other rock and roll performers did when they attacked their guitars. But the piano was different from the guitar in cultural status; it was associated less closely with the country roots of rock and roll and more closely with classical and other urban music. Jumping on the piano was more shocking to some viewers and at the same time safer than beating up a guitar, because the piano was unlikely to be destroyed in a shower of splinters. It is no coincidence that classical pianists were becoming more careful of their pianos as popular pianists were becoming rougher on theirs. By the 1950s, when Lewis was starting to test the durability of his pianos, classical pianists had long since learned to play a concert on a single instrument, even if they occasionally snapped a string on it—unlike Liszt, who had often needed several pianos to get through a performance. The difference was only partially that twentieth-century pianos stood up better than nineteenth-century ones to a heavy "touch." It was also that in the nineteenth century, because there were no Jerry Lee Lewises, Liszt could play the role of concert pianist as an act of aggression. But in the twentieth century, classical pianists, along with mock-classy pianists like Liberace, needed to shun aggressiveness in order to distinguish themselves from

Helen Morgan in Jerome Kern's *Showboat*, 1927

363

Jerry Lee Lewis in performance, June 1958

Opposite: Nam June Paik, *Klavier Intégral,* 1958–63 (Museum Moderner Kunst, Vienna)

rockers like Lewis, just as Lewis needed to pounce on the piano to prove that he was a real rocker, even if he did play the piano.

Nam June Paik's installation *Klavier Intégral* (1958–63) is another twentieth-century assault on a piano, another piano used more for provocative display than for musical play. This time the piano has been turned into an avant-garde art object, displayed in a museum. The display is an artistic overturning of the piano as a symbol of art; it is an attack, made in a museum, on the idea of art as it is found in the concert hall or the museum. It is an example from the world of happenings, installation art, and performance art—one of many examples in which pianos were displayed in unplayable states or were shown being rendered unplayable. All these displays targeted the piano for its cultural prestige, but they attacked it in different ways, drawing attention to different sides of its nature as an object and as a cultural symbol.

Events in which pianos were burned or dropped from a crane onto a parking

364

lot drew attention to its materiality and weight, as well as to the ease with which even the sturdiest cultural creations could be destroyed. A piano into which hundreds of nails had been hammered triggered thoughts of the instrument as a cultural coffin; one into which hundreds of flowers had been stuck drew attention to the piano as an object made from plants. In another instance a grand piano was wrapped in felt: in the words of the artist, Joseph Beuys, the piano was "condemned to silence."[1]

Of all these installations, Paik's is the most complexly symbolic. Here the piano is overwhelmed by objects from daily life, and although many of these objects themselves produce sound, inflicting them on the piano has destroyed its voice. We are urged to remember that the upright piano is itself an object from daily life, though one that promised to transport its owners out of the noise of their daily existence to a more artistic realm. This is a piano punished for being merely what it is, instead of what it promised to be.[2]

Twentieth-century musicians, like these twentieth-century artists, have been accused at times of ignoring what the piano is, of making it do things it wasn't designed to do, even of destroying perfectly good pianos. Some, regarding the beautiful piano sounds of Mozart or Brahms as the daily life of the piano, have searched for other sounds from it, as if wanting to save themselves and their audiences from being overwhelmed by the daily life of tradition. By contrast, for some classical pianists—"early music" specialists—the twentieth-century piano was too much a thing of the present to do justice to the richness of the musical past; they taught themselves to play Mozart on a Mozartian piano and Brahms on a Brahmsian one, leaving the modern piano—the piano of daily life—to cope with whatever was new. Meanwhile, in jazz and other branches of popular music, some keyboard players have accepted the unchanging piano as a "standard" that, like many of the tunes they played on it, challenged them to put their own stamp on it, and others have abandoned the piano for electronic instruments that belong to the piano family in their keyboard layout and touch, but that perform feats beyond the capacity of the piano.

Experimenting in the Museum: Piano Music of the Avant-Garde
James Parakilas

The search for new sounds, even if we explain it as the desire to get away from old sounds, is a quest for something precise. Schoenberg would not have wanted to use the new sounds discovered by Cage—who was briefly his student—and Cage would not have wanted to find Schoenberg's. To serve any musical purpose, a new sound has to provide the composer with some feeling of recognition. The piano began its life impersonating the sounds of the violin and the singing voice; in its

366

third century, it was still yielding up new sounds with which musicians could do new kinds of impressions.

The subjects of these impressions are often as surprising as the means used to draw them out of the piano. At the beginning of the century, for example, Debussy, in his preludes for piano, surveyed the world of musical impressions, from the dances of antiquity to the folk music of Europe and on to the rags and festivals of modern life. Where he was most lacking in musical models for his imagery—as in the depiction of the "terrace for moonlit audiences" in India that he had merely seen mentioned in the newspaper—he relied with sublime confidence on a sheer contrast of sonorities to give an impression of remoteness, setting winding scales against self-possessed triads and using different registers of his piano like unconnected planes (an effect well suited to his old-fashioned piano, which had a less blended sound than present-day instruments).

In the middle of the century, Olivier Messiaen made the piano do bird impressions—something that earlier composers had left largely to the flute—and do them in an immense *Catalog of Birds* (1956–58), relying like Debussy on registral color (especially the uppermost end of the keyboard) and extreme contrasts of texture to support his daring. He also imitated the organ—his own preferred instrument—at the piano, suggesting three keyboards played simultaneously, each with a different registration, in the "Regard du Fils sur le Fils" from his *Vingt Regards sur l'Enfant-Jésus* (1944); the compositional virtuosity of this movement lies in the way the piano, an old hand at imitating other instruments, here finds itself imitating an instrument that itself imitates other instruments, but by utterly different means.

In much of the piano music of Debussy, Messiaen, and their contemporaries, the impressions are made possible by regularly using the damper pedal in a way that was scarcely more than a special effect in the nineteenth century: to gather together and hold in suspension sounds that jar with each other harmonically and otherwise. The damper pedal allowed twentieth-century composers to write for the piano as they did for the orchestra, drawing together figures of many different characters and sonorities from all over the keyboard. It allowed them to suggest moods and dreams at the piano, whether blurring together individually sharp memories of a rosy past, as in the sonatas and songs of Charles Ives, or introducing a subjective distortion into a single, supposedly objective musical style, as in the neo-Baroque preludes and fugues of Dmitri Shostakovich. Piano composers from Prokofiev to Webern and from Bartók to Crawford are like silent-movie pianists. Playing to a movie that runs only in their minds, they hold that pedal down,

pulling together the musical voices and colors they need to bring out the emotional tenor of each new moment in an unfolding drama.

But pianists who performed this music were not meant to play in the background like movie-house pianists. The alterations to the piano and the alternate ways of drawing sound out of it pioneered by Cowell, Ives, Cage, and Crumb, for instance, are avant-garde creations; they are designed to be performed under the spotlights of the concert hall—the musical museum—because, like the piano installations of Nam June Paik (an associate of Cage) and other visual artists, they call into question the premises about the piano that the concert hall enshrines. They revel in the new barrier between piano music for the concert hall and for the home. Their innovations in sound are designed with little thought that they might be tried at home, because although harmless there, they would make little effect. This music is meant to have a visual impact, not just a sonic one.

Take the two most famous innovations of Henry Cowell. The first, the tone cluster—a spread of adjacent keys sounded all at once—appeared in his *Tides of Manaunaun* (1912), a work he wrote at the age of fifteen. The tone cluster was not a new idea in 1912; eighteenth-century battle pieces for piano had used such clusters to imitate the sounds of cannons. Cowell's tone-cluster effects are no less concerned with the musical dramatization of force, but the force he had in mind was cosmic, and his effect was heightened by the sight of the pianist slamming the keyboard with the full forearm. More original and even more challenging to the conventional notion of how to play the piano was Cowell's idea of playing directly on the strings, disregarding the keys. His first work using this technique is *Aeolian Harp* (1923), followed by *The Banshee* (1925) and others. In *The Banshee* the pianist stands in the curve of the piano (the damper pedal has to be held down by someone or something else) and by means of glissandi and a variety of other strokes produces unearthly sounds, for which Cowell found an apt title; but the unearthliness consists partly in seeing a performer stand at a piano and produce sounds unrecognizable as piano sounds.[3]

The sound of Charles Ives's Three Quarter-Tone Pieces for two pianos (1923–24) is perfectly recognizable as coming from a piano, even though the pianos need to be specially prepared for a performance: each tuned in the usual way to itself, but one tuned a quarter-tone above the other. Ives had considered creating a special quarter-tone piano with two keyboards connected to sets of strings tuned a quarter-tone apart, to be played by one pianist: the idea must have appealed to the organist in him. The third of these pieces ("Chorale") is derived from an earlier composition that he intended for strings. Indeed, strings seem like a more

Thomas Hart Benton, *The Sun Treader (Portrait of Carl Ruggles)*, 1934, tempera with oil on canvas mounted on panel, 45" × 38". Benton's painting, named for Ruggles's orchestral masterpiece, is a portrayal of a twentieth-century composer using the piano to search for new sounds. (The Nelson-Atkins Museum of Art, Kansas City, Mo. Gift of the Friends of Art. © T. H. Benton and R. P. Benton Testamentary Trusts/ Licensed by VAGA, New York, N.Y.)

369

congenial medium for a quarter-tone piece, but maybe Ives despaired of getting string players to realize it, whereas in the two-piano version, once the pianos were tuned, the intonation was set. In effect Ives had created a new instrument, and it remained to test what it could do. Finding himself in something like Lodovico Giustini's situation writing for the new soft-and-loud harpsichord two centuries earlier, Ives did something like what Giustini had done: he put his quarter-tone duo-piano through the paces of many styles that his listeners were familiar with on normally tuned pianos—character piece, rag, hymn, and patriotic song—but he arranged them so as to show the capabilities of the new medium in all of those styles. In fact, he poses the scales of the two instruments against each other with endless resourcefulness—creating, in Wiley Hitchcock's words, now a "vibrant shimmer," now a "sizzling, twanging music evocative of a crazy banjo."[4]

Ives's Quarter-Tone Pieces require pianos that have been specially prepared. The term *prepared piano,* however, is especially associated with John Cage, whose long list of works for piano or pianos "prepared" by the installation of tone-altering objects on certain strings began with his *Bacchanale* in 1940. These preparations resemble Cowell's string strumming in that they make the piano sound remarkably unlike itself. They also are like Ives's retuning in that they are done ahead of time, so that in the performance there is nothing visible indicating why the piano sounds unusual. The combination of these two effects makes this music far more unsettling to hear in concert than that of either Cowell or Ives. In fact, although many of the innovations in twentieth-century piano music that once outraged listeners have now ceased to offend, many continue to consider a sacrilege Cage's fastening of screws, bolts, rubber bands, and felt weather stripping on the strings of a piano.

This lingering discomfort says more about the cultural status of the piano than about Cage's music. The preparations that he prescribes are less dangerous to a piano than strumming the strings, and there is good advice available in print for anyone who wants to perform either inside-the-piano or prepared-piano music without harming the instrument.[5] The preparations Cage calls for take time and experimentation, but they are rewarding; the notes of those pieces can in some cases even be sight-read by an amateur. In terms of accessibility for performance, then, there is hardly any avant-garde piano music more suited for trying at home, so long as the home has a grand piano, of any size. And the sound of the music—unlike that of *The Banshee*—is quiet and tranquil, like a toy gamelan. The "script" for which this music might have been written has mystery, but no threat. What upsets people about a musician who fastens hardware on the strings is that we have been raised not to put our soda cans on the piano, not to think of it as a machine but as a work of art, not to dream of intruding on its inner mysteries but to leave its maintenance to its priest, the piano technician. But in his quiet way, Cage merely reminded us of what the piano has always been. It has always been a piece of hardware from which poetry could be drawn. It has always made singing, ringing sounds that couldn't entirely be predicted from its mechanism. And it has always been a transplanting instrument, capturing in its own terms the sounds of one musical site in order to carry them to another site—in this case transplanting into the concert hall not the bells and whistles of any human music, but the barely perceptible ringings and buzzings of the universe.[6]

While Cage was seeing what new sounds he could get out of one string of the piano, other composers on several continents were taking advantage of the liberation of the piano from amateurs to make ever more extreme demands on profes-

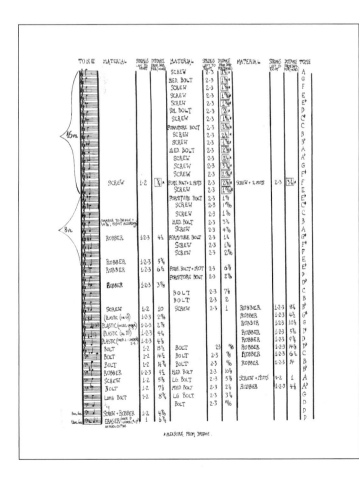

John Cage, Table of Preparations from *Sonatas and Interludes* (1948; published New York, 1960). The table is prefaced by a note that reads: "Mutes of various materials are placed between the strings of the keys used, thus effecting transformations of the piano sounds with respect to all of their characteristics."

sional performers. The complexities of rhythm, discontinuities of pitch, and varieties of attack required of pianists by composers like Karlheinz Stockhausen, Pierre Boulez, Milton Babbitt, and Elliott Carter provide their own unprecedented dramas, sonorities, and evocations. But the remarkable ability of pianists like David Tudor, David Burge, and Ursula Oppens to keep up with the demands of these composers seems in some cases only to have further liberated them—if that is the word for it—leading them to imagine feats for which no pianist had enough hands or could possibly have enough speed or control. One way out was to turn to computers to realize their dreams fully and faultlessly, whether in imitation piano sound or some other sonority. But not every composer had that option. An American composer who did not was Conlon Nancarrow, who isolated himself in Mexico in the early 1940s to escape the politically heavy hand of his own government and who had in any case long dreamed of "getting rid of the performers." He turned to a medium that had reached a dead end commercially at the time, but that gave him just the means he needed to realize the "tempo tornadoes" in his head: the player piano. In his more than fifty studies for player piano, he created dizzyingly crisp sonorities and energetic processes all his own—the results of considering the player piano an instrument in its own right, not just a playerless imitator of played pianos.[7]

Unlike the works of Cowell, Ives, Cage, and Nancarrow, a piano piece or chamber work with piano by George Crumb does not revolve around a single

Toy piano by Albert Schoenhut, Philadelphia, early twentieth century (Metropolitan Museum of Art, New York)

Charles M. Schulz, Peanuts cartoon. Schroeder's toy piano, no less than the attitudes all the Peanuts characters express, represents an adult amusement at putting adult thoughts into the minds of children.

untraditional use of the piano; it is a catalog of many. In the course of a single work, Crumb may call on his performer to amplify the piano; to play inside it in various ways; to play a key while muting its strings by hand; to play one set of notes while letting other strings vibrate by silently depressing their keys; and to switch to an unconventional piano (but not a player piano). Building on the explorations of novel piano sound by his avant-garde predecessors, Crumb has wielded the most stunning sonoric palette of all and been the most explicit in applying his sonic novelties to images, fantasies, and ideas, in texted as well as untexted works.

In Crumb's *Ancient Voices of Children* (1970), a song cycle for soprano, boy soprano, and a small group of instruments on poems of García Lorca, the singers sometimes sing into the amplified piano, its lid and dampers lifted, for the aura of vibrations that their voices set off inside the instrument. The fourth song has the devastating text "Each afternoon in Granada, a child dies each afternoon," and a devastating way of representing a child who dies. After the singer has intoned the text in a whisper, the pianist, who has not yet played in this song, begins to play a toy piano. The toy piano, a nineteenth-century invention, is more toy than piano.[8] It is a device that allows children to imagine being adults more than an instrument on which they can learn music. It looks like a scaled-down piano, but it doesn't work like one: pressing its keys vibrates metal bars, not strings. As a result, it doesn't sound like a piano. And that is exactly what makes it serve Crumb's purpose: the toy piano creates its own sonority, the sound of childhood. Instead of a child imagining herself or himself as an adult, the listener is coaxed into imagining the adult pianist as a child. On this tiny instrument the pianist now plays phrases of "Bist du bei mir," a song familiar from Bach's Notebook for Anna Magdalena Bach. The words are not heard here, but anyone who knows them will be haunted by them in this new context: "With you by my side, I go with gladness to death and to my rest." And just as the final phrase of the song is about to resolve into its final chord, the toy piano breaks off.

The Piano in Jazz
Mark Tucker

Trumpeters and saxophonists play the romantic leads. With gleaming horns held erect to the lips or curving out from their bodies, they excel in the art of musical seduction. Look at the photographs: the commanding authority of Louis Armstrong, the transcendent cool of Lester Young, the intensity of Charlie Parker, the mystique of Miles Davis. Behind these magnetic stars, bassists and drummers make up the supporting cast. They keep time, monitor flow and continuity, and comment, choruslike, on the unfolding action. They are crucial yet secondary.

Pianists in jazz occupy the middle. They can step forward into the spotlight to shine as soloists or stay in the background to join bass and drums in rhythm section chores. They all share one physical disadvantage, though: it is hard to look hip or erotically charged while seated at a large box-shaped instrument staring down at your fingers. (Rock pianists solved the problem by strapping on compact electric keyboards and playing them like guitars; when they hit expressive high notes they could bend knees, swivel hips, and grimace, making their bodies part of the performance.) Yet the piano's versatility keeps players from being relegated to a merely subordinate status. Jazz pianists can state themes as boldly as any trumpeter and unleash flurries of improvised lines to rival any saxophonist. They can create contrapuntal interest, punctuate with chords, apply washes of harmonic color, drive the rhythm forward, pound out the beat, or dance on top of it. They can do it all—and this affects their personality and character.

Pianists in jazz are authority figures, sages, intellectuals, teachers, control freaks. Sitting upright at their keyboards, they resemble engineers behind a console board or flight controllers operating a complicated series of switches, levers, and buttons. They have a formal, bookish air. In the glory days of ragtime and the school of Harlem stride, back in the 1910s and 1920s, the most accomplished pianists were called "professors." Other players stood in awe of them, striving to acquire their polished technique, harmonic know-how, and consummate musicianship. Later Dr. Billy Taylor would assume the "professor" role, expounding on the history of jazz from his keyboard podium. The maverick Lennie Tristano taught in private, passing on esoteric knowledge to his students—many of them not even pianists. A legendary professor of harmony and the improvised line, Barry Harris has instructed several generations of players from the 1950s to the present.

Learning how to operate a complex mechanism can take years of study. One way jazz pianists convey their studiousness, the intense labor they have invested in their art, is by wearing glasses. Horn players shun these props or hide behind dark shades. But consider the great bespectacled pianists: Bill Evans, Herbie Hancock, Billy Taylor, Dave Brubeck, Dick Hyman, Tommy Flanagan, Jimmy Rowles, Dick Wellstood, Phineas Newborn, Jr.—on the list goes. The glasses worn by these players suggest an arduous process of acquiring knowledge, of paying dues, but also a certain vulnerability. Jazz pianists have not been afraid to look vulnerable. Glasses are a symbol of their trade, just as they are for scientists and scholars.

Herbie Hancock, photographed by Francis Wolff, December 1964

Mary Lou Williams, photographed by Charles Stewart, 1957

Being a figure of control and authority can swell the ego to grandiose proportions. Jelly Roll Morton and Willie "the Lion" Smith were two from the old school renowned for their cocky arrogance. Morton took credit for inventing jazz; in 1938 he told Alan Lomax that everyone who played in a jazz style was indebted to him. "The Lion" would loudly proclaim the superiority of his abilities, then take the stool in his derby hat, bow tie, and thick-framed glasses to give a convincing demonstration of his prowess. Art Tatum knew that he was extraordinary. There once was a headstrong pianist who challenged Tatum to a pianistic duel and put on an impressive display of virtuosity, only to have Tatum turn to his companion, an accomplished though lesser mortal, and calmly say, "Take him, Marlowe." Another time, Fats Waller was playing in a club when he acknowledged Tatum in the audience by proclaiming, "God is in the house tonight." Who but a pianist would refer to a fellow player this way?

Such hubris is forgivable. Like God, pianists have the whole wide world in their hands. Cecil Taylor conjures up a planet wracked by violent forces—surging waves, howling winds, explosive eruptions. Marian McPartland paints softly glowing landscapes of slanting light and subtle tonal shifts. Dave McKenna recreates a lost realm of beauty and romance that existed long ago in the dreams of songwriters.

The pianist as Creator: when Keith Jarrett began playing epic-length improvisations at his solo concerts, he said that before going out on stage he would try to clear away from his consciousness every preexisting musical idea, wiping the slate clean of knowledge and experience in order to create anew.

God is in the house tonight.

Pianists gain authority and control by creating music for others to play. They tend to be composers, arrangers, orchestrators, bandleaders, and musical directors. Standing in the group portrait with Morton are Duke Ellington, Fletcher Henderson, Mary Lou Williams, Thelonious Monk, John Lewis, Tadd Dameron, Billy Strayhorn, Toshiko Akiyoshi, McCoy Tyner, Chick Corea, and Joe Zawinul. Drummer Art Blakey had a series of gifted pianists serve as musical directors of his Jazz Messengers, among them Horace Silver, Bobby Timmons, Cedar Walton, James Williams, and Mulgrew Miller. Dick Hyman is cast exactly to type: he can play fluently in any style, write film scores and transcribe arrangements from old recordings, compose originals and arrange standards, lead groups and conduct orchestras, perform flawlessly as soloist or sideman. A brainy, knowledgeable musician, he's got the whole jazz tradition in his hands. He is that professorial gentleman over there in glasses, seated at the keyboard.

For years women excelled in jazz either by singing or playing the piano. (Some, like Sarah Vaughan, Nina Simone, Shirley Horn, and Diana Krall, have been adept at both.) These were traditionally feminized musical activities, considered more proper for young ladies than blowing trumpet in a brass band or plucking bass in an orchestra. Working as pianists in jazz gave women some of the same power and perquisites enjoyed by their male counterparts. Lillian Hardin contributed original pieces to the repertory of bands led by King Oliver and her husband Louis Armstrong. Mary Lou Williams composed, arranged, and held the piano chair in the Kansas City–based orchestra of Andy Kirk. Marian McPartland has used trios as showcases for her playing and writing talents, while Toshiko Akiyoshi and Carla Bley have fronted big bands for the same purpose. From the 1970s on, many women pianists have emerged as prominent figures on the contemporary jazz scene, among them Joanne Brackeen, Geri Allen, Renee Rosnes, Michelle Rosewoman, Jessica Williams, Peggy Stern, Eliane Elias, and Myra Melford. The instrument has empowered women to carve out a profession in a field dominated by men.

The piano did not always carry prestige and power in jazz. Early on it was a humble accompanying instrument, plunking chords alongside banjo or guitar, pounding out the rhythm with drums and tuba (or string bass). The signature sound of early jazz came from brass and reeds—trumpet, trombone, clarinet, and saxophone. These were the instruments that got listeners hot and bothered with their bluesy smears, piercing high notes, and deep moaning growls. The piano outlined harmonies, thickened textures, and raised the volume a few notches, but it lacked a distinctive jazz identity. Playing piano in a jazz band required no special techniques or improvising abilities—if you had a basic knowledge of chords and could keep time you were qualified, as both Lillian Hardin and Fletcher Henderson discovered in the early 1920s. One major problem faced by pianists was purely acoustical: they could not be heard well over other instruments, which is why on early band recordings everyone else usually dropped out during piano solos. Another problem was stylistic: how to make the self-sufficient idiom of pi-

Inventing Jazz Piano

ano ragtime work in an ensemble context, blending with and complementing the other instruments.

On recordings from the mid to late 1920s, a few players can be heard making headway in these areas. Jelly Roll Morton, who had already developed formidable soloing skills as a young man in New Orleans, began finding ways for a band pianist to do more than simply provide background oompah accompaniment. He played countermelodies behind soloists. He broke up repetitive accompanying patterns by inserting short melodic figures in the bass, connecting the musical syntax in the manner of a trombone or tuba. He used treble octaves to make the piano ring out amid brass and reeds—a device also employed by Earl Hines with Louis Armstrong's small groups and Count Basie with Bennie Moten's orchestra. Beyond broadening the range of accompanying options, Morton emulated the sound of other instruments playing jazz. He could simulate the clarinet's ornate filigree lines, the trumpet's penetrating tone, the trombone's jocular interjections, and the bass drum's thumping beat. He taught the piano how to play jazz.

The piano came into its own as a jazz instrument in the 1930s. In the solo

Jelly Roll Morton at RCA
Victor studio, July 1929

Art Tatum, photographed
by Charles Peterson at
Café Society Downtown,
1940

arena, Art Tatum demonstrated a degree of virtuosity previously unknown in jazz, nearly beyond belief. Combining the rhythmic drive and textural clarity of Fats Waller with the rococo imagination of Earl Hines, and incorporating technical devices associated with the nineteenth-century school of virtuosity—rapid scales in single notes and thirds, sweeping arpeggiated flourishes, hammering octaves— Tatum invented a new musical persona for the jazz pianist. He was a force of liberation proving that anything and everything was possible on the instrument. If only a few who followed came close to reaching Tatum's level of virtuosity (Oscar Peterson, Adam Mackowicz, Dick Hyman), many more were inspired by him to take advantage of the instrument's full resources—all its registers, textures, harmonies, and expressive capabilities.

Swing-era pianists expanded and refined their instrument's role in ensembles. With sparkling touch and elegant phrasing, Teddy Wilson made the piano a sophisticated partner in the chamber music conversations of clarinetist Benny Goodman's small groups, as in the quartet he joined together with vibraphonist Lionel Hampton and drummer Gene Krupa. There Wilson flowed smoothly with the liquid counterpoint and floated effortlessly above the rhythm. Neither aggressive solo exhibitionist nor deferential accompanist, Wilson brought subtlety and flexibility to jazz piano style. Billy Kyle cultivated these same qualities in John Kirby's sextet, his facility and precision well suited for the group's arrangements of pieces from the classical repertory. Pianists with big bands also began favoring a lighter touch and sparer textures. Schooled in the luxurious, full-bodied style of Harlem stride piano, Count Basie undertook a major pruning job, getting rid of the pumping left hand and flashy figuration, cutting back to simple riffs and clean single-note lines played high in the treble. He turned his four-piece rhythm section (piano, guitar, bass, drums) into a band within a band, featuring it prominently in arrangements and thus raising his own profile as the leading solo voice in this quartet. Together with Duke Ellington, another bandleader who sat at the keyboard, Basie used the piano to conduct his orchestra: cuing with chords, setting tempos, calling and responding, connecting phrases, segueing from one piece to the next.

Small-group pianists playing "bebop" in the 1940s and 1950s continued the process of paring down textures and simplifying chord structures to enhance the music's supple rhythmic character. When accompanying, they favored short staccato chords voiced in the middle register. Instead of hitting every chord in a harmonic sequence, they skipped some and only alluded to others. While earlier pianists might have played a full F^7 chord (F, A, C, E-flat), Bud Powell or Thelonious Monk might play only a shell consisting of the outer interval (F and E-flat). They edited themselves rigorously, applying the less-is-more principle that Basie had found effective in a big-band context.

A similar reductive impulse governed the soloing techniques of bebop pianists. With left hands providing sporadic chordal punctuation, they constructed chains of single-note phrases with their right, articulating in the manner of a saxophonist or trumpeter. The relative parity between hands in earlier jazz soloing styles gave way to a more lopsided arrangement in which one hand underplayed and the other performed most of the work. In a way, the leaner right-hand lines reflected a more transparent textural ideal; at the same time they seemed a form of horn envy, with pianists straining to emulate the speed and agility of such players as Charlie Parker, Dizzy Gillespie, and Clifford Brown. A variation of this technique was the block chord, "locked hands" style popularized by George Shearing, Milt Buckner, and others. In this a melody line in the top voice was harmonized in close position by both hands, the resulting chords moving together in synchrony. Although perfectly suited to the keyboard, the block chord style often suggested a harmonized horn line or ensemble writing for massed brass and reeds in big-band arrangements. Like Jelly Roll Morton before them, bebop pia-

nists had become expert mimics of other instruments in the jazz family. Stationed at their keyboards, they could fashion replicas of the greater jazz world around them—gods of the microcosm.

During the 1950s, jazz pianists began to tire of self-imposed stylistic limitations in which the right hand sought to play horn lines and the left supplied only light rhythmic punctuation. Not content to imitate or replicate others, they started sa-

Count Basie and his band at the Famous Door, 1938

Reinventing Jazz Piano

voring the unique properties of their instrument: the gratifying pop of hammers hitting strings; the gorgeous clang of a metal harp resonating inside a wooden chamber; the infinite tonal gradations achieved by changing weight, pressure, articulation. At their feet they discovered a damper pedal that could sustain chords and transform timbres. Having accomplished the task of integrating the piano into jazz—clarifying its functions and developing techniques to carry them out—they now set about to explore its worlds of sound.

Some were drawn to the piano's percussive character. Earlier African-American musicians had turned stringed instruments like banjo, guitar, and bass into drumlike creations, hitting and slapping strings, knocking on hollow bodies, laying down beats. A strong percussive tradition had also characterized African-American keyboard styles in ragtime, stride, blues, gospel, and boogie-woogie. The jazz pianist who placed this legacy at the center of his art was Thelonious Monk. With fingers flat and splayed, Monk struck the keys forcefully, jabbing dissonant chords and clusters and releasing them abruptly. (His wife Nellie referred to him playfully as Melodious Thunk.) Around the same time that composer Conlon Nancarrow was getting the player piano to do what was humanly impossible—perform complex, densely textured music at racing tempos with no mistakes—Monk went after a radically different aesthetic, reminding listeners that it was he, the fallible pianist, who took full responsibility for the apparent "wrong" notes, smudged intervals, and "accidents" that, lo and behold, turned out to be right and deliberate after all. Monk was a magician specializing in illusions of imperfection. He Africanized the piano, not just by awakening the spirit of the drum, but also by making his melodies sing the blues and his rhythms swing through space and time with the grace of a tap dancer. He inspired others to do the same: Horace Silver, Herbie Nichols, Andrew Hill, Cecil Taylor, Abdullah Ibrahim, Geri Allen, and especially Randy Weston, the Brooklyn-born musician who played on the piano like a master drummer, using traditional African materials—ebony, ivory, strings—to summon the ancestral spirits.

Other pianists in the 1950s cultivated a more lyrical style and softer touch, basing their techniques on principles of tone production that had long prevailed in Europe. They gave the piano a voice of sweet intimacy perfect for singing romantic ballads and whispering secrets. Instead of brittle, hard-edged chords, they produced velvety cushions soothing to the ear. Instead of drumming on the keyboard, they caressed it. Red Garland with the Miles Davis quintet; Ahmad Jamal, Nat "King" Cole, and Marian McPartland with their trios; and exceptional accompanists like Hank Jones, Tommy Flanagan, Jimmy Jones, and Ellis Larkins

Thelonious Monk, photographed by Bob Parent at the Open Door, 1953

—these were some of the players who helped define a characteristic identity for jazz piano that conveyed laid-back cool and worldly sophistication. They spawned a genre that, in the hands of some practitioners, would become equated with "cocktail piano," implying tinkling harmonies in the background conducive to drinking and conversing. But behind the pleasing sheen of their sound, these jazz pianists worked on a deeper level, telling intricate stories for those who listened closely, creating urban nocturnes that channeled inner emotional lives into public discourse.

A leading figure in this romantic school of jazz piano was Bill Evans, who performed with Miles Davis in the late 1950s and went on to lead trios for the rest of his career. In his autobiography, Davis recalled how Evans had sparked his interest in twentieth-century classical music, introducing him to works by Ravel and Khachaturian and recordings by Italian pianist Arturo Benedetti Michelangeli. Davis especially prized Evans for his sound. That sound came from the rich chromatic vocabulary of bebop, the bittersweet dissonance of Debussy and Ravel, and the sober air of ancient modes—Dorian, Phrygian, Mixolydian. His right hand had a singing, legato touch; his left arranged familiar chords in new ways, and these left-hand "voicings" were not merely functional harmonic shells but supplied a melodic component that caught the ear's attention. Instead of the right hand playing "soloist" to the left hand's "accompanist," the two carried on a conversation. The recordings Evans made with his trio at the Village Vanguard in 1961 reveal the modest eloquence of his melodic statements and the aqueous tints of his tonal palette.

Evans's poignant lyricism and luminous harmonies came to define a school of jazz piano that produced many distinguished graduates in the 1960s and after—players who took his conception as a starting point for finding their own voice on the instrument. One was Herbie Hancock, who possessed a solid classical technique and lavish harmonic imagination but also wanted the piano to produce funky grooves for dancing. Electronic keyboards and synthesizers helped him accomplish this, as heard on the recordings *Headhunters* (1973) and *Secrets* (1976). Chick Corea, similarly, could enter into Evans's world of tender chords and meditative moods, then crank up the volume with Return to Forever and the Elektric Band, his right-hand lines skittering up and down the keyboard and charged with rock-and-roll energy. The cantabile quality of Keith Jarrett's lines owed something to Evans as well as classical practice, while the loose, discursive structures of his improvisations came from elsewhere—Miles Davis or psychedelic rock, perhaps, or the uncharted waters of Jarrett's unconscious. Pianists who emerged in the 1980s and 1990s also drew spiritual and musical sustenance from the intertwined legacy of Evans, Hancock, Corea, and Jarrett, among them Stephen Scott, Renee Rosnes, Brad Mehldau, and Bruce Barth.

Together with the percussive, blues-rooted tradition of Monk and the Romantic impressionism of Evans, there were two other main streams of jazz piano that emerged in the late 1950s and 1960s and served as exemplary models for younger players in the decades that followed. During his years with John Coltrane's quartet, McCoy Tyner developed an energized style that incorporated many of the saxophonist's signal traits: surging rhythmic energy, ferocious speed and power, modal harmonies, free-ranging chromaticism, melodic sequencing, and motivic play. Tyner gave back to the lower half of the keyboard both the vigor and the volume that had ebbed during the reign of bebop. His left hand sparred with busy right-hand lines to create polyphonic interest and pounded out open intervals (octaves, fifths, quartal chords) to build great waves of sound.

A more adventurous musical and pianistic conception grew up in tandem with free jazz and the avant-garde. Cecil Taylor spearheaded the movement, which also drew in such figures as Sun Ra, Don Pullen, Muhal Richard Abrams, Borah Bergman, Mischa Mengelberg, Myra Melford, and Matthew Shipp. These players frequently dismantled or discarded tonality while shunning the familiar scales, modes, harmonies, textures, and gestural vocabulary of earlier jazz pianists. Like Tyner and his school, the free players were dedicated to exploiting the total sound resources of the piano. They held down the damper pedal to construct thickly layered textures, played crunching chord clusters and rapid-fire atonal runs, struck strings inside the piano, exploited extremes of register, and attacked the keys with maximum force. Although the work of these pianists grew out of jazz and its improvisatory practice, it bore hallmarks of the experimental modernism that had animated twentieth-century composers from Webern and Cowell to Cage and Stockhausen.

Despite stereotypes that have grown up around those who play jazz for a living—images of flighty creative types, colorful eccentrics, free spirits off in their own orbits—they tend to be, like most professional musicians, eminently practical souls. They make the best of their circumstances, putting up with unpredictable venues, odd hours, rigorous travel, and audiences with widely varied expectations. They strive for optimal musical results from available resources—whether it

Using the Piano in Jazz

is a gifted touring soloist in concert adapting to mediocre local accompanists, or members of a pickup group at a record date striving to sound relaxed and authoritative playing pieces they have never seen before.

The practical advantages of the piano account partly for its popularity throughout the history of jazz. As many gifted solo players have shown, from Morton and Tatum to Jarrett and Taylor, the instrument on its own can provide a complete and satisfying musical experience for listeners. It can fill out the sound of a big band or small combo or shrink down to smaller scale with one or two other instruments—as in the duos of Duke Ellington and bassist Jimmy Blanton, Butch Thompson and trumpeter Doc Cheatham, and Myra Melford and drummer Han Bennink, or the many accomplished piano trios that have formed over the years. The piano also blends wonderfully with vocalists: one of the most luscious tonal combinations in jazz was Ella Fitzgerald and Ellis Larkins performing a set of Gershwin songs, with her limpid phrases floating over his warm, relaxed accompaniment like clouds on a summer afternoon.

But these examples only give a sense of the piano's visible, public functions; it also figures prominently behind the scenes in the jazz world. The piano has been indispensable for teaching jazz harmony and invaluable for giving a solid theoretical base to those who play single-line instruments. When the new harmonic language of bebop was being formulated in the early 1940s, the piano was a kind of sketch pad on which musicians worked out their ideas. Trumpeters Dizzy Gillespie and Miles Davis recalled how Thelonious Monk would explain harmonies to them at the keyboard—and it was from one such demonstration that Gillespie learned a chord that inspired the melody of his piece "Woody 'n You" and the introduction to his version of Monk's "'Round Midnight."[9] Although today one can take courses in jazz harmony and buy books devoted to the subject, the piano is still a preferred medium for translating theory into practice.

For many in jazz, the piano is a tool for composition and an outlet for private music making. One of the earliest glimpses of a jazz composer using the piano is in the film *Black and Tan* (1929), in which Duke Ellington sits at the keyboard to try out his "latest" composition, "Black and Tan Fantasy" (actually dating from 1927), accompanied by Arthur Whetsol on muted trumpet. In a later film, *Symphony in Black* (1935), Ellington is shown composing at the piano in his studio, writing a new work for the concert hall. Another composer in jazz, bassist Charles Mingus, was proficient enough at the piano to record an entire album on the instrument, *Mingus/Oh Yeah* (1962). Listening to Mingus play piano—on this recording, and in *Mingus*, the 1968 film documentary by Tom Reichman—one hears him exploring chords, noodling, searching for something, all part of a larger creative process. Then there are those with keyboard facility—saxophonists Ben Webster and Wayne Shorter, for example, and trumpeter Wynton Marsalis—who rarely perform or record on the piano, instead turning to it for personal pleasure and instruction, using it to enter a vast sound world outside the reach of their primary instruments.

Keith Jarrett, photographed by Gene Martin, 1991

Beyond its practical uses, the piano also has a symbolic function in jazz. Sitting on stage or in a club, alone or grouped with other instruments, it resembles a venerable antique chest containing knowledge, lore, and principles. Its shape and bulk convey these impressions, as do its associations with musical traditions that predate jazz—particularly the art music of western Europe. How fitting it seemed for orchestra leaders like Ellington, Basie, Stan Kenton, and Toshiko Akiyoshi to direct their groups from the keyboard, just as composer-performer-conductors had done for centuries. And how natural when such jazz pianists as John Lewis, Keith Jarrett, and Chick Corea played works from the classical repertory, revealing their own musical roots and tastes while acknowledging the broader historical tradition that produced them.

At the same time, the imposing history of the piano has given jazz musicians something to rebel against. It has forced them to invent new sounds and techniques that are not merely borrowed from other traditions. For while the piano can impart musical knowledge, it can also prove inhibiting—which is why some in the past, like saxophonists Gerry Mulligan and Ornette Coleman, have eliminated it from their groups, seeking escape from its harmonic strictures and musty aroma of tradition. Technological developments—the electric piano, synthesizer, and digital keyboards—have also been embraced by jazz players seeking to make their music "now" instead of "then."

But many others have stuck by the old piano, turning it into a modern jazz machine through their distinctive styles and compelling musicianship. Sometimes their physical position at the keyboard shows them actively struggling with this transformation, as they seek to extract sounds and expression that the instrument was not designed to produce. Bill Evans hunched down over the keys, a perfect model of "incorrect" posture, tilting his head to the side as if calibrating the weight of each chord. Keith Jarrett, in the heat of improvisation, lifts himself up and away from the keyboard, rising to his feet and looking skyward; for him, the piano is merely a vehicle for transport: his true goal lies beyond. And Thelonious Sphere Monk, what did he do when his playing soared and his band swung hard and the music took on a life of its own? He got up and started moving, catching the rhythm in his body, spinning in circles, showing us that jazz was a music of freedom and possibility in which pianists had earned the right to do anything they pleased.

New Specialties in the Musical Marketplace
James Parakilas

Any symbolic representation of the musical marketplace in the industrial world at the beginning of the twentieth century would undoubtedly show the piano right at the center of things. A representation of the equivalent marketplace at the end of that century, however, would need to show the piano pushed to the side by the guitar and above all by the electronic production and reproduction of sound. The piano might still play a central role in classical music and its avant-garde extensions, as well as in jazz, but those branches of music account for relatively little of the worldwide music industry. Given this situation, it would be easy to think of the piano as a holdover from the past, retained in certain settings for sentimental or snobbish reasons, but inexorably losing ground to newer keyboard instruments or to situations in which no keyboard instrument is required at all.

The truth is richer. Take the singing pianist. When Bobby Short accompanies his own singing at the Carlyle Hotel in New York, he is as likely as Horowitz to be playing a Steinway grand; he clings to tradition in his choice of piano as he does in his repertory of classic twentieth-century American popular songs. For his well-heeled and at-least-middle-aged listeners, his gentle touch on the Steinway embodies social and musical sophistication, reassuringly blocking out the louder, cruder music of the masses, especially the young masses. But the intimate interplay of his voice and his playing depends on twentieth-century amplification, even if it is more discreetly measured out at a nightclub than at any popular-music concert. And as a singer who accompanies himself, amplified, he is not so much sustaining the eighteenth- and nineteenth-century tradition of singing from the piano as he is resurrecting it in a musical world where the practice of singing to one's own playing has become commonplace again, because of the guitar. In that sense the guitar might even be thought of as holding the door open for the piano.

The list of musicians who have sung from the piano in the twentieth century is long, criss-crossing the fields and styles of popular music, from Professor Longhair to Aretha Franklin, from Ray Charles to Elton John, from Jerry Lee Lewis to Billy Joel. Some, like Short, have milked the long-standing upper-class associations of the piano, even while practicing new styles of music making on it. Others, like Charles and Franklin, have brought traditional African-American styles of singing and playing to audiences that include all races and classes. Together, all have added something new, which they themselves sometimes proclaim in song, to the older image of the pianist who communicates solely through the keys—the image of an Artur Rubinstein or a George Shearing (the image that even Victor Borge plays on when he stops talking long enough to sit down at the piano and play). These newer images, created by stars of the music business, have in turn affected conditions for gigging musicians; Bruce MacLeod, in a 1993 study of musicians who played the party circuit in New York, concluded that "the keyboard player who is also a strong vocalist has become perhaps *the* most important single band member."[10]

Twentieth-century popular and commercial music, unlike classical and jazz, has overwhelmingly favored vocal over purely instrumental sounds, and especially over the sound of instrumental solos. But where there are instrumental solos in those fields, the piano gets the lion's share of them. There, too, the piano has not simply hung on to past styles, outdated images, and old audiences, but has played an important part in the creation of the new. In New Age music, for instance, the piano solo—represented by George Winston's recordings or Michael Nyman's soundtrack to Jane Campion's movie *The Piano*—has been a leading force. Part of what was new about New Age was the extent to which it was the creature of the recording industry, relying relatively little on concert performances to build its audience. In the industrial, or postindustrial, world of the late twentieth century, New Age was a product of the technology of social escape; it was preeminently the music of the commuter's car audio system and weekend getaways. It is hardly surprising that the piano found a central place in this style, because it had long established itself as the companion and sound of solitude in the days before recorded sound. For that matter, the attraction of live piano sound is not just a distant memory for many fans of New Age music, and some of them, treasuring the music as a solitary experience, are driven to play it for themselves. As a result, New Age has kept people learning the piano.

The world of recorded music has given new twists to other long-established aptitudes and associations of the piano. It is often called on, for instance, in mood-manipulating recordings, whether background music made to increase sales when heard by customers or foreground music made to help people reduce stress, get through childbirth, or go to sleep. In many of these recordings, music that is presumed to be familiar to the listener in one arrangement is presented in a "cooler" arrangement, which typically means that words, the sound of the human voice, and any indications of passion are stripped away. It is hardly surprising that the piano is often used in this process of paring down: from the time it was invented, it has been used in musical arrangements as a substitute for voices and other instruments. Nor is there anything new in giving the piano the job of cooling things down: nineteenth-century albums of piano music for the home are filled with social dance music that was made by bowdlerizing the most passionate arias from Donizetti and Verdi operas. What makes these bowdlerizations of the late twentieth century interesting, in fact, is not any new musical tricks that the piano is being asked to perform, but the new social situations in which, thanks to the technology of recording, the piano is now able to perform its old tricks.

In movie soundtracks, the piano may be used to keep the music stripped down—sung words have traditionally been saved for special situations and the credits—without necessarily keeping it cool. Even in Hugh Hudson's 1981 movie *Chariots of Fire*, with its synthesized score by Vangelis Papathanassiou, the sound of the piano appears in the theme song. Its effect there depends on it not being heard solo but posed against other instrumental sounds, as in a piano concerto. According to the conventional wisdom about classical music, the piano concerto typically represents heroic, solitary struggles of individuals against powers greater than themselves. The *Chariots of Fire* theme draws on that symbolism in that it is heard in a movie about Olympic runners determined to win gold medals against the odds. But the theme does not sound much like a piano concerto, nor does it invoke the 1920s—the era in which the movie is set—by means of musical style. Those who saw the movie in the 1980s no more heard the piano sonority on the soundtrack as a dated sound than they thought of the Olympic ambitions of the runners as a dated quest; the sound of the piano is no more a simple holdover or throwback, then, in the music of this movie than it is in a piano bar, a George Winston CD, or a tape played in a restaurant.

Finally there are the dance bands in which the piano has played a role in the twentieth century, not just jazz bands, but also mambo bands, polka bands, tango bands, and many others. In some of these the piano has shared the stage with accordions, guitars, or other instruments capable of supplying some of the same melody, rhythm, and harmony as the piano. But the place of the piano does not seem to be endangered by these other instruments; each has its distinctive sound, and the music usually provides enough different musical tasks to keep several of these workhorse instruments busy. The piano has often been replaced, however, by an electronic keyboard. Why? In the first place, the piano was the one instrument that a band didn't bring with it, so that a keyboard player needed to have a portable keyboard for those venues where there was no piano, or no good one. Then, once keyboardists all started having their own keyboards, there was less pressure on the owners of the performance sites to have and maintain a piano. Finally, keyboards developed such a spectacular menu of sounds that keyboard players could put some of their fellow band members out of work at the same time that they put the instrument they themselves originally played—the piano—out of business.

The Piano in the Plugged-In World
Michael Chanan

"The history of the piano," Arthur Loesser observes, "does not coincide with the development of musical genius; it follows the development of industry and commerce."[11] The rise of the electronic keyboard provides only the latest instance in the twentieth century of new technological products of industry and commerce usurping traditional uses of the piano, making inroads into piano sales, and leading to predictions of the demise of the piano, only to produce a cultural situation in which the piano plays an altered, but not necessarily diminished, role. In the decades after World War I, the piano industry was crippled by competition from alternative and cheaper sources of domestic musical entertainment, the radio and the phonograph, and the coming of the talkies. In the United States, where motor cars were recognized by the piano trade as formidable competitors as symbols of consumer status, piano production reached 370,000 in 1910 and then began to fall—although player pianos increased their sales and in 1923 actually overtook those of conventional instruments. At the end of the 1920s, with the onset of the Great Depression, the collapse was immediate and dramatic: production fell to 120,000 in 1930, and five years later to little more than half of that. The same happened worldwide: almost 600,000 instruments in 1910, down to 212,000 in 1930, and less than 150,000 five years later. Despite attempts in the 1930s to rebuild the market with smaller and therefore cheaper instruments (many of which were also substandard), recovery, delayed by the war, was to take decades.[12]

The contraction of production of new instruments did not in itself signify a loss of pianism in the populace. Pianos were highly durable; they did not disappear from their locations quickly; and plenty of people played them. Nevertheless, as early as 1925 a London music critic prophesied "The Passing of the

Pianoforte," quoting "a well known English musician" who opined that "wireless and gramophone have broken the head of the amateur" and predicting that in another fifty years the piano would be as extinct as the viol and the harpsichord. Six years later, a writer in an Austrian musical journal asked, "Is the piano still a domestic instrument?"[13] And well after World War II, Roland Barthes took a negative answer to that question for granted when he described the decline of the amateur musical practice of the nineteenth century: "initially the province of the idle (aristocratic) class, it lapsed into an insipid social rite with the coming of the democracy of the bourgeoisie (the piano, the young lady, the drawing room, the nocturne), and then faded out altogether (who plays the piano today?)."[14]

Yet the truth is that today more people play keyboards, after a fashion, than at any previous time, and the piano remains at the apex of keyboard artistry. To be sure, there are many bands where the piano seems to be fighting a losing battle with the electronic versions of itself, almost as the 78 did with the LP and the LP did in turn with the CD. But there is a difference between mechanical reproduction and practical music making that makes this analogy deceptive: in the field of the former, new technologies have a tendency to supersede old ones, whereas in the latter, the new is added to the old, and both of them thrive. The story of the development of the synthesizer can therefore be told here not as the end of the piano's history, but as a transformation of the piano into something with new capacities and limitations, an instrument that gives broader meaning to the concept of the keyboard, leaving the place of the piano itself altered but not diminished. And if the synthesizer is the technological development that offers most direct competition to the piano as an instrument, twentieth-century developments in sound reproduction, worldwide communications, and instrument manufacture—some of the very technologies that have been supposed to be killing the piano off—will be shown to have contributed instead to its adaptation and survival.

Behind the transformation of the piano into the synthesizer lies a prehistory in-

Soprano Luella Melins in an early radio broadcast session at the WJZ studio, New York, 1922. Radio, like recording, separated performers from audiences, at the same time that it brought concertlike performances by professional musicians into people's homes. In this photograph, it is striking how much the broadcast studio is set up to look like the music room of a home.

A music classroom with both piano and audio equipment, Bates College, Maine, 1998. The two sound sources have complementary rather than competing functions in music instruction.

cluding the search for new musical sonorities that has inspired instrument makers in every age, accentuated by the modernist search for novelty, and crossed with radio and recording. Nothing now survives of Thaddeus Cahill's Telharmonium of 1906 except a few photographs, but within a generation, and following the technological development of oscillators, amplifiers, and loudspeakers, new electronic pitched instruments became legion, bearing fanciful names like Aetherophon, Electrochord, Electronde, Electrone, Klaviatur, Magnetton, Ondes Martenot, Ondes Musicales, Orgatron, Pianotron, Rangertone, Superpiano, Theremin, and Wave Organ. Some of these instruments use keyboards and virtually all have become museum pieces; two of them, both named after their inventors, continue to make occasional appearances: the ondes martenot on the concert platform, the theremin in the film music recording studio. But their successor, the keyboard synthesizer, is now ubiquitous.

The central issue in the design of electrophonic instruments can be stated baldly enough: without a rich envelope of partials—the overtones that normally accompany the sounding of a note—the tone is thin and patently synthetic. Most researchers pursued the model of the harmonium or organ and tried to produce a band of tones controlled by a conventional-looking keyboard with knobs on it. To produce such a complex timbre, the instrument must produce multiple tones that are overlaid, modulated, filtered, and amplified in various ways before reaching

393

the loudspeaker, a highly complicated business. Even so, the rate of experiment increased at the end of World War I with the rapid dissemination of knowledge of radio technology, and assorted researchers in university laboratories engaged in a host of undocumented and half-remembered attempts to build their own instruments. The main obstacle to progress—the lack of an effective mechanism for varying the timbre—began to find solutions around the end of the 1920s, and the prototype of the synthesizer is the electronic organ devised in 1934 by Laurens Hammond, an American inventor who already held patents for an electric clock and a small synchronous motor. Hammond employed the motor to drive a series of tone generators, using alternating current to produce the component tones, which are synthesized to create the instrument's timbre.

The problems of synthetic sound remained—indifference to the touch of the player, sluggish response, distortion, and a monotonous timbre—demonstrating that it is one thing to synthesize a complex tone, quite another to give it the mobile character of the sound of the traditional instrument. But the Hammond organ was practical to build, simple enough to play, and sufficiently cheap to find a market, especially when it was endorsed by famous purchasers like Henry Ford and George Gershwin. Surviving a legal challenge by the Federal Trade Commission over whether it was entitled to call itself an organ, it was taken up after World War II by a new generation of popular musicians, many of them untutored, who thus acquired enough keyboard technique to speed the adoption of the electronic synthesizer, which arrived in the late 1960s.

Popular music and the electronic keyboard both entered a new phase in the 1960s, when engineers began taking advantage of transistor technology to produce the first commercial synthesizers. The devices introduced in 1964 by Donald Buchla in California and Robert Moog in New York, building on technology first developed in the laboratory by RCA, had a modular construction and were oriented to the electronic music studio; Moog began to incorporate a keyboard, and by the end of the decade he produced smaller portable models that married the circuitry to the keyboard in a single case, effectively turning it into a performing instrument that anyone with knowledge of piano or organ could play. In the same way that the Hammond organ had been used as a novelty in the 1950s by jazz musicians like Count Basie, the keyboard synthesizer was now taken up by pop musicians; in 1969 the Beatles, who had already employed tape effects on their albums, incorporated some discreet synthesizer sounds in *Abbey Road,* and, in the words of a progressive DJ on a New York radio station, "electronic rock was off and running."[15] The first instruments were monophonic, hardly more developed than the electronic instruments of the 1920s, although well suited to providing bass lines and solo breaks; the first models with "polyphonic" capabilities appeared around 1975.

The incorporation of electronics into rock and pop provided the market that stimulated the integration of the various electronic technologies of musical production and reproduction into a unified system, integrated by digitization, in which sounds are translated into the strings of zeros and ones of computerized information. The 1950s had seen small keyboard devices like the Mellotron, intended not for the studio but to provide backing in performance, in which the keys operated individual tape loops, designed to produce the sound of, say, a string orchestra. If the polyphonic digital keyboard synthesizer is as far from such devices as it is from, say, a mechanical fairground organ, it also supersedes the electronic organ (the Hammond company shut up shop in 1975) to become a full-fledged instrument in its own right, employing electronic circuitry to generate both the imitation of the sounds of other instruments (including, of course, the Hammond) and newly synthesized tones of its own making.

The digital keyboard synthesizer emerged when Yamaha, which now dominates the market, incorporated digital technology to replace the oscillators of the original design, adding new capabilities. The appearance of the Yamaha DX7 in 1983, says one writer, signaled the rise to dominance of Japanese computer-based technologies. The technique employed in this instrument came from an American academic and composer, John Chowning: Yamaha took it on when he found no American company prepared to put in the necessary investment to bring the idea to mass production. The success of the new instrument was extraordinary. In 1989, says Andrew Blake in his book *The Music Business*, a series of eight BBC television programs, *Under African Skies*, featured music from all over Africa. "Among the many different percussion instruments, brass, and guitars, the DX7 appeared on all the programs, as the only electronic performance keyboard in popular music groups from Ethiopia to South Africa."[16]

It is easy to see the advantages the synthesizer has over the piano for many uses. It is cheaper, and even if the keyboard is shorter, it is always exactly in tune, no attention needed at all. The lower-priced models are musically so much more limited than the cheapest piano as to represent no direct competition. The more sophisticated jobs, on the other hand, with proper touch-sensitive keys and multiple banks of programmable oscillators, or nowadays digital data banks, offer entirely new sonic worlds. They are not a replacement for the piano so much as an entirely different instrument, which has had a major effect not only within popular music but in many areas of musical production where music is made for dissemination through loudspeakers (and earphones). But demand for pianos is unquenched, and recent reports even speak of an upturn in sales for instruments both new and restored.[17]

One reason is that "wireless and gramophone" did not in fact "break the head of the amateur" but turned it in new directions. Popular pianism, succored by Tin Pan Alley, parted company with that of high art early in the century, and an entirely new form appeared that actually thrived on the phonograph. Jazz was not just a repertory that was given a wider dissemination by recordings; it was an idiom whose essence was improvisation, and recordings extended its space as a form of musical practice—or musica practica, to use the medieval term that Barthes revived. Recordings helped make jazz a field in which entirely new forms of pianistic art developed, and so gave people new reasons to keep learning to play the piano.

In the field of classical piano music, too, recordings—along with radio and eventually television—provided for wider dissemination than ever before, with serious effects on musical culture. National schools of performance and lineages from one teacher to another were dissipated by the internationalization of musical life, to which the spread of recordings contributed. At the same time, the nature of musical interpretation was altered by the experience of playing into the microphone. Busoni complained as early as 1919 about the strain and artificiality of recording, of the fear of inaccuracy and being conscious the whole time that every note was going to be there for eternity, which eliminated inspiration, freedom, swing, or poetry from the performance. Alejo Carpentier quotes the declaration of "a famous interpreter" in 1951 that "in the presence of an audience you play with heat, but the disc is recorded cold." What is missing is the human contact of the live performance, which produces "a type of collective emotion" that is lost to the recording. (He is quite philosophical about it, however. "The disc is to live performance what color reproduction is to an original painting . . . if we in [Latin] America want to have an idea of the work of Gauguin, Cézanne, Picasso, we have no other option.")[18]

According to the musicologist Richard Taruskin, the result is the demise, whatever the school, of a "vitalist" style of performance—romantic, emotionally intense, full of fluctuating dynamics and tempo, a tendency toward bombast and histrionics—in favor of a "geometrical" one, not only more angular and precise, but inelastic in dynamics and generally faster.[19] The whole approach is more cerebral and analytic, in which a flawless technique is combined with a cool self-

Sergei Rachmaninoff listening to a recording of himself playing, from *Ladies' Home Journal*, December 1920. A pianist who grew up unaffected by recordings hears himself in a new way, with what consequences for his playing?

effacing manner at the keyboard. Indeed the very persona of the performer, as Barthes pointed out, has changed. First, he wrote, "there was the performer, the actor of music, then the interpreter (the great romantic voice), finally the technician, who relieves the auditor of every activity, however vicarious." Because musical amateurs, he says, are now so much rarer, there are no longer musicians like the pianist Lipatti or the singer Panzéra, who appeared the perfect amateurs because they stirred in us "not satisfaction but desire—the desire to make such music."[20] Instead we have professionals with an esoteric training, and we are cast, as auditors, in the cold and objective role of judges. We listen differently in this condition. Symptomatic of the change is the rise of the international piano competition—like the Tchaikovsky in Moscow and the Leeds International, which date from 1958 and 1963, respectively—where command of physical technique is taken for granted, and despite the protestations of the judges that musicality is really unquantifiable, there is always a winner, who practically always goes on to a highly successful career; for these, after all, are the pianists who know how play upon the keys of our skeptical postmodern sensibilities.

These competitions are indicative of a new stage in the international organization of musical life in which, within the domain of classical music, there are no longer any composer-pianists, and professional concert pianists are in the hands of agents, managers, promoters, and committees of every sort, who are increasingly beholden to the interests of the transnational corporations who control the vast apparatus of commercialized culture. The bread-and-butter concert becomes parasitic upon fame and success cultivated in the music festival; the festival is the showcase that the agent needs to capture for the artist's promotion; the artist, to garner attention, must now win an international competition. All are parasitical upon the record industry, which in turn is a parasite on the print media, radio, and above all television. There are tie-ins between promoters, various types of music and record companies, television stations, and the video market. Yamaha, anxious to promote its pianos in North America, provides the instruments for a new competition in Toronto. In the 1990s, competitions like the Cliburn in America (Van Cliburn himself had won the Tchaikovsky) and the Leeds in Britain have become a kind of televised gladiatorial contest. Some even allow the viewers to participate in the judging by calling in their choices for the winner. Here, to assuage the elitist associations of the music, the anonymous member of the television audience is given the chance to assert a virtual democracy of taste.

In the piano industry itself, meanwhile, technological and other innovations have not been simply a threat but have provided means of rescue. Piano manufac-

Frederic Chiu at the Ninth Van Cliburn International Piano Competition, 1993. Television audiences for piano competitions see only pianists and pianos onstage; the pianists themselves—sharing the stage with and even hemmed in by photographers and their equipment, facing the constant glare of television lights—may be more aware of the media through which they reach their worldwide audience than of the audience actually present with them in the hall.

ture everywhere at the end of World War II was in a sad and depleted state, but it was slowly renovated with the benefit of new technical advances—new types of glue developed by aircraft manufacturers during the war, new types of kiln, the introduction of plastics for parts of the action, and new alloys for the frames, making them lighter. These improvements were all in place by 1960. Modernization in the piano industry was typically introduced by the large-scale manufacturers of the cheapest uprights and resisted most strenuously by the most prestigious makers of concert grands. But even that pattern yielded in the late twentieth century as multinational corporations and conglomerates extended their ownership across one branch after another of the media and cultural industries, and even world-famous independent piano companies became specialized units within an international corporate system. The Steinway company, for instance, was sold to CBS in the early 1970s and then to two private investors in 1985; these two new owners, the Birmingham brothers, brought high technology to the tradition of hand craftsmanship, with the introduction of computer-aided design techniques already employed by competitors like Baldwin. Computers, for example, took over the job of fitting the soundboard to the rim, previously done by hand and eye, with the fitter shaving the board with a blade to achieve a tight fit—a highly skilled job. The press subsequently reported teething troubles.

High-tech industries have also provided models for new marketing schemes in the piano industry. The Kawai company, finding that universities can't afford to buy pianos, loans them and gets exclusive rights to sell new and used pianos once a year on campus. The inspiration for this scheme is explained by a Kawai sales manager: "Apple Computers pioneered this type of program. We followed Apple's strategy."[21] And while the electronic keyboard has been brought to success by Yamaha, a prime producer of conventional pianos, the bankrupt piano maker Mason and Hamlin was rescued in 1996 by the California-based music-technology company Music Systems Research, maker of the electronic PianoDisc automatic piano. In the manufacture of musical instruments, as in the practice of music making, it seems, the new does not necessarily displace the old, but the two may actually nourish each other.

Moreover, the latest communications medium that might be thought to represent a serious threat to traditional cultural pursuits actually reveals strong indications of a lively pianistic culture concerned with the instrument's support, promotion, and defense. A simple Internet search on the word *piano* brings up more than 642,000 items, starting with "The Piano Education Page," offering tips for piano lessons, activities, music, reviews, and interviews for "parents, students, teachers and fans of the piano." There are pages for piano sellers, restorers, and resellers; for piano tuners and piano movers; for sheet music, recordings, videos, player pianos, and piano rolls; for college courses; and even sites that promise to teach you to play the piano over the net. The active form of this virtual community, which is spread through the advanced economies of the English-speaking world, is found in e-mail discussion groups. One such, intended for pianists and piano teachers, with members in North America, Europe, Australia, and Japan, has a score or more of daily postings on topics such as how to finger certain passages, where to find this or that edition of a certain piece or composer, how to treat or avoid typical pianists' injuries, memory and practice techniques, pedagogical advice about sight-reading and memory, and how to deal with performance anxiety.

The truth is that the piano is no ordinary commodity. It inspires an affection and acquires an identity that may sometimes stand up to the logic of economics. When the Bechstein company, whose pianos were admired by Liszt and Wagner, collapsed in 1993, public upset at the loss of the celebrated name resulted in a rescue plan by Berlin's ruling senate, which exercised an option to buy back the company's headquarters on a valuable site near the former Checkpoint Charlie. The piano even inspires people to defy governments. A television documentary tells the story of Ben Truehaft, a California piano tuner, who defies the U.S. embargo against Cuba in order to take donated pianos and a brigade of piano tuners to Havana.[22] Pianos in Cuba suffer from the humidity; they get eaten by termites, and the strings rust in the salt air. A Cuban conservationist tells us that old Steinways are more resistant, because of their better wood; the Soviet pianos that began to arrive after the revolution were never designed for such conditions, and the collapse of the Soviet bloc has left the island not only in desperate economic straits but also increasingly bereft of playable pianos. On pianos completely beyond repair, Cubans play everything from Bach, Chopin, and Debussy to their own classic composers of nineteenth-century danzón, Lecuona and Cervantes, and contemporary Latin jazz. On instruments painfully out of tune, with broken hammers, they display their impeccable sense of rhythm, and the film becomes an eloquent testimony to the piano's magic in circumstances in which you might have thought people had more important things to worry about. But not at all, for as a piano teacher in an urban neighborhood puts it, comparing playing piano to getting a buzz on rum, the piano "is our drug, and our drink, and our family."

*I*n the early nineteenth century, it was possible to dust a harpsichord off and play it, as an exercise in historical rediscovery, because the harpsichord was a dead instrument by then. It was much more complicated—and much less inviting—to dust off an eighteenth-century piano at that time and try to learn something about history from it. The piano was a living, developing creation, and it was impossible to take too great an interest in its past state without threatening its present. After all, the historical activity that most occupied nineteenth-century keyboard players was to perform the harpsichord music of Couperin or Bach on the piano, appropriating it—to repeat the language of Chapter 5—into the empire of the piano. To play the same music on the harpsichord, as a few hardy women and men did at various times in that century, was to resist that appropriation, to reclaim the music not only for its own instrument but also for its own age. It was to let everyone who heard them play on the harpsichord know that playing that music on the piano meant transcribing and therefore altering it. To play a Couperin or Bach harpsichord suite on the harpsichord was to ask that it be heard as an example of "the pastness of the past" (a phrase of T. S. Eliot's that Richard Taruskin has drawn into this question of musical performance) and to assert that pegging the music in the past could in fact be a path toward appreciating its universality.[1] These were formidable claims to sustain at the time; cultural thinking was then dominated by evolutionary ideologies that made it difficult for people to think of the harpsichord as anything but a piano manqué. As if proving the point, the surviving harpsichords were all in a state of greater or lesser disrepair.

The practical problem at least could be addressed: by the 1880s the two leading French piano manufacturers were building harpsichords, however ill conceived those were by today's standards. But almost a whole century passed—until the 1970s—before instrument makers made sustained efforts to reproduce early pianos. The early piano posed no greater challenge in construction than the harpsichord; it must have been the idea of the early piano that provoked so much more resistance than the idea of the harpsichord. To understand this resistance, it is worth considering the case of a nineteenth-century musician whose studies encompassed both instruments.

Alfred Hipkins was born in 1826, tuned pianos for Chopin's last tour of Britain in 1848, worked for the Broadwood company for more than half a century, and by the 1880s was publishing the results of his lifetime study of the history of the piano and of earlier keyboard instruments.[2] In his lectures on the subject, he performed keyboard music of the seventeenth and early eighteenth centuries on clavichords and harpsichords—museum pieces that had presumably been restored to working order. With the history of the piano, however, he was in a dilemma. As a historian he belonged to his age; he thought of the piano as a single instrument being improved steadily as generation after generation of builders solved its design problems. But as a musician he seems to have rejected some important new developments in the instrument he loved, and as a living institution within the Broadwood company late in the nineteenth century, he used his considerable influence to prevent the adoption of important new design features—like cross-stringing—that might have kept Broadwood pianos competitive with Steinways, Bechsteins, and the other leading concert grands of the day. For this he is blamed today, however much he is honored for his pioneering historical work.[3]

The trouble, perhaps, lay in Hipkins's concept of the piano as a single instrument. Having heard Chopin play his music on Broadwoods that were among the best, most advanced pianos of their day, Hipkins evidently felt inclined to keep Broadwoods the way they had been, so that they could continue to provide the sound he remembered in Chopin's playing. But the world of piano design had marched on, producing instruments of louder, richer, more blended sound—all the better, presumably, for using to play the concert repertory. Ironically, the concert repertory was increasingly a repertory of classics; the new, improved pianos were therefore being presumed to be better than the pianos of Beethoven's day for playing Beethoven, better than the pianos of Chopin's day for playing Chopin.

Other developments in the musical world were strengthening this presumption: concert halls were being built larger, piano concerto performances were posing pianos against ever larger and louder orchestras, and newer works written for newer pianos were coloring the expectations that performers and listeners brought to the older works of the repertory. But Hipkins, with his long musical memory, may have felt that if an instrument of the present were going to be used to play the music of the past, it would be best if the piano of the present retained a recognizable relationship to the pianos of the past. Historical pianos may have been the stepping-stones of progress, but they also constituted a tradition that asserted itself against the pull of progress.

About the time of Hipkins's death in 1903, it became apparent that tradition and progress could go their separate ways. As even the most conservative of piano makers, like Broadwood and Erard, came to accept changes that had been introduced to the design of grand pianos half a century earlier, performers like Arnold Dolmetsch and Wanda Landowska, who had already created a stir playing harpsichords, began giving performances on early pianos. A society was founded in Munich to sponsor performances of eighteenth-century piano music on historic pianos.[4] The music of Mozart or Beethoven or Chopin was performed—and later recorded—on pianos that had once belonged to or been played by those masters. This use of composers' pianos was musically problematic, because playing those instruments without restoring and repairing them gave no good idea of anything, whereas any alteration to them destroyed evidence of what they had been.

Conceptually, however, this was a most important move. The idea of Mozart's own piano had an aura about it, and that aura was useful to pose against the aura of the modern concert grand—the "Instrument of the Immortals" (see Chapter 2). By playing on Mozart's piano, a performer could assert that Mozart conceived his music for a particular kind of piano, not an ideal piano, and that there is much about his music that could be learned only by playing it on that kind of piano. The idea that the piano is one instrument, and that therefore the most "advanced" model was the best instrument for all music and all situations, was no longer unchallenged.

There were still problems to solve. Replicas of old instruments turned out to be more satisfactory for demonstrating what old instruments could do than were restorations of the instruments themselves. Before the end of the twentieth century, there were instrument builders on several continents replicating early models of pianos, from Cristofori's to those of the mid–nineteenth century. These were specialty builders, unconnected to the companies building modern pianos, and their operations themselves replicated the workshops of eighteenth- and early-nineteenth-century piano builders in scale and method of production. Once these builders gave players workable models of early pianos, the players still had to learn how to play them, and scholars have collaborated with them in finding out about the differences in musical performance practice between one or another time, place, or musician and in making musical sense of those discoveries. The results have been more than a novelty, more than a jolt at how different an eighteenth- or even nineteenth-century piano sounded from a twentieth-century one: treasured repertories have been made new for countless listeners.

In one sense this process can be seen as just like the earlier process of re-claiming Couperin and Bach for the harpsichord. Another slice of keyboard repertory is reclaimed for its own instrument; another period of music history, liberated from the homogenizing rule of the modern piano, regains its own identity. The difference is that a piano by Cristofori, Stein, or Pleyel—or a replica of one of those pianos—is a piano, just as much as a Steinway or a Yamaha is, and that was

In the replication of early pianos, as in the original production of those instruments, the clientele is wealthy and select (if no longer noble), the workshops small; the materials, tools, and methods are a blend of old and new. Seen here is Rodney Regier in his workshop in Freeport, Maine, adjusting dampers on a five-octave fortepiano he and his assistant have built, modeled on instruments made by the Viennese builder Anton Walter around 1785–90 and played by Mozart and his contemporaries.

the cause of the delay in bringing the early-music process to the piano in the first place. Once the process had moved from the harpsichord to the early piano, there was no longer any natural boundary between the historical and the classic; the whole classical repertory, in fact all the music in the world that uses the piano, became—at least theoretically—historical. "The very phrase 'early music revival' has become something of an anachronism," Harry Haskell writes, because that revival caught up to the era of piano music.[5] When Malcolm Bilson plays Schubert on a replica of an 1820s Conrad Graf piano made in the 1990s by Rodney Regier, he reveals beauties in Schubert's music that can be heard in no other way; but that is what modern harpsichordists and harpsichord makers have done for Bach. Bilson does something else. He puts his listeners in a remarkable position to consider what a piano is. The experience he gives them makes clear that no piano is the piano; that every piano is historical, but no piano—"modern" or "early"—embodies the history of the instrument; that there is no such thing as the modern piano any more than there is such a thing as the early piano.

The cultural history of the piano is like the early-piano revival: it is a network of differences, not the history of the single-minded pursuit of an ideal form. Just as there has never been an ideal piano, there has also never been an ideal use of the piano, an ideal site for the piano, an ideal role for the piano to play in people's lives. D. H. Lawrence's mother, playing hymns for her family on a Sunday night, was not failing to be Paderewski on the stage of the Crystal Palace. But because she knew about a cultural world defined by his playing—and in particular because she felt excluded from that world—she spent what to her was a fortune to buy a piano for herself and her children. The cultural history of the piano is the story of how people like Lawrence's mother have turned such differences—even such exclusions—into connections, just as the early-piano revival is the story of how musicians like Malcolm Bilson have turned the difference between Schubert's piano and George Crumb's—between Schubert's way of playing and Rudolf Serkin's—into music.

Notes

Introduction

1. On Lydia Beardsall Lawrence, D. H. Lawrence's childhood, and their family piano, see John Worthen, *D. H. Lawrence: The Early Years, 1885–1912* (Cambridge, 1991), chaps. 1 and 2, esp. p. 39.

Chapter 1. 1700 to 1770s: The Need for the Piano

1. For a succinct survey of eighteenth-century stringed keyboard instruments, explaining their mechanisms, capabilities, and uses, see Laurence Libin, "The Instruments," chap. 1 of *Eighteenth-Century Keyboard Music*, ed. Robert L. Marshall (New York, 1994).

2. Melvin Kranzberg and Carroll W. Pursell, Jr., eds., *Technology in Western Civilization*, vol. 1: *The Emergence of Modern Industrial Society, Earliest Times to 1900* (New York, 1967), chap. 19: John B. Rae, "The Invention of Invention."

3. Stewart Pollens, in the authoritative work on the earliest stages in the development of the piano, denies Cristofori the title of "inventor," preferring to see his work as the "rediscovery of the principle of striking the string," which in turn "marked the beginning of a continuum of developments that led to the modern piano." Stewart Pollens, *The Early Pianoforte* (Cambridge, 1995), p. 5.

4. Arthur Loesser, *Men, Women, and Pianos: A Social History* (1954; repr. New York, 1990), p. 16.

5. Pollens, *The Early Pianoforte*, p. 56.

6. Eric Cochrane, *Florence in the Forgotten Centuries, 1527–1800* (Chicago, 1973), p. 318.

7. The full text of Maffei's article, "Nuova invenzione d'un gravecembalo col piano e forte," orig. published in *Giornale de' letterati d'Italia* 5 (Venice, 1711): 144–59, is translated into English in Pollens, *The Early Pianoforte*, pp. 57–62, with the orig. Italian reproduced in app. 3, pp. 238–43.

8. In 1753, Carl Philipp Emanuel Bach could still write that the piano "sounds well by itself and in small ensembles." See the introduction to part 1 of his *Versuch über die wahre Art das Clavier zu spielen*, trans. by William J. Mitchell as *Essay on the True Art of Playing Keyboard Instruments* (New York, 1949), p. 39.

9. See Simon McVeigh, *Concert Life in London from Mozart to Haydn* (Cambridge, 1993), pp. 211–19. The piano kept its place in London orchestras for many years to come, though elsewhere the days of keyboard continuo in orchestras were numbered.

10. Lodovico Giustini, *Sonate da cimbalo di piano, e forte, detto volgarmente di martelletti* (1732; repr. Geneva, 1986).

11. According to Daniel Freeman, these violinistic passages may represent Giustini's keyboard imitation of the style of the violin sonatas of his fellow Tuscan, Francesco Maria Veracini. Daniel Freeman, "Johann Christian Bach and the Early Classical Italian Masters," in *Eighteenth-Century Keyboard Music*, ed. Marshall, p. 242.

12. See Pollens, *The Early Pianoforte*, pp. 53, 122–23.

13. A list of these performances is given in Libin, "The Instruments," p. 21. There may of course have been earlier public performances to which no reference has yet been found.

14. A list of these publications is given by Katalin Komlós in *Fortepianos and Their Music: Germany, Austria, and England, 1760–1800* (Oxford, 1995), p. 37.

15. Ibid., pp. 38, 49.

16. See McVeigh, *Concert Life in London*, p. 90.

17. Ibid., p. 104.

18. See Komlós, *Fortepianos and Their Music*, pp. 45–47.

Chapter 2. Designing, Making, and Selling Pianos

1. Maffei's notes are reproduced, in the original Italian as well as an English translation, in Stewart Pollens, *The Early Pianoforte* (Cambridge, 1995), pp. 232–37.

2. "Bartolomeo Cristofori, Paduan, inventor, made [it,] Florence."

3. Pollens, *The Early Pianoforte*, p. 48. For some of the bills submitted by Cristofori to reimburse the artisans, see app. 1 in Raymond Russell, *The Harpsichord and Clavichord* (London, 1959), pp. 125–30.

4. The pitch of a string (the note it sounds) matches the rapidity of its vibration, which is determined by the combination of the string's length, the tension with which it is stretched, and its mass (or, somewhat inaccurately, thickness). Change one of these, and at least one other must change. Using strings of the same lengths as in his harpsichords under higher tension, Cristofori had to have thicker strings.

5. The double case construction was discovered by Stewart Pollens when he used an X-ray device to examine the New York piano's inner construction. Figures on p. 78 of Pollens, *The Early Pianoforte*, reproduce the X-ray and show a diagram of the double case and soundboard.

6. The instrument is in the Conservatorio Luigi Cherubini in Florence. Its inscription is: "P. Domenicus del Mela de Gagliano inventr: fecit anno: MDCCXXXIX" (P[adre] Domenico del Mela of Gagliano, inventor, made [it in] the year 1739). A similar instrument, attributed to del Mela but not signed, is in the Museo degli Strumenti Musicali, Castello Sforzesco, in Milan. Both of Cristofori's wills mention a del Mela family as heirs. That suggests but does not prove Domenico del Mela's connection with him.

7. See Michael Cole, *The Pianoforte in the Classical Era* (Oxford, 1998), pp. 23–42.

8. Ibid., p. 47; see also pp. 61–62.

9. Ibid., pp. 60–62.

10. Quoted by Philip James in *Early Keyboard Instruments* (1930; repr. London, 1967), p. 80.

11. Cole, *Pianoforte in the Classical Era*, pp. 52–53, 62–63. Cyril Ehrlich writes in *The Piano: A History*, rev. ed. (Oxford, 1990), p. 39, that piano prices in England "were always quoted in the dignifying unit of guineas."

12. Cole, *Pianoforte in the Classical Era*, pp. 50–53. Burney is quoted from his article "Harpsichord" in Abraham Rees, *The Cyclopaedia, or Universal Directory of the Arts, Sciences, and Literature* (London, 1819).

13. Dunlap's *Pennsylvania Packet*, March 13, 1775. It is possible that John Sheybli made pianos earlier in America, but the claim in his advertisement of 1774 is less clear.

14. Letter of Oct. 17, 1777, Emily Anderson, ed. and trans., *The Letters of Mozart and his Family*, 3d ed. (London, 1985), pp. 327–30.

15. Cole, *Pianoforte in the Classical Era*, p. 133.

16. David Wainwright, *Broadwood by Appointment: A History* (London, 1982), p. 79.

17. Ibid., pp. 78, 103; Nancy Groce, "Musical Instrument Making in New York during the Eighteenth and Nineteenth Centuries," Ph.D. diss., University of Michigan, 1982, pp. 51, 136, 138.

18. Charles Taws in *Philadelphia Aurora*, March 15, 1799.

19. Wainwright, *Broadwood by Appointment*, p. 98.

20. *Musical Opinion*, Oct. 1921. Quoted by Ehrlich in *The Piano*, p. 40.

21. When Burkat Shudi retired in 1771 from his partnership with John Broadwood, he conveyed the entire building on Great Pulteney Street to Broadwood but reserved space, "particularly the use of the Dining Room," to show and sell the remaining new Shudi harpsichords (Russell, *Harpsichord and Clavichord*, p. 164). The 1778 inventory of Americus Backers lists a Piano Forte in the dining room along with the table, chairs, carpets, bureaus, and "Cast iron Bath Stove" (Cole, *Pianoforte in the Classical Era*, p. 372).

22. *New-York Gazette and Weekly Mercury*, Oct. 10, 1774.

23. For Broadwood, see Wainwright, *Broadwood by Appointment*, p. 76; for Steinway, see Cynthia Adams Hoover, "The Steinways and Their Pianos in the Nineteenth Century," *Journal of the American Musical Instrument Society* 7 (1982): 55.

24. The 1778 London inventory of Americus Backers lists six benches (Cole, *Pianoforte in the Classical Era*, pp. 282, 375); that of George Albright in Baltimore in 1802 lists two (*Baltimore County Inventory*, 22:269–70). Albright was brother and former partner of piano maker Charles Albrecht in Philadelphia.

25. The strict guild statutes in France allowed a master to train only one apprentice at a time; see Frank Hubbard, *Three Centuries of Harpsichord Making* (Cambridge, Mass., 1965), p. 195. In Vienna, Anton Walter was said to have had twenty apprentices, Conrad Graf about ten in the 1830s; see Deborah Wyethe, "Conrad Graf, 1782–1851: Imperial Royal Court Fortepiano Maker in Vienna," Ph.D diss., New York University, 1990, p. 45. W. J. Rorabaugh, in *The Craft Apprentice from Franklin to the Machine Age in America* (New York, 1986), provides an excellent account of the erosion of the master's authority and the rise of the cash wage in America. One instance of a legal apprenticeship in America is found in an 1805 indenture binding John Fielding (age thirteen) to piano maker John Sellers in Alexandria, Virginia, until Fielding became twenty-one (Alexandria County, Virginia, Orphans Court Records, 1801–1805, Feb. 20, 1805, p. 244). Sellers died four years later.

26. Ehrlich, *The Piano*, p. 18; Wainwright, *Broadwood by Appointment*, pp. 60, 81; Geib advertisement from New York's *Spectator*, March 19, 1800; Chickering numbers are from the factory books now at the Smithsonian's National Museum of American History Archives; Steinway numbers are from a speech by Charles Steinway at the opening of their factory in 1860 (Hoover, "The Steinways and Their Pianos," p. 54).

27. The gluing and installation of the soundboard by journeyman Broadwood and master Shudi are the only specific tasks mentioned in the 1767 affidavit filed to dispute nephew Joshua Shudi's claims of having himself made all the Shudi harpsichords for Frederick the Great (Russell, *Harpsichord and Clavichord*, p. 169). Since the soundboard is often regarded as the "soul" of the instrument, this may have been an early attempt to create the mystique of the personal supervision that still is present in twentieth-century piano advertising.

28. The Chickering information is from *New York Musical World & Times*, Dec. 18, 1852. He purchased his keyboards from Pratt, Brother & Co. of Deep River, Connecticut; his wire from Washburn in Worcester, Massachusetts; and his iron frames from Alger's foundry in South Boston.

29. On the Broadwood factory fire of 1856, see Wainwright, *Broadwood by Appointment*, pp. 172–73. In New York, after the fire of the Lighte & Bradbury factory in 1860, the organization of journeymen piano makers collected funds. Even in the 1930s employees of the Sohmer piano factory on Long Island had to furnish their own tools—and benches. See Groce, "Musical Instrument Making," p. 133.

30. Ehrlich, *The Piano*, p. 42.

31. The only known copy of the *Book of Prices* is in the Print Department of the Metropolitan Museum of Art. The Steinway data is from Joseph D. Weeks, *Report on the Statistics of Wages in Manufacturing Industries*, vol. 20 (Washington, D. C., 1886), p. 292.

32. For Graf, see Wyethe, "Conrad Graf," p. 48. Broadwood production statistics and the 1867 number of divisions are from Wainwright, *Broadwood by Appointment*, pp. 109, 150, 194. The forty-two steps at Broadwood are cited in William Pole, *Musical Instruments in the Great Industrial Exhibition of 1851* (London, 1851), pp. 18–20. The Chickering material is from the *New York Musical World & Times*, Dec. 18, 1852.

33. The term was applied principally to the harpsichord-shaped instruments, though William Stodart's "upright grand piano in the form of a bookcase" meant a vertical harpsichord-shaped piano in a rectangular case. John Isaac Hawkins's "Portable Grand Piano" was a piece of advertising puffery and in some ways a contradiction in terms. In German-speaking Europe, the harpsichord shape was called a *Flügel* (wing-shaped), and in France it came to be known as a *piano à queue* (piano with a tail).

34. See Christoph Wolff, "New Research on Bach's Musical Offering," *Musical Quarterly* 57 (July 1971): 403.

35. "Janissary" or "Janizary" was a term for crack regiments in the Turkish army. The Turkish monarch gave a military band to King Augustus the Strong of Poland at some time after 1710, and the new sounds of drums, cymbals, bells, and various ringing and jingling objects became extremely popular, as evidenced in

works like Haydn's "Military" Symphony and Mozart's opera *The Abduction from the Seraglio,* both of which featured Janissary effects in the orchestra. Mozart's "Rondo alla turca," the famous last movement of his Sonata in A Major, K. 331, imitates bells and drums in the piano, and many were the pianists in the early nineteenth century who gleefully used the Janissary stop to embellish it.

36. Melvin Kranzberg, "Prerequisites for Industrialization," in *Technology in Western Civilization,* vol. 1 (New York, 1967), pp. 218–19.

37. Ehrlich, *The Piano,* p. 504; Wainwright, *Broadwood by Appointment,* pp. 149–50, 126; George Dodd, "A Day at a Pianoforte Factory," in *Days at the Factories* (London, 1843), from *Reprints of Economic Classics* (London, 1968), pp. 387–408.

38. Dodd, *Days at the Factories,* pp. 407; Wainwright, *Broadwood by Appointment,* pp. 172, 180; Ehrlich, *The Piano,* pp. 37–38.

39. Descriptions of the factories prior to the fire are from *New York Musical World & Times,* Dec. 18, 1852.

40. Accounts of the new Chickering factory appeared in *Frank Leslie's Illustrated Newspaper* (April 16, 1859), Ballou's *Pictorial Drawing-Room Companion* (July 23, 1859), and *New York Musical Review & Choral Advocate.*

41. The Boardman & Gray factory is well described and illustrated in "Boardman & Gray's Dolce Campana Attachment Piano-fortes," *Godey's Lady's Book* (Philadelphia, Jan. 1854), pp. 5–13; (Feb. 1854), pp. 101–7.

42. Edward Rothstein, "At Steinway, It's All Craft," and Henry Scott Stokes, "On Yamaha's Assembly Line," both in *New York Times,* Feb. 22, 1981.

43. Squares warped "like a banana," writes Cole in *Pianoforte in the Classical Era,* p. 109.

44. The term *tension bars* is misleading. Tension is the force applied by stretching: strings are under tension. The bars do not apply tension but resist it. They should probably be called compression bars.

45. Patent document. The U.S. Patent Office burned in 1837, and patents prior to that date had to be reconstructed. No new number was given to Babcock's patent, and the original number has been lost.

46. Chickering patents no. 1802 for cast iron frame for squares (Nov. 8, 1840) and no. 3238 for grands (Sept. 1, 1843).

47. Albert-Louis Blondel, "Le Piano et sa facture," in *Encyclopédie de la musique et dictionnaire du Conservatoire,* ed. Albert Lavignac and Lionel de la Laurencie (Paris, 1927), p. 2069. Blondel included cross-stringing in his indictment, though Erard had made instruments with cross-stringing since 1901. I have not found any evidence on when Erard actually introduced a one-piece frame.

48. *Music Trade Review,* July 19, 1879, p. 19.

49. *Music & Dramatic Times,* June 3, 1876; *Music Trade Review,* July 19, 1879.

50. D. W. Fostle, *The Steinway Saga: An American Dynasty* (New York, 1995), pp. 215–17.

51. Dun reports are available for reference at the Baker Library, Harvard Business School; Fostle, *Steinway Saga,* p. 248; Alfred Dolge, *Pianos and Their Makers* (1911; repr. New York, 1972), p. 181.

52. The sales promotion, written by Hale's brother-in-law Albert G. Cone (who was also Kimball treasurer and head of advertising), is quoted by Van Allen Bradley in *Music for the Millions: The Kimball Piano and Organ Story, 1857–1957* (Chicago, 1957), pp. 3–18, 35.

53. Baldwin material from Craig H. Roell, *The Piano in America, 1890–1940* (Chapel Hill, N.C., 1989), pp. 100–105, 170, 250. The 1882 quotation of H. C. Hazen, Billings & Co., is from the *Musical Courier* 4 (March 16, 1882): 11, 123.

54. Bradley, *Music for the Millions,* pp. 47, 102–4, 76, 49, 209. Bradley cites the source of the 1886 quotation as the *Music Trades Free Press,* Feb. 27, 1886.

55. Sears, Roebuck catalog (Chicago, spring 1896), pp. 511–14; Sears, Roebuck catalog (1902; repr. New York, 1969), pp. 1, 175. The 1926 Montgomery Ward information is from Harvey N. Roehl, *Player Piano Treasury* (Vestal, N.Y., 1961), p. 37.

56. Epworth Pianos, *A Satisfactory Piano at a Satisfactory Price,* catalogue 18-B (Chicago, [1902]).

57. Comment about men and player pianos is from Ehrlich, *The Piano,* p. 134. Statistics (which did not al-

ways agree) are from ibid., 134; Roell, *Piano in America*, pp. 216–17; and Roehl, *Player Piano Treasury*, p. 51.

58. Dolge, *Pianos and Their Makers*, p. 181.

59. Fostle, *Steinway Saga*, p. 450; Roell, *Piano in America*, pp. 180–81.

60. Fostle, *Steinway Saga*, pp. 451, 537; Loesser, *Men, Women, and Pianos*, p. 554; Richard K. Lieberman, *Steinway & Sons* (New Haven, 1995), pp. 143–44.

61. It is interesting that what used to be called "electronic pianos" are now simply called "keyboards"—not even "electronic keyboards." One of the reasons, of course, is that they incorporate many hundreds of sounds besides piano. But it is oddly reminiscent of the eighteenth century's *cembalo*, properly harpsichord but also used almost as "keyboard," or the more general German *Klavier*, which is quite literally "keyboard" and could be used to mean that—as in J. S. Bach's *Well-Tempered Clavier*, which could be and was played on organ, harpsichord, clavichord, or piano. And when you look at the typical contemporary keyboard on its stand, you see something strangely reminiscent of Johannes Zumpe's little squares.

62. More detailed information on all these systems is to be found in Larry Fine, *The Piano Book*, 3d ed. (Boston, 1994), pp. 95–96, 107–9, 126–27.

63. On sampling, see John R. Pierce, *The Science of Musical Sound* (New York, 1983), pp. 211–16. Pierce discusses the subject in terms of the computer generation of sound, but it is also applicable to the computerized processing of recorded sound.

Inset: The Player Piano

1. Arthur Loesser, *Men, Women, and Pianos* (1954; repr. New York, 1990), p. 580.

2. Ibid., p. 581.

3. Quoted in Arthur Ord-Hume, *Player Piano: The History of the Mechanical Piano and How to Repair It* (London, 1970), p. 35.

4. Ernest Newman, *The Piano-Player and Its Music* (London, 1920).

5. Quoted by Edward Jablonski and Lawrence D. Stewart, *The Gershwin Years* (New York, 1996), p. 33.

6. Quoted in Edward Jablonski, *Gershwin Remembered* (London, 1992), pp. 7–8.

Chapter 3. 1770s to 1820s: The Piano Revolution in the Age of Revolutions

1. Wolfgang Mozart to Leopold Mozart, Jan. 12, 1782, in Wolfgang Amadeus Mozart, *Briefe und Aufzeichnungen: Gesamtausgabe*, vol. 3 (Kassel, 1962–75). My translation.

2. "Memoir of Muzio Clementi," unsigned article in *The Harmonicon*, Aug. 1831, p. 183.

3. Leon Plantinga, *Clementi: His Life and Music* (London, 1977), p. 290.

4. Quoted in Katalin Komlós, *Fortepianos and Their Music: Germany, Austria, and England, 1760–1800* (Oxford, 1995), p. 15.

5. Preface to *Music Made Easy, or a New Musical Vade-Mecum: Being a Complete Book of Instructions for Beginners on the Piano-forte or Harpsichord* (London, 1798).

6. For an impressive list of these English and foreign editions compiled by Sandra Rosenblum, see the Da Capo reprint of Clementi, *Introduction to the Art of Playing on the Piano Forte* (New York, 1974), pp. xxi–xxxix.

7. See Plantinga, *Clementi*, p. 238.

8. Plantinga, in *Clementi*, p. 238, passes on this citation from Max Unger, *Muzio Clementis Leben* (Langensalza, 1914), p. 217.

9. A tremendous resource for studying the periodicals of this period and their contents is Imogen Fellinger, *Periodica Musicalia (1789–1830)* (Regensburg, 1986).

10. D. W. Krummel, "Music Publishing," in *The Romantic Age, 1800–1914*, ed. Nicholas Temperley, vol. 5 of *The Athlone History of Music in Britain* (London, 1981), p. 57.

11. Arthur Loesser, *Men, Women, and Pianos: A Social History* (1954; repr. New York, 1990), p. 267.

12. On the culture of reading in this period, see Roger Chartier, "The Practical Impact of Writing," in *Passions of the Renaissance*, ed. Roger Chartier, trans.

Arthur Goldhammer, vol. 3 of *A History of Private Life* (Cambridge, Mass., 1989).

13. On Austen's life with the piano, see "Jane Austen at the Keyboard," app. 1 in Robert K. Wallace, *Jane Austen and Mozart: Classical Equilibrium in Fiction and Music* (Athens, Ga., 1983).

14. Richard Leppert, *Music and Image: Domesticity, Ideology, and Socio-Cultural Formation in Eighteenth-Century England* (Cambridge, 1988), pp. 31, 28.

15. A fascinating account of the development of postal service in this period and its effects on daily life can be found in G. E. Mitton, *Jane Austen and Her Times*, 2d ed. (London, 1906), chap. 6: "Letters and Post."

16. Caroline Austen-Leigh, *My Aunt Jane Austen: A Memoir* (London, 1952), pp. 6–7; cited in Wallace, *Jane Austen and Mozart*, p. 251.

17. Mary Burgan, in "Heroines at the Piano: Women and Music in Nineteenth-Century Fiction," *Victorian Studies* 30 (1986): 51–76, begins her survey of the piano in English literature with Austen.

18. "Ionych," in Anton Chekhov, *"Lady with Lapdog" and Other Stories*, trans. David Magarshack (Harmondsworth, Eng., 1964), pp. 235–36.

19. James Weldon Johnson, *The Autobiography of an Ex-Colored Man* (1912), reprinted in *Three Negro Classics*, intro. by John Hope Franklin (New York, 1965), chap. 1 (pp. 395–96) and chap. 11 (p. 509).

20. Danièle Pistone, in "Le Piano dans la littérature française des origines jusqu'en 1900," Ph.D. diss., Université de Lille III, 1975, gives a survey of the piano as a theme in French literature that is unrivaled for any other national literature.

21. Leo Tolstoy, *The Kreutzer Sonata*, trans. Aylmer Maude (1924), in Tolstoy, *"The Kreutzer Sonata" and Other Stories*, ed. Richard Gustafson (Oxford, 1997), pp. 135, 145.

22. Tolstoy's novella is interpreted by Richard Leppert in "The Piano, Misogyny, and 'The Kreutzer Sonata,'" chap. 7 of *The Sight of Sound: Music, Representation, and the History of the Body* (Berkeley, 1993).

23. August Wilson, *The Piano Lesson* (New York, 1990), p. 45.

24. For a discussion of keyboard tutors and instructional treatises in this period, see Komlós, *Fortepianos and Their Music*, pp. 122–32.

25. Johann Ferdinand von Schönfeld, *Jahrbuch der Tonkunst von Wien und Prag* (Vienna, 1796; facs. repr., ed. Otto Biba, Munich and Salzburg, 1976), pp. 87–91. Extended passages, from which these extracts are drawn, are quoted in the original German and in translation in ibid., pp. 11–12.

26. László Somfai, *The Keyboard Sonatas of Joseph Haydn*, translated by the author in collaboration with Charlotte Greenspan (Chicago, 1995), pp. 154–55.

27. On the keyboard instruments of Haydn and others in this period, see ibid., pp. 3–29; and A. Peter Brown, *Joseph Haydn's Keyboard Music: Sources and Style* (Bloomington, Ind., 1986), pp. 134–44, citation from p. 161. Brown includes a useful chart of instrument choice in relation to specific works at pp. 166–70. Sandra P. Rosenblum's *Performance Practices in Classic Piano Music* (Bloomington, Ind., 1988) is another excellent text for discussions of instruments and notation in this period.

28. In the entire set of six "Esterházy" Sonatas (Hob. XVI:21–26) of 1774, for example, there is only one dynamic marking (a forte indication in the first movement of the E Major Sonata, Hob. 22, just before the recapitulation), and among the so-called 1776 Sonatas (Hob. XVI:27–32), only one—the F Major, Hob. 29—has dynamic indications in early sources, markings that are lacking in the autograph.

29. Elaine R. Sisman, "Haydn's Solo Keyboard Music," in *Eighteenth-Century Keyboard Music*, ed. Robert L. Marshall (New York, 1994), p. 288.

30. Johann Peter Milchmeyer, *Die wahre Art das Pianoforte zu spielen* (Dresden, 1797), p. 69; trans. in Komlós, *Fortepianos and Their Music*, p. 85.

31. Loesser, *Men, Women, and Pianos*, pp. 64–67, 267–83.

32. Haydn to the publisher Artaria, Feb. 25, 1780, in *The Collected Correspondence and London Notebooks of Joseph Haydn*, ed. H. C. Robbins Landon (London, 1959), p. 25.

33. Schönfeld, *Jahrbuch der Tonkunst von Wien und Prag*,

p. 68, trans. in Somfai, *Keyboard Sonatas of Joseph Haydn*, p. 177n.35.

34. Michael Kelly, *Reminiscences of Michael Kelly, of the King's Theatre . . .* (London, 1826), quoted in Brown, *Joseph Haydn's Keyboard Music*, p. 11.

35. Johann Reichardt, *Vertraute Briefe geschrieben auf einer Reise nach Wien . . .* (Amsterdam, 1810), p. 145, trans. in Brown, *Joseph Haydn's Keyboard Music*, p. 53.

36. Plantinga, *Clementi*, p. 152.

37. It has been suggested that the work played was the D Major Concerto, Hob. XVIII:11; see Brown, *Joseph Haydn's Keyboard Music*, pp. 33, 419n.79.

38. Ibid., p. 235. See Somfai's discussion of these sonata types, *Keyboard Sonatas of Joseph Haydn*, pp. 175–80, and his response to Brown's criticism, p. 175n.33. For a thoughtful discussion of the *Kenner-Liebhaber* and *Virtuosen-Dilettanten* distinction, see Komlós, *Fortepianos and Their Music*, pp. 109–21.

39. Landon, ed., *Collected Correspondence and London Notebooks of Joseph Haydn*, p. 79.

40. Haydn's letters to Frau von Genzinger, dated June 10 and 27 and July 4, 1790, are translated in H. C. Robbins Landon, *Joseph Haydn: Chronicle and Works*, vol. 2: *Haydn at Eszterháza, 1766–1790* (London and Bloomington, 1976), pp. 743–46.

41. Carl F. Cramer, *Magazin der Musik* (Hamburg, 1785), p. 535, trans. in Brown, *Joseph Haydn's Keyboard Music*, p. 27.

42. Ibid.

43. Two recent accounts of the concertos admirably address a surprising gap in historical scholarship on these works: Robert D. Levin, "Mozart's Keyboard Concertos," in *Eighteenth-Century Keyboard Music*, ed. Robert L. Marshall (New York, 1994), pp. 350–94; and Neal Zaslaw, ed., *Mozart's Piano Concertos: Text, Context, Interpretation* (Ann Arbor, 1996).

44. Levin, "Mozart's Keyboard Concertos," p. 357.

45. Mozart retrieved this concerto for a performance with his student Josepha Barbara Auernhammer in Vienna in 1782, an occasion that may account for new scoring to include clarinets, trumpets, and timpani; see pref-ace to Christoph Wolff, ed., *Neue Mozart Ausgabe (NMA)*, V/15/iii, p. ix.

46. Levin, "Mozart's Keyboard Concertos," p. 371.

47. See the preface to Wolff, ed., *NMA*, V/15/ii, p. viii.

48. Wolfgang Mozart to Leopold Mozart, Dec. 28, 1782, no. 476 in Emily Anderson, ed. and trans., *The Letters of Mozart and His Family*, 3d ed., (London, 1985), p. 833.

49. See the preface to Wolff, ed., *NMA*, V/15/iii, p. x; the occasions for the performances in question were Mozart's own "Academy" concert on March 23 and that of the singer Mlle Teyber on March 30.

50. Robert D. Levin summarizes the arguments of various scholars regarding continuo playing in the concertos in "Instrumental Ornamentation, Improvisation, and Cadenzas," in *Performance Practices: Music after 1660*, ed. Howard Mayer Brown and Stanley Sadie (New York, 1990), pp. 287–89; see also Faye Ferguson, "Mozart's Keyboard Concertos: Tutti Notations and Performance Models," in *Mozart-Jahrbuch, 1984–85*, pp. 32–39.

51. Wolfgang Mozart to Leopold Mozart, May 26, 1784, no. 514 in Anderson, ed., *Letters of Mozart*, p. 877.

52. Reproduced in the *Kritischer Bericht* that accompanies Wolff, ed., *NMA*, V/15/vii, and discussed by Frederick Neumann in *Ornamentation and Improvisation in Mozart* (Princeton, N.J., 1986), pp. 251–53.

53. On cadenzas and improvised embellishment, see esp. Levin, "Instrumental Ornamentation, Improvisation, and Cadenzas," pp. 267–91. Christoph Wolff argues that in copying out his cadenzas, Mozart provided himself with a template for performance; Christoph Wolff, "Cadenzas and Styles of Improvisation in Mozart's Piano Concertos," in *Perspectives on Mozart Performance*, ed. R. Larry Todd and Peter Williams (Cambridge, 1991), pp. 228–38. Levin is himself a notable exception to the rarity of improvisation in current performances of Mozart's concertos. In both live and recorded performances, he plays extended cadenzas ex tempore, demonstrating that this practice would not have to be rehearsed, much less written down by the composer.

54. As noted above, K. 537 was scored with ad libitum

winds, trumpets, and timpani; its standard orchestral version stems from André's first printed edition. See preface to Wolfgang Rehm, ed., *NMA,* V/15/viii.

55. The recent recording *Beethoven: The Complete Piano Sonatas on Period Instruments* (Claves Records, CD 50-9707/10), by Malcolm Bilson and his former students on nine different fortepianos, makes the best case for matching a given work with the kind of piano for which it was written.

56. William S. Newman, *Beethoven on Beethoven: Playing His Piano Music His Way* (New York, 1988), pp. 50–57, quotation from p. 51. On the particular qualities of Beethoven's instruments, see also Malcolm Bilson, "Beethoven and the Piano," *Clavier* 22 (Oct. 1983): 18–21; and, more generally, his chapter on "Keyboards" in *Performance Practice,* ed. Brown and Sadie, pp. 223–38.

57. Quoted by Eva Badura-Skoda, "Performance Conventions in Beethoven's Early Works," in *Beethoven, Performers, and Critics,* ed. Robert Winter and Bruce Carr (Detroit, 1980), p. 53. This essay is a valuable exploration of various notational and performance practices in relation to Beethoven's works and their subsequent printings. For more on concert life in Vienna during Beethoven's lifetime, see Otto Biba, "Concert Life in Beethoven's Vienna," in ibid., pp. 77–93; and Mary Sue Morrow, *Concert Life in Haydn's Vienna* (Stuyvesant, N.Y., 1989).

58. *Allgemeine musikalische Zeitung* 24 (1822): 310, cited in Newman, *Beethoven on Beethoven,* pp. 78–79.

59. Carl Czerny, *On the Proper Performance of All Beethoven's Works for the Piano,* trans. and ed. with commentary by Paul Badura-Skoda (Vienna, 1970), pp. 22, 16.

60. Beethoven to Streicher, May 6, 1810, in Emily Anderson, ed. and trans., *The Letters of Beethoven* (New York, 1961), 1:271.

61. For a thorough account of this movement in relation to the special qualities of Viennese pianos, as well as its programmatic content, see Owen Jander, "Beethoven's 'Orpheus in Hades': The *Andante con moto* of the Fourth Piano Concerto," in *Nineteenth Century Music* 8 (1985): 195–212.

62. Beethoven himself acceded to this fashion in a collaboration with Mälzel that produced the "Wellington's Victory" overture of 1813, which met with an enthusiastic reception in Vienna.

63. *Thayer's Life of Beethoven,* rev. and ed. Elliot Forbes (Princeton, N.J., 1970), pp. 360–61.

64. Franz Wegeler and Ferdinand Ries, "Biographical Notes," in *Beethoven Remembered,* trans. Frederick Noonan (Arlington, Va., 1957), p. 32; cited in Tia DeNora, *Beethoven and the Construction of Genius: Musical Politics in Vienna, 1792–1803* (Berkeley, 1995), p. 134. DeNora's is a fresh and provocative consideration of reception history relative to Beethoven. On the keyboard works, see esp. chap. 6, "Beethoven in the Salons."

65. On the female students of Beethoven's early years in Vienna, see *Thayer's Life of Beethoven,* pp. 233–34. Among students to whom Beethoven dedicated solo piano sonatas are several women, including Princess Barbara Keglevics, later Odescalchi (Op. 7); Princess Anna Margarete von Browne (Op. 10); Baroness Josepha von Braun (Op. 14); Princess Josephine Sophia von Liechtenstein (Op. 27, no. 1); Countess Giulietta Guicciardi (Op. 27, no. 2); Countess Thérèse von Brunswick (Op. 78); and Baroness Dorothea von Ertmann (Op. 101).

66. *Thayer's Life of Beethoven,* p. 412.

67. Ibid., p. 669.

Chapter 4. The Piano Lesson

1. Daniel Gottlob Türk, *School of Clavier Playing,* trans. Raymond H. Haggh (orig. German ed., 1789; Lincoln, Neb., 1982), p. 26. In a footnote to this sentence, Türk allows for the case of keyboard teachers who do not play another instrument.

2. Ibid., pp. 19–20.

3. Johann Peter Milchmeyer, *Die wahre Art das Pianoforte zu spielen* (Dresden, 1797), p. 2.

4. The art of basso continuo playing is taught in some piano methods published well into the nineteenth century, but there it is taught as a purely academic subject.

5. Friedrich Wilhelm Marpurg, *Die Kunst das Clavier zu spielen*, 4th ed. (Berlin, 1762), p. 6.

6. Türk, *School of Clavier Playing*, p. 19.

7. Grete Wehmeyer, *Carl Czerny und die Einzelhaft am Klavier, oder Die Kunst der Fingerfertigkeit und die industrielle Arbeitsideologie* (Kassel, 1983).

8. Jérôme-Joseph de Momigny, *La Première année de leçons de piano-forte* (1802–3; new ed. Winterthur, Switz., 1980).

9. Carl Czerny, *Letters to a Young Lady, on the Art of Playing the Pianoforte* (1837; reprint New York, 1982; trans. of *Briefe über den Unterricht auf dem Pianoforte* (Vienna, 1830), pp. 5, 11–12, 16, 23–24, 30.

10. As a former student of Beethoven, Czerny even claimed the authority to apply his ideas of regularity to the performance of Beethoven's sonatas. See George Barth, *The Pianist as Orator: Beethoven and the Transformation of Keyboard Style* (Ithaca, N.Y., 1992).

11. Czerny, *Letters*, p. 29.

12. Johann Nepomuk Hummel, *Ausführliche theoretisch-practische Anweisung zum Pianoforte-Spiel* (1828; reprint Geneva, 1981); Charles Louis Hanon, *Le Pianiste virtuose* (Boulogne-sur-Mer, 1874; many subsequent editions). The subtitle of the Hanon reveals its purpose: *Sixty exercises calculated for the acquisition of agility, independence, strength, and the most perfect equality of the fingers as well as suppleness of the wrists.*

13. Friedrich Wieck, "Secrets: A Paper on the Study of the Piano," in Friedrich Wieck, *Piano and Song (Didactic and Polemical)*, trans. and ed. Henry Pleasants (orig. German ed., 1853; Stuyvesant, N.Y., 1988), pp. 42–43. Logier patented the chiroplast, the most highly promoted and controversial of many mechanical devices for practicing, in 1814.

14. Schumann's "Rules" *(Musikalische Haus- und Lebensregeln)*, which he originally intended to intersperse throughout the *Album für die Jugend* (Album for the young), were in the end published separately in his music journal, the *Neue Zeitschrift für Musik*, in 1850.

15. The term *Repos de l'étude* is used in Franz Hünten, *Nouvelle méthode pour le piano-forte* (Paris, 1833); *Recreation* is used in *The New England Conservatory Method for the Piano-Forte* (Boston, 1870); *Amusements* is used in Nathan Richardson, *Richardson's New Method for the Piano-Forte* (Boston, 1859).

16. Czerny, *Letters*, pp. 1–2.

17. See Judith Tick, *American Women Composers before 1870* (Ann Arbor, Mich., 1983), chap. 4: "Music in Female Seminaries."

18. Czerny, *Letters*, p. 48.

19. See the report on the competition of 1835 in the journal *Le Pianiste* 2, no. 20 (Aug. 20, 1835; repr. Geneva, 1972): 160.

20. Arthur Loesser, *Men, Women, and Pianos: A Social History* (1954; repr. New York, 1990), p. 53.

21. Ramón Ruiz Amado, *La educación femenina* (Barcelona, 1912), p. 115; quoted in English in Michela De Giorgio, "The Catholic Model," trans. Joan Bond Sax, in *A History of Women in the West*, vol. 4: *Emerging Feminism from Revolution to World War*, ed. Geneviève Fraisse and Michelle Perrot (Cambridge, Mass., 1993), p. 183.

22. See Sheryl Maureen Peterson Mueller, "Concepts of Nineteenth-Century Piano Pedagogy in the United States," Ph.D. diss., University of Colorado, 1995; UMI 9613292, pp. 129–33.

23. [Thomas] Ridley Prentice, *Hand Gymnastics, for the Scientific Development of the Muscles Used in Playing the Pianoforte* (London, 1891), p. 8.

24. See *The Alexander Technique: The Essential Writings of F. Matthias Alexander*, intro. Edward Maisel (New York, 1990).

25. See Robert R. Alford and Andras Szanto, "Orpheus Wounded: The Experience of Pain in the Professional Worlds of the Piano," *Theory and Society* 25 (1966): 1–44.

26. On the early history of the Conservatoire, see Cynthia M. Gessele, "The Conservatoire de Musique and National Music Education in France, 1795–1801," in *Music and the French Revolution*, ed. Malcolm Boyd (Cambridge, 1992), pp. 191–210; and Jean Mongrédien, *French Music from the Enlightenment to Roman-*

ticism: 1789–1830, trans. Sylvain Frémaux (Portland, Oreg., 1996).

27. For a discussion of Luigi Cherubini's role in limiting the size of the piano classes and banning contemporary virtuoso repertoire during his tenure as director (1822–42), see Cécile Reynaud, "Une Vertu contestée: L'idéal de virtuosité dans la formation des élèves des classes de piano au Conservatoire de Musique (l'époque Cherubini)," in *Le Conservatoire de Musique de Paris: Regards sur une institution et son histoire*, ed. Emmanuel Hondré (Paris, 1995), 109–23.

28. The rationale for private lessons is defended in W. S. B. Mathews, "Private Teacher vs. Conservatory: A Pedagogical Polemic," *Music* 8, no. 5 (Sept. 1895): 487–97.

29. Hugo Riemann, "Unsere Konservatorien," in *Präludien und Studien* (Leipzig, [1895]), 1:22–23, trans., ed., and introduced by E. Douglas Bomberger as "Our Conservatories," *Bulletin of Historical Research in Music Education* 15, no. 3 (May 1994): 226.

30. Rudolf Lüdeke, "Zur Geschichte der Privatmusikerziehung im 19. und 20. Jahrhundert," 2 vols., Ph.D. diss., Humboldt University, Berlin, 1958, 2:216.

31. For further discussion, see Leonard M. Phillips, "The Influence of the Leipzig Conservatory on Music in Nineteenth-Century America," chap. 9 of "The Leipzig Conservatory: 1843–1881," Ph.D. diss., Indiana University, 1979 (UMI 79-16, 957), pp. 221–39.

32. For a discussion of the changes that took place after Mendelssohn's death and the evolution of the institution into a bastion of conservatism, see Johannes Forner, "Leipziger Konservatorium und 'Leipziger Schule': Ein Beitrag zur Klassizismus-Diskussion," *Die Musikforschung* 50, no. 1 (Jan.–March 1997): 31–36.

33. Riemann, "Our Conservatories," p. 235.

34. The eminent Berlin critic Heinrich Ehrlich, for instance, believed that the open admission policies of Germany's private conservatories would lead to a "wretched proletariat of musicians"; Heinrich Ehrlich, "Das Musikerproletariat und die Konservatorien," in *Modernes Musikleben* (Berlin, 1895), pp. 83–90.

35. Peter Cahn, *Das Hoch'sche Konservatorium in Frankfurt am Main, 1878–1978* (Frankfurt am Main, 1979), p. 104.

36. Amy Fay, *Music-Study in Germany* (1880; reprint New York, 1965), pp. 206–7.

37. A complete account of the trial may be found in "Ein Klavier-Prozess," *Der Klavier-Lehrer* 6, no. 1 (Jan. 1, 1883): 5–6.

38. *Catalogue of Dana's Musical Institute* (Philadelphia, 1875), pp. vii, 27.

39. The Schumann legacy is discussed at length in Peter Cahn, "Die Tradition Clara Schumanns," in *Das Hoch'sche Konservatorium*, pp. 125–29. Cahn notes that the school attempted to maintain her tradition by hiring former students as teachers in the years following her retirement. This policy backfired, as the resultant inbreeding led to an era of pedantry and conservatism.

40. For further discussion of the Lebert-Stark method, see Reginald R. Gerig, *Famous Pianists and Their Technique* (Washington, D.C., 1974), pp. 230–33; and E. Douglas Bomberger, "Kelley vs. Lebert: An American Confronts a German Piano Method," *American Music Teacher* 43, no. 4 (Feb.–March 1994): 14–17, 81.

41. Fay, *Music-Study in Germany*, 264–66.

42. These and numerous other anecdotes illustrating Liszt's attitude toward conservatories may be found in August Göllerich, *The Piano Master Classes of Franz Liszt, 1884–1886: Diary Notes of August Göllerich*, ed. Wilhelm Jerger, trans., ed., and enlarged by Richard Louis Zimdars (Bloomington, Ind., 1996); and Carl Lachmund, *Living with Liszt*, ed., annotated, and introduced by Alan Walker, Franz Liszt Studies Series 4 (Stuyvesant, N.Y., 1995).

43. Riemann, "Our Conservatories," p. 227.

44. This aspect of musical conservatories and university music departments is discussed at length in two ethnomusicological examinations of musical training in the United States: Bruno Nettl, *Heartland Excursions: Ethnomusicological Reflections on Schools of Music* (Urbana, Ill., 1995); and Henry Kingsbury, *Music, Tal-*

ent, and Performance: A Conservatory Cultural System (Philadelphia, 1988).

45. Eliza Leslie, *Amelia; or, A Young Lady's Vicissitudes. A Novel* (Philadelphia, 1848).

46. Philadelphia *Public Ledger*, Sept. 5, 1850.

47. Elizabeth Lindsay Lomax, *Leaves from an Old Washington Diary, 1854–1863*, ed. Lindsay Lomax Wood (New York, 1943), p. 27.

48. Mrs. A. W. Fairbanks, ed., *Emma Willard and Her Pupils; or, Fifty Years of Troy Female Seminary, 1822–1872* (New York, 1898), pp. 511–12; Tick, *American Women Composers before 1870*, pp. 162–88.

49. "Miscellaneous Music News," *New York Musical World and Times*, Sept. 17, 1853, p. 20.

50. Eliza R. to a friend, Dec. 27, 1825, Way-Champlain Correspondence, American Antiquarian Society, Worcester, Mass. (collection on loan, quoted with permission of donor).

51. Letitia M. Burwell, *A Girl's Life in Virginia before the War*, 2d ed. (New York, 1895), p. 192.

52. Millie Gray, *The Diary of Millie Gray, 1832–1840*, ed. William B. Graham (Houston, 1967), p. 26.

53. "Pittsfield Seminary for Young Ladies" (advertisement), *Boston Recorder and Telegraph*, Oct. 12, 1827.

54. Artur Schnabel, *My Life and Music* (New York, 1963), p. 125.

55. Malvine Brée, *Die Grundlage der Methode Leschetizky* (Mainz, 1902; English trans. as *The Groundwork of the Leschetizky Method*, 1902).

56. Ignace Jan Paderewski and Mary Lawton, *The Paderewski Memoirs* (1938; repr. New York, 1980), p. 96.

57. Ibid., p. 95.

58. Artur Schnabel, "Theodor Leschetizky zum achtzigsten Geburtstage," *Allgemeine Musik-Zeitung* 37, no. 25 (June 17, 1910): 600.

59. See Mercer Ellington with Stanley Dance, *Duke Ellington in Person: An Intimate Memoir* (1978; repr. New York, 1979), p. 10.

60. Barry Ulanov, *Duke Ellington* (1946; repr. New York, 1975), pp. 14, 10–11.

61. Mercer Cook to Mark Tucker, June 24, 1984.

62. Herbert Saal, "The Duke at 70," *Newsweek*, May 12, 1968, p. 117.

63. Duke Ellington, *Music Is My Mistress* (1973; repr. New York, 1976), p. 28.

64. Judith Tick, "Passed Away Is the Piano Girl: Changes in American Musical Life, 1870–1900," in *Women Making Music: The Western Art Tradition, 1150–1950*, ed. Jane Bowers and Judith Tick (Urbana, Ill., 1986), p. 327.

Inset: The Metronome

Tsvetaeva published the autobiographical essay "Mat' i Muzyka" (Mother and music) in Paris in the journal *Sovremennye Zapiski* (1934); it is reprinted in Marina Tsvetaeva, *Proza* (Moscow: Sovremennik, 1989), pp. 58–83. An English translation of the entire essay is found in Marina Tsvetaeva, *A Captive Spirit: Selected Prose*, trans. J. Marin King (Ann Arbor, Mich., 1980), pp. 271–94.

Chapter 5. 1820s to 1870s: The Piano Calls the Tune

1. Charles Dickens, *American Notes* (1842), repr. in *American Notes and Pictures from Italy* (Oxford, 1957, 1987), p. 68.

2. According to Thomas Dublin, in *Women at Work: The Transformation of Work and Community in Lowell, Massachusetts, 1826–1860* (New York, 1979), p. 150, "there is no doubt that mill managers considered literate, educated workers more productive," even though Dublin's own research suggests to him that they were not. He also provides an account of a mill worker in Clinton, Massachusetts, in 1851 who saved her earnings so that she could go to college (pp. 37–38).

3. *Musical Times*, Aug. 1, 1873, p. 175.

4. Nikolai Gogol, *Dead Souls* (1842), trans. Richard Pevear and Larissa Volokhonsky (New York, 1996), vol. 1, p. 23.

5. This ad, which appeared in the *Gazette musicale* (Paris), March 26, 1837, is reproduced in facsimile in Ernst Burger, *Franz Liszt: A Chronicle of His Life in Pictures and Documents*, trans. Stewart Spencer (orig. German ed., 1986; Princeton, N.J., 1989), p. 89.

6. See Alan Walker, *Franz Liszt*, vol. 1: *The Virtuoso*

Years, 1811–1847, rev. ed. (Ithaca, N.Y., 1987), pp. 364–65.

7. See Arthur Loesser, *Men, Women, and Pianos: A Social History* (1954; repr. New York, 1990), sec. 6, chaps. 12 and 16.

8. Anonymous report in *Dwight's Journal of Music,* Aug. 22, 1857, pp. 166–67.

9. The nineteenth-century publication that gives the most comprehensive idea of what music was in print at a given date is not the catalog of any one publisher, but the *Handbuch der musikalischen Literatur* (Handbook of music literature) prepared by Carl Friedrich Whistling (eventually with the help of his sons) and published in Leipzig starting in 1817. The *Handbuch* (which is known as the Whistling-Hofmeister catalog because its publication was assumed by Friedrich Hofmeister in 1819) is international in scope, though it covers German music publishers more comprehensively than foreign ones.

10. Dublin, *Women at Work,* pp. 4–6.

11. John Rosselli, "Opera Production, 1780–1880," in *Opera Production and Its Resources,* trans. Lydia G. Cochrane, pt. 2, vol. 4 of *The History of Italian Opera,* ed. Lorenzo Bianconi and Giorgio Pestelli (orig. Italian ed., 1987; Chicago, 1998), p. 158.

12. This feat is reported by Charles Hallé in his autobiography; doubts about when this concert took place and which movement of the Symphonie Liszt played are evaluated by Adrian Williams in *Portrait of Liszt, By Himself and His Contemporaries* (Oxford, 1990), p. 85.

13. Review in the *Courrier de l'Europe,* Feb. 22, 1809, cited in Jean Mongrédien, "Les Premiers exercices publics d'élèves d'aprés la presse contemporaine (1800–1815)," in *Le Conservatoire de Paris: Des Menus-Plaisirs à la Cité de la musique, 1795–1995,* ed. Anne Bongrain and Yves Gérard (Paris, 1996), p. 27.

14. Sigismond Thalberg, *L'Art du chant appliqué au piano,* Op. 70 (Paris, n.d.).

15. On the reception of Mattmann's performance, see Katharine Ellis, "Female Pianists and Their Male Critics in Nineteenth-Century Paris," *Journal of the American Musicological Society* 50, nos. 2–3

(summer–fall 1997): 367. Student performances of Thalberg opera fantasies are listed in two programs at the Cherry Valley Seminary in New York, one on Aug. 22, 1851, the other undated; see Judith Tick, *American Women Composers before 1870* (Ann Arbor, Mich., 1983), pp. 46–49.

16. On Chopin and the damper pedal, see Sandra P. Rosenblum, "Some Enigmas of Chopin's Pedal Indications: What Do the Sources Tell Us?" *Journal of Musicological Research* 16, no. 1 (1996): 41–61.

17. Gottlieb Graupner, *Rudiments of the Art of Playing on the Piano Forte,* 2d ed. (Boston, 1827).

18. Schubert's song cycle *Die schöne Müllerin* waited thirty-two years after its publication for a complete performance in public, and even then (1856) such programming seemed ridiculous to the famous Viennese critic Eduard Hanslick; see Susan Youens, *Schubert: Die schöne Müllerin* (Cambridge, 1992), pp. 22–27.

19. See Jürgen Thym, "Crosscurrents in Song: Five Distinctive Voices," in *German Lieder in the Nineteenth Century,* ed. Rufus Hallmark, (New York, 1996), p. 156.

20. See George Barth, *The Pianist as Orator: Beethoven and the Transformation of Keyboard Style* (Ithaca, N.Y., 1992).

21. George Bernard Shaw, "The Religion of the Pianoforte," *Fortnightly Review* (Feb. 1894); repr. in Shaw, *How to Become a Musical Critic,* ed. Dan H. Laurence (New York, 1961), p. 214.

22. Adam, *Méthode de piano,* "De l'art d'accompagner la partition," pp. 227–29.

23. On the history of opera rehearsing, see "Rehearsal" in *The New Grove Dictionary of Opera.*

24. William Crotch, *Specimens of Various Styles of Music Referred to in a Course of Lectures, Read at Oxford and London, and Adapted to Keyed Instruments,* 3 vols. (London, [1808]). He published the lectures themselves as *Substance of Several Courses of Lectures on Music* (London, 1831; repr. Clarabricken, Ireland, 1986).

25. Albert Lavignac and Lionel de la Laurencie, *Encyclo-*

pédie de la musique et dictionnaire du Conservatoire, pt. 2 (Paris, 1927), p. 2083.

26. Adam, *Méthode de piano*, p. 234.

27. Vaughan Williams is the source of the story. See Ursula Vaughan Williams, *R.V.W.: A Biography of Ralph Vaughan Williams* (Oxford, 1964; new ed., 1988), p. 80.

28. See Charlotte N. Eyerman, "The Composition of Femininity: The Significance of the 'Woman at the Piano' Motif in Nineteenth-Century French Visual Culture from Daumier to Renoir," Ph.D. diss., University of California, Berkeley, 1997; UMI 9828680, 1998. Although the "woman at the piano" motif is not limited to French visual culture, the French case provides a compelling case study because of the prominence of Paris as a visual and musical capital in the nineteenth century.

29. In fact, the piano had become so commonplace in the home by midcentury that the 1852 edition of the Manuels-Roret assumes that its readers possess one; see *Nouveau manuel complet de la maîtresse de la maison, ou lettres sur l'économie domestique* (Paris, 1852), p. 17.

30. These skills were obtained at a dear price, however, for fifteen francs per month was indeed a major investment.

31. The print was later republished simultaneously by houses in Paris and London during the 1850s or 1860s.

32. Louis Huart, *Les Prodiges de l'industrie. Revue philosophique, critique, comique, et fantastique de l'Exposition de 1844* (Paris, 1844), p. 48.

33. Charles Forster, *Quinze ans à Paris (1832–1848)*, vol. 1 (Paris, 1848), p. 263.

34. Honoré de Balzac, *Physiologie du mariage, ou méditation de philosophie eclectique sur le bonheur et le malheur conjugal*, vol. 1. (Paris: Levasseur, 1830), 93.

35. The lithographer Bouchot employs a similar approach to the "duet" as a seduction scenario in his fourth lithograph in the "Bonnes Têtes Musicales" series, *Le Charivari* (1846).

36. Published in *Le Charivari*, March 6, 1843. Daumier did not write the captions that accompanied his caricatures.

37. Richard Leppert explores these and related issues in *The Sight of Sound: Music, Representation, and the History of the Body* (Berkeley and Los Angeles, 1993).

38. See Wayne E. Franits, *Paragons of Virtue: Women and Domesticity in Seventeenth-Century Dutch Art* (Cambridge, 1993).

39. Vermeer was not alone in receiving attention, for the critic Edmond Duranty (who championed Degas's painting) enthused about Metsu's *The Music Lesson* in his "Promenades au Louvre" in the 1870s; reprinted in Carol Armstrong, *Odd Man Out: Readings of the Work and Reputation of Edgar Degas* (Chicago, 1991), p. 89.

40. Charles Blanc published his "Histoire des peintres 1861" and Thoré-Bürger published "Van der Meer de Delft" in Blanc's journal *Gazette des Beaux-Arts* 21 (1866): 297–330, 458–70, 542–75.

41. Bob Kirsch, "Paul Cézanne: *Jeune fille au piano* and Some Portraits of His Wife; an Investigation of His Painting in the Late 1870s," *Gazette des Beaux-Arts* 110 (July–Aug. 1987): 21–26. See also Lawrence Gowing, *Cézanne: The Early Years, 1859–1872*, exhib. cat. (Washington D.C., National Gallery of Art, 1988), p. 158. Both Kirsch and Gowing rely on Alfred H. Barr, Jr., "Cézanne and Wagner," trans. Margaret Scolari, *Magazine of Art* 31 (May 1938): 288–91.

42. Cézanne was well acquainted with the lithographic tradition; he even looked through women's fashion magazines. See John Rewald, *The History of Impressionism*, 4th ed. (New York, 1973), p. 208.

43. Champfleury [Jules Fleury], *Richard Wagner* (Paris, 1860), p. 11.

44. Roger Delage, *Chabrier* (Geneva, 1982), plate 98, n.p.

45. See Française Cachin et al., *Manet, 1832–1883* (Paris, 1983), pp. 286–87; and Gary Tinterow and Henri Loyrette, *Origins of Impressionism*, exhib. cat. (New York: Metropolitan Museum of Art, 1994), pp. 414–15. Jean Sutherland Boggs cites an 1871 letter written to Berthe Morisot by her mother that describes the Manet salon in somewhat less flattering terms. See

her *Portraits by Degas* (Berkeley and Los Angeles, 1962), p. 22.

46. Boggs, *Portraits by Degas*, p. 24. Apparently, Manet had offered Degas a still-life depicting plums that was returned after the debacle (Cachin, *Manet*, p. 286, and Boggs, *Portraits by Degas*, pp. 22–23). The tension surrounding the event is also recounted in Otto Friedrich, *Olympia: Paris in the Age of Manet* (New York, 1992), pp. 102–3. Boggs reports that both George Moore and the painter Jacques-Emile Blanche commented on the verisimilitude of the portrait of Manet (Boggs, *Portraits by Degas*, p. 23). Degas had previously painted the subject of woman at the piano in 1865 (location unknown, Lemoisne, no. 130); see Albert Kostenevich, *Hidden Treasures Revealed: Impressionist Masterpieces and Other Important French Paintings Preserved by the State Hermitage Museum, St. Petersburg*, ed. James Leggio, trans., Elena Kolesnikova, Catherine A. Fitzpatrick, and Stan Rabinovich (New York, 1995), p. 112.

47. See Theodore Reff, *Degas, The Artist's Mind* (New York, 1976), p. 124. He also made numerous paintings of the pianist Mademoiselle Dihau. See also Denys Sutton, *Edgar Degas: Life and Work* (New York, 1986), p. 73.

48. Duranty's essay is reprinted in Charles Moffett, *The New Painting: Impressionism, 1874–1884* (San Francisco, 1986), pp. 38–50 and (in French) 477–84.

49. Ibid., p. 44. For a fascinating account of the complex relationship between the public and private spheres, see Martha Ward, "Impressionist Installations and Private Exhibitions," *The Art Bulletin* 73, no. 4 (Dec. 1991): 599–622. Ward's article demonstrates that a domestic aesthetic (associated with femininity) informs commercial-artistic space. Her argument raises important issues regarding the display and consumption of small, intimate genre pictures (such as "woman at piano" paintings), for they were often exhibited in "domestic" gallery settings.

50. According to Gloria Groom's extremely informative catalog entry on this work in *Gustave Caillebotte, Urban Impressionist*, ed. Anne Distel (New York, 1995), p. 213.

51. Ibid.

52. They were habitués of Berthe Morisot's evening salons. See Anne Higonnet, *Berthe Morisot* (New York, 1990), p. 181. Her source for this information is Stéphane Mallarmé, "Berthe Morisot," in *Oeuvres* (Paris, 1961), p. 533.

53. For a comprehensive discussion of this series and the woman at the piano theme in Renoir's oeuvre, see Charlotte N. Eyerman, "Models of Melomania: Renoir's *Jeunes filles au piano* Series," in *Modern Art and the Condition of Music*, ed. James Leggio (New York, Garland, forthcoming).

54. See Anne Distel, "Renoir's Collectors," in *Renoir* (London, 1985), pp. 28–29n.76; and Kostenevich, *Hidden Treasures Revealed*, p. 114, on the Hermitage painting (formerly in the Krebs collection). The provenance of this unfinished work is not provided in the *Hidden Treasures* catalog.

55. Mallarmé discusses the procedure in letters that date to April 1892 to Berthe Morisot (Manet's sister-in-law, Renoir's friend, and fellow painter) and to Roger Marx (a prominent art critic). See Stéphane Mallarmé, *Correspondance*, vol. 5 (Paris, 1981), pp. 61–62. The dossier on the purchase is housed at the Archives Nationales, F21 2147. According to those documents, Renoir's work was registered on May 31, 1892; Renoir's fee of four thousand francs was approved on June 18, 1892.

56. The thematic and visual similarities between Monet's series and Renoir's *Jeunes filles au piano* pictures were pointed out to me by Kermit S. Champa in discussions and in the text of an unpublished lecture, "Impressionist Impressions—Lasting, Fleeting, or Cumulative?" Newark Museum (Sept. 1993) and University of Western Ontario (April 1994). In the lecture, Champa explores the "musical" quality of Monet's and Renoir's "multiples" (his term), a theme explicitly addressed by Renoir's overtly music-referencing 1892 series. I am grateful to Professor Champa for his intellectual generosity. Apparently Michel Hoog has also noted this connection in *Catalogue de la collection Jean Walter-Paul Guillaume* (Paris, Musée de

l'Orangerie, 1984), p. 190, cited in Kostenevich, *Hidden Treasures Revealed*, p. 114.

57. Distel, *Renoir*, p. 266.

58. According to Julie Manet, cited in ibid., pp. 261, 266.

Inset: The Piano Tuner
I am indebted for this section to a communication from Owen Jorgensen, professor emeritus of music at Michigan State University and author of *Tuning* (Lansing, Mich., 1991).

Chapter 6. The Concert and the Virtuoso

1. Thurston Dart, *The Interpretation of Music* (London, 1954), pp. 56–57.

2. See William Weber, *The Rise of Musical Classics in Eighteenth-Century England: A Study in Canon, Ritual, and Ideology* (Oxford, 1992), pp. 1–17.

3. For a reproduction of the Mozart notice, see Michael Forsyth, *Buildings for Music: The Architect, the Musician, and the Listener from the Seventeenth Century to the Present Day* (Cambridge, Mass., 1985), p. 30.

4. See ibid., p. 39, for a listing of London concert halls (according to the *General Evening Post*, Feb. 25, 1784). For concert halls in Dublin, see Brian Boydell, *A Dublin Musical Calendar, 1700–1760* (Dublin, 1988), pp. 11–24, esp. p. 15.

5. See Simon McVeigh, *Concert Life in London from Mozart to Haydn* (Cambridge, 1993), p. 90. The successful violinists in England had also been "foreigners."

6. Nicholas Temperley, "Piano Music: 1800–1870," in *Music in Britain: The Romantic Age, 1800–1914*, ed. Nicholas Temperley (Bath, 1988), pp. 401–2.

7. Arthur Loesser, *Men, Women, and Pianos: A Social History* (New York, 1954; repr. New York, 1990), p. 122. After his death, concerts continued in this hall, the Mehlgrube.

8. The lighter Viennese actions were preferred by many of the better-known pianists, perhaps as late as the 1830s. See Jane Ritterman, "Piano Music and the Public Concert, 1800–1850," in *The Cambridge Companion to Chopin*, ed. Jim Samson (Cambridge, 1992),

pp. 11–31, esp. p. 18; she quotes for example Hummel's *A Complete Theoretical and Practical Course*, pt. 3 (1828), p. 64.

9. William Weber, *Music and the Middle Class: The Social Structure of Concert Life in London, Paris, and Vienna* (New York, 1975), pp. 12–14; Alice M. Hanson, *Musical Life in Biedermeier Vienna* (Cambridge, 1985), pp. 6–11.

10. By contrast, London in 1750 had already a dozen shops (according to Thomas Busby); other directories list as many as thirty shops by 1797, and 150 in 1824. See Loesser, *Men, Women, and Pianos*, pp. 122, 251–52.

11. For a delineation of the roles of these halls and the few other appropriate alternatives for solo musicians in Vienna at the time, see Hermann Ullrich, "Aus vormärzlichen Konzertsällen Wiens," in *Jahrbuch des Vereines für die Geschichte der Stadt Wien* 28 (1972): 106–30.

12. Hanson, *Musical Life*, pp. 61–86.

13. In Helga Haupt's compendium of 207 Viennese instrument builders around the turn of the century, more than half were occupied with building keyboard instruments; see her "Wiener Instrumentenbauer von 1791 bis 1815," *Studien zur Musikwissenschaft* 25 (1960): 120–84.

14. See Ullrich, "Aus vormärzlichen Konzertsällen Wiens," p. 109; and Weber, *Music and the Middle Class*, p. 6: "The middle class did not yet wield much power in musical life through communications media. Neither magazines nor newspapers played powerful roles in the concert world, such as they were to achieve by the middle of the nineteenth century." The notice referred to, from the *Wiener Zeitung*, Feb. 3, 1820, is quoted in Hanson, *Musical Life*, p. 30.

15. Hanson, *Musical Life*, pp. 94–97.

16. Eduard Hanslick, *Geschichte des Concertwesens in Wien* (Vienna, 1869), vol. 1, pp. 178–84, esp. 183–84.

17. Reviews may be found in translation in William Atwood's *Fryderyk Chopin: Pianist from Warsaw* (New York, 1987), app. B. See also Ritterman, "Piano Music," p. 11.

18. *Mercure de France*, Oct. 1768, p. 149, and Dec. 1768,

p. 175; quoted in Georges Favre, *La Musique française de piano avant 1830* (Paris, 1953), p. 5. Two most helpful sources on Paris concert life in this period are Jean Mongrédien, *French Music from the Enlightenment to Romanticism, 1789–1830*, trans. from the French by Sylvain Frémaux (Portland, Oreg., 1986); and Jeffrey Cooper, *The Rise of Instrumental Music and Concert Series in Paris, 1828–1871* (Ann Arbor, Mich., 1983).

19. Mongrédien, *French Music*, p. 209.

20. Letter of Oct. 6, 1796, quoted in Mongrédien, *French Music*, p. 227. "Pont-neufs" were popular songs, after the name of the bridge.

21. It mattered little to Fétis whether the piano was used for solo or for collaborative purposes: "Soirées musicales de quatuors et de quintetti, données par M. Baillot," *Revue musicale* 1, no. 1 (Feb. 1827): 37–39, and "Concerts," *Revue musicale* 2 (1827–28): 523–24, quoted in Cooper, *Rise of Instrumental Music*, p. 140.

22. *Correspondance des professeurs et amateurs de musique*, Jan. 15, 1803, quoted in Mongrédien, *French Music*, pp. 206–7. He also cites other contemporary expressions of similar viewpoints.

23. Ibid., p. 206.

24. See the last volume of Fétis's *Revue musicale*, April 12, 1835, pp. 115–16: "Concert de M. Liszt, Au Bénéfice d'une famille pauvre."

25. Cooper, *Rise of Instrumental Music*, p. 19, referring to "Nouvelles de Paris," *Revue musicale* 7 (1830): 266–68.

26. Percy M. Young, "Orchestral Music," in *Music in Britain*, ed. Temperley, p. 361.

27. George F. Root, *The Story of a Musical Life: An Autobiography by Geo. F. Root* (1891; repr. New York, 1970), p. 67.

28. The concert is described in Loesser, *Men, Women, and Pianos*, pp. 363–64. According to Loesser, the "multipiano vogue lasted for twenty-five years or so" (p. 365).

29. Nancy B. Reich, *Clara Schumann: The Artist and the Woman* (Ithaca, N.Y., 1985), p. 53.

30. See Emil F. Smidak, *Isaak-Ignaz Moscheles: Das Leben des Komponisten und seine Begegnungen mit Beethoven, Liszt, Chopin, Mendelssohn* (Vienna, 1988), "Erste Bekanntschaft mit Paris," pp. 23–24.

31. See Jean Mongrédien, "Les Premiers exercices publics d'élèves (1800–1815) d'après la presse contemporaine," in *Le Conservatoire de Paris: Des Menus-Plaisirs à la Cité de la musique, 1795–1995*, ed. Anne Bongrain and Yves Gérard (Paris, 1996), pp. 15–37.

32. *Allgemeine musikalische Zeitung*, Aug. 23, 1809, quoted in ibid., p. 18.

33. See Elisabeth Delafon-Bernard, "Habeneck et la Société des Concerts du Conservatoire: Un destin exemplaire," in *Le Conservatoire de Paris, 1795–1995*, pp. 97–116; and A. Elwart, *Histoire de la Société des Concerts du Conservatoire Impérial de Musique* (Paris, 1860), pp. 171–72.

34. Loesser, *Men, Women, and Pianos*, pp. 346–47.

35. See William Weber's entry "Recital" in the forthcoming edition of Grove's Dictionary. I wish to thank Professor Weber for providing an advance copy of the article.

36. Reich, *Clara Schumann*, pp. 259–60, quoting Sterndale Bennett's correspondence in the Staatsbibliothek, Preussischer Kulturbesitz, Musikabteilung, Berlin.

37. A generous sample of programs from the whole history of piano concerts can be found in George Kehler, *The Piano in Concert*, 2 vols. (Metuchen, N.J., 1982).

38. *London Music in 1888–89 as Heard by Corno di Bassetto (Later Known as Bernard Shaw), with Some Further Autobiographical Particulars* (New York, 1973), pp. 43–47 (concert of Dec. 12, 1888); p. 338 (concert of March 7, 1890).

39. Andrew C. Minor, "Piano Concerts in New York City, 1849–1865," (master's thesis, University of Michigan, 1947), pp. 470, 475.

40. Ibid., pp. 463, 474.

41. W. S. B. Mathews, assoc. ed., *A Hundred Years of Music in America: An Account of Musical Effort in America . . .* (Chicago, 1889; repr., New York, 1970), pp. 141–44.

42. Alfred Dolge, *Pianos and Their Makers* (1911; repr. New York, 1972), p. 393.

43. See Mathews, *A Hundred Years of Music*, p. 145; Florence Ffrench, *Music and Musicians in Chicago: The*

City's Leading Artists, Organizations, and Art Buildings, Progress and Development (Chicago, 1899; repr. New York, 1979), pp. 196–97.

44. Forsyth, *Buildings for Music*, p. 259–60.

45. Ibid., pp. 276, 306.

46. The opening line in Peter Gay, *The Naked Heart: Victoria to Freud*, vol. 4 of *The Bourgeois Experience* (New York, 1995), p. 3. See pp. 11–35 for an excellent summation of the emergence of bourgeois "inner life" and its relation to music and listening practices. For an excellent prehistory to the period of my concern, see William Weber, "Did People Listen in the Eighteenth Century?" *Early Music* 23, no. 4 (Nov. 1997): 678–91.

47. On the changing history of the words *virtuoso* and *virtuosity*, which could carry pejorative or adulatory meaning by the nineteenth century, see Robert Wangermée, "Tradition et innovation dans la virtuosité romantique," *Acta Musicologica* 42 (1970): 5–32; and Marc Pincherle, "Virtuosity," trans. Willis Wager, *Musical Quarterly* 35, no. 2 (April 1949): 226–43.

48. La Mara, ed., *Letters of Franz Liszt*, trans. Constance Bache, 2 vols. (London, 1894), 1:31 (emphasis in original). For citation of contemporaneous confusion over "reciting" on the piano, see Adrian Williams, *Portrait of Liszt: By Himself and His Contemporaries* (Oxford, 1990), p. 133.

49. Pietro Mechetti in the *Wiener Zeitschrift für Kunst*, May 5, 1838, quoted in Williams, *Portrait of Liszt*, p. 104.

50. Williams, *Portrait of Liszt*, pp. 87–88.

51. Michel Foucault, *The Order of Things: An Archaeology of the Human Sciences* (Eng. trans., New York, 1970); Jonathan Crary, *Techniques of the Observer: On Vision and Modernity in the Nineteenth Century* (Cambridge, Mass., 1990); and Martin Jay, *Downcast Eyes: The Denigration of Vision in Twentieth-Century French Thought* (Berkeley and Los Angeles, 1993).

52. Donald M. Lowe, *History of Bourgeois Perception* (Chicago, 1982).

53. See Richard Leppert, *The Sight of Sound: Music, Representation, and the History of the Body* (Berkeley and Los Angeles, 1993).

54. For an example, see James H. Johnson, *Listening in Paris: A Cultural History* (Berkeley and Los Angeles, 1995), p. 232.

55. Timothy J. Clark, "Preliminaries to a Possible Treatment of *Olympia* in 1865," *Screen* 21 (1980): 21. See also Leppert, *Sight of Sound*, pp. 139, 192, 267n.41.

56. Michelle Perrot, ed., *From the Fires of Revolution to the Great War*, trans. Arthur Goldhammer, vol. 4 of *A History of Private Life* (Cambridge, Mass., 1990), p. 533 (emphasis mine).

57. Quoted in Williams, *Portrait of Liszt*, p. 167.

58. Ibid., p. 172.

59. Richard Sennett, *The Fall of Public Man: On the Social Psychology of Capitalism* (New York, 1978), p. 191.

60. Friedrich Schlegel, *Critical Fragments* [1797–1801], reprinted in *Theory as Practice: A Critical Anthology of Early German Romantic Writings*, ed. and trans. Jochen Schulte-Sasse et al. (Minneapolis, 1997), p. 244 (emphasis in original).

61. *The Musical World* 13 (June 11, 1840): 361, 363–64 (emphasis and punctuation in original).

62. *The Musical World* 20 (Aug. 28, 1845): 269 (emphasis in original).

63. *The Musical World* 15 (June 17, 1841): 395.

64. Heinrich Adami in the *Allgemeine Theaterzeitung*, May 5, 1838; quoted in Williams, *Portrait of Liszt*, p. 104 (emphasis in original).

65. See further Arthur Loesser, *Men, Women, and Pianos*, pp. 411–12.

66. Johnson, *Listening in Paris*, p. 29.

67. Gay, *Naked Heart*, p. 18.

68. Sennett, *Fall of Public Man*, p. 206. According to Sennett (p. 207), disciplined silence was foremost a phenomenon of urban centers, less so provincial outposts. As he further notes, the dimming of house lights, which began in the 1850s and was virtually universal by the 1890s, contributed to audience self-restraint.

69. Johnson, *Listening in Paris*, p. 232.

70. Sennett, *Fall of Public Man*, p. 210. See also Gay, *Naked Heart*, pp. 18–19.

71. See for example, Walter Salmen, *Das Konzert: Eine*

Kulturgeschichte (Munich, 1988), pp. 28–29, 31, 47, 114–15, 123, 129, 133, 136, 165, 175.

72. The best published sample of images is Ernst Burger, *Franz Liszt: A Chronicle of His Life in Pictures and Documents*, trans. Stewart Spencer (Princeton, 1989).

73. Robert Schumann, *On Music and Musicians*, ed. Konrad Wolff, trans. Paul Rosenfeld (New York, 1969), p. 150 (emphasis mine); and Sennett, *Fall of Public Man*, p. 203. On Liszt's technique, see Michael Saffle, *Liszt in Germany, 1840–1845: A Study in Sources, Documents, and the History of Reception*, Franz Liszt Studies, no. 2 (Stuyvesant, N.Y., 1994), pp. 207–8.

74. Saffle, *Liszt in Germany*, p. 117.

75. On the conductor as "Führer," see Theodor W. Adorno, *Introduction to the Sociology of Music*, trans. E. B. Aston (New York, 1976), pp. 104–17.

76. Williams, *Portrait of Liszt*, p. 203.

77. Harvey Sachs, *Virtuoso* (London, 1982), p. 53.

78. The caricature was published in *Borsszem Jankó*, April 6, 1873. See Burger, *Franz Liszt*, p. 256; and Sachs, *Virtuoso*, p. 46. For more on Jankó, see Géza Buzinkay, *Borsszem Jankó és társai: Magyar élclapok és karikatúráik a Xix. század mádodik felében* (Budapest, 1983); more on Liszt at pp. 131–32, 159.

79. Alan Walker, *Franz Liszt: The Virtuoso Years, 1811–1847*, rev. ed. (Ithaca, N.Y., 1988), pp. 289–90.

80. Quoted in Burger, *Franz Liszt*, pp. 118, 336. The performance occurred on Nov. 27, 1839; the review appeared in *Wiener Theaterzeitung*, Nov. 30, 1839 (no. 240), pp. 1175–76.

81. John Knox Laughton, *Memoirs of the Life and Correspondence of Henry Reeve, C.B., D.C.L.*, 2 vols. (London, 1898), 1:49. For more on Liszt's appearance while performing, see Williams, *Portrait of Liszt*, pp. 84, 89, 146.

82. Michel Foucault, *The History of Sexuality*, vol. 1, *An Introduction*, trans. Robert Hurley (New York, 1978), pp. 104, 121, 146–47.

83. See Wilhelm Seidel, "Olympia: Uber die Magie der Herzlosigkeit," *Die Mechanik in den Künsten: Studien zur ästhetischen Bedeutung von Naturwissenschaft und Technologie* (Marburg, 1990), pp. 201–12; and Loesser, *Men, Women, and Pianos*, pp. 233–35, 367.

84. Walker, *Franz Liszt*, p. 285.

85. Robert S. Winter, "Orthodoxies, Paradoxes, and Contradictions: Performance Practices in Nineteenth-Century Piano Music," in *Nineteenth-Century Piano Music*, ed. R. Larry Todd (New York, 1990), p. 17.

86. Quoted in Williams, *Portrait of Liszt*, p. 100.

87. See Walker, *Franz Liszt*, pp. 232–43; and Katherine Ellis, *Music Criticism in Nineteenth-Century France: La Revue et Gazette musicale de Paris, 1834–1880* (Cambridge, 1995), pp. 149–52.

88. Walker, *Franz Liszt*, p. 233.

89. See reproductions in Burger, *Franz Liszt*, p. 171.

90. *Dwight's Journal of Music* 38, no. 2 (April 27, 1878): 220.

91. Burger, *Franz Liszt*, p. 336.

92. *Neue Zeitschrift für Musik*, no. 12 (1840): 118–20; quoted from Walker, *Franz Liszt*, p. 350.

93. Walker, *Franz Liszt*, p. 288.

94. See ibid., p. 327.

95. *The Musical World* 13, no. 5 (1855): 257.

96. Richard Leppert, *Music and Image: Domesticity, Ideology, and Socio-Cultural Formation in Eighteenth-Century England* (Cambridge, 1988), pp. 122–25.

97. See Foucault, *The History of Sexuality*, vol. 1, *An Introduction*.

98. Reich, *Clara Schumann*, p. 211.

99. On the fragility of the earlier nineteenth-century pianos that Liszt played, see Walker, *Franz Liszt*, pp. 286–87. For a satiric American account from 1849 of the piano-damaging virtuoso "Herr Smash," probably Maurice Strakosch, see Loesser, *Men, Women, and Pianos*, pp. 489–90.

100. Heinrich Heine, *Florentine Nights*, trans. Kirke Boylan Fitz-Gerald (Boston, 1929), p. 69; Burger, *Franz Liszt*, pp. 158, 340; concert of Oct. 8, 1845, reviewed in *Grossherzoglich Hessische Zeitung*, Oct. 10, 1845.

101. Loesser, *Men, Women, and Pianos*, p. 369. Concerning the range of praise and damnation that attended Liszt's playing, see Saffle, *Liszt in Germany*, pp. 42–43, 75–76.

102. Henry F. Chorley, *Modern German Music: Recollections and Criticisms*, 2 vols. (London, 1854), 2:245; Walker, *Franz Liszt*, p. 372. Ignacy Paderewski's fa-

mous and abundant mop of hair excited an enormous amount of commentary by men late in the century relative to its (purported) effects on women; his hair likewise inspired a number of caricatures and cartoons. See Adam Zamoyski, *Paderewski* (New York, 1982), pp. 86–87, 90–91, 99–101. Liszt's long hair became something of a political issue with the Russian tsar in 1842; see Williams, *Portrait of Liszt*, pp. 187–89.

103. *Dwight's Journal of Music* 30, no. 5 (May 21, 1870), p. 242.

104. Arthur Schopenhauer, *Die Welt als Wille und Vorstellung* [1819], excerpted and reprinted in *Music and Aesthetics in the Eighteenth and Nineteenth Centuries*, ed. Peter Le Hurray and James Day (Cambridge, 1981), p. 330.

105. Schumann, *On Music and Musicians*, p. 156. See also the comments by Lawrence Kramer, *Music as Cultural Practice, 1800–1900* (Berkeley and Los Angeles, 1990), pp. 90–91.

Chapter 7. 1870s to 1920s: The World's the Limit

1. Figures on piano production are from Cyril Ehrlich, *The Piano: A History* (London, 1976), esp. app. 2, p. 221; and Craig H. Roell, *The Piano in America, 1890–1940* (Chapel Hill, N.C., 1989), esp. chap. 5.

2. See Ehrlich, *The Piano*, esp. chap. 5.

3. On Bethune's career, see Eileen Southern, *The Music of Black Americans: A History* (New York, 1971), pp. 251–54. A fuller study is Geneva Southall, *Blind Tom: The Post–Civil War Enslavement of a Black Musical Genius* (Minneapolis, 1979) and *The Continuing Enslavement of Blind Tom, the Black Pianist-Composer, 1865–1887* (Minneapolis, 1983).

4. Jerre Mangione, *Mount Allegro: A Memoir of Italian American Life*, (1943; repr. New York, 1981), pp. 212–13.

5. Nicholas Tawa, *A Sound of Strangers: Musical Culture, Acculturation, and the Post–Civil War Ethnic American* (Metuchen, N.J., 1982), pp. 56–61.

6. Mangione, *Mount Allegro*, p. 218.

7. Advertisement in the program of a concert by Samuel Coleridge-Taylor on April 23, 1907, preserved in the Daniel Murray pamphlet collection, vol. 18, no. 8, in the Rare Book and Special Collections Divisions of the Library of Congress (microfilmed by the Library of Congress photoduplication service, 1990).

8. Cited in Roell, *Piano in America*, p. 33. See also the chapter "The Ragtime Debate" in Edward A. Berlin, *Ragtime: A Musical and Cultural History* (Berkeley and Los Angeles, 1980).

9. On the Broadwood art-case pianos, see David Wainwright, *Broadwood by Appointment: A History* (London, 1982), pp. 208–14. On the Steinway art-case pianos, see Ronald V. Ratcliffe, *Steinway* (San Francisco, 1989), chap. 5.

10. Edward Grieg, preface to *Norwegische Bauerntänze (Slåtter)*, Op. 72 (Leipzig, 1903).

11. On the creation and reception of Grieg's *Slåtter*, see Finn Benestad and Dag Schjelderup-Ebbe, *Edvard Grieg: The Man and the Artist*, trans. William H. Halverson and Leland B. Sateren (orig. Norwegian ed., 1980; trans. Lincoln, Neb., 1988), pp. 363–70.

12. William Christopher Handy, *Father of the Blues: An Autobiography* (New York, 1941), p. 99.

13. LeRoi Jones, *Blues People: Negro Music in White America* (New York, 1963), p. 148.

14. Benestad and Schjelderup-Ebbe, *Edvard Grieg*, p. 365.

15. Handy, *Father of the Blues*, p. 10.

16. On Nazareth's life and music, see David Appleby, *The Music of Brazil* (Austin, 1983), pp. 78–83; on the position of his music in Brazilian culture, see Vasco Mariz, *História da Música no Brasil*, 4th ed. (Rio de Janeiro, 1994), pp. 124–26.

17. Burmese piano music, played by U Yee Nwe, can be heard on the CD *Sandya: The Spellbinding Piano of Burma* (Shanachie 66007), with notes by Rick Heizman.

18. In this section, Japanese personal names are given with the person's family name before his or her given name, following the Japanese custom.

19. The embassy's multivolume official report to the Meiji government was edited by its chief secretary,

Kume Kunitake, under the heading *Tokumei zenken taishi Bei-O kairan jikki* (Record of the journey of the embassy extraordinary and plenipotentiary to America and Europe). The quotation is from its current publication edited by Tanaka Akira (Tokyo, 1992), 1:147.

20. Ibid., 1:88.

21. In obtaining this information, I am indebted to Kumaya Kōzō, director of the Kumaya Museum, which owns the piano, as well as Katsura Ryōko, who mobilized her machine on my behalf. Cf. Martha Novak Clinkscale, *Makers of the Piano, 1700–1820* (Oxford, 1993), p. 229. At the time of Siebold's visit, Japan was closed to Western countries except Holland. Siebold was asked by a shogun's interpreter why he did not speak the same Dutch as his fellow Dutchmen. He survived the query by replying that he was "mountain Dutch."

22. Akiyama Tatsuhide, ed., *Nihon no yōgaku hyakunenshi* (A century of Western music in Japan) (Tokyo, 1966), p. 7. Both the army and the navy had for some time been equipped with Western-style brass bands trained by officers from various Western countries.

23. There are many publications on Mason's life and work in both Japanese and English. In Japanese, see, for example, Nakamura Rihei, *Yōgaku dōnyūsha no kiseki: Nihon kindai yōgakushi josetsu* (The life histories of the importers of Western music: Introduction to the history of Western music in modern Japan) (Tokyo, 1993), chap. 9. In English, the most recent addition is Sondra Wieland Howe, *Luther Whiting Mason: International Music Educator* (Warren, Mich., 1997).

24. Endō Hiroshi, *Meiji ongakushi kō* (Reflections on the history of music in the Meiji period) (Tokyo, 1948), pp. 95–99. The organ was completed in 1881.

25. Endō, *Meiji ongakushi kō*, pp. 83–84.

26. Edward S. Morse, *Japan Day by Day* (Boston, 1917), 1:399, 400, 401, 402. Elsewhere Morse described a performance of a flute, a small reed pipe, and a shō as follows: "It was impossible to catch any air or strain. The music sounded weird and solemn. The shō kept up a continuous note, or rather a humming sound,

which varied slightly" (p. 292).

27. Ibid., 2:225, 226.

28. The textbook of songs is Monbushō Ongaku Torishirabe-gakari, ed., *Shōgaku shōkashū* (Songs for primary schools) (Tokyo, 1881), in *Nihon kyōkasho taikei kindaihen* (Encyclopedia of Japanese textbooks, modern), ed. Kaigo Munekoki and Naka Shin, vol. 25, *Shōka* (Songs) (Tokyo, 1965), pp. 5–43. The publication did not acknowledge Mason, but he was the teacher at Ongaku Torishirabe-gakari (the music school) of Monbushō (the ministry of education), which is noted as the editor.

29. Program note of a two-day concert (Jan. 30–31, 1882) written by the Education Ministry's Ongaku Torishirabe-gakari. The concert was a part of the school's "activities report." Quoted in Endō, *Meiji ongakushi kō*, pp. 107–25, 134.

30. The verse describes the proper relationships between father and son, lord and subject, husband and wife, elder brother and younger brother, and friends. Song 33 in Kaigo and Naka, eds., *Shōka*, p. 18.

31. Song 18, ibid., p. 12.

32. Song 23, ibid., p. 14.

33. See Julia Meech-Pekarik, *The World of the Meiji Print: Impressions of a New Civilization* (New York, 1986), p. 152. On Anna Lohr, the best source is Nakamura, *Yōgaku*, chap. 8.

34. On Bigot, see Meech-Pekarik, *World of the Meiji Print*, pp. 185–94.

35. "Kēberu" (Koeber) in *Iwanami tetsugaku jiten* (The Iwanami dictionary of philosophy); Furuta Akira, "Kēberu" (Koeber), in *Kokushi daijiten* (Encyclopedia of Japanese history) (Tokyo, 1985), 5:75. Koeber attributed his professional choice to his distaste for performing music in public.

36. Endō, *Meiji ongakushi kō*, p. 42.

37. Yoshimoto Mitsuaki, ed., *Miura Tamaki: "O-Chō fujin"* (Tamaki Miura: Madama Butterfly) (Tokyo, 1997), pp. 76, 169–70.

38. Yoshimoto, *Miura Tamaki*, p. 166.

39. Endō, *Meiji ongakushi kō*, p. 39.

40. Concert Hall, Tokyo School of Music, March 1905;

Akiyama, *Nihon no yōgaku*, p. 135; Endō, *Meiji onga-kushi kō*, p. 40.

41. "Ongaku gakkō ensōkai" (School of Music concert), *Miyako shinbun*, March 23, 1905, in Akiyama, *Nihon no yōgaku*, p. 139.

42. Concert programs, Akiyama, *Nihon no yōgaku*, passim.

43. Programs in those days did not always include the opus number or key signature of a work.

44. Judith Ann Herd, "Piano Industry in Japan," in *Encyclopedia of the Piano*, ed. Robert Palmieri (New York, 1996); "Nihon gakki no meiyo" (The honor of the Japanese musical instrument), *Ongakukai* (Dec. 1909), vol. 2, no. 12, in Akiyama, *Nihon no yōgaku*, p. 209.

45. "Chūgakkō no gakki hoyūsū" (The number of musical instruments at middle schools), *Ongakukai* (Feb. 1910), vol. 3, no. 2, in Akiyama, *Nihon no yōgaku*, p. 215. This was neither a scientific nor a comprehensive survey. As such, it did not specify how large a "large" school was. "Middle school," coming after the six-year primary school, was not compulsory. Few went to a middle school in those days.

46. Natsume Sōseki, *Gubijinsō* (Red poppy), in *Sōseki zenshū* (Complete works of Natsume Sōseki) (Tokyo, 1966), 3:152.

47. The list of lessons a young woman takes in another of Natsume's novels, *Meian* (Light and darkness), in *Sōseki zenshū*, 7:190.

48. Natsume Sōseki, *Nikki* (Diaries), entries for June 21 and 30, 1909, in *Sōseki zenshū*, vol. 13, pp. 396, 398. For four hundred yen, one could buy a midprice Yamaha upright.

49. Tamagawa Yūko, "Akogare to genjitsu—piano o tō-shite miru Taishō no yōgaku shakaishi" (Aspirations and realities—the social history of Western music in the Taishō period as seen through the piano), *Oto no shakaishi—jūkyū seiki ni okeru sono hensen*, March 1992, pp. 60, 62–63, 65.

50. Ibid., pp. 64–65.

51. "Osaka-shi kaku shōgakkō ongakujō no setsubi" (Music facilities at primary schools in Osaka," *Ongaku-*

kai, no. 185, in Akiyama, *Nihon no yōgaku*, p. 307. "Aomori ongakukai zappō" (Miscellaneous news on music in Aomori), *Ongakukai*, July 1922, in ibid., p. 355.

52. *Ongaku zasshi* (April 1892), vol. 19, in Akiyama, *Nihon no yōgaku*, p. 56.

53. These numbers were computed from the programs of concerts given between August 1886 and December 1912 and collected by Akiyama in *Nihon no yōgaku*.

54. Watanabe Tatsukiyo, "Ongakudan" (Conversation on music), *Fujinkai* (Sept. 1902), vol. 1, no. 4, in Akiyama, *Nihon no yōgaku*, p. 166.

55. See Roell, *Piano in America*, chap. 2, "The Origins of a Musical Democracy."

56. Gillian Anderson, *Music for Silent Films, 1894–1929: A Guide* (Washington, 1988), pp. xlii–xliii.

57. Timothy J. Gilfoyle, *City of Eros: New York City, Prostitution, and the Commercialization of Sex, 1790–1920* (New York, 1992), p. 225.

58. See Gordon Cox, *A History of Music Education in England, 1872–1928* (Aldershot, England, 1993); and James A. Keene, *A History of Music Education in the United States* (Hanover, N.H., 1982).

59. I am grateful to George Eberts of the Southeast Psychiatric Hospital—successor to the Athens Lunatic Asylum—for supplying me with the photograph of the ballroom, along with an informal history of the uses of the room and of pianos in the institution.

60. This story was related to me by Rachelle Smith, formerly a teacher in the English prison system.

Inset: Silent Movies with Piano

1. Cyril Ehrlich, *The Music Profession in Britain since the Eighteenth Century: A Social History* (Oxford, 1985), p. 197.

2. See Michael Chanan, *The Dream that Kicks: The Prehistory and Early Years of Cinema in Britain*, 2d ed. (London, 1980), pp. 259–65.

3. Quoted in ibid., p. 260.

4. Bert Ennis, quoted in ibid., p. 263.

5. Terry Lewis of the Yamaha Corporation of America. Personal communication from James Parakilas.

Chapter 8. Hollywood's Embattled Icon

1. Gwendolyn Brooks's "Piano after War" was published in *A Street in Bronzeville* (New York, 1945), shortly before the Japanese surrender that ended World War II.

2. Arthur Loesser, *Men, Women, and Pianos: A Social History* (1954; repr. New York, 1990), p. 608.

3. John Huntley, *British Film Music* (London, 1947), pp. 124, 110.

4. Quote from pressbook at British Film Institute (London).

5. Robert Jay Nash and Stanley Ralph Ross, *Motion Picture Guide* (Chicago, 1985–), p. 3032.

6. *Motion Picture Herald*, Nov. 18, 1944.

7. *NS-Kurier* (Stuttgart). No date is included on this press clipping as found in the file on *Abschiedswalzer* at the Bundesarchiv/Filmarchiv in Berlin.

8. Press materials on *Chopins Jugend* at the Bundesarchiv/Filmarchiv.

9. Lawrence Morton, "Chopin's New Audience," *Hollywood Quarterly [Film Quarterly]* 1, no. 1 (Oct. 1945): 31–33.

10. Liner notes on Liberace's *Concertos for You* album, which includes the "Warsaw Concerto" as well as movie concerto themes from *Love Story* and *Spellbound*. Columbia Masterworks, ML-4764 (1953).

11. Director Edgar G. Ulmer, an assistant to the legendary German expressionist director Fritz Murnau before fleeing the Nazi regime, made a subsequent film on this very subject: in *Carnegie Hall* (1947), a woman works as a janitor to support her son's piano career.

12. Martin M. Goldsmith, *Detour: An Extraordinary Tale* (New York, 1939), p. 53.

13. Caryl Flinn discusses *Detour*'s Chopin motif as "an emblem of better times," a soundtrack device constructing "this failed musical utopia" of Al's Oedipal condition. See Flinn, *Strains of Utopia: Gender, Nostalgia, and Hollywood Film Music* (Princeton, N.J., 1992), pp. 125, 131.

14. Roger Cohen, "Music Helps Sarajevo Stay Sane during War," *New York Times*, Oct. 23, 1994.

15. Ibid.

16. Ibid.

17. Ernst Lothar, *The Angel with the Trumpet*, trans. Elizabeth Reynolds Hapgood (Garden City, N.Y., 1944).

Chapter 9. 1920s to 2000: New Voices from the Old Impersonator

1. The piano with nails, Günther Uecker's *Piano* (1964), and the one with flowers, Joseph Beuys's *Revolution Piano* (1969), are both pictured in Karin von Maur, ed., *Vom Klang der Bilder: Die Musik in der Kunst des 20. Jahrhunderts* (Munich, 1985), p. 23. Quotation in Caroline Tisdall, *Joseph Beuys* (New York, 1979), p. 168. The work, called "Infiltration-Homogen for Grand Piano," was made at the Staatliche Kunstakademie in Düsseldorf in 1966 and later displayed at the Pompidou Center in Paris.

2. See John G. Hanhardt, *Nam June Paik* (New York, 1982), pp. 74–75.

3. See David Burge, *Twentieth-Century Piano Music* (New York, 1990), pp. 123–25.

4. H. Wiley Hitchcock, *Ives: A Survey of the Music* (New York, 1977), p. 49.

5. On preparing pianos, see Richard Bunger, *The Well-Prepared Piano* (Colorado Springs, 1973). On playing inside the piano, see Burge, *Twentieth-Century Piano Music*, pp. 216–17.

6. See the section "The Prepared Piano" in James Pritchett, *The Music of John Cage* (Cambridge, 1993), pp. 22–35.

7. See Philip Carlsen, *The Player-Piano Music of Conlon Nancarrow: An Analysis of Selected Studies* (New York, 1988); Kyle Gann, "Conlon Nancarrow's Tempo Tornadoes," *Village Voice*, Oct. 5, 1993, pp. 93, 97; Kyle Gann, *The Music of Conlon Nancarrow* (Cambridge, 1995).

8. On the history of the toy piano, see Margaret Leng Tan, "Toy Pianos No Longer Toys!" *Piano and Keyboard*, Nov.–Dec. 1997, pp. 51–54.

9. Dizzy Gillespie, *To Be, or Not . . . to Bop* (Garden City, N.Y., 1979), pp. 134–35. See also Miles Davis with

Quincy Troupe, *Miles: The Autobiography* (New York, 1989), pp. 79–80.

10. Bruce A. MacLeod, *Club Date Musicians: Playing the New York Party Circuit* (Urbana, Ill., 1993), p. 167.

11. Arthur Loesser, *Men, Women, and Pianos: A Social History* (1954; repr. New York, 1990), p. 391.

12. Estimated figures, taken from *The Piano: The New Grove Dictionary of Musical Instruments* (London, 1988), p. 57; and Cyril Ehrlich, *The Piano: A History* (London, 1976), p. 129.

13. Loesser, *Men, Women, and Pianos*, pp. 603, 610.

14. Roland Barthes, "Musica Practica," in *Image-Music-Text* (London, 1977).

15. John Schaeffer, "New Sounds," *The Virgin Guide to New Music* (London, 1990), p. 5.

16. Andrew Blake, *The Music Business* (London, 1992), pp. 50, 54.

17. "A Piano Crescendo Lifts Sales of New and Restored Instruments," *Wall Street Journal*, July 17, 1997.

18. Alejo Carpentier, *Esa musico que llevo dentro*, vol. 2 (Havana, 1980), pp. 246–56.

19. Richard Taruskin, "The Pastness of the Present and the Presence of the Past," in *Authenticity and Early Music*, ed. Nicholas Kenyon (Oxford, 1988).

20. Barthes, "Musica Practica."

21. See "Music Retailers Strive to Drum Out Piano Sales at Universities," *Detroit News*, March 31, 1996.

22. "Tuning with the Enemy," dir. Tricia O'Leary and Helen Gallacher, transmitted Channel 4, United Kingdom, Aug. 16, 1998.

Afterword

1. Richard Taruskin, "On Letting the Music Speak for Itself," reprinted in his *Text and Act: Essays on Music and Performance* (New York and Oxford, 1995), p. 57.

2. Alfred Hipkins, *Musical Instruments, Historic, Rare, and Unique* (Edinburgh, 1888), and *A Description and History of the Pianoforte and of the Older Keyboard Stringed Instruments* (London, 1896).

3. See David Wainwright, *Broadwood by Appointment: A History* (London, 1982), pp. 215–18, or Cyril Ehrlich, *The Piano: A History* (London, 1976), pp. 146–47.

4. See Harry Haskell, *The Early Music Revival: A History* (London, 1988), p. 190.

5. Haskell, *Early Music Revival*, p. 189.

Recommended Readings

The following short list is intended simply to provide a few leads to readers who are interested in pursuing topics raised in this book or in discovering some of the richness of recent writing about the piano. Other leads can be found in the references throughout this book.

The cultural history of the piano deserves to be considered in the context that more general cultural histories provide, whether or not they themselves give much attention to musical life. Some monumental examples include Philippe Ariès and Georges Duby, eds., *A History of Private Life* (English trans., Cambridge, Mass., 1987–91), Georges Duby and Michelle Perrot, eds., *A History of Women in the West* (English trans., Cambridge, Mass., 1992–94), and Peter Gay, *The Bourgeois Experience: Victoria to Freud* (New York and London, 1984–98).

For a survey of modern Western musical life in the context of social and political developments, consult the volumes of the *Music and Society* series, Stanley Sadie, general editor (Englewood Cliffs, N.J., 1989–94). A brief history of Western music as a social practice, with a chapter on "The Age of the Piano," is Michael Chanan's *Musica Practica* (London and New York, 1994). Three histories of the piano that provide social historical perspectives are *The Book of the Piano*, ed. Dominic Gill (Oxford, 1981), *The Lives of the Piano*, ed. James R. Gaines (New York, 1981), and the classic of the subject, Arthur Loesser, *Men, Women, and Pianos* (1954; reprint New York, 1990). Two studies of the piano as a women's instrument are Stefana Sabin, *Frauen am Klavier: Skizze einer Kulturgeschichte* (Frankfurt, 1998), and Joan Berman Mizrahi, "The American Image of Women as Musicians and Pianists, 1850–1900" (Ph.D. dissertation, University of Maryland, 1989).

The literature on the piano from standpoints other than cultural or social history is staggering. Maurice Hinson's recent bibliography, *The Pianist's Bookshelf: A Practical Guide to Books, Videos, and Other Resources* (Bloomington, 1998), gives an idea of how staggering, and that covers just ten years of publications in English only and ignores nonclassical repertories as well as the cultural and social historical sides of the subject. Three recent works on pianos, piano playing, and piano music are *The New Grove Piano* (New York and London, 1988), Garland's *Encyclopedia of the Piano*, ed. Robert Palmieri with Margaret W. Palmieri (New York and London, 1996), and *The Cambridge Companion to the Piano*, ed. David Rowland (Cambridge, 1998).

From here on, this list follows the outline of the book. On the creation of the piano, centering on the work of Cristofori, two comprehensive studies are Stewart Pollens, *The Early Pianoforte* (Cambridge, 1995), and Konstantin Restle, *Bartolomeo Cristofori und die Anfänge des Hammerclaviers* (Munich, 1991).

On the history of piano design, see Edwin M. Good, *Giraffes, Black Dragons, and Other Pianos: A Technological History from Cristofori to the Modern Concert Grand* (Stanford, Calif., 1982). On design developments in the period from Zumpe to the early nineteenth century, see Michael Cole, *The Pianoforte in the Classical Era* (Oxford, 1998). The instruments produced by early piano manufacturers are cataloged in Martha Novak Clinkscale, *Makers of the Piano, 1700–1820* (Oxford, 1993), and *Makers of the Piano, 1820–1860* (Oxford, 1998). Among books of photographs of historic pianos, David Crombie, *Piano* (San Francisco, 1995), is a particular feast. For the history of the piano industry, see Cyril Ehrlich, *The Piano: A History* (London, 1976). Studies of national piano industries and of individual piano manufacturers are listed in the entries of Garland's *Encyclopedia of the Piano*.

On pianos, piano music, and piano performance

in the age of revolutions, Katalin Komlós's *Fortepianos and Their Music: Germany, Austria, and England, 1760–1800* (Oxford, 1995) is complemented geographically by Adélaïde de Place, *Le Piano-forte à Paris entre 1760 et 1822* (Paris, 1986). A pictorial study of domestic music making in this period is Walter Salmen, *Haus- und Kammermusik*, vol. 4/3 of *Musikgeschichte in Bildern*, ed. Heinrich Besseler and Werner Bachmann (Leipzig, 1969). The cultural roles of domestic musical life in England in this period are analyzed in Richard Leppert, *Music and Image: Domesticity, Ideology, and Socio-Cultural Formation in Eighteenth-Century England* (Cambridge, 1988). Two studies of the theme of the piano in literature also serve incidentally to point out a multitude of novels worth reading: Mary Burgan, "Heroines at the Piano: Women and Music in Nineteenth-Century Fiction," *Victorian Studies* 30 (1986): 51–76, and Danièle Pistone, "Le Piano dans la littérature française des origines jusqu'en 1900" (Ph.D. diss., University of Lille III, 1975).

For the history of the piano lesson, Da Capo, Minkoff, and other publishers have been providing a valuable service by reprinting a number of important historical piano methods. Among histories of piano pedagogy based on these methods is Debra Brubaker, "A History and Critical Analysis of Piano Methods Published in the United States from 1796 to 1995" (Ph.D. dissertation, University of Minnesota, 1996). A history of piano technique based on the practices of great teachers and performers is Reginald R. Gerig, *Famous Pianists and Their Technique* (Washington and New York, 1974). Another kind of history of piano study could be constructed from the memoirs of teachers and students; the American classic in this field is Amy Fay, *Music-Study in Germany* (1880; repr. New York, 1965); the book that Noah Adams refers to in his Foreword to this book is his *Piano Lessons: Music, Love, and True Adventures* (New York, 1996). Among histories of individual conservatories, two readable examples are Bruce McPherson and

James Klein, *Measure by Measure: A History of New England Conservatory from 1867* (Boston, 1995), and Laetitia Chassain-Dolliou, *Le Conservatoire de Paris, ou Les voies de la création* (Paris, 1995).

Nothing provides a clearer window into mid-nineteenth-century musical life than the music journals that provided it to the (largely piano-playing) public of the time. Two books that cull rich samples of articles from individual journals of that period are Percy A. Scholes, *The Mirror of Music, 1844–1944: A Century of Musical Life in Britain as Reflected in the Pages of the Musical Times*, 2 vols. (Oxford, 1947), and Irving Sablosky, *What They Heard: Music in America, 1852–1881, from the Pages of Dwight's Journal of Music* (Baton Rouge and London, 1986). Dieter Hildebrandt's *Pianoforte: A Social History of the Piano*, translated by Harriet Goodman (New York, 1988), is really a story of nineteenth-century piano composers and musical life. Domestic musical life in the nineteenth century is the subject of Andreas Ballstaedt and Tobia Widmaier, *Salonmusik: zur Geschichte und Funktion einer bürgerlichen Musikpraxis* (Stuttgart, 1989). Philip Brett explores piano duet playing as a scene of social intimacies and identities in "Piano Four-Hands: Schubert and the Performance of Gay Male Desire," *Nineteenth-Century Music* 21 (fall 1997), pp. 149–76. For the study of representations of the piano and other music in visual culture, Tom Phillips, *Music in Art through the Ages* (Munich and New York, 1997), presents an artist's perspective, and Richard Leppert, *The Sight of Sound: Music, Representation, and the History of the Body* (Berkeley, 1993), a cultural theorist's perspective.

The classic social history of the concert in the era of the piano is William Weber, *Music and the Middle Class: The Social Structure of Concert Life in London, Paris, and Vienna* (New York, 1975). A rich pictorial source for the history of the concert is Heinrich W. Schwab, *Konzert*, vol. 4/2 of *Musikgeschichte in Bildern*, ed. Heinrich Besseler and Werner Bachmann (Leipzig,

1971). A revealing sampler of recital programs by many of the greatest pianists in history is George Kehler, *The Piano in Concert*, 2 vols. (Metuchen, N.J., 1982). Notices of two centuries of piano performances can be found in collections of the reviews of Berlioz, Hanslick, Shaw, and many other important music critics. A festival of filmed documents of great pianists (recitals, interviews, and such) is beautifully cataloged in Christian Labrande and Pierre-Martin Juban, eds., *Classique en images 1998: Les grands pianistes du XXème siècle* (Paris, 1998). The history of pictorial representations of Liszt is amply displayed in Ernst Burger, *Franz Liszt: A Chronicle of His Life in Pictures and Documents*, trans. Stewart Spencer (Princeton, N.J., 1989).

Craig H. Roell, in *The Piano in America, 1890–1940* (Chapel Hill, N.C., 1989), provides a splendid cultural history as well as business history of turn of the century America. The history of Western music in the rest of the world is just beginning to be written. A work about the piano that shows what can be done in this field (covering in this case a period well into the twentieth century) is Richard Curt Kraus, *Pianos and Politics in China: Middle-Class Ambitions and the Struggle over Western Music* (Oxford, 1989).

Two brief articles on the presence of pianists in movies are Sarah Cahill, "Eighty-eight Keys to Terror," *Piano & Keyboard*, May–June 1994, pp. 42–47, and Ivan Raykoff, "Great Pianists on Film," *Piano & Keyboard*, May–June 1998, pp. 21–23.

Twentieth-century artists' images of the piano, as well as fascinating interpenetrations of music and the visual arts in the twentieth century, are presented in *Vom Klang der Bilder: Die Musik in der Kunst des 20. Jahrhunderts* (Munich, 1985). David Burge, in *Twentieth-Century Piano Music* (New York, 1990), surveys the concert repertory. Billy Taylor's *Jazz Piano: A Jazz History* (Dubuque, Iowa, 1982) is not so much a history of the piano in jazz as a history of jazz from the piano bench. Michael Chanan studies the transforming effects of recording on musical culture in *Repeated Takes: A Short History of Recording and its Effects on Music* (London and New York, 1995).

Contributors

E. DOUGLAS BOMBERGER is an associate professor at the University of Hawaii at Manoa, where he teaches courses in music history and literature. He holds a Ph.D. in musicology from the University of Maryland and an M.M. in piano performance from the University of North Carolina. The subject of his dissertation—a topic he continues to pursue—is nineteenth-century American music students in Germany, and he is also investigating American composers' concerts of the 1880s and 1890s. Among his many publications on nineteenth-century music is a forthcoming edition of biographical sketches of American musicians from *Brainard's Musical World*.

MARTHA DENNIS BURNS, a doctoral candidate in history at Brown University, is completing a dissertation on music, gender, and politics in the period of the Compromise of 1850. Her focus is the press portrayal of the Jenny Lind concert tour. She has received fellowships from the American Antiquarian Society, the Huntington Library, the Newberry Library, the Pew Program in Religion and American History at Yale University, the Virginia Historical Society, and the Smithsonian Institution.

MICHAEL CHANAN, born in London in 1946, studied philosophy at Sussex and Oxford. A music critic since 1967, he is also a documentary film maker, beginning with documentaries on music for BBC Television; in the 1980s, he made several films on Latin American subjects, mostly for Channel 4 in London. He is the author, editor, and translator of books and articles on film history in Britain and Latin America, the media, and music, and teaches film and video in London. His next books are *From Handel to Hendrix: The Composer in the Public Sphere* and a new edition of *The Cuban Image: Cinema and Cultural Politics in Cuba*.

JANE COSTLOW received her Ph.D. in Slavic languages and literatures at Yale University and is associate professor of Russian at Bates College. She is the author of *Worlds within Worlds: The Novels of Ivan Turgenev*, a co-editor of *Representations of the Body and Sexuality in Russian Culture*, and the translator of Lydia Zinovieva-Annibal's *The Tragic Menagerie*. She has twice won the Heldt Prize for the best article in Slavic women's studies.

CHARLOTTE N. EYERMAN received her Ph.D. in the history of art from the University of California in 1997 and is an assistant professor at Union College. She has published essays on nineteenth-century European art and visual culture and is presently revising her doctoral dissertation, a cultural history of the "woman at the piano" motif in nineteenth-century French visual representations, for publication as a book.

EDWIN M. GOOD is professor emeritus of religious studies at Stanford University and research collaborator in the Division of Cultural History at the Smithsonian Institution. Besides his many publications in biblical studies, he is the author of the award-winning *Giraffes, Black Dragons, and Other Pianos: A Technological History from Cristofori to the Modern Concert Grand* and of other studies in the history of the piano. In collaboration with Cynthia Adams Hoover, he is editing the diaries of William Steinway and planning the Piano 300 exhibition and events at the Smithsonian. He is the pianist of the Rock Creek Chamber Players and a member of the Friday Morning Music Club in Washington.

ATSUKO HIRAI, a native of Japan, came to the United States for her graduate education. She received a Ph.D. in government from Harvard University. Called back to music by "life after the Ph.D.," she took weekly voice lessons for five years from Leona Scheunemann Witter, a student of Anna Schoen-René. She is Kazushige Hirasawa Professor of History at Bates College. In addition to her teaching and writing on Japanese history, she occasionally gives a concert with pianist Frank Glazer.

CYNTHIA ADAMS HOOVER, curator of musical instruments at the Smithsonian Institution, has had the privilege of working with the Smithsonian's superb collection of more than 180 pianos since 1961. Through the support of a Guggenheim Foundation fellowship she has studied the changing intersections of technology, culture, and commerce during the piano's three hundred years. Along with promoting the Piano 300 project, she has written articles about the piano (especially the developments in America) and is co-editor with Edwin M. Good of the annotated diary of William Steinway. The piano has been part of her life since her youth in western Nebraska and through her years at Wellesley College and Harvard and Brandeis universities.

RICHARD LEPPERT is Morse Alumni Distinguished Teaching Professor of Comparative Studies in Discourse and Society and chair of the Department of Cultural Studies and Comparative Literature at the University of Minnesota. His work is concentrated on the relations of music and imagery to social and cultural construction, principally revolving around issues of gender, class, and race. His most recent books include *Art and the Committed Eye: The Cultural Functions of Imagery* and *The Sight of Sound: Music, Representation, and the History of the Body.*

JAMES PARAKILAS is professor of music and chair of the Humanities Division at Bates College, where he has taught since receiving his doctorate in musicology from Cornell University in 1979. His scholarly work on piano music includes the book *Ballads without Words:*

Chopin and the Tradition of the Instrumental Ballade and a critical edition entitled *The Nineteenth-Century Piano Ballade: An Anthology.* He also writes on opera and on the uses of music in the past and present. As a pianist he performs and records with the chamber trio Penumbra.

IVAN RAYKOFF is receiving his Ph.D. from the University of California at San Diego, with a dissertation on the mythology of the Romantic pianist in twentieth-century popular culture. He has served as co-writer and research consultant for a documentary film, *Hollywood Loves the Piano.* A native of Buffalo, New York, he studied piano at the Eastman School of Music and at the Liszt Academy of Music in Budapest on a Fulbright scholarship. He performs regularly with new-music ensembles and as a soloist, and pursues research and teaching interests in contemporary music and film studies.

JUDITH TICK, professor of music at Northeastern University, is a music historian who writes about American music and women's history. Her biography *Ruth Crawford Seeger: A Composer's Search for American Music* has received an ASCAP Deems Taylor award for excellence. Previous publications include articles about Charles Ives and the co-edited anthology *Women Making Music: The Western Art Tradition, 1150–1950,* which also received an ASCAP award. She serves as an associate editor for the journal *Musical Quarterly.*

MARK TUCKER was born in Seattle, Washington. He began piano lessons at age eight in Cincinnati, continuing in high school with Findlay Cockrell at SUNY-Albany. He studied with John Kirkpatrick, William Westney, and Donald Currier at Yale, where he received his B.A. in 1975 and a master's in piano in 1976. After graduate studies in musicology at the University of Michigan (Ph.D., 1986), he taught at Columbia University from 1987 to 1997. His writings include *Ellington: The Early Years, The Duke Ellington Reader,* and (with Garvin Bushell) *Jazz from the Beginning.* Currently he is at work on a study of Thelonious Monk. As a pianist he has given many lecture-recitals on Ellington's solo keyboard works. He is on the faculty of the College of William and Mary.

GRETCHEN A. WHEELOCK is associate professor and director of graduate studies in musicology at the Eastman School of Music. She earned her Ph.D. at Yale University, where she studied piano with Bruce Symonds and Donald Currier. Her research and teaching interests have focused on music of the late eighteenth century, especially of Haydn and Mozart, aesthetics and performance practice, reception history, and issues of gender in music history and analysis. She is the author of *Haydn's Ingenious Jesting with Art: Contexts of Musical Wit and Humor,* along with many articles and reviews.

STEPHEN ZANK began studying piano and composition at age seven in Binghamton, New York, with Mildred Lyon and Alice Lohse, two followers of the Polish teacher Theodor Leschetizky. His training in performance at the New England Conservatory in Boston was followed by four years of study in Paris with Gaby Casadesus and Philippe Entremont and graduate studies in historical musicology (Ph.D., Duke University). He has taught at the State University of New York campuses at Binghamton and Oneonta, at Hartwick College in New York, and at Denison University in Ohio. He is an assistant professor of music at the University of Illinois, Urbana-Champaign.

Acknowledgments

This book is an element of Piano 300, a project examining and commemorating the three-hundred-year history of the piano in its cultural contexts. The concept of the book emerged largely from the meetings and discussions of a planning group made up of Lynn Edwards, H. Wiley Hitchcock, Cynthia Hoover, Richard Leppert, Sandra Rosenblum, Ruth Solie, Mark Tucker, and me. As Cynthia Hoover drew the Smithsonian Institution into the overall project, her colleagues Edwin Good, Patrick Rucker, and James Weaver became crucial in planning, supporting, and leading it. Several of these people have contributed to the book as authors; each of them has lent invaluable help of some sort to its creation.

The contributors to the book are true co-authors. Beyond providing the texts that bear their names, they have provided ideas for the whole book and answers to one another's queries, as well as supplying or suggesting illustrations. They could all, I'm sure, supply their own list of names to acknowledge. Julie Carlson's name should be on every page. Charged with blending the writing of more than a dozen authors together to tell a single story, working on the project with peerless dedication, she turned our motley scripts into a book.

This book conveys its message in pictures as much as in words, and two groups of students deserve the credit for carrying the pictorial work from research to publication. Three—Timothy Bakland, Nils van Otterloo, and Karen Grady—worked as summer research apprentices at Bates College, discovering and combing through pictorial sources of every description, filing photocopies, and supplying information to the press. Four others—Rosalie Metro, Jennifer Korn, Chris Mooney, and K. C. Choi—worked at Yale University Press tracking down the pictures, securing permission to reproduce them, and ordering the reproductions.

Courtney Elf at Bates produced a handful of beautiful musical examples.

Bates College provided generous institutional support for the book; for this I thank especially Deans Martha Crunkleton and Ann Besser Scott and the members of the committee on student research. The librarians of the Ladd Library—especially Elaine Ardia, Thomas Hayward, Laura Juraska, Janice Lee, Gilbert Marcotte, Paula Matthews, Sharon Saunders, and LaVerne Winn—provided years of support to this work, but their moment of glory came in the summer of 1998, when the library was closed for renovation and they nevertheless made it possible for research on the book to reach its peak.

In a larger sense, this project was sustained by the whole Bates community—by endless conversations that showed me what important roles pianos play in many people's memories and consciousness, as well as by favors that I owe to particular individuals. Besides two of my colleagues, Jane Costlow and Atsuko Hirai, who are among the authors, I thank Judith Head, who provided crucial editorial help; William Matthews, who made the project fit into the life of our department; my students in a course that mapped out the subject of this book; Max Andrucki, Dennis Browne, Timothy Chin, Rebecca Corrie, Craig Decker, Laura Gagnon, Frank Glazer, Sylvia Hawks, Mark Howard, Phyllis Graber Jensen, Melville McLean, Lillian Nayder, John Strong, Sarah Strong, and many others who provided both ideas and material help. And I remember the wonderful lesson I received in researching nineteenth-century American culture from Bob Branham.

For help on the subject of piano tuning, I thank Owen Jorgensen; on the subject of pianos in institutional settings, Rachelle Smith; and on the book as a whole, William Weber. For references, advice, and answers to queries, I thank David Appleby, Isabelle Belance-Zank, Jennifer Bloxam, Martha Clinkscale, Martha Cox, Mária Eckhardt, George Eberts, David Engle, David Fuller, Lee Glazer, Charles Hamm, Maria Anna Harley, John Hasse, Marshall Hawkins, Roland Hoover, Ann Kuebler, Terry Lewis, Paige Lily, Ralph Locke, Cristina Magaldi, Judith McCullough, Julia Meech, Zvi Meniker, Jean-Paul Montagnier, Lyle Neff, Leon Plantinga, Tom Pniewski, Regula Qureshi, Rodney Regier, Tim Stone, Thomas Stoner, William Summers, Nicholas Tawa, Susan Wegner, William Williams, Susan Youens, and Neal Zaslaw.

Librarians at institutions from neighboring Bowdoin College to the Modern Music Library in Tokyo put their resources at the service of this project. So did people at museums, conservatories, and other institutions both profit and nonprofit. In many cases I do not know the names of the people I should thank. Let Sarah Adams and Suzanne Eggleston of the music libraries at Harvard and Yale universities stand for many.

Likewise, at Yale University Press many people known and unknown to me made the production of the book possible. I would like to thank by name those whom I worked with directly: Kathleen Cunningham, Phillip King, Nancy Ovedovitz, and above all Harry Haskell, who stood behind the project at every turn.

Pianos are family fixtures, and in the making of this book about the piano many questions have been answered and many crises eased by the members of my family—Mary Hunter, Sandy and Jacob Parakilas, George and Shelagh Hunter. In all my work I count on support from Mary that is miraculously spousal and collegial at the same time; in this case she also supported our family single-handedly for half a year so that I could write.

Illustration Credits

Page xii Courtesy of the Academy of Motion Picture Arts and Sciences; p. 3 Photograph, Yale University Library; p. 5 Agence Photographique de la Réunion des Musées Nationaux, © Photo RMN–Gérard Blot; p. 8 Reprinted from *La galleria armonica: Catalogo del Museo degli Strumenti Musicali di Roma* (Rome, 1994), Yale University Music Library; p. 12 (top) Loan: The Netherlands Institute of Cultural Heritage, Museum Boijmans van Beuningen, Rotterdam; p. 12 (bottom) Photograph, Scala/Art Resource, New York; p. 13 (top) Yale Center for British Art, Paul Mellon Collection; p. 14 Photograph courtesy of Tony Bingham; p. 15 Seeley Mudd Library, Yale University; p. 21 Beinecke Rare Book and Manuscript Library, Yale University; p. 25 Photograph, Yale University Music Library; p. 27 Sächsische Landesbibliothek, Staats-und-Universitätsbibliothek, Dresden; p. 32 Photograph by Edwin M. Good; p. 33 Reprinted from *The New Grove Piano* (New York: Norton, 1988), courtesy of New Grove Dictionaries; p. 35 Reprinted from Franz Josef Hirt, *Stringed Keyboard Instruments* (Zurich, 1981); p. 39 Yale Center for British Art, Paul Mellon Collection; pp. 43, 45 Photographs, Smithsonian Institution; pp. 47, 48, 49 Reprinted from *The New Grove Piano* (New York: Norton, 1988), courtesy of New Grove Dictionaries; pp. 54, 55, 56 Photographs, Smithsonian Institution; p. 57 Photographs courtesy of Yamaha Corporation of America; p. 63 Photograph, Smithsonian Institution; p. 69 (top) Photograph courtesy of Hammacher Schlemmer; p. 69 (bottom) Reprinted from Larry Fine, *The Piano Book* (Boston: Brookside, 1994); p. 78 Photograph, Yale University Music Library, Wilshire Collection; p. 79 (top) Reprinted from Arthur Hutchings, *Mozart: The Man, The Musician* (New York: Schirmer, 1976); p. 79 (bottom) Photograph, Lauros-Giraudon; p. 80 Photograph, British Library, London; p. 85 Photograph, Sibley Music Library, Ruth T. Watanabe Special Collections, Eastman School of Music, University of Rochester; pp. 90–91 Eda Kuhn Loeb Music Library, Harvard University; p. 95 Photograph, Beinecke Rare Book and Manuscript Library, Yale University; p. 97 Courtesy of Spink-Leger, London; p. 99 Photograph by Hans Petersen; p. 100 Reprinted from Georges Duby and Michelle Perrot, eds., *History of Women in the West*, vol. 4 (Cambridge, Mass., 1992–94); p. 101 Yale Center for British Art, Paul Mellon Collection; p. 107 Tate Gallery, London/Art Resource, New York; pp. 127, 132, 136, 139 Photographs, Yale University Music Library; p. 140 Photograph, Yale University Music Library; p. 141 Photograph, Smithsonian Institution; p. 142 Photograph, Yale University Library; p. 145 Beinecke Rare Book and Manuscript Library, Yale University; p. 146 Eda Kuhn Loeb Music Library, Harvard University; p. 147 Yale University Library; p. 149 Willis Music Company, Florence, Kentucky; p. 150 Photograph, Sibley Music Library, Eastman School of Music, University of Rochester; p. 154 Photograph, Yale University Library; pp. 156, 157 Reprinted from Johannes Forner, Hansachim Schiller, and Martin Wehnert, eds., *Hochschule für Musik Leipzig: gegründet als Conservatorium der Musik* (Leipzig, 1968); p. 160 Photograph, Princeton University Library; p. 167 Photograph by Martha Dennis Burns; p. 170 Photograph, Bildarchiv, ÖNB Wien; p. 172 Reprinted from Duke Ellington, *Music Is My Mistress* (New York: Da Capo, 1973), photograph, Yale University Music Library; p. 175 Photograph courtesy of Judith Tick; p. 179 Photograph, Harvard University Library, courtesy of Ardis Publishing; p. 180 Photograph, Beinecke Rare Book and Manuscript Library, Yale University; p. 183 Jacob Marling (American, 1774–1833), *The Crowning of Flora*, 1816, oil on canvas, 30⅛" × 39⅛", Chrysler Museum of Art, Norfolk, Virginia, gift of Edgar William and Bernice Chrysler Garbisch (80.181.20); pp. 184, 186 Photographs, Yale University Library; pp. 189, 191, 194 Photographs, Yale University Music Library; p. 197 By permission of the Houghton Library, Harvard University; p. 201 Photograph courtesy Bildarchiv Preussischer Kulturbesitz; p. 204 Ladd Library, Bates College, Lewiston, Maine, photograph by Melville McLean; p. 207 Photograph, Yale University Library; p. 209 (top) The Metropolitan Museum of Art, H. O. Havemeyer Collection, bequest of Mrs. H. O. Havemeyer, 1929 (29.100.184), photograph by Malcolm Varon; p. 209 (bottom) Alfred Eisenstaedt/*Life* magazine © Time Inc.; p. 210 Photograph, Yale University Music Library; p. 212 (top) Reprinted from I. F. Kunin, *Nikolai Andreevich Rimsky-Korsakov* (Moscow: Muzyka Editions, 1988); p. 212 (bottom) Photograph, Giraudon/Art Resource, New York; p. 213 (top) Photograph © Photothèque des Musées de la Ville de Paris; p. 213 (lower right) Photograph, Yale University Library; p. 213 (lower left) Michael Okoniewski/NYT Pictures; pp. 217, 218, 220, 221 Photographs courtesy of Charlotte Eyerman; p. 223 Agence Photographique de la Réunion des Musées Nationaux, © Photo RMN–Gérard Blot; p. 228 Agence Photographique de la Réunion des Musées Nationaux, © Photo RMN; p. 230 Photograph courtesy Photographie Giraudon; p. 233 Agence Photographique de la Réunion des Musées Nationaux, © RMN; p. 234 Agence Photographique de la Réunion des Musées Nationaux, © Photo RMN–C. Jean; p. 244 Photograph, Yale University Library; p. 248 Photograph, Corbis/Bettman; p. 249 Reprinted from Alfred Dolge, *Pianos and Their Makers* (1911), photograph, Yale University Music Library; p. 250 Collection Ferenc Bónis, Budapest; p. 256 Photograph, Bildarchiv Preussischer Kulturbesitz; p. 258 Photograph courtesy of Richard Leppert; p. 261 Reprinted by permission of Rice University Library; pp. 263, 266 Photographs courtesy of Richard Leppert; pp. 270, 274 Photographs, Yale University Library; p. 276 Photograph courtesy of Laurence Ac-

land; p. 277 Photograph courtesy of Richard Leppert; p. 289 Courtesy the Lilly Library, Indiana University, Bloomington, Indiana; p. 291 Bangor, Maine, Public Library, photograph by Melville McLean; p. 292 Photograph © Sterling and Francine Clark Art Institute, Williamstown, Massachusetts; p. 295 James Parakilas, photograph by Melville McLean; p. 297 Photograph by Melville McLean; p. 300 Mangione & Filhos, São Paulo, Brazil; p. 306 The Metropolitan Museum of Art, gift of Lincoln Kirstein, 1959 (JP 3276), photograph by Otto E. Nelson, © 1986 The Metropolitan Museum of Art; p. 308 Photograph, Shogakukan; p. 309 Photograph, Department of Printing and Graphic Arts, Houghton Library, Harvard University; p. 311 Reprinted from *Illustrirte Zeitung*, vol. 124 (1905), 276; p. 317 Photograph, Yale University Library; p. 318 Museum of Modern Art, Film Stills Archive; p. 319 Agence Photographique de la Réunion des Musées Nationaux, © Photo RMN–Hervé Lewandowski; p. 320 (top) Unknown artist, *Front Parlor, Mary Humphrey's, Cheyenne, Wyoming*, ca. 1900 (P1976.13) © Amon Carter Museum, Fort Worth, Texas; p. 320 (bottom) Bangor, Maine, Public Library, photograph by Melville McLean; p. 321 Photograph, Yale University Library; p. 322 Photograph, Athens Mental Health Center, Athens, Ohio; p. 323 (top) Photograph, Yale University Library, courtesy New York Institute for Special Education; p. 323 (bottom) Reprinted from James A. Johnston, *Prison Life Is Different* (Boston: Houghton Mifflin, 1937), by permission of Houghton Mifflin; p. 324 Culver Pictures, New York; p. 326 Photograph, Northeast Historic Film, Bucksport, Maine; pp. 328, 333, 334 Courtesy of the Academy of Motion Picture Arts and Sciences; p. 335 Bundesarchiv/Filmarchiv, Berlin; p. 337 Courtesy of the Academy of Motion Picture Arts and Sciences; p. 339 (top) Bundesarchiv/Filmarchiv, Berlin; p. 339 (bottom) Courtesy of the Academy of Motion Picture Arts and Sciences; p. 340 (top) Bundesarchiv/Filmarchiv, Berlin; p. 340 (bottom) Museum of Modern Art, Film Stills Archive; p. 341

445

Index